DISCARD

CHAUCER'S ENGLISH

THE LANGUAGE LIBRARY

EDITED BY ERIC PARTRIDGE AND SIMEON POTTER

Ralph W. V. Elliott

CHAUCER'S ENGLISH

Exclusive distributor for U.S.
and Canada:
WESTVIEW PRESS
1898 Flatiron Court
Boulder, Colorado 80301

ANDRE DEUTSCH

First published 1974 by
André Deutsch Limited
105 Great Russell Street London WC1

Printed in Great Britain by
William Clowes & Sons, Limited
London, Beccles and Colchester

ISBN 0 233 96539 4

For
ERIC PARTRIDGE
a modest tribute
on his eightieth birthday

Contents

🔯🔯🔯🔯🔯🔯

Preface

🢒🢒🢒🢒🢒🢒

IT is easier to say what this book is not than what it is. It is neither a systematic linguistic study of Chaucer's English, nor 'the kind of inquiry . . . into the art and language of Chaucer' which Dr F. R. Leavis thought, in *Sociology and Literature*, ought to be undertaken by someone. If anything, it might be described as a modest thrust in the latter direction. My aim in this book is twofold. The first chapter endeavours to provide with a minimum of technicalities the more important facts of Chaucer's pronunciation and grammar and a few hints about his prosody. Appropriate quotations take the place of formal paradigms and an attempt is made to look critically rather than linguistically at some of the forms Chaucer used. The remaining chapters of the book are a conducted tour along some of the more interesting highways and byways of Chaucer's English: his use of colloquialisms and slang, technical language, literary terms, proper names, oaths, and the like. Chapter 3 looks at the language of the four prose works, again with a critic's rather than a linguist's eye, and indeed this approach characterizes the whole work. The final chapter, perhaps the most venturesome of them all, probes the question of characterization through language in Chaucer's poetry: did he in any way create different idioms for different characters and how far was he successful?

Inevitably, there is considerable speculation in a work of this kind; but anchored, I hope, wherever possible to facts of language and to acceptable interpretations of Chaucer's art. If such speculations achieve no more for the reader than another look, with renewed curiosity, at, say *The Tale of Melibee* or *The Canon's Yeoman's Tale*, or make him aware of the interest of what might be called Chaucer's '*un*-phase' in the early thirteen-eighties, or make him assess afresh the likely impact upon Chaucer's audience of the many words which were distinctly unusual, rare, not to say modish, in Chaucer's work – then they will have served a useful purpose.

9

Preface

Much of the book is concerned with Chaucer's vocabulary, and in this respect it may be said to complement rather than duplicate the most recent study of Chaucer's language, Professor Norman E. Eliason's *The Language of Chaucer's Poetry: An Appraisal of the Verse, Style, and Structure* (Copenhagen, 1972), which reached me shortly after the completion of my own manuscript. 'The vocabulary likewise receives scant treatment,' writes Professor Eliason in his Introduction (p. 8), 'for only certain words or types of words that seem to merit it especially are singled out for discussion.' My own contention is that a very large number of Chaucer's words merit attention and a glance at the Index of Words will show that they have received it here.

The study of Chaucer's diction is beset with difficulties: manuscript transmission often makes uncertain what Chaucer wrote; the connotations, occasionally even the primary meanings, of some words are not easy to ascertain; the one and a half major dictionaries (the *OED* and *MED*) at the disposal of the modern scholar cannot determine with absolute certainty whether Chaucer was the first English writer to use a given word in literature; and so on. Even that indispensable work, Tatlock and Kennedy's *A Concordance to the Complete Works of Geoffrey Chaucer*, to which the present book owes a particular debt, has certain limitations which made impossible the complete statistical accuracy occasionally felt desirable. Future scholars, using a computer, may be able to overcome such handicaps. Hence my references to Chaucer's using a word in English literature for the first time, or to a word not found recorded elsewhere in Middle English, or to some word having a distinctly 'modern' look in the late fourteenth century, need to be taken with a little salt, and the reader is asked to bear patiently with the fact that my own language is, in Mr F. W. Bateson's characteristic phrase, 'tiresomely peppered with qualifications' like 'probably', 'perhaps', 'apparently', and the like. I trust that there is nonetheless some value in the kind of scrutiny to which many of Chaucer's words and forms of words have been subjected in the following pages.

The present book ranges over all of Chaucer's accepted work except the *Romaunt of the Rose*. Although part of the extant Middle English version of this poem is regarded by most scholars as probably Chaucer's, an element of doubt remains, and, apart from an occasional sideways glance at the *Romaunt*, I thought it wiser to ignore it. The text used is that of the second edition of F. N. Robinson's *The Works of Geoffrey Chaucer* (London, 1957), except where otherwise indicated. As the book is addressed primarily to the general reader of Chaucer rather than to expert medievalists, unfamiliar words are glossed in quotations where this was thought helpful, and all quotations from *The General Prologue* and from specific tales in *The Canterbury Tales* are accompanied by abbreviated titles. Only where quotations come from the links and interludes between tales, which include all except the first of Harry Bailly's utterances, are line references preceded by *CT* (i.e. *Canterbury Tales*) followed by Robinson's fragment number, e.g. *CT* II, 16. In order to distinguish between the words of the narrators of poems, as in *Troilus and Criseyde* or the separate tales in *The Canterbury Tales*, and those of characters within the poems or tales, the latter are placed in quotation marks in all indented quotations.

The English used by Chaucer, however much it bears the imprint of his particular genius, is of course the language of his contemporaries also, and to study it in relation to the latter is to see both the common pursuit and the individual talent.

Quotations from Chaucer's contemporaries in the present book are mainly from those with whom most readers of Chaucer are likely to have some acquaintance, the *Gawain*-poet, Langland, and Gower. To go much beyond these, to attempt anything approaching a more thoroughgoing comparative study, would have radically altered the scope of this book and would have lessened its immediate interest and possible usefulness for readers of Chaucer. But such a study remains to be undertaken, perhaps when the *Middle English Dictionary* has been completed and the use of computers has become established as a normal research method in the humanities.

The indebtedness of this book to generations of Chaucerian scholarship and criticism 'with tonge unnethe may discryved bee'. I have tried to acknowledge every debt of which I am aware, but realize that there may be omissions. To students and colleagues who have read and discussed Chaucer with me I owe much inspiration and insight. To Carolyn Angas and Wendy Reid I am particularly grateful for help with research and the preparation of the typescript. To the Librarians and staff at the Flinders University Library, the British Museum, the Bodleian Library, and the Oxford English Faculty Library, I am indebted for their un-

Preface

failing courtesy and helpfulness. My special thanks must go to the general editors of The Language Library for their encouragement, criticism, and patience, and to my wife and children for 'letting daddy get on with his work' when there were much more important demands like games to be played or stories to be told. Finally, I acknowledge gratefully the financial help provided by the Flinders University of South Australia and the Australian Research Grants Committee.

WEDGE ACRE   RALPH W. V. ELLIOTT
COROMANDEL VALLEY
SOUTH AUSTRALIA.
APRIL 1973

Abbreviations

ᔕᔕᔕᔕᔕ

CHAUCER'S WORKS

ABC	*An ABC*	*Mel*	*The Tale of Melibee*
Adam	*Adam Scriveyn*	*MerchT*	*The Merchant's Tale*
Anel	*Anelida and Arcite*	*MillT*	*The Miller's Tale*
Astr	*A Treatise on the Astrolabe*	*MkT*	*The Monk's Tale*
		MLT	*The Man of Law's Tale*
Bal Compl	*A Balade of Complaint*	*NPT*	*The Nun's Priest's Tale*
BD	*The Book of the Duchess*		
		PardT	*The Pardoner's Tale*
Bo	*Boece*	*ParsT*	*The Parson's Tale*
Buk	*Lenvoy de Chaucer a Bukton*	*PF*	*The Parliament of Fowls*
CkT	*The Cook's Tale*	*PhysT*	*The Physician's Tale*
CLT	*The Clerk's Tale*	*Pity*	*The Complaint unto Pity*
Compl d'Am	*Complaynt d'Amours*		
CT	*The Canterbury Tales*	*PrT*	*The Prioress's Tale*
CYT	*The Canon's Yeoman's Tale*	*Purse*	*The Complaint of Chaucer to his Purse*
Form Age	*The Former Age*	*Rom*	*The Romaunt of the Rose*
Fort	*Fortune*		
FranklT	*The Franklin's Tale*	*RvT*	*The Reeve's Tale*
FrT	*The Friar's Tale*	*SecNT*	*The Second Nun's Tale*
Gen Prol	*The General Prologue*	*ShipT*	*The Shipman's Tale*
HF	*The House of Fame*	*SqT*	*The Squire's Tale*
KnT	*The Knight's Tale*	*SumT*	*The Summoner's Tale*
Lady	*A Complaint to his Lady*	*Thop*	*The Tale of Sir Thopas*
		Tr	*Troilus and Criseyde*
LGW	*The Legend of Good Women*	*Ven*	*The Complaint of Venus*
MancT	*The Manciple's Tale*	*WBT*	*The Wife of Bath's Tale*
Mars	*The Complaint of Mars*		

EDITIONS OF CHAUCER

DONALDSON Donaldson, E. T., ed. *Chaucer's Poetry‡: An Anthology for the Modern Reader.* New York, 1958.

GLOBE Pollard, Alfred W., Heath, Frank H., Liddell, Mark H., and McCormick, W. S., eds. *The Works of Geoffrey Chaucer.* London, 1898, repr. 1960.

MANLY AND RICKERT Manly, John M., and Rickert, Edith, eds. *The Text of the Canterbury Tales.* 8 vols, Chicago and London, 1940.

ROBINSON Robinson, F. N., ed. *The Works of Geoffrey Chaucer.* Boston, 1933, 2nd edn., Boston and London, 1957.

ROOT Root, Robert Kilburn, ed. *The Book of Troilus and Criseyde.* Princeton, 1926.

SKEAT Skeat, Walter W., ed. *The Complete Works of Geoffrey Chaucer.* 7 vols, Oxford, 1894–7, 2nd edn. 1899.

BOOKS AND PUBLICATIONS

BRYAN AND DEMPSTER Bryan, W. F. and Dempster, Germaine, eds. *Sources and Analogues of Chaucer's Canterbury Tales.* Chicago, 1941, repr. New York, 1958.

CLEMEN Clemen, Wolfgang. *Chaucer's Early Poetry.* Translated by C. A. M. Sym. London, 1963.

CONF AM Gower, John. *Confessio Amantis. The English Works of John Gower.* Edited by G. C. Macaulay. 2 vols, E.E.T.S., E.S. 81, 82, 1900–1.

CURRY Curry, W. C. *Chaucer and the Mediaeval Sciences.* Oxford, 1926, rev. edn, London, 1960.

DONALDSON, *Speaking* Donaldson, E. Talbot. *Speaking of Chaucer.* London, 1970.

E.E.T.S., O.S. AND E.S. The Early English Text Society, Original Series and Extra Series.

GORDON Gordon, Ida L. *The Double Sorrow of Troilus: A Study of Ambiguities in Troilus and Criseyde.* Oxford, 1970.

HUPPÉ Huppé, Bernard F. *A Reading of the Canterbury Tales.* Albany, N.Y., 1964, rev. edn, 1967.

JEFFERSON Jefferson, Bernard L. *Chaucer and the Consolation of Philosophy of Boethius.* Princeton, 1917, repr. New York, 1968.

KERKHOF   Kerkhof, J. *Studies in the Language of Geoffrey Chaucer.* Leiden, 1966.

MASUI   Masui, Michio. *The Structure of Chaucer's Rime Words: An Exploration into the Poetic Language of Chaucer.* Tokyo, 1964.

MED   Kurath, Hans, Kuhn, Sherman M., and Reidy, John, eds. *The Middle English Dictionary.* Michigan, 1956 *et seq.*

MUSCATINE   Muscatine, Charles. *Chaucer and the French Tradition: A Study in Style and Meaning.* Berkeley and Los Angeles, 1957, repr. 1966.

MUSTANOJA   Mustanoja, Tauno F. *A Middle English Syntax.* Part I: *Parts of Speech.* Helsinki, 1960.

OED   Murray, J. A. H., Bradley, Henry, Craigie, W. A. and Onions, C. T., eds. *The Oxford English Dictionary on Historical Principles.* Oxford, 1884–1928. Corrected reissue with Supplement, 13 vols, 1933.

PMLA   *Publications of the Modern Language Association of America.*

PP   Langland, William. *Piers the Plowman and Richard the Redeless.* Edited by Walter W. Skeat, 2 vols, Oxford, 1886.

SGGK   *Sir Gawain and the Green Knight.* Edited by J. R. R. Tolkien and E. V. Gordon, revised by Norman Davis, Oxford, 1967.

TATLOCK AND KENNEDY   Tatlock, John S. P., and Kennedy, Arthur G., eds. *A Concordance to the Complete Works of Geoffrey Chaucer.* Washington, 1927, repro. 1973.

TEN BRINK   ten Brink, Bernhard. *The Language and Metre of Chaucer.* Translated by M. Bentinck Smith. London, 1901.

OTHER ABBREVIATIONS

Fr.	*French*
M.E.	*Middle English*
O.E.	*Old English*
O.Fr.	*Old French*
O.N.	*Old Norse*

Phonetic Symbols

𝔊𝔊𝔊𝔊𝔊𝔊

The following letters are used as phonetic symbols with their usual English values: p, b, t, d, k, g, f, v, s, z, h, r, m, n. Other symbols are used with the values indicated by the italicized letters in the keywords which follow:

CONSONANTS

ʃ	*sh*ip		ç	German i*ch*
ʤ	*j*u*dge*		x	Scots lo*ch*
θ	*th*in		ʀ	French *r*ue
ð	*th*en			

VOWELS

i:	s*ee*		ɔ:	s*aw*
e	g*e*t		o:	t*o*ne
ɛ	th*e*re		u	p*u*t
e:	d*a*te		u:	s*oo*n
a	f*a*t		ü	French nat*u*re
ɑ:	f*a*ther		ʌ	b*u*t
ɔ	h*o*t			

DIPHTHONGS

ɔu	see p. 37		ui	r*ui*n
ou	g*o*		iu	n*ew*
ai	fl*y*		ɛu	see p. 36
au	n*ow*			

Square brackets enclose phonetic symbols. A colon after a phonetic symbol indicates length. // enclose phonemic symbols.

CHAPTER I

Myn Englissh

ﺤﺤﺤﺤﺤﺤ

CHAUCER'S English is that of an educated Londoner of the second half of the fourteenth century, but like his counterpart six centuries later who will use occasional provincialisms or Americanisms, Chaucer sometimes uses words or forms of words which did not normally figure in the London English of his time. Moreover, because Chaucer probably felt, as his Squire did, that his 'Englissh eek is insufficient' (*SqT* 37) sometimes for his purposes, he readily turns elsewhere for inspiration and reinforcement: to 'provincialisms', as we would now consider them; to the popular spoken idiom of his time which had not hitherto made a particularly noticeable impression upon literary English; and to the other languages with which he was familiar: Latin, French and Italian. Occasionally, though not very often, Chaucer even coined a new word.

The word *insufficient* just cited is a case in point. We do not know where Chaucer first came across it. He uses the word only twice, in *The Squire's Tale*, 37, and in *The Summoner's Tale*, 1960, yet it is unlikely that Chaucer invented the word except in the medieval sense of 'inventing', that is finding or coming upon something. The modern word 'sufficient' generally appears as *suffisant* or *suffisaunt* in Chaucer, although *sufficient* also occurs a few times. His contemporaries also knew both versions, but Chaucer appears to have been the first to use *insufficient* in writing, although at about the same time as Chaucer was writing *The Canterbury Tales* John of Trevisa used the adverb *insufficiantly* to translate the Latin *insufficienter*. The word may have been current in educated spoken usage and Chaucer may have heard it first in conversation with some courtier or some fellow writer of his acquaintance. Communication with men like John Gower may help to explain the almost simultaneous appearance in the work of both poets of words not previously recorded in English. Or else Chaucer may have read the word in a French or Latin book whence it entered his own English vocabulary. This was often the case where Chaucer worked closely from a source in one of these languages, as we shall note in subsequent chapters of this book. One important aspect of Chaucer's linguistic genius illustrated by the example of *insufficient* is his readiness to employ words from any available source for specific literary purposes, in these two given instances for use in rhyme, since, as he says elsewhere, 'rym in Englissh hath such skarsete' (*Ven* 80).

Rhyme is also responsible for occasional dialectal forms in Chaucer. Not all of these would be felt to be 'provincialisms' in the London English of the later fourteenth century, a word which in any case has acquired derogatory connotations in later English not appropriate to Chaucer's time. For the various purposes of the vernacular the major regional dialects of England enjoyed about equal status, and literary works of considerable merit, like the north-west midland alliterative poems ascribed to the *Gawain*-poet, emanated from different parts of the country. Yet at the same time, increasing importance probably attached to the speech of London during the sixty years of Chaucer's life, a development assisted by the geographical position of London and its steadily growing political and economic importance, and perhaps accelerated by the work of influential writers like Chaucer and Wyclif. Hence there is some justification for believing that, as Rodolpho Jacobson puts it, 'the London speech of the fourteenth century had grown into a prestige dialect developing features which made it the forerunner of present day English', and that 'a more or less uniform language must have been in use in London much before the time usually allotted to the appearance of Modern English'.[1]

Among dialectal features of Chaucer's English not characteristic of London are the northern words and speech forms used in *The Reeve's Tale* for a specific artistic purpose (see below, ch. 7, pp. 390–3), and some other northernisms used for the sake of rhyme. The ending -*es* for the third person singular of the present indica-

---

1. Rodolfo Jacobson, *The London Dialect of the Late Fourteenth Century: A Transformational Analysis in Historical Linguistics* (The Hague and Paris, 1970), pp. 12 f. At the same time one must doubt Jacobson's wisdom in regarding examples of Chaucer's literary, often mannered, prose as reflecting 'the language *spoken* in London during the second half of the century' (my italics), and of using these as the data on which to base such an analysis. See *op. cit.*, pp. 54 ff.

tive of verbs is characteristic of northern and north-west midland usage in the second half of the fourteenth century. Chaucer normally uses *-eth*, as in *folweth* 'follows' (*HF* 5), but an occasional northern *-es* is introduced for the sake of, and is attested by, rhyme. In *The Book of the Duchess* occurs *it telles* (73) rhyming with *elles* 'else', the same pair recurring in *The House of Fame*, 425–6; also in *The Book of the Duchess* the singular verb *falles* (257) rhymes with the plural noun *halles*. The northern and north-midland *second* person singular present indicative ending *-es* is used exceptionally in *The House of Fame*, 1908, 'thou . . . brynges' to rhyme with the plural noun *tydynges*.

The occasional south-eastern form of a word with a root vowel *e* instead of Chaucer's usual *i* (from O.E. *y*) as in *kesse* 'kiss' (*CLT* 1057) rhyming with *stedfastnesse*, compared with *kisse* (*ibid.* 553) rhyming with *blisse*, was probably familiar enough in fourteenth-century London English. Chaucer's close association with Kent, where this [e] was the usual pronunciation in such words, further explains his readiness to make use of forms in *e* for rhyme. Other examples are *ken* (*BD* 438), normally *kin* 'kind, mankind', rhyming with *ten*; *knette* (*PF* 438), normally *knitte* 'knit', rhyming, *inter alia*, with *lette*, similarly in *The Complaint of Mars*, 183; and the very frequent forms with *e* of *leste* 'to please' in phrases like 'if the lest', if it pleases you (*Tr* II, 1394), usually *list*, and the corresponding noun *lest* 'pleasure, desire, wish', as in 'as was his lest' (*KnT* 2984) rhyming with *brest*, usually *lust*, as in that ringing alliterating line

> Hyr lyf, hir love, hir lust, hir lord.
> (*HF* 258)

Chaucer was well aware of the varieties of English which he so readily exploited for literary purposes:

> And for ther is so gret diversite
> In Englissh and in writyng of oure tonge,
> (*Tr* V, 1793–4)

he says at the end of *Troilus and Criseyde*, anxious that scribal vagaries, or secretarial incompetence of the kind hinted at in the little poem *Unto Adam, His Owne Scriveyn*, or, worst of all, dialectal distortions and substitutions, should not disfigure his poem. Hence his prayer in the lines that follow:

So prey I God that non myswrite the,
Ne the mysmetre for defaute of tonge.
And red whereso thow be, or elles songe,
That thow be understonde, God I biseche!

(ibid. 1795–8)

Chaucer's anxiety was certainly not without good cause, as the two Selden manuscripts of *Troilus and Criseyde* in the Bodleian Library at Oxford illustrate. MS Selden B 24 contains among other poems the unique copy of the fifteenth-century poem *Kingis Quair* and its Scottish scribe has managed to give even Chaucer's thoroughly English poem something of a Scottish appearance by altering spellings and replacing Chaucer's pronominal form *hir(e)* and *hem* by the northern *thair* and *them*. MS Selden, Supra 56 contains only *Troilus and Criseyde*, strongly impregnated with northern dialect characteristics.[2]

And if mis-writing, for whatever reason, was bad, mis-metring was presumably worse. Chaucer was an accomplished metrical craftsman despite the Man of Law's belittling comment

'That Chaucer, thogh he kan but lewedly
On metres and on rymyng craftily,
Hath seyd hem [i.e. tales] in swich Englissh as he kan'.

(CT II, 47–9)

The main problem of 'metring' Chaucer's verse satisfactorily is to know when to sound and when not to sound the final *-e* which developed ubiquitously from various Old English inflectional endings or came into the language in words of romance origin, like *corage* or *compaignye*, and which sounded like the *a* in *china*. It was his failure to treat Chaucer's *-e* with due respect that caused Dryden to scan Chaucer's verse as if it were 'rym dogerel' (as Harry Bailly calls *Sir Thopas, CT* VII, 925) and to claim that 'it were an easie Matter to produce some thousands of his Verses, which are lame for want of half a Foot, and sometimes a whole one, and which no Pronunciation can make otherwise'.[3]

Much erudition has been expended since then on what to do about Chaucer's *-e*'s, whether and when to pronounce or suppress them, whether grammatical or metrical canons can be established

2. Cp. Root, pp. lix f.
3. Preface to *Fables Ancient and Modern,* in *The Poems and Fables of John Dryden,* ed. James Kinsley (London, 1961), p. 529.

as guide-lines, whether Chaucer himself was being systematic and consistent, and whether, in fact, there was a time in the later fourteenth century when speakers of London English had a free choice in this particular matter of pronunciation. The last question is perhaps the easiest to answer. A living language is always to some extent in a state of transition, as Chaucer himself was well aware –

Ye knowe ek that in forme of speche is chaunge,
(*Tr* II, 22)

– and there are instances of the co-existence of alternative meanings, forms, pronunciations at any given time in the history of English. There is nothing improbable about a similar state of affairs as regards final *-e* in Chaucer's time; perhaps the older generation tended to retain it, and the younger to drop it, while a poet of Chaucer's eclectic tendencies would readily subscribe to either party as it suited his literary needs. One recalls H. C. Wyld's wistful comment under the word *chemist* in his *Universal Dictionary of the English Language* (1932): 'Some good old-fashioned speakers still say [k*í*m*i*st]', at a time when more recent fashion was favouring our current pronunciation. Chaucer was unlikely to have been wistful about such matters; as a poet he knew how to utilize them, although he had his moments of anxiety, as we saw, about the fate of his poems in the hands of people whose linguistic habits were different from his own or liable to blunders ('defaute of tonge').

Another point that can be made about final *-e*'s is that where they possessed a grammatical function they were as a rule more likely to be pronounced by people speaking reasonably careful fourteenth-century London English, which would include people reciting poems to an audience. One such function is the plural of monosyllabic adjectives ending in a consonant, like *good-e* and *old-e* in

The thre were goode men, and riche, and olde
(*WBT* 197)

where *riche* also has plural function but is indistinguishable from the singular in form and its final *-e* is elided in pronunciation, as was usual before a following vowel or *h*.

Where no grammatical criteria apply, and even these are not

23

rigidly observed, the reader of Chaucer's verse, which included Chaucer himself in the first instance, is forced to decide for himself how he wants the verse to sound. It is quite possible to ignore most or all of the final -*e*'s and still produce what Dryden, in the same Preface, called 'the rude Sweetness of a *Scotch* Tune in it, which is natural and pleasing, though not perfect'. Most people since Dryden, however, have preferred to read Chaucer's short lines in *The Book of the Duchess* and *The House of Fame* as octosyllables, and the long lines as lines of ten syllables, or eleven where a 'feminine' ending is added, and to scan these, subject to appropriate variations, as iambic pentameters. Such 'appropriate variations' may be so frequent and so radical, however, particularly if the reader is to avoid stressing unimportant words or syllables and to try to catch the right phrasal patterns of Chaucer's often colloquial tone, that any underlying iambic pentameters may be hard to recognize. In the following examples only the first can be regarded as a regular iambic pentameter where every one of the five stresses falls on a word that qualifies semantically for emphasis, and even here a reader might wish to give emphasis to the repeated *ful*, an emphatic adverb used three times in the Wife of Bath's portrait and ironically appropriate to her in several ways, in which case the line would have seven stresses (the symbol ∕ denotes a stressed syllable, ∪ an unstressed syllable, | a momentary pause, and (e) a silent *e*):

Fŭl strei̇́t(e) y̆téyd | ănd shóes fŭl móyst(e) ănd néw(e).
(Gen Prol 457)

Lines of four semantically justifiable stresses are common in Chaucer. In the next example the alternation of stresses and pauses creates the rhythm of a neatly itemized catalogue:

Hĕ koŭdĕ róost(e) | ănd séth(e) | ănd bróill(e) | ănd frý(e).
(Gen Prol 383)

Here, as quite often in Chaucer, it would be possible to alter the effect of the line by forgetting about the iambic pentameter and pronouncing all the final -*e*'s, mouthing each word voluptuously, as Keats did his claret, as if it suggested palpably the gastronomic achievements implied:

He koude rооste | and sethe | and broille | and frye.

Here are two examples of three stresses:

He was a verray | parfit praktisour.
(*ibid.* 422)

Nor of the knobbes sittyng(e) on his chekes.
(*ibid.* 633)

In the following example the conversational rhythm of the two lines reduces the number of semantically justifiable stresses to two in each line:

And eek ye knowen wel | how that a jay

Kan clepen 'Watt(e)' | as wel as kan the pop(e).
(*ibid.* 642–3)

Finally, there are lines like the following in which none of the words stands out sufficiently distinctly to merit stressing, although individual readers may of course feel inclined to stress one or the other, perhaps the rhyming words:

But er that he hadde maad al this array.
(*MillT* 3630)
'Who evere herde of swich a thyng er now?'
(*SumT* 2229)
And thus he seyde unto us everichon.
(*CT* VII, 2819)

In cases like these one can probably do no better than try to approximate to corresponding modern English conversational speech rhythms, in the hope that the Chaucerian rhythms were rather similar. One of the merits of Nevill Coghill's modern renderings of *Troilus and Criseyde* and *The Canterbury Tales* is that they suggest so plausibly the Chaucerian rhythms in modern garb.

Considering how infinitely variable Chaucer's prosody is – a variety at which a handful of examples can merely hint, but which a reading of Chaucer's poetry soon confirms – it is not surprising that some modern critics have eagerly cast the whole question of Chaucerian prosody back into the melting pot of scholarly debate.[4] James G. Southworth rejects 'the iambic decasyllabic theory' (*op. cit.*, p. 70) and with it all final -*e*'s, and substitutes a rhythmical prosody akin to that of the alliterative poets. Ian Robinson's verdict on the final -*e* is to sound it where this achieves 'rhetorical effectiveness' (*op. cit.*, p. 103) or 'helps the expressiveness of Chaucer's poetry' (p. 107); and his general conclusion is that the metre of Chaucer's long line is a 'compound of pentameter with half-line movement' (p. 172), combining the basic regularity of a five-foot line with the balanced pattern of the alliterative long line as it existed in Old English and as it was used by some of Chaucer's contemporaries. Since the alliterative line expresses particularly well the short phrasal units of the English of its age which also figure markedly in Chaucer's verse, and since the pentameter confirms the steady rhythmic movement felt by most readers to be inherent in the verse, Robinson's conclusion is an acceptable if not particularly startling one. It means that the reader still needs to attend to the -*e*'s to gain a sense of the underlying rhythmical pattern of the line, while at the same time achieving with the help of balance and appropriate pauses a phrasal rhythm which does no injury to the meaning.

One further point about Chaucer's prosody should be mentioned. Scholars are divided about the final -*e* which frequently figures in rhyme at the end of the line, whether the line is short or long. Ian Robinson comes out strongly against sounding them: 'they make Chaucer's poetry sound second-rate, bad in an uncharacteristic way: they make him sound stilted, sing-song and artificial '(*op. cit.*, p. 108). Basil Cottle, on the other hand, takes the view that 'Chaucer obviously liked "feminine" rhymes . . . and at a line-ending we shall be safe in sounding every final -*e*'.[5] Some readers prefer the consonantal stop to the line; others like the variety achieved by contrasting consonantal and vocalic couplets. Such variety is certainly characteristic of Chaucer, but

---

4. See, for example, James G. Southworth, *Verses of Cadence: An Introduction to the Prosody of Chaucer and his Followers* (Oxford, 1954), and Ian Robinson, *Chaucer's Prosody: A Study of the Middle English Verse Tradition* (Cambridge, 1971). A good summary of the scholarly debate is Tauno F. Mustanoja's chapter, 'Chaucer's Prosody' in *Companion to Chaucer Studies*, ed. Beryl Rowland (Toronto, 1968), pp. 58 ff.

5. Basil Cottle, *The Triumph of English 1350–1400* (London, 1969), p. 32. Helge Kökeritz, *A Guide to Chaucer's Pronunciation* (Stockholm and New Haven, 1954, 1961; New York, 1962), p. 18, recommends sounding -*e* at the end of the line.

whether it makes him sound all the things Robinson claims is a matter of personal response. Once again, objective criteria are hard to establish, as even -*e* in its grammatical function is not used consistently. In the following line, the plural endings of the adjectives *alle* and *grete* are probably not intended to be pronounced because of elision, so that the -*e* of *smale* may also be meant to be silent:

Amonges alle his gestes, grete and smale.

(*ShipT* 24)

Yet it is possible to argue that sounding the -*e* in *smale* sums up, as it were, the plural function of all three adjectives in the line, thus restoring at least a semblance of grammatical 'correctness'. In the lines from *The General Prologue* cited earlier it could be argued that the sounding or not sounding of the final syllable of the line depends on the rhythmical balance of the line as a whole. Thus in the line

Nor of the knobbes sittynge on his chekes

the words *knobbes* and *chekes* are rhythmically and semantically linked and would therefore be sounded with the same number of syllables. Similarly, in the line

Kan clepen 'Watte' as wel as kan the pope

the words *Watte* and *pope* should both be sounded as monosyllables because *Watte* has its final -*e* elided before the following vowel, so that for the sake of rhythmical balance the -*e* in *pope* should be silent also.

Another grammatical function of the final -*e* is that it indicates the infinitive. Chaucer's infinitives end either in -*e* or in -*en*, representing the development of the Old English infinitive ending -*an* as in O.E. *tellan* 'to count, state, tell'. Chaucer uses both *tellen* and *telle*. In rhyme the distribution of the two forms is surprisingly uneven: in *Troilus and Criseyde* he uses *telle* thirty times in rhyme,[6] but *tellen* only once, in the first line of the poem:

The double sorwe of Troilus to tellen,

(*Tr* I, 1)

where it rhymes with the plural past tense *fellen* 'fell, happened'. In

6. The statistics are those of Masui.

27

The Canterbury Tales telle occurs fifty times in rhyme, *tellen* not at all. In interior positions in the line Chaucer presumably intends *tellen* to be disyllabic,

> But, for to tellen yow of his array,
>
> *(Gen Prol* 73)

while *telle* could be either disyllabic, where this enhances the sound of the line, as in

> 'To telle me the fyn of his entente',
>
> *(Tr* III, 125)

or monosyllabic when elision of the *-e* takes place before a vowel or *h*, as in

> To tell(e) in short, withouten wordes mo.
>
> *(ibid.* 234)

Even allowing for the uncertainty of manuscript transmission, the evidence is inconclusive as a guide to the sounding or not sounding of infinitive *-e* in rhyme. Nor is the evidence of French-derived words ending in *-e* any more conclusive. The word *compaignye*, for example, in order to achieve a smooth rhythm, can be pronounced either with three syllables in the interior of a line:

> 'For I wol(e) holde compaigny(e) with thee',
>
> *(FrT* 1521)

or with four:

> 'And in his compaignye moot I goon.'
>
> *(ShipT* 362)

When therefore the word occurs in rhyme, as it frequently does (forty-eight times in *The Canterbury Tales*), the modern reader of Chaucer must decide for himself which pronunciation he consider preferable, especially since, as Masui points out,[7] 'nouns of Romance origin generally rime with each other' and are thus of no help in solving this particular dilemma.

No matter how the modern reader approaches Chaucer's verse, he will soon become delighted with what Matthew Arnold called 'his divine fluidity of movement',[8] a uniquely successful com-

7. Masui, p. 17.

8. In his comments on Chaucer in 'The Study of Poetry', *Essays in Criticism*, Second Series (London, 1888).

bination of formal metrical patterning with a variety of rhythms frequently suggesting conversational English. Chaucer's prayer not to be mis-metred suggests that there is a right and a wrong way of reading him and that linguistic blunders can play havoc with his verse. His comment that his poetry ought to please,

> Though som vers fayle in a sillable,
> (*HF* 1098)

also suggests that he was conscious of regular metres and was presumably endeavouring to achieve them. If at the same time as coming to terms with Chaucer's prosody, the modern reader makes some attempt to recapture the sounds of Chaucer's English, he is indeed well on the way not to 'mysmetre for defaute of tonge'.

The standard work on Chaucer's pronunciation is Helge Kökeritz's *Guide* previously mentioned,[9] still the most useful introduction to the subject for the student of Chaucer, although some interesting attempts have been made since to apply recent linguistic theories to the study of Middle English sounds.[10] The consonants of the London English of Chaucer's time were probably for the most part pronounced as they are today, with some important exceptions. Where modern English has silenced the initial consonants in words beginning with *gn-* and *kn-*, Chaucer still pronounced them in *gnat, gnawen, gnof* 'churl, lout, boor', *knave, knyght, knotte,* and similar cases. In words of French origin, like *benygne, digne, resigne,* however, the *g* was not pronounced. These words occur rarely in rhymes, incidentally, and where they do, they generally rhyme with each other, as in *Troilus and Criseyde* I, 429 ff., or *The Man of Law's Tale,* 778 ff., but other rhymes like that of *resygne* with *medicyne* (*ABC* 78 ff.) make the pronunciation clear. The group *ng* was probably pronounced as in modern English *finger* in words like *honge* 'hang', *singen, strong, thyng;* but it was pronounced as in modern English *sing* in the ending *-ing* or *-yng* which was generally unstressed, but could nonetheless figure in rhyme as in *The Monk's Tale,* 2304 ff., where *clothyng, huntyng, knowyng,* and *likyng* rhyme with one another.

---

9. See n. 5 above. I gladly acknowledge the debt which the following pages owe to Professor Kökeritz's work.

10. For example by Charles Jones in ch. 3 of *An Introduction to Middle English* (New York, 1972).

Two other consonants which are silent in certain combinations in modern English were pronounced in Chaucer's day: initial *w* when followed by *r* in words like *wrappe* (hence the alliteration in 'wynde and wrappe', *CLT* 583), *wrecche* (another example of alliteration in 'I, wrecche, which that wepe and wayle thus', *KnT* 931), *writen, wrooth* 'angry'; and *l* when followed by *f, k* or *m* in such words as *half, stalke, calm.* Initial *h* was either a very weak aspirate or was becoming silent altogether in the course of Chaucer's lifetime. It is generally agreed that it was not pronounced in words adopted from the French, like *hoost* 'host', where spellings like 'the Grekis oost', the army of the Greeks (*Tr* IV, 599), bear this out. In words of Old English or Scandinavian origin, spellings without *h* also occur in the later fourteenth century and increasingly in the first half of the fifteenth. This is true of weakly stressed forms like the pronouns *him, his,* and so on, which tend to retain *h* in spelling, and in words occupying stressed positions in the sentence.[11] However, initial *h* tended to be lost early in the pronoun *it,* from O.E. *hit,* although the latter form is also found in Chaucer. The elision of final *-e* before *h* as well as before vowels, which we noted earlier, usually applies to words with initial *h*-irrespective of origin. This points to a weakening of the aspiration almost to the point of disappearance. By the turn of the fifteenth century, the younger generation was probably dropping its aitches frequently. Chaucer's readiness to make use of alliterating phrases, which will occupy us further in the next chapter, gives some hint of his treatment of *h*-. In pairs consisting of words beginning with *h*- where one is of French origin and another from Old English, the latter presumably also lost its aspiration, as in 'heel and honour' (*LGW* Prol F, 296), that is health or prosperity and honour, similarly in *The Franklin's Tale,* 1087 and elsewhere. Hence it is not unreasonable to assume that where both words in such pairs are of English origin, both might lose or almost lose their aspirates, for example, 'hyde and hele' (*Mel* 1089), hide and conceal, 'hoole herte' (*Gen Prol* 533), and so forth.

Several consonantal spellings signal more than one possible pronunciation: *c* can represent, as in modern English, either the

11. Cp. Rolf Berndt, *Einführung in das Studium des Mittelenglischen unter Zugrundelegung des Prologs der 'Canterbury Tales'* (Halle, 1960), p. 162. Jacek Fisiak, *A Short Grammar of Middle English* (Warsaw and London, 1968), p. 61, notes that '/h/ was sometimes dropped in unstressed words'.

sound [s] as in *celle, citee*, when preceding an *e* or *i*; or it can have the sound [k] when preceding an *a* or *o* or *u*, as in *castel, come, cursen*, or before a consonant as in *clad, craft*. The letter *g* has the sound of modern English [g] where we so pronounce it, as in *game, gete* 'to get', *good, guttes* 'guts', *glad, gnat, grene, dogge*, and so on; and it was sounded [dʒ] like the *dge* in modern English *edge* in words like *gentillesse, engendred, religioun* where modern English has the same phoneme. The same sound [dʒ] attaches to the letter *j*, as in *Jakke* 'Jack', *joye, justice*. As in modern English also, the letter *s* is pronounced in Chaucer's English either like modern English [s], as in *song, mous* 'mouse', or like modern English [z] where we would so pronounce it, as in *as, bisy* 'busy', *houses*, and so forth. The pronunciation of *th* was, as it is in modern English, either [θ] as in *thyng, with*, or [ð] as in *the, that, they, ther, ferther* 'further', *hethen* 'heathen'. The phoneme /r/ probably had two allophones in Chaucer's English, a trilled sound at the beginning of words, hence the peculiar aptness of Criseyde's

'O, rolled shal I ben on many a tonge!'

(*Tr* V, 1061)

and a weaker sound more like uvular [R] before a consonant as in the mild expletive *pardee*, or at the end of a word, as in *flour* 'flower'. The letters *gh* indicate either the sound [x] as in Scots *loch* or German *Achtung*, in such words as *taughte, droghte* 'drought', *thurgh* 'through', where the sound follows a vowel or diphthong pronounced in the back of the mouth; or else the sound [ç] as in German *Reich* after a vowel or diphthong pronounced forward in the mouth, as in *eight, knyght, nyght*.

Of the short vowels in Chaucer's English, *e* was pronounced as in modern English *get*, *i* (spelt either *i* or *y*) as in modern received standard English *bit*, and *u* as in modern English *full*. The latter sound was also pronounced in a number of words where the Middle English spelling was *o* or *ou*, for the most part words which had *u* or initial *w(e)o-* in Old English, or had *o* or *u*, later *ou*, in Old French; for example: *come* (O.E. *cuman*), *love* (O.E. *lufu*), *monk* (O.E. *munuc*), *sone* 'son' (O.E. *sunu*), *world* (O.E. *w(e)orold*), *double* (O.Fr. *doble, duble, double*). Short *o* was pronounced as in modern English (although not in American) *pot*, except before *gh* or *ght* where it had a diphthongal pronunciation rather like the *ow* in modern English (although not in Australian) *crow*; for

31

example: *ynogh* 'enough', *thoght*. In these cases the spelling in Middle English was often *ou* besides *o*. Short *a* was pronounced as in the German name *Hans*, a sound which has no exact equivalent in modern English but can be approximated by shortening the long *a* sound in *enhance*. Before *l*, however, in words like *al, halle, smal, talke*, the *a* was pronounced much like the vowel in modern American (although this time not in British) English *pot*.

The scribes who copied out the manuscripts of the later fourteenth and fifteenth centuries sometimes made the attempt to distinguish between short and long vowels, mainly by doubling letters, like *ee* and *oo*, to indicate length. Unfortunately, this was by no means a consistent practice, although where it is done it obviously helps the reader of Chaucer, as in the opening lines of *The General Prologue* to *The Canterbury Tales*, for example, where these spellings occur:[12] *soote* (1), *roote* (2), *eek, sweete, breeth* (5), *heeth* (6), *goon* (12). These spellings may help with the quantity but not with the quality of the vowels involved, which is regrettable because there were two distinct pronunciations for long *e* and two for long *o*. The distinction is a phonemic one, hence its importance: in the portrait of the Clerk, for example, occur the words *heed* 'head' (*Gen Prol* 293) rhyming with *reed* 'red', and *heede* 'heed' (303) rhyming with *neede*. Only the correct pronunciations [hɛ:d] and [he:d] respectively can keep the two words apart. Similarly, Chaucer would distinguish between *brood* 'brood' (*LGW* Prol F, 133) rhyming with *good*, and *brode* 'broad' (*KnT* 2917) rhyming with *lode* 'load', for as a rule he is careful to use only like sounds in rhyme.[13] True, he uses an occasional dialect variant in pronunciation to help with a rhyme, just as he uses an occasional grammatical form not usual in London English for the same reason, but these are exceptions.

The two sounds of long *e* are represented in spelling usually by *e* or *ee*; they are, firstly, the close long [e:] heard in German *gehen*, French *été*, and rather as in modern English *take*. This is usually spelt *e* or *ee* in corresponding modern English words, and is occasionally spelt *ie* in Chaucerian English; for example, *sweete*

12. In the editions of Robinson, Manly and Rickert, and Donaldson.
13. 'Rimes of *ę̄* and *ę̆* (i.e. [ɛ:] and [e:]) are avoided only by poets who rime strictly, and in popular poetry are common, especially before dentals, where *ę̄* seems to have had a closer pronunciation in some districts, particularly in the North'. Karl Brunner, *An Outline of Middle English Grammar*, trans. by Grahame Johnston (Oxford, 1963), p. 13.

and *eek* 'also' (cp. 'to eke out'), cited above. Other examples are: *seke* 'to seek', *slepen* 'to sleep', *grief*, and the second syllables in *degree*, *meschief*. The other sound is [ɛ:] as in modern English *there*, which is usually spelt *ea* in corresponding modern English words; for example, *breeth* 'breath' and *heeth* 'heath', cited above. Other examples are *heed* 'head', *grece* 'grease', *speken* 'speak', *plesaunt* 'pleasant'. While the modern English spellings are a helpful guide in most cases, there are a few exceptions, like the Chaucerian *deere* and *heere* which have *ea* spellings in modern English 'dear' and 'hear' but have the close [e:] sound in Chaucerian pronunciation. Similarly, *speche* has *ee* spelling in modern English 'speech', but could have the open [ɛ:] sound in Chaucer's verse, derived from the pronunciation current in the south and south-west of England. In the south-east and east Midlands, *speche* and some other words normally had the closed [e:], so that Chaucer, familiar in his London English with both pronunciations, was able to sound such words in rhyme as it suited him. Hence such rhymes as *speche* and *teche* 'teach' (*Gen Prol* 307–8), which Kökeritz reads with their south-eastern sounds [e:], but *preche* 'preach' and *teche* (*ibid.* 481–2), to which he gives the sound [ɛ:][14] which represents the normal Middle English pronunciation of *preche* derived from O.Fr. *prechier* and the open sound in *teche* as it was pronounced in all parts of England outside Kent. Elsewhere Chaucer uses *speche* as a rhyme for *preche*, presumably pronouncing both words with open [ɛ:] this time (*PardT* 329–30; *Tr* II, 57–9; II, 496–7), and twice with the addition of a third rhyme word, *leche* 'physician, leech' (O.E. *læce*) in *Troilus and Criseyde* II, 569–72, and *teche* in IV, 1472–5. Chaucer is certainly right in claiming that

> ther is so gret diversite
> In Englissh and in writyng of oure tonge,
> (*Tr* V, 1793–4)

and he responded to it in matters of pronunciation as in other ways with characteristic alacrity.

Modern English has in many cases lost the difference in pronunciation between Chaucerian words with closed and open long *e*; thus *seek, grief, heath, speak, speech, teach*, all now have the same [i:] sound. In the case of Middle English long *o* this has not happened, although here too there were two distinct pronuncia-

14. Kökeritz, *op. cit.*, p. 24.

tions, an open [ɔ:] as in modern English *saw*, and a closed [o:] pronounced rather like modern English *tone*, with as little diphthongization as an English speaker can manage, or more accurately like German *Sohn* or French *chose*. Both sounds were spelt indiscriminately *o* or *oo* by medieval scribes, whereas in modern English the spellings are generally *o* or *oa* for the open sound, and *o* or *oo* for the closed one. Examples of Chaucerian open [ɔ:] are: *goon* 'go', cited earlier from *The General Prologue*, *hooly* 'holy', *hoom* 'home', *wo* 'woe', *cote* 'coat'. Examples of closed [o:] are: *roote*, cited earlier, *book*, *do* (or *doo* or *doon*), *oother* 'other', *sothe* 'sooth, truth', *to* 'too', or 'to' when stressed in the sentence. From these examples it will be noted that the first group, Chaucer's [ɔ:], represents words which in modern English have developed the diphthong [ou], to which should be added the common Chaucerian words *oon* 'one' and *noon* 'none', which also had the open [ɔ:]. The second group consists of words which today have the sound [u:] as in *root*, or [u] as in *book*, or [ʌ] as in *other*.

The dialectal differences affecting the distribution of the long *e* sounds in southern and midland regions of England have no exact parallel in the case of [ɔ:] and [o:]. Only north of the Humber did these sounds undergo rather different development, a fact which Chaucer put to good use in characterizing northern pronunciation in *The Reeve's Tale*. Nevertheless there are instances of Chaucer's rhyming the two sounds occasionally, which could be explained as carelessness (Gower does it too), but is perhaps better explained as a tendency for some words with open [ɔ:] to approach the close [o:] pronunciation in northern and eastern parts of England including London.[15] Such a tendency would make acceptable to Chaucer's audience rhymes like *doom*: *hoom* (*CT* VII, 1937-8), strictly [o:] : [ɔ:], but presumably both intended to be sounded [o:], or similarly *forsothe*: *bothe* (*Tr* IV, 1035-6), or the treatment meted out to some words figuring in rhyme on the not very frequent occasions when Chaucer places the word *to* at the end of a line. Apart from rhymes with *do*, which has the close [o:] one expects in *to*, there are several rhymes involving words with [ɔ:]: *also* and *so* (*BD* 771-2, *FranklT* 797-8, 1329-30), *therfro* (*HF* 735-6), *tho* 'those' (*WBT* 369-70), *two* (*WBT* 1251-2), all of which presumably are to be pronounced with close [o:]

15. Cp. E. J. Dobson, *English Pronunciation 1500-1700* (Oxford, 1957), Vol. II, pp. 674 ff.

on these occasions on the assumption that Chaucer intended these words to rhyme.

The remaining long vowels of Chaucer's English are rather less complicated. Long *a*, as in Middle English *name, space, take*, or the stressed syllable *-age* in *corage, pilgrimage*, has a sound somewhere between modern English *rather* and modern English *rare*, but whether closer to the one or to the other is a moot point.[16] The sound is occasionally spelt *aa*, a fact Chaucer may have made use of in *The Reeve's Tale* where the northern long *a* figures instead of long open *o* in the speech of Aleyn and John, but medieval scribal and modern editorial practices make it impossible to be certain what Chaucer's own practice was. In Manly and Rickert, line 4086 of *The Reeve's Tale* reads:

I is ful wight god waat as is a ra

while Robinson doubles the *a* in *ra* 'roe' as well as in *waat* 'knows':

'I is ful wight, God waat, as is a raa'.

Long *i* was spelt either *i* or *y*, but was uniformly pronounced as in modern English *feet*. Examples are *nyne* 'nine', *ryde* 'ride', *write*, the second (stressed) syllable in *dyvyne* 'divine'. In all these cases modern English has developed the diphthongal pronunciation [ai].

The long *u* sound as in modern English *boot* was generally spelt *ou* or *ow* as in *flour* 'flower', *yow* 'you', or in the second (stressed) syllable of *licour* 'liquid', or the final syllable of *condicioun* 'condition'. The spellings *ou* and *ow* could, however, also indicate a diphthongal pronunciation, which will be noted below. The letter *u* could indicate either the short [u] sound as in *ful* 'full, fully', mentioned earlier, or a long [ü:] sound as in German *Tür* or modern French *nature* in words adapted into Middle English from Romance sources, like *nature* or *vertu* or *aventure* in the opening passage of *The General Prologue*, all stressed on the *u*. But at the same time as this long [ü:] sound was pronounced in such words by educated speakers of Chaucer's time, an alternative pronunciation [iu], as in modern English *new*, was current in fourteenth-century colloquial English. Occasional spellings like *eu, ew, iw* indicate scribal attempts to render the diphthongal sound.

16. See the long note on p. 118 in John Williams Clark, *Early English: A Study of Old and Middle English* (London, rev. edn, 1967).

35

Chaucer very likely exploited this popular pronunciation much as a modern speaker of English might differentiate between what are commonly regarded as more 'refined' and more 'vulgar' pronunciations of words like *amateur* or *garage*; but where a writer like Dickens or D. H. Lawrence could indicate the desired pronunciation in print, Chaucer was at the mercy of scribes who were more than likely to 'myswrite' possible orthographic subtleties. Yet the fact remains that appropriate pronunciation will enhance a Chaucerian character or add a touch of irony: Harry Bailly's pronunciation of *aventure* was probably different from the Knight's, and a Chaucerian audience would have been likely to respond with a hearty laugh to hearing *excused* and *rude* pronounced in the more 'vulgar' manner in the Franklin's disingenuous

'Have me excused of my rude speche.'
(*FranklT* 718)

The same diphthong [iu], as in modern English *new*, had regularly developed in Middle English in words like *hewe* 'hue', *knew*, *newe*, *trewe* 'true', generally spelt either *ew* or *eu*. The same spellings were used to indicate another diphthong, [ɛu], which has no close modern English parallel, but which is not unlike the English [au] sound as pronounced by some speakers of broad Australian,[17] or perhaps like the *yƏ-oo* 'you' and *tƏ-oo* 'too' of Eliza's 'Lisson Grove lingo' in Shaw's *Pygmalion*. Examples of Chaucerian words with [ɛu] are: *fewe*, *lewed* 'ignorant, rude', *rewe* 'row, order, line', *shewe* 'show', *shrewe* 'shrew'. Pairs of words like *rewe* 'rue, sorrow, distress' with [iu] and *rewe* 'row, order, line' with [ɛu], and *hewe* 'hue' with [iu] and *hewe* 'to hew' with [ɛu], show that the distinction between the diphthongs is a phonemic one. Chaucer carefully keeps the two sounds apart in rhyme: among words with the [ɛu]diphthong, typical rhymes are *shewe*:*fewe* (*PardT* 343–4; *CT* VIII, 618–19; *Tr* V, 631–3; etc.); *dronkelewe* 'addicted to drink'; *shrewe* (*SumT* 2043–4, *MerchT* 1533–4, etc.); *shewed*:*lewed* (*HF* 1095–6, *PF* 44–7, with the additional rhyme *ithewed* '(well) conducted'). As a representative specimen of rhymes in [iu], here is a stanza from *Anelida and Arcite*, the same four rhymes recurring in a later stanza (281 ff.):

17. See A. G. Mitchell and Arthur Delbridge, *The Pronunciation of English in Australia* (Sydney, rev. edn, 1965), pp. 35 f.

So thirleth with the poynt of remembraunce
The swerd of sorowe, ywhet with fals plesaunce,
Myn herte, bare of blis and blak of hewe,
That turned is in quakyng al my daunce,
My surete in awhaped countenaunce,
Sith hit availeth not for to ben trewe;
For whoso trewest is, hit shal hir rewe,
That serveth love and doth her observaunce
Alwey til oon, and chaungeth for no newe.

(Anel 211–19)

Some other diphthongal pronunciations are illustrated by this
stanza, notably the several rhymes in -*aunce*, all of which are
stressed on this syllable. The sound was probably similar to the
[au] in modern English *cow*, although in some words, before the
labial consonants [f], [v], [m], an alternative monophthongal
pronunciation developed in the course of the fourteenth century,
its sound being the long [a:] as in Middle English *name*, *space*,
take, discussed earlier. Whether other words, like *daunce* or
chaunce developed a similar variant pronunciation at this time
is less certain.[18] The modern reader who gives to all these Chaucerian *au*-words the diphthongal value [au] will not be far wrong,
even if he would have sounded a little old-fashioned to Chaucer's
younger contemporaries.

The diphthong represented by *ai* in *availeth* and by *ey* in *alwey*
in the stanza from *Anelida and Arcite*, and elsewhere also spelt
ay or *ei*, had a Chaucerian pronunciation very close to the modern
one in the same words. Strictly, it was sounded a little lower in
the mouth than modern English *avail* or *way*, closer to the sound of
modern English *file*. Further examples are: *day*, *veyne* 'vein' and
'vain', *they*, *preye*.

We saw earlier that the spellings *ou* and *ow* could signal either
the long [u:] sound as in modern English *boot*, or a diphthong.
The latter had a pronunciation rather like the [ɔ] in modern
English *dog* followed by the [u:] in *boot*, transcribed [ɔu]. This
sound occurs in words which today have the sound [ou] as in
know (*knowe* in Chaucer's day), or a long [ɔ:] before *ght* as in
nought (*noght* in Chaucer).

The diphthong *oi*, also spelt *oy* as in *poynt* in the stanza above,
has much the same pronunciation in Chaucer's English as it has

18. Thus Kökeritz, *op. cit.*, p. 15. For the opposite view see Berndt, *op. cit.*, p. 111.

today. It may be that Chaucer's Prioress carried over from the local French dialect she spoke,

After the scole of Stratford atte Bowe,
For Frenssh of Parys was to hire unknowe,
(Gen Prol 125–6)

the Anglo-French pronunciation [ui] in words adopted from French into Middle English, like *boy (PrT* 562),[19] but it is unlikely that many of Chaucer's contemporaries retained this sound, despite the occurrence of occasional spellings like *juinen* 'join' or *puint* 'point' in the fourteenth century.[20] In the case of the Prioress Chaucer does not in any obvious way elaborate in her tale the kind of provincial French she spoke; we can only surmise whether in reading her tale aloud he indicated such Anglo-French features of her English as the [ui] sound in *boy* or possible peculiarities of accentuation. Such attention to certain linguistic minutiae, as we shall see in a later chapter, characterizes some of the portraits in *The Canterbury Tales*, and in the case of the Prioress would make all the more poignant the poet's ironic comment 'and Frenssh she spak ful faire and fetisly [elegantly]' *(Gen Prol* 124).

But accentuation, particularly of words adopted from French, is as difficult to establish precisely in Chaucer's English as are some of its sounds. Words derived from Germanic sources normally carried the stress on the stem syllable, or, in the case of compounds whose second element was a noun or adjective, on the first element of the compound, as in *wóful* and *sórwful* in the opening stanzas of *Troilus and Criseyde*. But the accentuation of Chaucer's verse may sometimes be a different matter from the way the poet himself might have talked English. In the third and fourth stanzas of Book I of *Troilus and Criseyde* several words ending in *-nesse* are made to rhyme on that syllable. That Chaucer stressed these syllables in ordinary speech is improbable, and to what extent he might have wished to vary normal accentual patterns for the sake of emphasizing rhymes is a question for individual readers to decide for themselves. Kökeritz stresses all these words, *un-*

19. A rare word in Chaucer, used elsewhere only by Friar and Pardoner. For its probable derivation from Old French, with the sound [ui], see *The Oxford Dictionary of English Etymology*, ed. C. T. Onions (Oxford, 1966), p. 112.
20. Cp. R. Jordan, *Handbuch der mittelenglischen Grammatik* (Heidelberg, 1925), pp. 210 f., and Berndt, *op. cit.*, pp. 106 ff.

liklynésse, derknésse, gladnésse, hevynésse, firmly on the *-nesse* suffix, although he indicates secondary stresses (\) on the stem syllables of *unlìklynésse* and *hèvynésse.*[21] Other readers may prefer to stress these words, and similar ones throughout Chaucer's works,[22] in the usual colloquial way, perhaps placing just enough subsidiary stress on the suffixes to indicate the rhymes. One's preference will be determined by the relative importance one wishes to attach to the underlying metrical structure of Chaucer's verse, or to the phrasal and accentual patterns of colloquial fourteenth-century English which Chaucer appears often to be reproducing, or to the level of speech – vulgar, informal, formal, highly rhetorical, and so on – suggested by the context. The opening stanzas of *Troilus and Criseyde*, with their apostrophe to 'thow goddesse of torment, | Thow cruwel Furie' (*Tr* I, 8–9), or the proem to Book III, equally formal and making use of some of the same rhymes, are presumably to be read somehow differently from the colloquial banter, for example, of Pandarus, who also uses such rhymes (as in I, 793 ff.).

Similar comments may be made about words of French origin in Chaucer's English. As a rule these continued to be stressed on the final syllable on adoption into English, as certain rhymes make clear, for example *licour: flour* (*Gen Prol* 3–4), *melodye:ye* 'eye' (9–10). In the case of polysyllabic words like *melodye* or *pilgrimages* or *servysable*, the first syllables probably received secondary stress, and this tendency, coupled with the habit of stressing native words on the stem syllable, probably helped gradually to shift the main stress to the stem of Romance words also. In Chaucer's time 'vulgar' characters, *cherles* as he calls them (*CT* I, 3169), or 'the lewed peple' (*PardT* 392), probably accented such French words as they used in the same way as the words derived from Old English or Scandinavian, while more educated speakers tended to retain the French accentual patterns longer. Chaucer's Miller bursts upon the Canterbury pilgrimage with a mouthful of oaths, a series of clichés ('for the nones', 'go my wey', 'alle and some', *CT* I, 3126 ff.), an assurance that he is drunk, advice to the audience to blame 'the ale of Southwerk' if he should 'mysspeke or seye', and to crown it all blunders with comic ineptitude onto

---

21. Kökeritz, *op. cit.*, pp. 31–2, in his phonetic transcription of *Tr* I, 1–35.
22. Like the rhyming *clothyng, huntyng, knowyng*, and *likyng* in *The Monk's Tale*, 2304 ff., noted on p. 29 above.

the erudite French word *protestacioun*, used elsewhere in *The Canterbury Tales* only once by the Parson, and outside that poem only by Criseyde (twice) and the false Egistus in the Legend of Hypermnestra in *The Legend of Good Women*. The Miller rhymes the word with *soun* 'sound'. According to strict pentametrical rules the word ought to be stressed prótĕstáciŏun and according to educated usage probably pròtestacioún (cp. Kökeritz's stressing of *lymytacióun* in his transcription of the opening lines of *The Wife of Bath's Tale, op. cit.*, p. 26). How was a drunken Chaucerian Miller likely to pronounce such a word in a richly colloquial passage? Slowly, haltingly, 'mis-spoken', no doubt; probably starting with an emphatic *pró-* and then laboriously uttering each painful syllable one after the other, as any *lewed* man would do, and distorting sounds here and there in the manner of any 'rolling English drunkard' on a pilgrimage along a 'rolling English road', something like [ˈprɔː ˈteʃˈtaːˈʃiːˈuːn] perhaps. This, of course, is conjecture based on the evidence provided by listening to modern English drunks struggling with long words, but it makes sense of the Miller's 'I knowe it by my soun' in the next line, and better sense of the words 'if that I mysspeke or seye' than is usually attached to them, and it explains moreover why such a rare word, fit for the Parson indeed, is ascribed to the Miller at this point in the proceedings.

One could cite other examples. Roger the Cook plunges into the fray, like the Miller, with a strong oath and a string of colloquial idioms, adorning his opening remarks with an impressive selection of Romance words, like *conclusion, argument, perilous, herbergage* 'abode, lodging', some of which, like the last, are distinctly learned words in Chaucer. Only the Clerk, the Man of Law, and the erudite cock Chauntecleer in *The Nun's Priest's Tale* use *herbergage* besides the Cook. Presumably the latter's pronunciation of such words would be more English than French, particularly in the matter of accentuation.

These comments are offered in the hope that they may help towards a more imaginative reading of Chaucer's verse, less stilted and mechanical than is often the case. No one knows how Chaucer himself read his verses aloud; the only time I myself was strongly reminded of the Chaucerian *cadence* (Chaucer's own word in *The House of Fame*, 623) when listening to a poet reciting his own verse was when hearing the versatile American poet James Dickey reading his 'Cherrylog Road', a distant descendant of the medieval fabliau that gave us among others *The Shipman's Tale* and similar Chaucerian masterpieces. Modern scholarship can draw up guidelines to Chaucer's grammar and pronunciation and stress and scansion, but only our individual response to Chaucer's poetry will ultimately determine how we read the Cook's words or the cock's and all the other voices Chaucer created in his work.[23]

As far as grammatical guidelines are concerned, it will be necessary here to comment on only a few aspects of Chaucer's grammar, because grammatical as well as syntactical topics will be discussed in various contexts in subsequent chapters of this book.[24] For the most part, Chaucer's grammar, like his pronunciation, is that of educated fourteenth-century Londoners, diversified by occasional 'provincialisms' for artistic, mainly prosodic, reasons, like the *-es* ending in rhymes for the third person singular of the present indicative which we have already noted. A comparison with a contemporary London prose text like Thomas Usk's Appeal against John Northampton of 1384[25] shows that Chaucer's grammar conforms to contemporary London usage when not influenced by literary considerations of a prosodic or rhetorical nature. Chaucer himself only once uses the word *grammeere*, when in *The Prioress's Tale* the 'litel clergeon's' older friend apologizes for his limitations as an instructor with the words

> 'I kan namoore expounde in this mateere;
> I lerne song, I kan but smal grammeere.'
> *(PrT* 535–6)

The word here has the usual Middle English meaning of Latin grammar, and a 'mayster of gramere', like the Iohan Cornwal

---

23. Some of these ideas first came to me some years ago when broadcasting *The Nun's Priest's Tale* for the Australian Broadcasting Commission. The girl student who read Pertelote's lines, in a passable approximation to Chaucer's English, did so in an attractive but rather high-pitched voice which combined astonishingly well (as I thought) the Chaucerian poetic tone with an unmistakable gallinaceous cackle. I like to think that Chaucer would have approved.

24. Most editions of Chaucer discuss his grammar. Systematic studies go back as far as B. ten Brink's original German edition of 1884, and are as recent as J. Kerkhof's. A concise summary of 'the main differences in grammar between Chaucerian and Modern English' is given in *An Introduction to Chaucer* by Maurice Hussey, A. C. Spearing, and James Winny (Cambridge, 1965), pp. 93–6.

25. This is printed in R. W. Chambers and Marjorie Daunt, *A Book of London English 1384–1425* (Oxford, 1931, repr. 1967), pp. 22–31.

and Richard Pencrych mentioned by John of Trevisa in his up-
dating of Ranulph Higden's *Polychronicon*,[26] was one who taught
his pupils how to *construen* Latin grammar. It is in this sense of 'to
translate by parsing' that Chaucer uses *construe* in the same context
in *The Prioress's Tale* (528), a word used only twice elsewhere
with the more general meaning of 'to form an opinion, pass
judgment' on something (*MED*) (*Tr* III, 33; *LGW* Prol F, 152).[27]
Trevisa's well-known passage is not intended to suggest any
growing concern with English grammar in 1385, but is clearly
interested in the substitution of English for French in 'construing'
Latin 'in al þe gramerscoles of Engelond'. Chaucer himself shows
no conspicuous interest in the grammar of his English comparable
to the attention which he pays to other facets of his language
and of his 'art poetical'; he simply uses it, but not, as we shall see,
without discrimination.

Most of the parts of speech in Chaucer's English display considerable morphological simplification compared with Old
English, especially perhaps the nouns, where the development of
unstressed final *-e* from various Old English vocalic noun endings
and the progressive loss of final *-n* in inflectional endings brought
about the disappearance of gender as a grammatical category
and helped to establish a simpler and more uniform system of
noun declension. Chaucer's nouns usually have only one distinctive inflectional ending which appears as *-s* or *-es*. This is one
method used to indicate the possessive function, as in 'the
Knyghtes Tale', or 'Loves folk' (*Tr* I, 34), alongside which could
be used constructions with *of* as in modern English: 'the double
sorwe of Troilus' (*Tr* I, 1). Group genitives like the modern
English 'The Wife of Bath's Prologue' are very rare in Chaucer;
he appears to have been the first to use them in poetry. Alongside
the more usual construction as in 'The Prologe of the Wyves Tale
of Bathe', Chaucer has 'the god of slepes heyr' (*BD* 168), 'that God
of Loves servantz' (*Tr* I, 15), and 'the grete god of Loves name'
(*HF* 1489), all involving the noun *god*. Some nouns are used
without *-(e)s* in the possessive case, mainly proper names ending
in *-s*, as in 'Thomas lyf of Inde' (*SumT* 1980), 'Epicurus owene

---

26. In ch. lix of Trevisa's translation. The passage is familiar to many students of
Middle English from Kenneth Sisam's *Fourteenth Century Verse and Prose* (Oxford,
1921 *et seq.*), p. 149.
27. Troilus once uses the antonym *mysconstruwe* in *Tr* I, 346.

sone' (*Gen Prol* 336); and some nouns occur in the possessive case
both with and without the -(*e*)*s* ending. These are mainly nouns of
relationship, like *fader* and *brother*, as in 'thi brother wif' (*Tr* I, 678)
or 'thy brotheres wyf' (*SecNT* 296), probably both disyllabic,
but *doghter* occurs only once in the possessive as 'hir doghter
name' (*CIT* 608), while *mooder* 'mother' always has the possessive
form *moodres* as in 'moodres pitee' (*PrT* 593). The word *herte* usually has the -*s* possessive, except in what are compounds, like
hertespoon, perhaps 'breast-bone' (*KnT* 2606), and practically
compounds, like *herte roote* (*WBT* 471, *LGW* 1993), and *herte
blood* (*WBT* 718, *ABC* 164, etc.). Similarly, the word *hevene*
'heaven' has the -*s* possessive in most cases, as in 'hevenes lilie'
(*SecNT* 87) or 'hevenes fyr' (*LGW* 1221), but has the possessive
hevene in combination with *kyng* (e.g. *MillT* 3464) or *blisse* (e.g.
PF 72). 'Hevene queene' occurs (*ABC* 24, 149) as well as 'hevenes
queene' (*CYT* 1089, *Tr* IV, 1594).

Perhaps in some cases Chaucer preferred one form to the other
for artistic reasons. In *Troilus and Criseyde* V, 675, the form *ladys*
(in Root, *ladis*) adds another sibilant to all the surrounding *s*'s in
initial, medial, and final positions – all suggestive of the wind and
the sighs referred to in the stanza:

'And hardily this wynd, that more and moore
Thus stoundemele encresseth in my face,
Is of my ladys depe sikes soore. . . .'
(*Tr* V, 673-5)

The only other example of this possessive form, *ladys*, in place of
Chaucer's usual possessive form *lady*, occurs in the doubtfully
Chaucerian poem *Complaynt d'Amours* (61), where there is a
similar contextual association with sighs. Perhaps this is too far-
fetched. But Chaucer did have a 'good ear', as Dorothy Everett
noted in a classic essay,[28] and even when due allowance is made
for scribal mis-writing and the erratic nature of manuscript
transmission, one is left with the impression that such grammatical
niceties could be, and sometimes were, part of Chaucer's poetic
art.

This impression is not diminished by comparing, for example,
the occurrences in Chaucer's verse of the possessive forms *fader*

28. Dorothy Everett, 'Chaucer's "Good Ear"', in her *Essays on Middle English
Literature* (Oxford, 1955), pp. 139–48.

and *fadres* as they appear in the edited texts of Robinson, Manly and Rickert, and Root. The first form, *fader*, is used rather less frequently than the other (fifteen times, as against twenty-three), and occurs almost wholly in idiomatic phrases, mainly oaths of the kind 'by my fader soule' or 'by youre fader kyn', and in the phrase 'after his fader day'. Not surprisingly, the oaths are confined to pilgrims like Harry Bailly, the Manciple, and the Canon's Yeoman, and to characters in certain tales who, like Pertelote, or John in *The Reeve's Tale*, swear manfully – or henfully. On only three occasions is *fader* used as a possessive in more straightforward narrative contexts ('his fader carte', *Tr* V, 665, and *HF* 943, referring to the sun's chariot, and *CLT* 896, with reference to the ousted Griselda's return to 'hir fadre hous'). On the other hand, *fadres* occurs normally in narrative contexts, most of them, as it happens, of a singularly pathetic or of a reverential kind, like the starving boy lying down 'in his fadres barm' to die, in the story of Ugolino of Pisa (*MkT* 2440), or Constance's pitiful

'So kys hym ones in his fadres name!'
(*MLT* 861)

Similar pathetic occurrences are in *The Physician's Tale* ('with fadres pitee', 211); in *The Franklin's Tale* ('and in hir fadres blood they made hem daunce', 1373); in *Troilus and Criseyde* ('hire fadres shame', I, 107); in *The Legend of Good Women* ('my faderes gost', 1295); and elsewhere. The context is reverential in devotional or biblical passages where the contrast with the *fader*-oaths is particularly obvious. Such passages occur in *The Prioress's Tale* ('the Fadres sapience', 472); in *The Second Nun's Tale* ('that Fadres Sone', 326); in *The Clerk's Tale* twice in quick succession:

And ay she kepe hir fadres lyf on-lofte
With everich obeisaunce and diligence
That child may doon to fadres reverence.
(*CLT* 229–31)

And similarly elsewhere. Perhaps Chaucer even intended a subtle difference, in *The Clerk's Tale*, between the *narrator's* use of 'hir fadre hous' (896), already mentioned, and the use by Walter of 'youre fadres hous' (809) and by Griselda of 'in my fadres place' (862) and 'my fadres hous' (871). Be that as it may, there is at least one instance of the -*s* form which no doubt every reader

44

would accept as a deliberate choice on Chaucer's part, namely towards the end of *The Legend of Good Women* in a passage where the *-s* possessive prevents three otherwise uninflected nouns of relationship coming one after the other in a double possessive construction:

> And thus Lyno hath of his fadres brother
> The doughter wedded.
>
> *(LGW* 2608–9)

It is an interesting fact that in his prose Chaucer uses the periphrastic construction with *of* more than ten times as often as the inflected possessive, whereas in his verse the proportion is about seven to five.[29] The more compact structure of the inflected type is often preferable in verse, whether in simple cases, like

> That he so ful stood in his lady grace,
>
> *(Tr* III, 472)

compared with

> To stonden in grace of his lady deere;
>
> *(CYT* 1348)

or in more complex patterns, like the emphatic

> 'Now by my moodres sires soule I swere',
>
> *(MerchT* 2265)

compared with the slower, more diffuse

> 'Up peril of my soule and of my lyf'.
>
> *(NPT* 2944)

The rhythms of Chaucer's prose, on the other hand, favour the frequent use of the periphrastic possessive: 'And right so ben we gladde somtyme of the face of the see whan it es cleer' *(Bo* II, pr. 5, 59–60); 'And forther over, sooth is that hooly ordre is chief of al the tresorie of God' *(ParsT* 893); 'The remenaunt of the bordure under the orisonte is the arch of the nyght' *(Astr* II, 7, 11–12) 'thurgh the benigne grace of hym that is kyng of kynges and preest over alle preestes, that boghte us with the precious blood of his herte; / so that I may been oon of hem at the day of doom that shulle be saved' *(CT* X, 1090–1).

The second function of the inflectional *-s* or *-es*, occasionally *-z*, is to indicate the plural of nouns, and this is in Chaucer's English

29. Cp. the table in Mustanoja, p. 75.

as in modern English the normal method: *shoures* 'showers', *croppes* 'crops', *nacions* 'nations', *marchauntz* 'merchants', and so on. Some words could form their plurals with or without inflectional -(*e*)*s*, especially nouns denoting quantities – numbers, sizes, amounts, periods of time, and the like – which are frequently left uninflected, particularly after, but not usually before, cardinal numbers. The following examples illustrate Chaucer's use of alternative plurals in verse:

Fyve thousand *folk* it was as greet mervaille
With loves [loaves] fyve and fisshes two to feede.
(*MLT* 502–3)

O yonge, fresshe *folkes*, he or she.
(*Tr* V, 1825)

But right anon a thousand *peple* in thraste.
(*PhysT* 260)

'Love, that with an holsom alliaunce
Halt *peples* joyned'.
(*Tr* III, 1746–7)

Er we hadde riden fully fyve *mile*
. . . .
It semed as he had priked *miles* three.
(*CT* VIII, 555, 561)

'Lo, Moyses fourty dayes and fourty *nyght*
Fasted. . . .'
(*SumT* 1885–6)

'The owle ek, which that hette Escaphilo,
Hath after me shright al thise *nyghtes* two'.
(*Tr* V, 319–20)

That falleth nat eft withinne a thousand *yeer*.
(*KnT* 1669)

But sooth is seyd, go sithen many *yeres*,
That 'feeld hath eyen and the wode hath eres'.
(*KnT* 1521–2)

The demands of rhyme clearly influence the plural form chosen where such alternatives exist, and occasionally even where they do not normally exist, as when the normal plural *organs*, as in 'the organs maden melodie' (*SecNT* 134), is left uninflected to provide a rhyme for the plural verb *gon*:

His voys was murier than the murie orgon
On messe-dayes that in the chirche gon.
(*NPT* 2851–2)

In the second quotation from *The Knyght's Tale* above *eres* is the usual plural for 'ears', but in some cases Chaucer leaves off the -*s* for the sake of rhyme, as in:

No wonder is, for to the peples ere
There cam no word, but that they mordred were.
(*CLT* 727–8)

Some nouns denoting animals have identical singular and plural forms in Chaucer's English, as some still have in modern English, as in 'thise wilde deer' (*FranklT* 1195) compared with the singular 'the leoun or the deer' (*KnT* 2150), or in this domestic catalogue:

His lordes sheep, his neet [cattle], his dayerye [dairy],
His swyn, his hors, his stoor [stock], and his pultrye
Was hoolly in this Reves governyng.
(*Gen Prol* 597–9)

The plural *hors* is the only form used by Chaucer in verse; in prose he also uses *horses*, as in this passage; 'Also the synne of aornement [adornment] or of apparaille is in thynges that aperteren to ridynge, as in to manye delicat horses that been hoolden for delit, that been so faire, fatte, and costlewe [costly]' (*ParsT* 432) – uttered, no doubt, with a disapproving glance at the Monk who had 'ful many a deyntee hors' in his stable and was riding a berry-brown palfrey 'in greet estaat'. Like *hors*, other nouns ending in -*s* are found uninflected in the plural, *caas* 'case, lawcase', for instance, in the line

In termes hadde he caas and doomes alle,
(*Gen Prol* 323)

or *paas* 'pace';

O fieble moone, unhappy been thy paas,
(*MLT* 306)

or *vers*:

These vers of gold and blak iwriten were.
(*PF* 141)

The form *eyen* 'eyes' in line 1522 of *The Knight's Tale*, quoted above, illustrates the plural formation in -*n* inherited from Old English and still found in a few nouns today, like *oxen* or *brethren*. Many more Middle English nouns formed their plurals thus than is the case today, particularly in the dialects of southern England, but the incidence of alternative plurals in -(*e*)*s* in the fourteenth century indicates the pressure of the more usual plural form. Among examples of alternative plurals in -*n* and -(*e*)*s* are these:[30] 'hir doghtren two' (*NPT* 2829) and 'hir doghtres two' (*ibid.* 3375); also:

Hir hosen weren of fyn scarlet reed,
(*Gen Prol* 456)

and

In hoses rede he wente fetisly;
(*MillT* 3319)

similarly, in rhyme, 'foes':

This false Brutus and his othere foon,
(*MkT* 2706)

and

'Right in dispit of alle your foos';
(*HF* 1668)

or, also in rhyme, 'toes':

Lyk asure were his legges and his toon,
(*NPT* 2862)

and

This Chauntecleer stood hye upon his toos.
(*ibid.* 3331)

---

30. Other examples are listed in Friedrich Wild, *Die Sprachlichen Eigentümlichkeiten der wichtigeren Chaucer-Handschriften und die Sprache Chaucers* (Wien and Leipzig, 1915), p. 267.

One other category of Old English plural formations that persists in modern English is the group of nouns which forms its plurals by changing its stem vowel, technically known as *umlaut* or mutation, as in 'a mows [mouse] among othere mys [mice]' (*Bo* II, pr, 6, 32), and similarly, among others, *foot, feet*; *goos, gees*; *man, men*; *womman, wommen*; but *lemman* 'sweetheart' has the plural *lemmans*, as in this piece of sound advice from one of Chaucer's disreputable friars:

Be war, my sone, and herkne paciently,
That twenty thousand men han lost hir lyves
For stryving with hir lemmans and hir wyves.
(*SumT* 1996-8)

A point worth noting is that plural subjects may occasionally be accompanied by singular verbs in Chaucer's English. One reason for this may be the fact that some nouns, like *sheep* or *swyn*, had identical singular and plural forms, as we have seen, while others had a collective meaning which justified a singular verb. The domestic catalogue from *The General Prologue* quoted above, for example, has a multiple subject including several nouns denoting animals which concludes with the collective noun *pultrye* 'poultry', the whole list being followed by the singular verb *was*. An instance of the singular *was* preceding the plural *mervailles*, rhyming with *batailles*, occurs in *The Squire's Tale*, 660:

That nevere yet was herd so grete mervailles.

'Marvels' is a curious anticipation of the modern English 'news', a collective plural form regularly treated as singular. There is an example of two plural nouns, perhaps also felt to have collective force, in the Parson's 'and ye shul understonde that orisouns or preyeres is for to seyn a pitous wyl of herte' (*ParsT* 1039).

Of other Old English noun inflections apart from the possessive and the plural forms discussed, only a few traces remain in Chaucer's English. These can be regarded as survivals of the Old English dative in such forms as *abedde* 'in bed' (*Tr* II, 1305) rhyming with the preterite *spedde*, compared with the normal form *bed* as in 'to the clerkes bed' (*RvT* 4219) rhyming with the past participle *ysped*. Similarly 'to shipe' (*MillT* 3540), compared with 'toward hir ship' (*MLT* 823); 'be with childe' (*KnT* 2310); 'yeer by yere' (*KnT* 1203); and some others. As with some of the other inflectional variants examined, Chaucer's choice was frequently determined by rhyme, and we cannot point to any evidence in our discussion so far that he toyed with grammatical innovations. Where alternatives were available, he availed himself of them; for the rest, it is probably fair to say that there is less *diversite* in Chaucer's grammar than in any other aspect of his 'Englissh'.

This conclusion holds as true for the remaining parts of speech as for the nouns so far considered. The personal pronouns, for example, as used by Chaucer, show no striking deviations from contemporary fourteenth-century London usage, though there are some differences from modern English usage. The most obvious difference is the medieval distinction, which persists in some modern European languages, between the polite (plural) form of the second personal pronoun, *ye*, with its oblique case *you* and possessive *youre*, and the informal or familiar (singular) form *thou, thee, thy(n)*. While in general Chaucer observes the conventions of his age in their use, he exploits the possibilities offered by a careful manipulation of these pronouns according to character and situation. As this topic will occupy us further in a later context (ch. 7, pp. 382 ff.), it may suffice to mention just one example here. In *Troilus and Criseyde* the lovers regularly employ the respectful, more formal plural pronoun in addressing one another, but at the central point in their relationship, at the unwelcome dawn of the morning following their first night of love together Criseyde interrupts the flow of *ye*'s and *yow*'s with a poignant

> 'For I am *thyn*, by God and by my trouthe!'
> (*Tr* III, 1512)

This reading is supported by the great majority of manuscripts of *Troilus and Criseyde* and probably represents what Chaucer wrote. It justifies the comment by D. S. and L. E. Brewer that 'the passion of this declaration is revealed by that rarest of grammatical uses between the lovers, the second person singular, though even here not as a pronoun',[31] that is, not in direct address but in the possessive case, though the latter is perhaps even more passionate here than *thou* would have been.

The forms of the pronouns also show some differences from their modern English equivalents. The first person singular,

---

31. *Troilus and Criseyde*, ed. D. S. and L. E. Brewer (London, 1969), p. 121.

usually *I*, occasionally appears as *ich* before a following vowel or *h*, as in

'Whi suffre ich it? Whi nyl ich it redresse?'
(*Tr* V, 40)

And similar alternatives exist in the case of the possessives *my* and *myn* and *thy* and *thyn*, where the forms in *-n* are used before a following vowel or *h*, as in:

'But I was hurt right now thurghout *myn* ye [eye]
Into *myn* herte, that wol *my* bane be.'
(*KnT* 1096–7)

The Chaucerian equivalent of modern *its* is *his*, for example: 'ecch contree hath his lawes' (*Tr* II, 42), and of modern *their* and *them* is *hir(e)* and *hem*, but *they* had replaced O.E. *hīe* by Chaucer's time:

'*They* wene that no man may *hem* bigyle,
But by my thrift, yet shal I blere *hir* ye [eye]'.
(*RvT* 4048–9)

Some Chaucerian constructions involving personal pronouns which look unfamiliar to the modern reader are quite idiomatic in Middle English. Such are the phrases 'it am I', as in 'Wostow naught wel that it am I, Pandare?' (*Tr* I, 588) and 'it were' with a plural noun, as in 'that it were gentil-men of gret degre' (*LGW* 1506); and the occurrence of the third personal pronoun with a demonstrative function, corresponding perhaps to modern English 'this' or 'a certain' or, where appropriate, the colloquial 'this 'ere', before a personal name or a personal noun (as in 'he þe comlokest kyng' in *SGGK* 53). A well-known example is Chaucer's 'certes, he Jakke Straw and his meynee' (*NPT* 3394); similarly, 'up roos he Julius, the conquerour' (*MkT* 2673), 'he Moyses' (*SqT* 250), 'hym Arcite' (*KnT* 1210), and others. Chaucer also uses personal pronouns frequently in reflexive functions which have disappeared in modern English; for example:

Repentynge *hym* that he hadde evere ijaped
Of Loves folk;
(*Tr* I, 318–19)

and similarly in prose: 'many men ne repenten *hem* nevere of swiche thoghtes' (*ParsT* 298). But the pronoun may be omitted, perhaps for metrical reasons, as in

> 'it shal nat bee
> That evere in word or werk I shal repente
> That I yow yaf myn herte in hool entente.'
> (*CLT* 859–61)

Verbs of motion, as in 'Up stirte hire Alison' (*MillT* 3824) or 'He goth hym hom' (*Tr* V, 1667), are also quite often used reflexively by Chaucer.

Impersonal constructions involving personal pronouns in their oblique forms are also common in Chaucer in connection with a number of verbs, either with *it*, as in modern English 'it seems to me', or without, as in the archaic 'methinks'. At the same time, Chaucer's usage reflects contemporary developments towards personal constructions making alternatives possible which once again helped to enrich the expressiveness of his English. Compare, for example, the impersonal construction

> 'so soore longeth me
> To eten of the smale peres grene',
> (*MerchT* 2332–3)

with the personal construction

> Thanne longen folk to goon on pilgrimages.
> (*Gen Prol* 12)

The latter denotes a straightforward desire, but the former, by making the desire to eat green pears the implied subject of the sentence and making the 'real' subject (*me*) the object, connotes an element of helplessness, a passive surrender to physical or psychological urges, which fit with appropriate irony into the strategy of 'this fresshe May' attempting to deceive her blind, doting husband. Among other verbs which employ personal pronouns in impersonal constructions are *liken*,

> 'For many a man that may nat stonde a pul,
> It liketh hym at the wrastlyng for to be';
> (*PF* 164–5)

metten 'to dream' ('me mette so ynly swete a sweven [dream]', *BD* 276); *remembren* –

'But, Lord Crist! whan that it remembreth me
Upon my yowthe, and on my jolitee,
It tikleth me aboute myn herte roote';

(*WBT* 469–71)

shamen ('to asken help thee shameth in thyn herte', *MLT* 101);
and others.

Chaucer occasionally employs what appear to be impersonal
constructions involving a noun as the subject of an infinitive,
although the noun may have been felt to be in an oblique case
rather than in the nominative. By using the preposition 'for',
modern English removes possible ambiguity in cases like 'time
for a lady to go hence', Chaucer's

'Now were it tyme a lady to gon henne!'

(*Tr* III, 630)

Similarly,

Lo, swich it is a millere to be fals!

(*RvT* 4318)

A kynges sone to ben in swich prysoun,
And ben devoured, thoughte hem gret pite.

(*LGW* 1975–6)

Chaucer uses as relative pronouns the words *which*a nd *what*,
which also function as interrogatives, and *that*. He does not use
who as a relative pronoun, but uses *whos* and *whom* with antecedents
denoting persons. *Which* and *that* may refer to persons or things,
whereas *what*, which occurs rarely in a strictly relative function,
is used with less definite antecedents like *al*. Thus the reading in
Troilus and Criseyde II, 1561 is usually given as 'but God and Pandare wist al what this mente', although several manuscripts have
instead the more modern sounding construction 'what al this
mente'. Other ways of expressing the relative function are by
adding *that* to *which* or *whom*, less commonly to *whos*; for
example:

'Hire fader, which that old is and ek hoor'.

(*Tr* V, 1284)

'Wel oghte a man avysed for to be
Whom that he broghte into his pryvetee'.
(*CT* I, 4333–4)

'Syk lay the goode man whos that the place is'.
(*SumT* 1768)

Occasionally Chaucer uses the combinations 'the which' or 'the which that' or 'which as' to introduce a relative clause, as in

'Whan that she comth, the which shal be right soone'.
(*Tr* V, 391)

Now was ther of that chirche a parissh clerk,
The which that was ycleped Absolon.
(*MillT* 3312–13)

Hir tretys, which as ye shal after heere.
(*CLT* 331)

Personal pronouns are sometimes combined with *that* to produce the equivalent of modern *who, whose, whom*; for example: 'A Knyght ther was ... / That ... / ... he loved chivalrie' (*Gen Prol* 43–5), where *he* not only helps the metre but holds the clause together, in this case an important function as another, grammatically different 'that he' intervenes:

A Knyght ther was, and that a worthy man,
That fro the tyme that he first bigan
To riden out, he loved chivalrie.

Perhaps this is not, syntactically, one of Chaucer's most successful sentences with its three rapidly succeeding *that*'s. Considering the number of possible methods of expressing relative function, Chaucer did not always opt for the best, as the last example illustrates, or the next with its duplicated *that*:

And taketh kep of that that I shal seyn,
(*PhysT* 90)

or this passage with its plethora of pronouns which are by no means easy to disentangle:

'For sith it may not here discussed be
Who loveth hire best, as seyde the tercelet,
Thanne wol I don hire this favour, that she

Shal han right hym on whom hire herte is set,
And he hire that his herte hath on hire knet'.
(*PF* 624–8)

Chaucer's use of one relative construction rather than another
was probably often quite mechanical, though Tauno Mustanoja
suggests that at least as far as *that* and *which* are concerned, 'it
seems possible to distinguish a few diverging trends in their uses'
in later Middle English.[32] But there appear to be too many exceptions to formulate rules. Chaucer may have preferred some
relative constructions to others, as is suggested by the great preponderance of plain *which* to *the which* in his work in contrast to
Gower, but mostly any conscious choice exercised will have been
determined by metrical or stylistic considerations, and not invariably crowned, as we have seen, with success.

In considering the grammatical function of final -*e* in Chaucerian
prosody earlier in this chapter we noted that monosyllabic adjectives ending in a consonant add -*e* when attached to a plural
noun, as in

The thre were goode men, and riche, and olde.
(*WBT* 197)

It is in fact only in adjectives of this type that any consistent
inflectional usage survives, and whether in the singular of the
original 'weak' declension or in the plural, the Chaucerian ending
is -*e*. In the case of *cold* the normal plural form is *colde*: 'the colde
sterres' (*Bo* II, m. 6, 20), 'in cares colde' (*Tr* V, 1747). In the
singular we find *cold* except in the following cases, where *colde*
is used: after the definite article ('the colde deeth', *KnT* 2008);
after demonstrative pronouns ('in thilke colde, frosty regioun',
KnT 1973); after possessive pronouns ('but ofte tyme hire colde
mowth he kiste', *Tr* IV, 1161); and before a proper name ('the
weie of the olde colde Saturnus', *Bo* IV, m. 1, 12–13). For two
other uses of the -*e* form in the singular Chaucer has no *colde*
examples; one is the form of an adjective before a noun in the
vocative, as in 'o yonge Hugh of Lyncoln' (*PrT* 684); and the
other when it follows a noun in the possessive case; for example
after *fadres*:

Whan that Criseyde unto hire bedde wente
Inwith hire fadres faire brighte tente.
(*Tr* V, 1021–2)

32. Mustanoja, p. 196.

When used predicatively the adjective remains uninflected in the singular ('swich was this ypocrite, bothe coold and hoot', *SqT* 520), but in the plural it could take either form, more commonly with -*e*: 'wommennes conseils been ful ofte colde' (*NPT* 3256). Adjectives adopted from French may retain an -*s* ending in the plural, as in 'oure othere goodes temporels' (*Mel* 998) rendering the French 'noz autres biens temporelz', or 'the foure principales plages' (*Astr* I, 5, 10–11), but 'these 3 principale cercles' (*Astr* I, 17, 45).

A handful of other inflexional relics survives in a few Chaucerian adjectival forms, for example in the phrase 'longe tyme' (*PardT* 436), that is 'for a long time', or in the descendant of the Old English genitive plural *ealra* in Chaucer's word *aller* 'of all':

And yet this Manciple sette hir aller cappe.
(*Gen Prol* 586)

Up roos oure Hoost, and was oure aller cok.
(*Gen Prol* 823)

The comparison of adjectives in Chaucer's English is much as it is today, using the ending -*er(e)* for the comparative, as in

Ther nas a man of gretter hardinesse,
(*Tr* I, 566)

and the ending -*est(e)* for the superlative, as in

And strengest folk ben therwith overcome,
The worthiest and grettest of degree.
(*Tr* I, 243–4)

The adverbs *moore* and *moost* are used by Chaucer to form comparatives and superlatives as in modern English: 'which partie is the bettre and moore profitable' (*Mel* 1211); 'which of hem been moost feithful and moost wise and eldest and most approved in conseillyng' (*ibid.* 1155).

Adverbs formed by adding -*ly* to adjectives are easily recognized as such by the modern reader of Chaucer: *shortly, fetisly, swetely*, as are adverbs formed with -*liche* –

And have a mantel roialliche ybore.
(*Gen Prol* 378)

Both types of adverb could be derived from the same adjective, providing yet more grammatical alternatives for Chaucer to exploit. The ending *-liche*, with the final *-e* silent, is often employed before a following vowel or *h*, but by no means invariably:

Right so this markys fulliche hath purposed.
(*CLT* 706)

And fully in his lady grace he stood.
(*MerchT* 2018)

A third method of deriving adverbs from adjectives was to add *-e*, as in

And Frenssh she spak ful faire and fetisly,
(*Gen Prol* 124)

except where the adjective already ended in *-e*, in which case adjective and adverb were formally indistinguishable unless another ending was employed. In the following passage *curteisly* is obviously an adverb; *narwe* could be both formally and syntactically either an adverb or an adjective qualifying *armes*, but the reference in the poem is plainly to the friar's tight embrace; and *sweete* could also be, formally, adverb or adjective, but the syntax demands the former:

The frere ariseth up ful curteisly,
And hire embraceth in his armes narwe,
And kiste hire sweete, and chirketh as a sparwe
With his lyppes.
(*SumT* 1802–5)

In a few cases, adjectives which do not end in *-e* function as adverbs without any ending being added; for example in the phrases 'plat and pleyn' and 'short and pleyn', as in Harry Bailly's

'This is the poynt, to speken short and pleyn'.
(*Gen Prol* 790)

Any suspicion aroused that this might be some vulgar solecism characteristic of the speaker is soon dispelled by the discovery that Knight, Monk, Second Nun, and other pilgrims use the same or similar phrases.

Verbs in Chaucer's English belong for the most part to either of the two main inflectional types inherited from Old English and still active in modern English. The first and larger group, the consonantal type (often referred to as 'weak verbs'), uses a *d* or *t* to form its preterite and past participle, as in modern English 'love', preterite 'loved', past participle 'loved', Chaucerian *love(n)*, *loved(e)*, *(y)loved*, or modern English 'greet', 'greeted', 'greeted', Chaucerian *grete(n)*, *grette*, *y-gret*. The second group, the vocalic type (often referred to as 'strong verbs'), forms its preterite and past participle by changing its root vowel or diphthong, as in modern English 'find', 'found', 'found', Chaucerian *fynde(n)*, preterite singular *foond*, plural *founde(n)*, past participle *founde*, *founden*, or *yfounde*, or modern English 'bear', 'bore', 'borne, born', Chaucerian *bere(n)*, preterite singular *bar*, plural *bare(n)*, past participle *bore*, *born*, *ybore*, *yborn*. Some forms obviously varied a good deal. Thus the past participle could be varied according to the needs of metre or rhyme, as in 'allas! that I was born!' rhyming with *lorn* in *The Book of the Duchess*, 686, and 'allas, that I was bore!' rhyming with *before* in line 1301 of the same poem. Similarly, Chaucer uses both *bar* and *beer* for modern English singular 'bore' in appropriate rhymes; for example:

> And for a contenaunce in his hand he *bar*
> An holwe stikke – taak kep and be war!
> *(CYT* 1264)

> And by the gargat hente Chauntecleer,
> And on his bak toward the wode hym *beer*.
> *(NPT* 3335–6)

Some verbs drew inflectional forms from both types, and again Chaucer exploits the alternatives in appropriate contexts, as with the verbs *wepen* 'to weep', *slepen* 'to sleep', and some others. For example:

> Allas! what wonder is it thogh she *wepte*,
> *(MLT* 267)

rhyming with *kepte*; or:

> And therwithal ful tenderly she *wep* [i.e. wept],
> *(LGW* 1732)

rhyming with the noun *kep*. Also in rhyme occur the variants 'she slepte' *(CLT* 224) and 'she slep' *(Anel* 137). Past participles may also belong to either type in some verbs, for example: 'thow hast wopen' *(Tr* I, 941), 'I have wept' *(MerchT* 1544), and so on.

The inflectional endings of the verbs in Chaucer's English conform, as we have noted, to contemporary London usage with a few deliberate exceptions. Consonantal and vocalic verbs have the same endings except in the imperative singular, where some consonantal verbs have an *-e* ending, others and the vocalic verbs none; in the past participle, where vocalic verbs have *-e* or *-en* and consonantal verbs *-d* or *-t*; and in the preterite indicative, where the vocalic verbs are inflected as shown in these examples of the verb *beren* 'to bear':

I bar hym on honde he hadde enchanted me.
(*WBT* 575)

'*Thou bare* hym in thy body trewely.'
(*CLT* 1068)

Under his belt *he bar* ful thriftily.
(*Gen Prol* 105)

How that *we baren* us that ilke nyght.
(*Gen Prol* 721)

Similarly *ye*, *they baren*.

Most of the remaining verbal inflections are illustrated in action in the following quotations:
Present indicative:

'*I love* another – and elles I were to blame'.
(*MillT* 3710)

'*Thou lovest* me, I woot it wel certeyn'.
(*CLT* 309)

She loveth hym, or whi *he loveth* here.
(*Tr* III, 34)

And somme seyen that *we loven* best.
(*WBT* 935)

'Now se I wel that *ye loven* nat myn honour ne my worshipe.'
(*Mel* 1681)

'They haten that *hir housbondes loven ay*.'
(*WBT* 781)

Preterite indicative:

'*I loved* alwey, as after my konnynge'.
(*PrT* 657)

'For love of hym *thow lovedest* in the shawe'.

(*Tr* III, 720)

And *he loved* hym al tendrely agayn.

(*KnT* 1197)

These Romeyn wyves lovede so here name.

(*LGW* 1812)

Similarly *we, ye lovede*. Alternatively, the plural for all three persons could be *loveden* (as in *The Parson's Tale*, 202). Occasionally forms occur like '[he] *lovede* venerie' (*Gen Prol* 166) which look tri-syllabic, but which Chaucer probably pronounced with two syllables by eliding either the medial or the final *e*.

Infinitive, either:

For soothly, nature dryveth us *to loven* oure freendes,

(*ParsT* 527)

or:

'*To love* hym best of any creature'.

(*MerchT* 1984)

Imperative, singular:

'*Love* thy neighebor as thyselve',

(*ParsT* 517)

plural:

'*Loveth* youre enemys, and *preyeth* for hem that speke yow harm, and eek for hem that yow chacen and pursewen, and *dooth* bountee to hem that yow haten.'

(*ibid.* 526)

Past participle, either:

'Which I have *loved* with al my myght',

(*BD* 478)

or:

'I have *yloved* yow ful many a day'.

(*LGW* 2115)

The prefix *y*-, from O.E. *ge-* (the equivalent of which is still regularly used in modern German), is used frequently in Chaucer's

English in both consonantal and vocalic past participles. Although generally uninflected, past participles occasionally have inflected forms in *-e*. This explains the difference in the form of 'fled' in these examples:

That Calkas traitour *fled was* and allied
With hem of Grece.

(*Tr* I, 87–8)

Alle other dredes *weren* from him *fledde*.

(*ibid.* 463)

The present participle ending of both consonantal and vocalic verbs in Chaucer's English is *-ing(e)* or *-yng(e)*:

For pitously ech other gan byholde,
As they that hadden al hire blisse ylorn,
Bywaylinge ay the day that they were born.

(*Tr* IV, 1249–51)

A povre wydwe, somdeel stape in age
Was whilom *dwellyng* in a narwe cotage,
Biside a grove, *stondynge* in a dale.

(*NPT* 2821–3)

There are many examples of words in Chaucer retaining the French present participle ending *-ant* or *-aunt*, but these normally function as adjectives and were probably regarded as such, as in 'an outlawe, or a theef *erraunt*' (*MancT* 224), or

The grete tour, that was so thikke and stroong
. . . .
Was evene *joynant* [directly adjacent] to the gardyn wal.

(*KnT* 1056–60)

The inflectional endings of the subjunctive in Chaucer's English are often indistinguishable from indicative endings. The following examples illustrate subjunctive forms contrasted, where appropriate, with corresponding indicatives:

Present subjunctive:

Lest I *myself falle* eft in swich dotage.

(*Buk* 8)

'And sacrifice to oure goddes, er *thou go*!'

(*SecNT* 488)

61

contrasted with the indicative '*thou goost* biforn' (*ibid.* 56)

'And if *he bereth* [indicative] a spere, hoold thee on the right syde,
and if *he bere* [subjunctive] a swerd, hoold thee on the lift syde.'
(*Mel* 1312)

'But God forbede that *we stynte* heere';
(*CT* I, 4339)

similarly *ye, they stynte* or *stynten*, as in the indicative.

Preterite subjunctive:

As though he wolde han slayn it er *he wente*,
(*CLT* 536)

and similarly for the other persons in the singular.

Bisekynge hym of grace, er that *they wenten*,
(*ibid.* 178)

and similarly for the other persons in the plural, or, alternatively,
without the final -*n*.

Apart from the two main types of verbs so far considered there
are some verbs which have their own inflectional peculiarities.
The common verbs *doon* 'do', *goon* 'go', *konnen* 'to be able', *willen*
'to will', all have consonantal preterites as well as change of
vowel or even word, *dide, wente, koude, wolde*, as they still have in
modern English.

An interesting verb with a bewildering number of variant
forms in Middle English is *hoten* which means principally either
'to name, or be named, be called', or 'to command', or 'to promise'. Chaucer uses several variant forms, as in these examples:

'How that ye sholde loven oon that *hatte* Horaste'.
(*Tr* III, 797)

'That loved a mayden, *heet* Stymphalides'.
(*FranklT* 1388)

Ther was a duc that *highte* Theseus.
(*KnT* 860)

His name *was hoote* deynous Symkyn.
(*RvT* 3941)

This last form appears in Manly and Rickert and in several other editions as *was hoten*. For the meaning 'promise' Chaucer prefers the form *he(e)te*, as in

'And swor, and hertely gan hir *hete*,
Ever to be stedfast and trewe'.
(BD 1226–7)

The verb 'to be', Chaucer's *be* or *been*, has alternative forms for the present indicative plural, *we* (*ye*, *they*) *be* or *been*, and *we* (*ye*, *they*) *arn* or *are*, of which only the last survives in modern standard English. Chaucer is quite capable of using both forms side by side, perhaps for the sake of variety: 'ther been two thynges that arn necessarie and nedefulle' (*Mel* 1643); but for the most part the choice of one form or the other seems quite arbitrary:

Thise arn the wordes that the markys sayde.
(CLT 342)

Thise been the cokkes wordes, and nat myne.
(NPT 3265)

That the latter form is by far the more common is obvious from its frequent use in rhyme, whereas *are*, *arn* do not occur in rhyme.[33] It is also instructive to note that in the line from *The Clerk's Tale* just quoted a considerable number of manuscripts prefer *ben* or *were* to *arn*, whereas in the line from *The Nun's Priest's Tale* only one manuscript, Royal 17 D XV, reads *arn* instead of *been*. Scribal transmission has its vagaries, however, as we have noted before. In *The Reeve's Tale*, where Chaucer probably intended 'ar ye' (4045) and 'are we' (4110) as deliberate northernisms in the speech of Aleyn and John, some manuscripts are sadly guilty of 'mis-writing' him by substituting *bee* or *ben*. No wonder he besought God to ensure accurate transmission of his 'Englissh'.

Parts of the verb *been*, as well as of *witen* and *haven*, combine with the negative particle to yield such forms as *nas* (for *ne was*), *nyl* (for *ne wil*), *noot* (for *ne woot*), *nyste* (for *ne wiste*), *nadde* (for *ne hadde*), and so on.

Even if Chaucer was occasionally unlucky in having his work miscopied by some of his scribes, he was fortunate in living in a period of considerable linguistic change. The frequent variants cited in this chapter are evidence not only of the diversity of forms

33. But note 'of which they first delyverid are' in *Rom* 6046, rhyming with *fare*.

with which a fourteenth-century Londoner was familiar, but of the poet's own readiness to use them to advantage. Rhyme and metre are obvious spurs to such linguistic eclecticism and probably explain a great part of Chaucer's more uncommon forms, like the retention of the French adjectival plural in

> And alle the mervelous signals
> Of the goddys *celestials*;
>
> (*HF* 459–60)

or the unusual occurrence of the preterite plural vowel in the third person singular *seet* rhyming with *feet* in *The Knight's Tale*, 2075, instead of Chaucer's normal *he sat*; or the dialectal *sende* rhyming with *amende* and *defende* in *Troilus and Criseyde* II, 1734, where the usual form is *he sente*. But sometimes more subtle artistic motives may have been at work. When the great downpour descends in Book III of *Troilus and Criseyde* the narrator twice uses the vocalic preterite form *ron* 'rained', once in the middle of the line:

> And syn it *ron*, and al was on a flod,
>
> (*Tr* III, 640)

and once in rhyme:

> And evere mo so sterneliche it *ron*.
>
> (*ibid.* 677)

This is a rare form and was probably something of an archaism by Chaucer's time, for the usual verb form was *reyne* 'to rain' with its preterite *reyned*. Pandarus uses the latter when speaking of the weather on the morning after the storm:

> Pandare, o-morwe which that comen was
> Unto his nece and gan hire faire grete,
> Seyde, 'Al this nyght so *reyned* it, allas. . . .'
>
> (*ibid.* 1555–7)

The archaic form supplies a monosyllabic word for line 640 and a useful rhyme for *anon* and *gon* in line 677; but there may have been more to its selection. The vocalic verb is mostly found in biblical contexts, as in *Piers Plowman* B XIV, 66) where the later C text substitutes *reynede*):

It is founden that fourty wynter folke lyued with-outen tulyinge,
And oute of the flynte spronge the flode that folke and bestes dronke.
And in Elyes tyme heuene was yclosed,
That no reyne ne *rone*; thus rede men in bokes.

This and similar uses dating back to Old English had perhaps
endowed *ron* with biblical connotations which Chaucer may be
exploiting by creating in *Troilus and Criseyde* an ironic link between
the great storm which leads to the union of Troilus and Criseyde
and the several theological implications of sin and redemption of
the biblical Flood.

Perhaps this is being over-subtle; for we can only surmise what
may have been the connotations of particular words or forms of
words for Chaucer and his contemporaries,[34] despite occasional
hints from the poet himself. And these hints may themselves be
tinged with characteristic Chaucerian irony, like the Merchant's
dismissal of Januarie's paraphrase of a passage from the Song of
Solomon in *The Merchant's Tale* with the comment 'Swiche olde
lewed wordes used he' (2149). *Olde*, certainly; *lewed*, hardly,
neither in the usual Chaucerian nor in the later sense. The poet's
audience would have recognized in Chaucer's diverse inflectional
and metrical usages the kind of linguistic plenty which the Eliza-
bethans responded to in their drama, and which in our own century is illustrated by such works as Hardy's *The Dynasts* or, in a
very different vein, Joyce's *Ulysses*.

Chaucer's good ear, his sense of linguistic propriety, generally
helped him to make the most of a language busily flexing its
muscles. The use of variants of the kind we have examined,
whether phonetic or prosodic, grammatical or dialectal, is merely
one of many facets of Chaucer's art. He can create ambiguities in
many other ways, some of which will be discussed in later contexts
of this book. The fact is indisputable, however, that Chaucer was
acutely conscious of his 'Englissh' and revealed in many passing
comments an awareness of language and style unequalled among
English poets until Shakespeare.

These comments cannot of course all be taken strictly at their
face value, for they are often uttered by Chaucer's creatures in
quite specific contexts. The Man of Law's

34. Cp. Donaldson, *Speaking*, p. 66.

O Donegild, I ne have noon Englissh digne
Unto thy malice and thy tirannye!

(*MLT* 778–9)

is paralleled by the Squire's avowal (perhaps he was more used to talking French):

Myn Englissh eek is insufficient.
It moste been a rethor excellent,
That koude his colours longynge for that art,
If he sholde hire discryven every part.
I am noon swich, I moot speke as I kan,

(*SqT* 37–41)

and by similar remarks elsewhere. But beneath the modest disclaimers of his characters lurks Chaucer's own persistent tendency to belittle his own art and his competence as a poet. Undoubtedly, this pose was a familiar medieval rhetorical mode which Chaucer readily exploited for ironic purposes, but it had some factual basis in the uncertainties of a rapidly developing language which faced every poet writing in the last thirty years of the fourteenth century. The narrator's comment in *Troilus and Criseyde* –

For myne wordes, heere and every part,
I speke hem alle under correccioun
Of yow that felyng han in loves art,

(*Tr* III, 1331–3)

– is a characteristic example of rhetorical *diminutio*, but it has the ring of truth in it. Caxton's pathetic exclamation a century later, 'Loo what sholde a man in thyse dayes now wryte. egges or eyren / certaynly it is harde to playse euery man / by cause of dyuersite & chaunge of langage',[35] might well have been uttered by Chaucer, and indeed was anticipated in some of his remarks, as he explored the 'gret diversite', the *amphibologies*, the hitherto largely unsuspected 'haboundances of rychesses' of his English. For Chaucer the artist there lay in this act of exploration the challenge which enabled him so to fashion his language that it became the vehicle of great poetry, and to 'ascertain' in Swift's sense and give permanence, as he puts it in *Boece* III, pr. 11, 190–1, to 'the thinges that whilom semeden uncerteyn to me'.

35. Prologue to *Eneydos* in *The Prologues and Epilogues of William Caxton*, ed. W. J. B. Crotch, E.E.T.S., O.S. 176 (London, 1928), p. 108.

CHAPTER 2

Thyng that I Speke, it Moot be Bare and Pleyn

🕲🕲🕲🕲🕲🕲

JUST as Chaucer's Franklin avows with a disarming show of innocence his ignorance of rhetoric –

I lerned nevere rethorik, certeyn;
Thyng that I speke, it moot be bare and pleyn,
                            (*FranklT* 719–20)

so his creator asserts in all his major works not only the inadequacy of his own 'wit' ('my wit is short, ye may wel understonde', *Gen Prol* 746; 'although that thow [Chaucer] be dul', *PF* 162), but his general incompetence as a writer: 'al be hit that he kan nat wel endite', Alceste is made to say of him in the Prologue (F 414) of *The Legend of Good Women*, or 'my rude endityng', as Chaucer puts it himself in the Introduction to the *Astrolabe* (43). The 'modesty topos', as Ernst Curtius calls it,[1] is a medieval commonplace, and a Chaucerian commonplace no less. It allows the Franklin to combine his opening disclaimer with a dazzling display of some seventy rhetorical forms in his tale,[2] and it affords Chaucer many similar opportunities, both in his own person and in those of his creatures, to achieve similar ironic incongruities. Chaucer's command of rhetorical forms of all kinds enabled him to embellish his poetry with all the recognized figures and 'colours', just as his artistic judgment made it possible for him, on the other hand, to do without them when he thought it proper. The Second Nun, for example, asks her audience's indulgence for telling a plain tale,

---

1. Ernst Robert Curtius, *European Literature and the Latin Middle Ages*, trans. by Willard R. Trask (New York, 1953), p. 84.

2. Cp. Benjamin S. Harrison, 'The Rhetorical Inconsistency of Chaucer's Franklin', *Studies in Philology* XXXII (1935), 55–61.

Foryeve me that I do no diligence
This ilke storie subtilly to endite;

(SecNT 79–80)

and she means it, for *The Second Nun's Tale* is indeed singularly free from rhetorical forms.

Such deliberate avoidance of rhetorical embellishment, however, is uncommon. Usually, Chaucer's art is strongly, though generally unobtrusively, affected by medieval rhetorical precept and practice, and his poetic 'wit' was certainly 'long' enough to find the appropriate language for different occasions. That this language, for all its rhetorical 'colouring', tends in the main to be of an informal, colloquial kind is another important characteristic of Chaucer's art. The opening lines of *The General Prologue* to *The Canterbury Tales* are perhaps the best known example of Chaucerian 'amplification', here in the form of *circumlocutio*, in all his work. Eighteen meandering lines are stretched into one long sentence to convey the simple fact that in spring people like going on pilgrimages. Except for its length, the passage is characteristic of much of Chaucer's style, with its astronomical reference and its classical allusion, its generous use of adjectives, mostly premodifying but occasionally postmodifying, its tendency to mingle common, homely words with some more learned ones, like the rare and in the thirteen-eighties relatively novel word *inspired* which occurs only three times elsewhere in Chaucer. The lyrical tone of the passage relies upon traditional echoes of May mornings and flowery meads and upon affective diction ('*sweete* breeth', '*tendre* croppes', '*smale* foweles', '*hooly blisful* martir') such as was to figure prominently in the later *Prioress's Tale*. But the dream-lands and classical settings of earlier poems are now firmly replaced by the familiar road to Canterbury, just as the characters themselves are changed: Alys of Bath is about to succeed the idealized Blanche of *The Book of the Duchess*, Chauntecleer is about to succeed the garrulous Eagle of *The House of Fame*, and that bold, hard-swearing publican Harry Bailly is about to succeed the avuncular Pandarus of *Troilus and Criseyde*. Only Chaucer himself remains, largely unchanged: the naïve dreamer, the monosyllabic listener, the incompetent inditer, are all recognizably present in the apologetic pilgrim of *The Canter-*

bury Tales and the prepetrator of *Sir Thopas* and, paradoxically, of *Melibee*.

As a *persona*, Chaucer maintains the pose; as narrator he continues to be the many-sided artist which his earlier poems had shown him to be. This many-sidedness, expressing itself in a variety of styles, shows Chaucer's remarkable confidence in a language which was as yet very largely untried. Parallel to the range and diversity of his diction – the principal theme of this book – is the flexibility of Chaucer's syntax. There is of course, as Tauno Mustanoja has stressed, 'an intimate connection between syntax and style, and it is often impossible to make a sharp distinction between the two.'[3] Chaucer's word-order, for example, frequently becomes the vehicle for different stylistic aims – emphasis, irony, rhetorical flourishes, and the like. Arcite's fatal illness, for instance, is introduced with the poignant inversion 'Swelleth the brest of Arcite' (*KnT* 2743); the Wife of Bath manages to infuse a neat modicum of irony into the positioning of 'that gentil text' in the lines

> Men may devyne and glosen, up and doun,
> But wel I woot, expres, withoute lye,
> God bad us for to wexe and multiplye;
> That gentil text kan I wel understonde;
>
> (*WBT* 26–9)

there is a business-like narrative movement in inversions like 'Goth Pandarus, and Troilus he soughte' (*Tr* IV, 946) or the Miller's 'Up stirte hire Alison and Nicholay' (*MillT* 3824). There are many instances, on the other hand, where the usual patterns of late fourteenth-century English are varied by Chaucer for less obviously stylistic reasons, for the sake of metre or rhyme perhaps, or simply because Chaucer was writing (as he no doubt often did) in a hurry. Hence such lines as 'ne telle hir durste I nat my thoght' (*BD* 1186), or the Shipman's line

> And richely this monk the chapman fedde,
> (*ShipT* 254)

which is simply confusing without inflexional endings to indicate that the subject 'the chapman' here follows the object 'this monk'.

3. Mustanoja, p. 41.

In the line

> Herde al this thyng Criseyde wel inough
> (*Tr* II, 1590)

the inverted order verb–object–subject is presumably simply a metrical matter, because neither *herde* nor the vague phrase 'al this thyng' is sufficiently trenchant to call for emphatic positioning at the beginning of the line or even, as here, of the stanza. But one cannot be dogmatic in such matters: in another instance Chaucer uses a similar inverted pattern, again at the head of a stanza, where the reason may be metrical also, but where the result seems much more arresting:

> Stood on a day in his malencolie
> This Troilus. . . .
> (*Tr* V, 1646–7)

The requirements of rhyme also play their part in determining Chaucer's word-order. The preposition *to*, for example, occurs fifteen times in rhyme in *The Canterbury Tales*, not without some resultant syntactical distortions, as in Januarie's

> 'I feele my lymes stark and suffisaunt
> To do al that a man bilongeth to'.
> (*MerchT* 1458–9)

Metre and rhyme may combine to produce a pleonasm as in

> And eek *in* what array that they were *inne*.
> (*Gen Prol* 41)

The positioning of adjectives is often determined by rhyme, Chaucer allowing himself considerable freedom in this, as these examples illustrate:

> Ful weel she song the service dyvyne.
> (*Gen Prol* 122)

> His newe sorwe, and ek his joies olde.
> (*Tr* V, 558)

> He syngeth in his voys gentil and smal.
> (*MillT* 3360)

> Or that the cruel lyf unsofte.
> (*HF* 36)

Of faire, yonge, fresshe Venus free.

(*KnT* 2386)

Frequently, it is rhythm, rather than rhyme, that determines the placing of adjectives in the interior of a line, as in the Man of Law's 'the woful day fatal' (*MLT* 261), or the Knight's 'of iren greet and square' (*KnT* 1076) or the narrator's 'and cheere good he made' (*Tr* II, 1575).

While some of the syntactical flexibility in Chaucer's writing may be ascribed to the stage of development reached by the language in the second half of the fourteenth century, much of it reflects Chaucer's own leanings towards more colloquial, more 'bare and pleyn', patterns of expression. The sudden appearance of a pronoun without any antecedent one might expect from the Wife of Bath; but it surprises the reader when it comes straight from the narrator in *The Book of the Duchess*, although the syntactical informality of the immediate context somehow lessens the impact:

And with that word ryght anoon
They gan to strake forth; al was doon,
For that tyme, the hert-huntyng.

(*BD* 1311–13)

But perhaps we have no business to be surprised, for right through the poem there runs a colloquial note, common to both the narrator and the Black Knight, which expresses itself in such syntactical arrangements as 'al was doon, / For that tyme, the hert-huntyng' or 'was never herd so swete a steven' (307) as well as in idiomatic turns of speech like 'what me is' (what the matter is with me, 31), or 'hyt sat me sore' (it afflicted me sorely, 1220).

In *Troilus and Criseyde* the narrator's role is a more complex one than in Chaucer's earlier poems, but there are similar examples, many of them, of the more colloquial tone of voice expressed through idiomatic phrases, dubious grammar, or loose syntax. For example, in the lines

She, this in blak, likynge to Troilus
Over alle thing, he stood for to biholde;

(*Tr* I, 309–10)

the grammatically incorrect, but emphatic *she* introduces a sentence of seven lines of loose construction, and it is not until the last line of the stanza that the grammatically correct 'on hire' restores some semblance of structural cohesion to the whole sentence. The syntactical disorder is probably quite deliberate, for it helps the narrator to mirror Troilus's confused state of mind:

> Ne his desir, ne wherfore he stood thus,
> He neither chere made, ne word tolde;
> But from afer, his manere for to holde,
> On other thing his look som tyme he caste,
> And eft on hire, while that the servyse laste.
> *(ibid.* 311–15)

Chaucer allows himself a different kind of syntactical liberty in the line

> Til neigh that he in salte teres dreynte,
> *(ibid.* 543)

which provides the only example in his work of the separation of 'til that' by an intervening word. There are other examples of loose syntax in *Troilus and Criseyde*: in the sixth stanza of Book II, for instance, the preterite *seyde* looks out of place among the gerunds in the lines

> As thus, in opyn doyng or in chere,
> In visityng, in forme, or seyde hire sawes,
> *(Tr* II, 40–1)

which E. T. Donaldson glosses 'or in speaking their speeches', as the reader is led to anticipate another gerund. An interesting syntactical ellipsis occurs later in the same book:

> But fle we now prolixitee best is;
> *(ibid.* 1564)

and there are other examples in this poem and elsewhere of similar ellipses as, for one reason or another, parts of speech are omitted. The subject ('everybody') is omitted in 'but boden [was commanded] go to bedde' *(Tr* III, 691); the verb is omitted in the middle clause of 'and took hire leve, and hom, and held hir stille' *(Tr* I, 126); similarly, a verbal form is omitted in 'and she to laughe' *(Tr* II, 1108); or again in 'but Pandare up, *(Tr* III, 548). A particularly effective syntactical ellipsis, as Donaldson has pointed out ('one of those syntactical ellipses that make Middle English so fluid a language'),[4] occurs towards the end of *Troilus and*

4. Donaldson, *Speaking*, p. 97.

Criseyde where there is a sudden switch to the plural verb *sholden*, but the subject *we* is omitted: 'and sholden al oure herte on heven caste' (V, 1825).

The colloquial tone which Chaucer's flexible syntax helped to achieve can be further illustrated by noting his marked preference for such an idiomatic usage as 'and so bifel' or 'bifel' as against the fuller 'it bifel'. The latter occurs twice in the octosyllabic metre of *The Book of the Duchess* (66, 1258), as it does in Gower's *Confessio Amantis* (e.g. Prol. 702; V, 3070; etc.), but only exceptionally in Chaucer's later work, as in the inverted order of the Miller's 'and so bifel it on a Saterday' (*MillT* 3399), or the Wife of Bath's 'and so bifel it that this kyng Arthour' (*WBT* 882), or in the prose occurrence of *Boece* I, pr. 4, 30. The elliptical form, on the other hand, occurs more than thirty times. The similar construction 'and happed that' shows much the same flexibility, but Chaucer is less partial to it and the distribution with or without the pronoun is roughly even. These and similar constructions are of course not unique to Chaucer in Middle English; Gower has various forms: 'so it befell' (*Conf Am* IV, 458), 'and fell . . . / This Piramus cam' (III, 1416 f.), 'and happeth that' (II, 868); and so have Langland and other fourteenth-century writers. The point is rather that wherever Chaucer found his language affording him a good deal of freedom and variety of syntactical arrangement, he readily availed himself of them, on the whole preferring more colloquial to more formal constructions. How great this freedom was and how readily Chaucer responded to it in a case like the present, a few typical examples will illustrate further. The more formal constructions are of the type 'it happened that', 'it befell that', as in

'Hit happed that I cam on a day',
(*BD* 805)

with inversion of pronoun and verb after conjunctive adverbs like *now*, *so*, *then*:

Now fil it that thise marchantz stode in grace
Of hym that was the Sowdan of Surrye.
(*MLT* 176–7)

The conjunctive *that* may be omitted, whether or not there is a preceding pronoun:

And on a day it happed, in a stounde,
Sik lay the maunciple on a maladye.
(R*v*T 3992–3)

And so bifel soone after, on a day,
This false juge, as telleth us the storie,
As he was wont, sat in his consistorie.
(*Phys*T 160–2)

On the other hand (and this is quite characteristic of Chaucer) the *that* may be repeated, especially when the syntax of the whole sentence gets rather involved:

It fel *that* in the seventhe yer, of May
The thridde nyght, (as olde bookes seyn,
That al this storie tellen moore pleyn)
Were it by aventure or destynee –
As, whan a thyng is shapen, it shal be –
That soone after the mydnyght Palamoun,
By helpyng of a freend, brak his prisoun
And fleeth the citee faste as he may go.
(*Kn*T 1462–9)

Another set of variations is to introduce an indirect object, nominal or pronominal, followed by a clause, with or without conjunction, or by an infinitive – 'it happede me for to beholde' (*PF* 18) – or by a mixture of different constructions juxtaposed, as happens in colloquial speech, without due regard for strict grammatical propriety:

And with that word *it happed hym*, par cas,
To take the botel ther the poyson was,
And drank, and yaf his felawe drynke also.
(*Pard*T 885–7)

Where 'it' is omitted in such cases, an impersonal construction results, of a type not uncommon in Middle English:

Yit happeth me ful ofte in bokes reede. . . .
(*PF* 10)

But the omission of 'it' is most common in phrases of the type 'and so bifel (that)', 'and happed (that)':

And so bifel that, longe er it were day,
This man mette in his bed. . . .
(*NPT* 3001–2)

And happed that he saugh bifore hym ryde
A gay yeman, under a forest syde.

(*FrT* 1379–80)

The result of such syntactical variety is a good deal of rhythmical
and consequently of narrative flexibility, even in a single line:

Ther *fil*, as *it bifalleth* tymes mo,
Whan that this child had souked but a throwe,
This markys in his herte longeth so. . . .

(*CLT* 449–51)

So shop it that *hym fil* that day a teene
In love. . . .

(*Tr* II, 61–2)

Occasional grammatical oddities or irregularities clearly did not
worry Chaucer. Middle English was indeed a 'fluid' language at
this time, and if he did notice anything odd, he may well have left
it alone as a permissible contemporary colloquial feature. Generally, such colloquial lapses fit well into the speech of particular
characters or into the narrator's own frequently informal idiom.
Even where the context is more formal, occasional irregularities
or, if we prefer, liberties, are unlikely to offend, as in the Pardoner's highly stylized sermon on the sins of the tavern, where
these lines occur:

And whan he cam, hym happede, par chaunce,
That alle the gretteste that were of that lond,
Pleyynge atte hasard he hem fond.

(*PardT* 606–8)

Whichever way one analyses this sentence, there is something
'not quite right' with it, but as in similar cases elsewhere in
Chaucer (e.g. *LGW* 1242–4) even an attentive reader hardly
notices that anything is amiss. This unobtrusive informality of
language Chaucer has made as much his own as Shakespeare has.

There are many other facets to this aspect of Chaucer's English,
some of them recognized rhetorical devices; the separation of
parts of a sentence, for example, which belong together, often for
the sake of rhyme (the rhetorical *transgressio*):

The colde wal they wolden kysse *of ston*,

(*LGW* 768)

Housbondes at chirche dore she hadde *fyve*,
(*Gen Prol* 460)

But now, paraunter, som man wayten wolde
That every word, or soonde, or look, or cheere
Of Troilus that I rehercen sholde,
In al this while *unto his lady deere*
(*Tr* III, 491–4)

– or changes of tense, as in the Reeve's

This millere *gooth* agayn, no word he *seyde*,
But *dooth* his note [business], and with the clerkes *pleyde*,
Til that hir corn *was* faire and weel ygrounde.
And whan the mele *is* sakked and ybounde. . . .
(*RvT* 4067–70)

Chaucer allows himself considerable freedom in the use of prepositions, not only as regards their positioning, but whether or not he uses them at all. Hence such contrasts as between

And thanne at erst he looked *upon me*,
(*CT* VII, 694)

and

'I durste nat ones loke *hir on*';
(*BD* 1217)

or between

On Theseus to helpe him to *werreye*,
(*KnT* 1484)

and

'Woltow *werreyen Thebes* the citee?'
(*ibid.* 1544)

where modern English 'make war' requires a preposition in either case.

Some rhetorical figures, as we have just noted, display similar freedom in syntactical structure. Although the context may be formal and the diction elevated, they yet subtly reinforce that grammatical and stylistic flexibility which is so marked a feature of Chaucer's English. The following examples illustrate the same grammatical point – omission of verb – but they range from an impatient, colloquial exclamation of Harry Bailly's to the nar-

76

rator's final, moving, highly stylized *conduplicatio* in *Troilus and Criseyde*:

> 'Namoore of this, for Goddes dignitee,'
> Quod oure Hooste. . . .
>
> > (*CT* VII, 919–20)

> Now to th'effect, now to the fruyt of al,
> Whi I have told this story, and telle shal.
>
> > (*LGW* 1160–1)

> O glotonye, ful of cursednesse!
> O cause first of oure confusioun!
> O original of oure dampnacioun,
> Til Crist hadde boght us with his blood agayn!
>
> > (*PardT* 498–501)

> Lo here, of payens corsed olde rites,
> Lo here, what alle hire goddes may availle;
> Lo here, thise wrecched worldes appetites;
> Lo here, the fyn and guerdoun for travaille
> Of Jove, Appollo, of Mars, of swich rascaille!
>
> > (*Tr* V, 1849–53)

Such language as in the last quotation is anything but 'bare and pleyn', of course, but is it being too fanciful to hear even in such phrases as the pagans' 'corsed olde rites' or in such a nonce Chaucerian usage as 'swich rascaille!' something of Chaucer's characteristic, often colloquial, idiom? Perhaps it is also in the little string of proper names, 'of Jove, Appollo, of Mars', so neatly summed up as 'swich rascaille', that a familiar Chaucerian note is heard, for Chaucer is fond of reeling off such lists, as well as sprinkling his verse with names of places and persons, whether saints or 'olde clerkes' or figures from biblical story or classical mythology. Even the most exotic names are often given a colloquial twist: India, for example, is Chaucer's 'down under' in such phrases as the Black Knight's

> 'But whether she knew, or knew it nowght,
> Algate she ne roughte of hem a stree!
> To gete her love no ner nas he
> That woned at hom, than he in Ynde',
>
> > (*BD* 886–9)

77

or the Pardoner's

'For I ne kan nat fynde
A man, though that I walked into Ynde'.
(*PardT* 721–2)

The Wife of Bath's world stretches from Denmark[5] to India:

God helpe me so, I was to hym as kynde
As any wyf from Denmark unto Ynde,
(*WBT* 823–4)

while the Shipman inhabits, as it were, several overlapping worlds: his expertise was unequalled 'from Hulle to Cartage' (*Gen Prol* 404), whereas his knowledge of ports extended

Fro Gootlond to the cape of Fynystere,
(*Gen Prol* 408)

as well as to 'every cryke [creek] in Britaigne and in Spayne' (*ibid.* 409).

The total extent of Chaucer's known world – Shakespeare's 'three-nook'd world' – is embraced in the line 'in Auffrike, Europe, and Asye' (*HF* 1339), and of the places mentioned within these continents most were familiar to the poet from his reading, a few from personal knowledge. He knew well how to use both the exotic quality of some names and the homely familiarity of others. Blanche of Lancaster, says the Black Knight, would not use 'suche knakkes smale', such petty tricks, as sending her admirers to such outlandish places as

'into Walakye [Wallachia],
To Pruyse [Prussia], and into Tartarye,
To Alysaundre [Alexandria], ne into Turkye,
And byd hym faste anoon that he
Goo hoodles to the Drye Se [Gobi Desert]
And come hom by the Carrenar [Lake Kara Nor in Mongolia]'.
(*BD* 1024–9)

The list of names detailing the Knight's campaigns in *The General Prologue*, 51 ff., is well known, as is that of the Wife of Bath's pilgrimages (*ibid.* 463 ff.), and many classical places figure in *The Legend of Good Women*. When referring to places nearer home, however, Chaucer could count on a different type of response. The contrast is much as in *The Waste Land* where the poet moves

5. *Denmark* is missing in Francis P. Magoun, Jr's *A Chaucer Gazetteer* (Chicago, 1961).

from 'Highbury . . . Richmond and Kew' to 'Jerusalem Athens Alexandria', or from the Starnbergersee to London Bridge. *Southwerk* and *Rouchestre, Stratford atte Bowe* and 'Trumpyngtoun, nat fer fro Cantebrigge [Cambridge]' are as much part of ordinary, colloquial Middle English as the Harley lyric poet's 'bituene Lyncolne ant Lyndeseye, Norhamptoun ant Lounde'. So are common personal names like Alysoun and John, or familiar saints like Peter and James.

Some place-names had become ordinary Middle English nouns, a process familiar enough in the history of the language. Items of manufacture or coins circulating in various countries were often called by their place of origin. One recalls the Genoese *jane*, a coin worth about a halfpenny, in *Sir Thopas*, 735 and *The Clerk's Tale*, 999, or Harry Bailly's *lussheburghes* (*CT* VII, 1962), an anglicized form of 'Luxemburg' to describe a spurious coin minted 'in imitation of the sterling or silver penny and imported from Luxemburg in the reign of Edward III' (*OED*). Langland refers to them in *Piers Plowman* B XV, 342:

As in Lussheborwes is a lyther alay [false alloy], and ȝet loketh he lyke a sterlynge.

Sir Thopas's 'shoon of *cordewane*' (*Thop* 732) are of Cordovan leather, from the Spanish town Cordoba; the Friar's 'double *worstede*' (*Gen Prol* 262) represents the Old English place-name Wurðestede, now Worstead, a village about ten miles north of Norwich; the Reeve mentions *chalons* 'blankets' (*RvT* 4140), so called because the fabric was manufactured in Châlons-sur-Marne in France; and likewise with several other words.

Some personal names as well as place-names tend to enter into colloquial usage as common nouns; of these the ubiquitous 'Jack' is the most obvious example. The Host's slangy 'Jakke of Dovere' (*CT* I, 4347) is a case in point; it designated some item of food, perhaps a pie or tart, possibly a fish (a Dover sole comes to mind), re-heated, as the context makes clear. Similarly, Alisoun addresses the amorous Absolon in *The Miller's Tale* (3708) as 'Jakke fool'. The name Jack had clearly acquired various colloquial connotations by Chaucer's time; in the following century the idiom 'jakke and gylle', Jack and Jill, came to mean simply everybody and anybody. A similar process is at work when

Chaucer turns the name Herod into a plural noun by making the Prioress exclaim:

> O cursed folk of Herodes al newe,
>
> (*PrT* 574)

or makes the name Judas into a common noun for a traitor by speaking of 'any Judas':

> If any Judas in youre covent be.
>
> (*CYT* 1007)

Chaucer's repertoire of biblical, classical and medieval personal names is very large, considerably larger than the approximately 300 geographical names to be found in his writings. Many are quoted as authorities in phrases characteristic of Chaucer's style, whether in prose or verse: 'and therfore seith Pamphilles' (*Mel* 1556); 'as seith Seint Augustyn' (*ParsT* 230); 'as saith Alkabucius' (*Astr* I, 8, 13); 'as writ myn auctor called Lollius' (*Tr* I, 394); 'as Guido tellith us' (*LGW* 1396); 'in hire Epistel Naso telleth al' (*ibid.* 2220); 'as telleth Titus Livius' (*PhysT* 1).

Lollius is one piece of erudite Chaucerian exhibitionism which has puzzled critics no end, but Chaucer obviously believed that there was such a writer and that he wrote about Troy; for Lollius not only figures twice in *Troilus and Criseyde* (I, 394; V, 1653), but also in a list of perfectly respectable authorities on Troy – Homer, Dares, Guido, among them – in *The House of Fame* (1468). The probability that Lollius owes his existence to a misreading of a line in Horace does not invalidate Chaucer's belief in him,[6] for Chaucer was careful with his names, as were some of his characters, witness the Pardoner's nicely pedantic

> What was comaunded unto Lamuel –
> Nat Samuel, but Lamuel, seye I.
>
> (*PardT* 584–5)

But names were also there to be played with, like words, and though Chaucer does not pun on Naso as Shakespeare's Holofernes does, he appears to be punning on the Jack Straw of the Peasants' Revolt of 1381 (mentioned in *NPT* 3394) in the narrator's

6. Cp. R. K. Root's remarks in his edition of *Troilus and Criseyde*, pp. xxxvi ff.

The noyse of peple up stirte thanne at ones,
As breme as blase of straw iset on-fire.

(Tr IV, 183–4)

Elsewhere he makes Harry Bailly talk of *galiones*, presumably
meant to be some medicine named after Galen, as if there really
was such a word (*CT* VI, 306). There is the narrator's play on
Calkas and *calkulynge* early in *Troilus and Criseyde* (I, 71); and possibly the name *Malkyn* (*CT* II, 30; *NPT* 3384), which may well be
the same as that of the Reeve's heroine *Malyne* (*RvT* 4236), carried already in Chaucer's day some of the unflattering domestic
connotations suggested by the synonyms and glosses – 'ovyn
swepyr: *Dorsorium . . . Tersorium*' – of the fifteenth-century *Promptorium Parvulorum*.[7] That *Malkyn* alliterates conveniently with
'maidenhead' both Langland (in *PP* B I, 182) and Chaucer demonstrate, the latter quite unequivocally suggesting wantonness,
perhaps proverbial, perhaps harking back to *The Reeve's Tale*
just completed, when Harry Bailly says:

'It wol nat come agayn, withouten drede,
Namoore than wole Malkynes maydenhede,
Whan she hath lost it in hir wantownesse.'

(CT II, 29–31)

Other connotations are possibly present in other names introduced into Chaucer's poetry: the Reeve's miller has a skull
'piled as an ape' (*RvT* 3935) and a simian face to match it:

Round was his face, and camus was his nose,

(RvT 3934)

so that his name, *Symkyn*, may well be something of a pun on
Latin *simia* 'ape', as well as on Latin *simus* 'flat-nosed, snub-nosed'.[8]
A different, more complex type of ambiguity attaches to the name
Damyan in *The Merchant's Tale*. St Damian was one of the two
patron saints of physicians, hence the appropriateness of the
name to the Merchant's love-sick squire whose astonishingly
rapid recovery from 'the loveris maladye / Of Hereos' (*KnT*
1373–4) is matched only by that of the Miller's Absolon. But

7. *The Promptorium Parvulorum: The First English–Latin Dictionary*, ed. A. L. Mayhew
(E.E.T.S., E.S. 102, 1908).

8. Cp. John M. Steadman, 'Simkin's Camus Nose: A Latin Pun in the *Reeve's Tale*?',
Modern Language Notes LXXV (1960), 4 ff.; and Dennis Biggins, 'Sym(e)kyn / *simia*:
The Ape in Chaucer's Millers', *Studies in Philology* LXV (1968), 44 ff.

more than that, for Damyan's dual function in the tale is pun-
ningly implied in the word *lechour* (*MerchT* 2257) which can mean
both 'lecher' and 'healer', the latter sense taking us back yet
again to St Damian.[9] Chaucer uses *lechere* in the sense of 'physician,
healer' alongside the more usual *leche* in *Boece* IV, pr. 6, 236, where
God is described as 'governour and lechere of thoughtes' rendering the Latin 'rector ac medicator mentium'. The *MED* records
no other instance of *lecher(e)* in this sense, but a Chaucerian
audience would not have missed the pun, particularly as either of
the two groups of words (*leche* 'physician', *lechen* 'to heal', *lechecraft*
'medicine', and *lechour* 'lecher', *lecherye* 'lechery', *lecherous* 'lecherous') was occasionally pronounced with the other's stem-vowel,
although usually the first group had a long closed [e:] and the
second a short [e]. May's explanation to her husband of what was
going on in the tree seems to clinch the pun:

'As me was taught, *to heele with youre eyen*,
Was no thyng bet, to make yow to see,
Than strugle with a man upon a tree.'

(*MerchT* 2372–4)

That there is more word-play in Chaucer than is acknowledged
by Robinson is clear from studies like those of Helge Kökeritz
and Paull F. Baum.[10] The subtlety of some of the punning may
belie its author's pose as a bare, plain, and rather witless inditer,
but it certainly bears witness to a pliable language with which an
imaginative poet could do some very clever things. That some
of the punning is bawdy, like the playing on *queynte*, on *ers* and
ars-metrike, or on *burdoun*, all discussed elsewhere,[11] is no more
surprising in Chaucer than it is in Shakespeare: both poets clearly
enjoyed playing with their language in both serious and comic
or vulgar contexts. Chaucer's puns include simple homonymic
juxtapositions, as well as more subtle word-play involving
deliberate ambiguity of meaning or double entendre, 'transla-

9. Cp. the notes by William Main in *The Explicator* XIV (1955) and Philip Mahone
Griffith in *The Explicator* XVI (1957), each under Item 13, 'Chaucer's *Merchant's
Tale*'.

10. Helge Kökeritz, 'Rhetorical Word-Play in Chaucer', *PMLA* LXIX (1954),
937 ff., and Paull F. Baum, 'Chaucer's Puns', *PMLA* LXXI (1956), 225 ff. and
LXXIII (1958), 167 ff.

11. Ch. 4, pp. 220 ff.

tion puns' involving other languages as in the case of *Symkyn*, and
the like. At its simplest, the Chaucerian pun plays on homonyms,
as in the Franklin's

> O blisful artow now, thou Dorigen,
> That hast thy lust housbonde in thyne *armes*,
> The fresshe knyght, the worthy man of *armes*,
>
> (*FranklT* 1090–2)

or the narrator's

> And in his *brest* the heped wo bygan
> Out *breste*,
>
> (*Tr* IV, 236–7)

or the Squire's rather more subtle example of a punning *rime
riche*:

> Al be it that I kan nat sowne his *stile*,
> Ne kan nat clymben over so heigh a *style*.
>
> (*SqT* 105–6)

No less subtle is the Summoner's friar's punning on 'chased' and
'chaste' with its contrasting prepositions *out* and *in*:

> 'Fro Paradys first, if I shal nat lye,
> Was man out *chaced* for his glotonye;
> And *chaast* was man in Paradys, certeyn.'
>
> (*SumT* 1915–17)

Of a different kind is the playing on *preamble, preambulacioun*, and

> 'What! amble, or trotte, or pees, or go sit doun!'

in the brief exchange between Friar and Summoner at the end of
the Wife of Bath's Prologue (*CT* III, 831 ff.).

Akin to the playing on *amble, trotte* and the rest, is the contrasting of opposites in such passages as these, with their added playing
on the several connotations of the words involved:

> 'Were his nayles poynted nevere so *sharpe*,
> It sholde maken every wight to *dulle*'.
>
> (*Tr* II, 1034–5)

> I am so sory, now that ye been *lyght*;
> For certes, but ye make me *hevy* chere.
>
> (*Purse* 3–4)

A particular kind of ambiguity derives from the co-existence in one word of strongly divergent meanings. What Huppé has called 'a remarkable piece of blasphemous word-play'[12] centres on the word *pryvetee* in the Miller's

'An housbonde shal nat been inquisityf
Of Goddes pryvetee, nor of his wyf.
So he may fynde Goddes foyson there,
Of the remenant nedeth nat enquere.'

(*CT* I, 3163–6)

The juxtaposition of God and of the wife declares the two meanings, 'divine mystery' and 'privy parts', beyond doubt: it does not pay to be too curious about either; what matters is to obtain 'Goddes foyson', God's plenty, from the wife's *pryvetee*. The other one, God's, is best left alone, as the carpenter in *The Miller's Tale* is later made to exclaim:

'Men sholde nat knowe of Goddes pryvetee.'

(*MillT* 3454)

The word occurs several more times in the tale and affords the Miller occasion not merely for blasphemous punning, but also for obscene wordplay on *queynte*:

And to his wyf he tolde his pryvetee,
And she was war, and knew it bet than he,
What al this queynte cast was for to seye.

(*ibid.* 3603–5)

Some well-known examples of punning on different connotations of the same word are the play on *philosophre* in *The General Prologue*, 297 and in *The Canon's Yeoman's Tale* (837 and 1122) meaning 'philosopher' and 'alchemist'; on *multiplie* in the same tale (669 etc.) meaning, simply, 'to increase', and, technically, 'to carry out the alchemical process'; or *makeles* 'without peer, matchless' and 'without spouse' in *Troilus and Criseyde* I, 172, a word not used elsewhere by Chaucer; on *divinistre* in *The Knight's Tale*, 2811, a word apparently made up by Chaucer (the *MED* records no other instance) to combine the idea of a *divine*, a theologian, with that of a *divinour*, a soothsayer or diviner. The word *venerye* unambiguously means 'hunting' when used by

12. Huppé, p. 78.

Emelye in her prayer to Diana in *The Knight's Tale*, 2308, but it is probable that when Chaucer applies it to the Monk, 'that lovede venerie' (*Gen Prol* 166), he was implying also the worship of Venus, that is venery in its sexual, etymologically distinct, meaning. Admittedly, the *OED* cites no example of this before the end of the fifteenth century, but neither Chaucer nor his audience was likely to miss the punning connection with Venus, obvious later on in the Wife of Bath's 'I am al Venerien' (*WBT* 609), especially as the hunting Monk is 'a manly man' (*Gen Prol* 167) on whose virility Harry Bailly was later to expatiate at considerable length.

A popular form of medieval word-play, the *adnominatio* of the rhetoricians, is the juxtaposition of closely similar words, like *whyle* 'while', *bygyle* 'beguile', and *whiel* 'wheel' in the opening stanza of Book IV of *Troilus and Criseyde*; or in such rhyming pairs as *afferme-conferme* (*Tr* II, 1588–9), *conserve-serve* (*KnT* 2329–30), *stonde-understonde* (*Gen Prol* 745–6), *assemble-resemble* (*WBT* 89–90). From such rhymes it was no great step to the occasional jingles, which Chaucer may well have acquired, as Kökeritz suggests, from 'reading his French masters',[13] and which no doubt appealed to his sense of fun with words. In *An A B C*, an early exercise of what Wolfgang Clemen called 'Chaucer's art of free creative transposition',[14] occurs the rhyme *merciable-merci able* (182, 184), while *The Book of the Duchess*, another early poem, rhymes *Morpheus* with *moo feës thus* (265–6), *floures* with *flour ys* (629–30), *Socrates* with *nat thre strees* (717–18), *harmed* with *harm hyd* (931–2), and so on. Once acquired, the habit (as Byron discovered) is not easily shaken off. Hence such jingles as *a tene is* and *Athenys* in *The House of Fame* (387–8), or *entrees* and *in trees* (*ibid.* 1945–6), and other so-called broken rhymes like *vices-vice is* (*Tr* I, 687, 689), *newe is-in hewis* (*Tr* II, 20–1), *fowles-foul is* (*Tr* V, 380, 383), *helle is-ellis* (*Tr* V, 1376–7). In cases like *harmed-harm hyd* or *newe is-in hewis* the fact that *h-* was not pronounced makes for more effective jingles. A familiar example, surely involving a pun, is the Pardoner's *beryed-a-blakeberyed* (*PardT* 405–6).

Unrecognized ambiguities may well be present in many passages of Chaucer's verse, and one critic at least has claimed that the 'poetical use of ambiguity' was 'already in full swing in the

13. Kökeritz, *op. cit.*, p. 948.
14. Clemen, p. 175.

English of Chaucer'.[15] One example cited by Empson is the use of *accesse* in one of its three occurrences in *Troilus and Criseyde*:

Compleyned ek Eleyne of his siknesse
So feythfully, that pite was to here,
And every wight gan waxen for accesse
A leche anon, and seyde, 'In this manere
Men curen folk.' – 'This charme I wol yow leere.'
But ther sat oon, al list hire nought to teche,
That thoughte, 'Best koud I yet ben his leche.'

(*Tr* II, 1576–82)

In all three occurrences in the poem (there are no others in Chaucer) the word *accesse* means, more generally, an attack of fever, and specifically Troilus's lovesickness. As a medical term it was familiar enough in the fourteenth century. Langland's Glutton has an *accesse* 'after al this surfet', in the A text (V, 210) of *Piers Plowman*, which in the later versions becomes 'and after al this excesse he hadde an accidie' (C VII, 417; similarly B V, 366). In the passage from *Troilus and Criseyde* quoted above, however, there is a hint of the modern meaning of 'access, approach' as Troilus's well-wishers crowd in to offer their counsel, just as a few stanzas before, the mention of *accesse* is followed by the line 'how men gan hym with clothes for to lade' (1544). Empson refers to Wyclif's use of *accesse* in the sense of Latin *accessus* 'a coming near, approach', a meaning well enough established by the middle of the fifteenth century, yet he doubts whether on balance Chaucer was in fact being ambiguous in the stanza under discussion: 'to Chaucer at any rate, I believe, the joke was strong enough to stand by itself, and too pointed to call up overtones; I have put it in to show a case where a plausible ambiguity may be unprofitable, and the sort of reasons that may make one refuse to accept it.'[16] The ambiguity is certainly a plausible one and is made more so by the obvious encroachment of the later meaning 'approach' on to the medical one in such an instance as 'þ' acces of anguych watȝ hid in my sawle' in *Patience*, 325, a poem closely contemporary with *Troilus and Criseyde*, and by the appearance of the adjective *accessyble* with its modern meaning by the end of the fourteenth century (see *MED s.v.*). Whether one accepts such an ambiguity in Chaucer's poetry depends upon one's own reading of it 'since

15. William Empson, *Seven Types of Ambiguity* (Harmondsworth, 1961), pp. 67 f.
16. Empson, *op. cit.*, p. 66.

it is left to the reader to decide', as Mrs Gordon says, 'whether, or in what ways, the ambiguity is part of the total effect intended'.[17] In the present instance, the ironic contrast between all the people crowding in with blankets and good advice and Criseyde sitting apart, knowing very well what would cure the patient, surely adds a further touch to the comedy of which Chaucer could hardly have been unaware.

There are numerous instances of two or more meanings 're-solved into one', as Empson puts it, in Chaucer's poetry, and the modern reader cannot really help missing many of them. An-other example from the same book of *Troilus and Criseyde* must suffice to illustrate the point. Pandarus 'leaps' into the sick-room to tell Troilus that Criseyde is about to be brought in to see him:

'God have thi soule, ibrought have I thi beere!'
(*Tr.* II, 1638)

The word *beere* is uniformly glossed 'bier' by the editors and translators as if this were all there was to the joke. But *beere* has a cluster of associations with bed, particularly *bere* 'child-bearing' and *bere* 'pillowcase' (as in *BD* 254, or the Pardoner's *pilwe-beer*, *Gen Prol* 694), which add just the right, bawdily ironic, note to Pandarus's remark. Again, it is improbable that Chaucer could have failed to be aware of or to intend the implied ambiguity.

Subtleties of this kind, not always easily recognized by the modern reader of Chaucer, can be expressed by various linguistic methods. The mood of a verb, for example, can express a shade of opinion, a hesitancy, a surmise, much as in modern English. A change from indicative to subjunctive mood occurs in the middle of the Pardoner's portrait, as the narrator speculates on the Par-doner's sexual condition.:

I trowe he *were* a geldyng or a mare.

(*Gen Prol* 691)

The word *trowe* may take either the indicative or the subjunctive, according to the certainty or lack of it in the statement. Thus Chaucer can write

And therwith she yaf me a ryng;
I trowe hyt *was* the firste thyng,

(*BD* 1273–4)

17. Gordon, p. 3.

or

> Ther was a monk, a fair man and a boold –
> I trowe a thritty wynter he *was* oold –
>
> (ShipT 25–6)

when no uncertainty is intended or when it is unimportant, as in
the latter case. The same idea can be expressed even more unequivocally by inserting the 'I trowe' parenthetically, as in the
Wife of Bath's

> He was, I trowe, a twenty wynter oold.
>
> (WBT 600)

When the subjunctive is used, however, some hesitancy is generally intended. The devil is not visible, but I believe that he may
well be around, says the Canon's Yeoman:

> Though that the feend noght in oure sighte hym shewe,
> I trowe he with us *be*, that ilke shrewe!
>
> (CYT 916–17)

And similarly with the Pardoner. Critics who all too readily accept
Curry's verdict that the Pardoner was '*a eunuchus ex nativitate*'
should remember that while Chaucer may be depicting an ef-
feminate character, the words 'he were a geldyng or a mare' are
not a statement of fact but a hesitant surmise, and that it is the
deliberate switch to the subjunctive mood which achieves this.
Most occurrences of the subjunctive in Chaucer present no
difficulty to the modern reader, except perhaps for the student
seeking to distinguish one mood from another, for indicative and
subjunctive or subjunctive and imperative forms are often the
same.[18] Hence one cannot be sure, for example, whether such as
the following forms are subjunctives or imperatives:

> 'Syn thou art mayde and kepere of us alle,
> My maydenhede thou *kepe* and wel *conserve*'.
>
> (KnT 2328–9)

A form of the imperative of which Chaucer appears to have been
fond varies the direct entreaty or command (as in 'Go, litel bok
. . .', *Tr* V, 1786) by introducing it with *as* or *so*:

18. For a fuller discussion of the moods see Kerkhof, pp. 33 ff., and Mustanoja, pp.
451 ff., and my discussion of this point in ch. 1, pp. 61 f.

'And for the love of God, my lady fre,
Whomso ye hate, *as beth* nat wroth with me'.

(*Tr* V, 144–5)

'For Goddes love, *so beth* me naught unkynde!'

(*Tr* IV, 1652)

A rare construction uses *that* with the second personal pronoun to introduce a subjunctive clause with obvious imperative intention:

'But, goode swete herte, that ye
Bury my body'. . . .

(*BD* 206–7)

'Mercy! and that ye nat discovere me,
For I am deed if that this thyng be kyd.'

(*MerchT* 1942–3)

In the latter example the second line illustrates neatly the contrast between Damyan's certainty that he *will* be dead should the truth ever become known and the awful possibility that the truth *might* become known.

Another rare Middle English construction,[19] this time involving infinitives, occurs when the causative verbs 'do' and 'let' are followed by two infinitives, namely *doon* 'do' and the main verb. The reason for the duplication may well be largely a metrical one for both Gower (cp. *Conf Am* II, 958, 3448, 3468) and for Chaucer:

And thus he *dide doon sleen* hem alle thre.

(*SumT* 2042)

He *leet* the feeste of his nativitee
Doon cryen thurghout Sarray his citee.

(*SqT* 45–6)

The latter construction is identical with Gower's 'and let do crien al aboute' (*Conf Am* II, 3468).

Such construction, and others like it – for example 'has done' followed by a past participle as in the Man of Law's 'thise marchantz han doon fraught hir shippes newe' (*MLT* 171), or the narrator's 'I was go walked' (*BD* 387) – may strike the modern

19. Skeat calls it 'remarkable', Robinson 'unusual', while Mustanoja speaks of its occurring 'occasionally' (p. 605) and cites an instance from Robert Mannyng as well as those from Chaucer and Gower cited above.

reader as odd, but they do not usually prevent a ready understanding of Chaucer's meaning. The same is true of some constructions involving other parts of speech: the use of the personal pronoun in a demonstrative role alongside a proper name,
for example, as in

> that ilke weddyng murie
> Of hire Philologie and hym Mercurie,
> *(MerchT* 1733–4)

where *hire* and *hym* have a similar function to *that ilke*. Or again, a
construction like 'oon the beste knyght' (*Tr* I, 1081) clearly has a
superlative function, although there is some dispute whether it
corresponds to modern English 'the very best knight', as Mustanoja argues,[20] or to 'one of the best knights', as other scholars
have maintained.[21] Although the distinction may not worry
most readers of Chaucer, it has subtle contextual implications. Is
Criseyde being proudly vain or reasonably modest when she says

> 'I am oon the faireste, out of drede,
> And goodlieste, whoso taketh hede,
> And so men seyn, in al the town of Troie'?
> *(Tr* II, 746–8)

Is the turtle-dove in *The Parliament of Fowls* being becomingly
humble or abjectly grovelling in front of her betters in describing
herself as 'a sed-foul [bird living on seeds], oon the unworthieste'
(*PF* 512)? In descriptions of particular heroes or heroines the
'absolute' superlative was customary, as in the Black Knight's
lengthy encomium on his lady in *The Book of the Duchess*, or in
some of the Harley lyrics, in romances and elsewhere, so that one
inclines to Mustanoja's explanation in interpreting such expressions as the Franklin's 'she was oon the faireste under sonne'
(*FranklT* 734) when introducing Dorigen, or the reference to
Troilus as 'oon the beste knyght' coming at the end of a series of
unequivocal superlatives:

> For he bicom the frendlieste wight,
> The gentilest, and ek the mooste fre,

20. Mustanoja, pp. 297 ff.
21. Thus Robinson in his note to *CLT* 212, Donaldson in glossing 'one of', and
earlier scholars; cp. Kerkhof, p. 129. In *SGGK* 2363, 'on þe fautlest freke', Davis
glosses 'the most faultless', despite the fact that three lines further on the Green
Knight points out that Gawain was *not* faultless: 'Bot here yow lakked a lyttel, sir,
and lewté yow wonted.'

The thriftiest and oon the beste knyght,
That in his tyme was or myghte be.
                                    (*Tr* I, 1079–82)

Such a view gains support from the fact that Chaucer has several
instances of a construction closer to the modern English one,
although the noun is still in the singular: 'oon of the gretteste
auctour that men rede' (*NPT* 2984): 'oon of the beste entecched
[endowed with good qualities] creature' (*Tr* V, 832); 'oon of the
gretteste and moost sovereyn thyng that is in this world is unytee
and pees' (*Mel* 1678).

The use of adjectives as nouns is found in Chaucer's English as
in present-day English, but some of Chaucer's usages are not
possible today. He uses, for example, the construction 'an impossible' on several occasions, as in

For trusteth wel, it is an impossible
That any clerk wol speke good of wyves,
                                    (*WBT* 688–9)

a construction rather more common in the fifteenth than in the
fourteenth century. Similarly, Chaucer uses 'a certeyn' as a substantive where modern English requires an additional noun of
quantity to complete the phrase: 'a certeyn frankes' (*ShipT* 334),
'with a certein of hire owen men' (*Tr* III, 596), that is, a certain
number of francs or of men. Langland has the same usage:

Kynges and knyghtes that kepen and defenden,
Hauen officers vnder hem and ech of hem a certayn,
                                    (*PP* C XXIII, 257–8)

elaborated a few lines later (267) into 'a certayn for a certayn'.

Such constructions, albeit different from present-day usage, do
not present much difficulty to the modern reader. We may pause
involuntarily when confronted by 'at the fulle' (e.g. *BD* 899)
corresponding to modern English 'fully, completely, thoroughly'
or 'at his large' corresponding to modern English 'at large, free
from imprisonment' (*KnT* 1327, *HF* 745, and similarly 'at thy
large', *KnT* 1283, 1292, 'at oure large', *WBT* 322), or even by such
seemingly pedantic phrasing as 'it am I' (*KnT* 1736), which is
quite normal Middle English, but we are unlikely to pause for
long. On the other hand, there are occasions when the pause may

be longer, when we may wonder whether Chaucer or his scribe or his modern editor hasn't made some mistake. The Miller's line

His owene hand he made laddres thre
(*MillT* 3624)

is not in fact anyone's blunder but a survival of the Old English inflected instrumental *his agenre handa* 'with his own hand', echoing Law Latin *manu propria*. Gower has several instances of such prepositionless instrumentals in the *Confessio Amantis*, including the variant 'his oghne mouth' (V, 5455).

More puzzling still is the Middle English use of *for* in conjunction with what Mustanoja calls 'semi-substantivised adjectives'.[22] Two instances occur in close proximity in *The Knight's Tale*:

He hadde a beres skyn, col-blak *for old*.
His longe heer was kembd bihynde his bak;
As any ravenes fethere it shoon *for blak*.
(*KnT* 2142–4)

Originally *for* served as an emphatic or intensifying prefix in Middle English as it had done in Old English, and as such it occurs in a number of verbs, like the Parson's 'for it [Sloth] *forsleweth* [delays] and *forsluggeth* [neglects] and destroyeth alle goodes temporeles by reccheleesnesse' (*ParsT* 685); or it could have a perfective or completive or causal function as in the narrator's description of Criseyde 'with broken vois, al hoors *for-shright*' (*Tr* IV, 1147), her voice all hoarse with so much shrieking. In *The Knight's Tale*, *for old* and *for blak* could be regarded as instances of intensive *for*, and some editors, among them Skeat in the Oxford *Chaucer*, print the words hyphenated: *for-old, for-blak*. Robinson, on the other hand (p. 678), prefers to regard *for* in these cases as a causal preposition combining with the adjective into the equivalent of a noun-phrase: 'because of age', 'because of blackness'. In some cases the construction is further elaborated so that the causal function is rather more obvious and what Skeat calls 'a curious idiom' results, apparently confined to the later fourteenth century, as in 'for pure ashamed' (*Tr* II, 656), glossed by Robinson 'for very shame'. Sometimes the function of *for* as an intensive prefix is the more apparent:

22. Mustanoja, p. 381. See also the entries in *OED* and *MED*.

'And sodeynly he was yslayn to-nyght,
Fordronke, as he sat on his bench upright.'

(PardT 673–4)

At other times some ambiguity is undeniable:

The Millere, that *for dronken* was al pale,
So that unnethe upon his hors he sat.

(CT I, 3120–1)

Amydde a tree, *for drye* as whit as chalk.

(SqT 409)

Chaucer was probably aware of possible ambiguity and may well have exploited it in such cases as the Wife of Bath's reference to her first three husbands:

Of wenches wolde I beren hem on honde,
Whan that *for syk* unnethes myghte they stonde.

(WBT 393–4)

Other writers beside Chaucer were familiar with this construction. Gower, for example, has 'for wroth' (*Conf Am* VI, 1696), and the more complex 'for pure abaissht' (*ibid.* IV, 1330), while the intensive prefix occurs in such words as 'al forwondered', very surprised (*SGGK* 1660), or Langland's *for-sleuthed* 'wasted through neglect' (*PP* C VIII, 52) which is associated with his description of Sloth, as is Chaucer's word *forsleweth* in *The Parson's Tale* for which one manuscript reading is *forslowthith*, the same word as Langland's.

A similar idiomatic usage occurs in connection with the word *wery* 'weary' linked to a past participle prefixed by *for*. Here the prefix seems to combine something of the emphatic function as in Chaucer's *fordronke* with that of the causal preposition as in Chaucer's 'for pure ashamed'. Langland has instructive examples in 'whan thow art *wery for-walked*', tired out with a lot of walking (*PP* B XIII, 204), and 'wery forwandred' in B Prologue, 7, where the A text has 'weori of wandringe' in Skeat's edition and 'wery [for]wandrit' in Kane's, and the C text has 'for weyrynesse of wandryng'. Chaucer has similar constructions in *The House of Fame*, 115, 'as he that *wery was forgo*', and in *The Man of Law's Tale*, 596–7:

Wery, *forwaked* in hire orisouns,
Slepeth Custance, and Hermengyld also.

93

Similar examples occur in other fourteenth-century poems.

That Chaucer's English is rich in such idiomatic turns of phrase used for a variety of artistic purposes is one of the principal themes of this book, and that some of these idioms may not be immediately intelligible to the modern reader is the inevitable consequence of the lapse of six hundred years. Sometimes a Chaucerian idiom may embody the meaning of a word which it no longer possesses today. Thus, for example, Chaucer is fond of the phrase 'it sit' in the sense of 'it befits, it suits', a usage influenced by a similar idiom in Old French, and found in other fourteenth-century writers:

> For wel sit it, the sothe for to seyne,
> A woful wight to han a drery feere [companion].
> 　　　　　(*Tr* I, 12–13)

> And trewely it sit wel to be so,
> That bacheleris have often peyne and wo.
> 　　　　　(*MerchT* 1277–8)

The verb *can* usually has for Chaucer its modern meaning of 'to be able', but occasionally the Old English meaning 'to know' survives in expressions like 'he that koude his good' (*Tr* V, 106) or 'this lady kan hire good' (*ibid.* 1149), where modern English has 'to know what is good for one'. The phrase can have a strongly colloquial ring, as in Harry Bailly's

> 'I se wel that ye lerned men in lore
> Can moche good, by Goddes dignitee!'
> 　　　　　(*CT* II, 1168–9)

The expression *been aboute* 'to go about something, undertake something' is common enough in Middle English; for example, in

> 'As of this thyng the whiche ye ben aboute',
> 　　　　　(*LGW* 1612)

but it takes on the more specific meaning of 'to waste one's time' in Diomede's colloquial 'certeynlich I am aboute nought' (*Tr* V, 100), well in keeping with the colloquial tenor of Diomede's amorous speculations:

> 'certeynlich I am aboute nought,
> If that I speke of love, or make it tough;

For douteles, if she have in hire thought
Hym that I gesse, he may nat ben ybrought
So soon awey; but I shal fynde a meene,
That she naught wite as yet shal what I mene.'

(Tr V, 100–5)

The expression 'make it tough' is used several times by Chaucer
and is glossed variously by different editors. Chaucer appears to
have distinguished between various, though related, senses. In
the above passage the sense 'to take great pains with any matter',
recorded by Halliwell,[23] accords particularly well with the accompanying idea of wasting time. In *Troilus and Criseyde* II, 1025,
'as make it with thise argumentes tough', and in *The Book of the
Duchess*, 531, 'he made hyt nouther towgh ne queynte', the sense
is probably simply 'to make it hard, to complicate matters', the
primary meaning recorded by the *OED*; while in *The Shipman's
Tale* the meaning is plainly bawdy:

Whan it was day, this marchant gan embrace
His wyf al newe, and kiste hire on hir face,
And up he gooth and maketh it ful tough.

(ShipT 377–9)

Structurally akin to 'been aboute' is the idiom 'been along on'
which both in the more general sense of 'to depend on' and in the
more specific sense of 'to be someone's fault' is used by Gower,
and, in Chaucer's work, by Pandarus. In the former sense Pandarus uses it in speaking to Criseyde:

'That, but it were on hym along, ye nolde
Hym nevere falsen while ye lyven sholde.'

(Tr III, 783–4)

In the latter sense Pandarus uses it when addressing Troilus:

'Do now as I shal seyn, and far aright;
And if thow nylt, wit al thiself thi care!
On me is nought along thyn yvel fare.'

(Tr II, 999–1001)

The same idiom occurs in the Ellesmere manuscript and some
others of *The Canterbury Tales* in two places in *The Canon's Yeoman's
Tale* (922 and 930) where Skeat, Robinson, and Manly and Rickert

23. James Orchard Halliwell, *A Dictionary of Archaic and Provincial Words* (London,
1847), Vol. II, p. 884, *s.v. tow* (1).

print *long*, the aphetic form of *along*, O.E. *gelang* 'dependent on'. But the Ellesmere reading is clearly preferable, particularly in the second instance, 'I kan nat telle wheron it was [a] long' (*CYT* 930), not only because the form *along* was quite acceptable in Chaucer's English, but because the idiomatic turn of phrase that befits Pandarus suits the Canon's Yeoman's lively account of the explosion in the laboratory just as well.

An apparently unique Chaucerian idiom, for which the *MED* cites no parallel, is the narrator's 'to come to hous upon an innocent!' in the Legend of Hypsipyle (*LGW* 1546). 'To come to hous upon' seems to mean 'to come to feel at home with someone', hence 'to become familiar with'.

A number of Chaucerian idioms involves numerals, and despite the mathematical precision which the poet may have intended, the modern reader sometimes remains puzzled. When Troilus rides past Criseyde's window, he does so 'with his tenthe som yfere' (*Tr* II, 1249). Learned opinion is about evenly divided whether Troilus is here one (*som*) of ten men, as in O.E. *fiftyna sum* 'one of fifteen' (*Beowulf* 207), that is Beowulf and fourteen others, or whether Troilus is accompanied by ten other men, a possible enough meaning of the phrase also in Middle English. In the context it matters little, but it is worth recalling that Chaucer was fond of round figures, twenty especially (books, winters, years, featherings of Pertelote, and so on), but also ten, twelve, hundred, thousand, and multiples thereof, occasionally reaching almost astronomical proportions:

> What pris were it to hym, though I yow tolde
> Of Darius, and an hundred thousand mo
> Of kynges, princes, dukes, erles bolde
> Whiche he conquered, and broghte hem into wo?
> (*MkT* 2647–50)

By comparison other round figures, forty and fifty for example, are quite rare in Chaucer.

Multiplication can be expressed in one or two idiomatic ways unfamiliar to the modern ear: by a cardinal number followed by *so*, as in 'ten so wod' (*LGW* 736), ten times as mad, or 'two so ryche' (*LGW* 2291), twice as rich; or by *swich* 'such' followed by a cardinal number, as in 'swiche seven', seven times as many:

To have moo floures, swiche seven,
As in the welken sterres bee,

(BD 408–9)

or 'swyche fyve', five times as many, said by Pandarus and
echoed by Criseyde in *Troilus* and *Criseyde* II, 126–8. The familiar
mode of multiplication (as in 'seven tymes seventene', *CT* VII,
3454) is also used by Chaucer. The calculation 'many thousand
tymes twelve' is made rather absurd (for so large a crowd) by
the addition of 'al be hemselve' in *The House of Fame*, 1215, but it
achieves the effect of a huge multitude towards the end of that
poem:

O, many a thousand tymes twelve
Saugh I eke of these pardoners,
Currours, and eke messagers,
With boystes crammed ful of lyes.

(HF 2126–9)

That Chaucer liked to express himself in mathematical terms may
have something to do with his interest in astronomy and his
enjoyment of mathematical calculation. He likes to get his dates
right, for example,

And this was on the sixte morwe of May,

(FranklT 906)

or his astronomical data,

For whan degrees fiftene weren ascended,
Thanne crew he.

(NPT 2857–8)

He likes to determine a person's age as nearly as possible, for it
may affect character or story. The young Squire is 'of twenty
yeer of age' (*Gen Prol* 82); the pathetic heroine of *The Physician's
Tale*, like Shakespeare's Juliet, is fourteen:

This mayde of age twelve yeer was and tweye.

(PhysT 30)

The Wife of Bath entered upon her marital career at the age of
twelve (*WBT* 4), a figure rich in connotations for the medieval
mind, in view of its chronological and monetary significance, the
twelve apostles, and the twelve signs of the Zodiac. 'Ten or
twelve' is a common Chaucerian phrase, fluctuating neatly

between decimal and duodecimal affiliation. The lusty Malyne of *The Reeve's Tale* has her bed 'ten foot or twelve' from the parental one; and in *The Book of the Duchess* there is the severity of a forestry commission plantation about the grove where

> every tree stood by hymselve
> Fro other wel ten foot or twelve.
>
> *(BD* 419–20)

One suspects that such bare and plain mathematics are prompted more by rhyme than by calculation, however; for not many lines further on in the latter poem the Black Knight's *compleynt* is measured in the same rather arbitrary fashion as consisting of 'ten vers or twelve' *(BD* 463), because rhymes in -*elve* have, along with others, at least in Chaucer's English 'such skarsete', as he puts it in *The Complaint of Venus*, 80; hence every occurrence of *twelve* at the end of a line rhymes with *hymselve* or *myselve* or some other variant of *selve*. Actually, the Black Knight's *compleynt* has eleven lines!

Another reason for the appeal of such numerical idioms may well have been their jingling alliteration. Gower also has examples of 'ten or twelve', in *Confessio Amantis*, Prologue, 526, or in II, 2063, for instance, and there are other pairs, like 'six or sevene'. In the English *Romaunt*, for example, the original 'vins en baris e en touniaus' *(Roman de la Rose*, 11776) is rendered as

> Barelles of wyn, by sixe or sevene,
>
> *(Rom* 7072)

and in *Troilus and Criseyde* IV, 622, Pandarus advises Troilus to 'manly sette the world on six and sevene', an idiom probably derived from the game of hazard where it referred to the odds being in certain circumstances against the person betting. The subsequent meaning of the phrase, 'to be in disorder or confusion', is attested in the Towneley Plays where Herod's anger at the Wise Men makes him exclaim 'I shall, and that in hy, set all on sex and seuen';[24] this may be Pandarus's meaning too, although the original sense of taking a chance irrespective of the odds fits the context equally well:

24. *The Wakefield Pageants in the Towneley Cycle*, ed. A. C. Cawley (Manchester, 1958), V, 128.

'Lat nat this wrecched wo thyn herte gnawe,
But manly sette the world on six and sevene;
And if thow deye a martyr, go to hevene!'
(Tr IV, 621-3)

Alliterating phrases are much more common in Chaucer's English than is often realized.[25] For the most part they are popular idioms, integral to the language, which contribute yet another ingredient to the colloquial register so prevalent in Chaucer's work. Structurally, these alliterating phrases are of several types, of which perhaps the most common are pairs of words alliterating on consonants or vowels (possibly with a trace of preceding aspiration); for example, nouns:

Inspired hath in every *holt and heeth.*
(Gen Prol 6)

'And first I shrewe myself, bothe *blood and bones'.*
(NPT 3427)

'In *word and werk,* bothe heere and everywheere'.
(CLT 167)

And brennen *hous and hoom,* and make al playn.[26]
(MancT 229)

The simple juxtaposition of two nouns may be elaborated by appropriate syntactic variation. Compare, for example, the simple 'of fissh and flessh' *(Gen Prol* 344) with Januarie's

'*Oold fissh and yong flessh* wolde I have ful fayn',
(MerchT 1418)

where the alliteration is reinforced by the common alliterating formula 'ful fayn' at the end of the line; similarly, the simple 'freend or foo' *(SqT* 136) is appropriately varied in the Monk's

Fortune was *first freend, and sitthe foo.*
(MkT 2723)

Adjectives and adverbs also frequently occur in alliterating pairs:

Ne me nys nothyng *leef nor looth.*
(BD 8)

25. Cp. the useful discussion by ten Brink, pp. 241 ff.

26. On such 'untransposable' pairs as 'word and werk', 'hous and hoom', whether alliterating or not, see Simeon Potter, 'Chaucer's Untransposable Binomials' *Neuphilologische Mitteilungen* LXXIII (1972), 309-14.

'Ther is a *long and large* difference'.
(*CT* IV, 1223)

'To thyng to come, al falle it *foule or faire*.'
(*Tr* IV, 1022)

Here too the pattern is often varied, as in 'that baggeth [squints] *foule* and loketh *faire*' (*BD* 623); and the same holds true of pairs of verbs, like 'dyke and delve' (*Gen Prol* 536), or 'hauke and hunte' (*CLT* 81), or 'wepe and wayle' (*KnT* 931), which are subject to similar elaboration:

To *wepe* ynogh, and *wailen* al my fille.
(*Lady* 13)

Or compare the end of the Envoy which concludes *The Clerk's Tale*,

And lat hym care, and *wepe*, and *wrynge*, and *waille*!
(*CIT* 1212)

with the Merchant's echoing

'*Wepyng and waylyng*, care and oother sorwe'.
(*CT* IV, 1213)

A common device is to link adjective and noun by alliteration:

'This *wyde world*, which that men seye is round'.
(*FranklT* 1228)

How looth hire was to been a *wikked wyf*.
(*FranklT* 1599)

'Herkneth thise *blisful briddes* how they synge,
And se the *fresshe floures* how they sprynge';
(*NPT* 3201–2)

fresshe floures being something of a Chaucerian commonplace, a basic theme on which the poet plays numerous linguistic variations; for example:

And *fressher* than the May with *floures* newe.
(*KnT* 1037)

The odour of *floures* and the *fresshe* sighte.
(*FranklT* 913)

To seen this *flour* so yong, so *fressh* of hewe.
(*LGW* Prol F, 104)

That maken hony of *floures freshe* of hewe.

(PF 354)

Verbs are often linked by alliteration with other parts of speech, as in the Parson's 'loved ful longe' (*ParsT* 562), the Prioress's 'synge a song' (*PrT* 584), the Knight's 'looketh lightly' (*KnT* 1870), the very common phrase 'sooth to seyn' (*Gen Prol* 284), and so on. Similarly, other phrases are common in which various parts of speech combine into alliterating patterns: 'water of the well' (*Thop* 915), 'hadde the hyer hond' (*Gen Prol* 399), or the more elaborate prose patterns of a passage like this: 'and som-tyme it semede that sche touchede the *hevene* with the *heghte* of *here heved*; and whan sche *hef hir heved heyer*, sche percede the selve *hevene* . . .' (*Bo* I, pr. 1, 15–18).

Similes sometimes involve alliteration, but these are usually the more commonplace, poetically less memorable ones, 'battered similes', as Eric Partridge calls them, which 'assault our sensibilities',[27] akin to some of the dead metaphors that clutter up contemporary English with clichés. Such a one is 'as meeke as is a mayde' (*Gen Prol* 69), the alliterative equivalent of 'as meke as evere was any lomb' (*SecNT* 199), both of them familiar enough to Chaucer and his contemporaries. Another common alliterative simile is 'as stille as any stoon', appropriate enough when it refers to some stationary object like the horse standing still in the courtyard in *The Squire's Tale*, 171, or the poet-dreamer kneeling motionless in the daisy meadow in the Prologue to *The Legend of Good Women* (F 308–10). But when silence is combined with movement, as in

In crepeth age alwey, as stille as stoon,

(CLT 121)

Chaucer's simile becomes 'battered', a mere mechanical device, a poetic opportunity missed: stones don't creep. The opportunity exists even with hackneyed diction like 'as stille as any stoon'. Perhaps it is not quite fair to cite an instance from an alliterative poem, for here the movement of the alliterating lines as well as the inherent tendency towards formulaic diction make such idioms more acceptable, but the *Gawain*-poet for example needs to add

27. Eric Partridge, *A Charm of Words* (London, 1960), p. 49. Cp. also the introductory essay to Partridge's *A Dictionary of Clichés* (London, 1940).

only a modicum of elaboration[28] to make even 'as stille as any stoon' come alive:

> Gawayn grayþely hit bydez, and glent with no membre,
> Bot stode stylle as þe ston, oþer a stubbe auþer
> Þat raþeled is in roché grounde with rotez a hundreth.
>
> *(SGGK* 2292–4)

That Chaucer was familiar with contemporary alliterative poetry is beyond doubt. The Parson's brief reference to 'geeste "rum, ram, ruf"', by lettre' (*CT* X, 43) is unmistakable, as are Chaucer's own occasional excursions into a more sustained alliterative mode. Besides, it is instructive to remember that Chaucer's patron John of Gaunt owned rich possessions in the north-west midlands where the alliterative revival flourished, that he kept paid entertainers there,[29] and that he may have been, for all we know, patron also to some of the alliterative poets active in Lancashire, Cheshire, or Staffordshire. It is in *The Knight's Tale* that Chaucer most successfully captures the idiom of the alliterative poets, both in occasional pithy phrases like

> With *hunte* and *horn* and *houndes hym* bisyde,
>
> *(KnT* 1678)

or

> With *knotty, knarry*, bareyne trees olde,
>
> *(KnT* 1977)

or

> In which ther *ran* a *rumbel* in a swough,
>
> *(KnT* 1979)

or

> That in the *bataille blowen blody* sounes,
>
> *(KnT* 2512)

and in the sustained passage describing the tournament in Part Four of the tale:

> Ther shyveren shaftes upon sheeldes thikke;
> He feeleth thurgh the herte-spoon the prikke.

28. 'Some increment of meaning', as J. A. Burrow calls it, *Ricardian Poetry* (London, 1971), p. 139.

29. At Tutbury Castle in Staffordshire, for example. Cp. Sydney Armitage-Smith, *John of Gaunt* (London, 1904, repr. 1964), p. 104.

Up spryngen speres twenty foot on highte;
Out goon the swerdes as the silver brighte;
The helmes they tohewen and toshrede;
Out brest the blood with stierne stremes rede;
With myghty maces the bones they tobreste.
He thurgh the thikkeste of the throng gan threste;
Ther stomblen steedes stronge, and doun gooth al;
He rolleth under foot as dooth a bal;
He foyneth on his feet with his tronchoun,
And he hym hurtleth with his hors adoun.

(KnT 2605–16)

Although only three of these lines are proper alliterative long lines (the first, eighth and twelfth lines), the general impression is very like that of similar battle passages in some of the alliterative poems of the fourteenth century. The diction of this passage contributes to this effect almost as much as the alliteration, some of it being noticeably un-Chaucerian: the compound *herte-spoon*, which refers to the concave part of the breast, is unique to this passage, and so are several other words: *shyveren* as a verb (but cp. *to-shyvered*, PF 493), *toshrede*, *throng* as a noun, *stomblen*, *tronchoun*. Some of the other words are of very limited occurrence: *shaft* occurs once in a simile elsewhere in *The Knight's Tale* (1362), and once in *The Parliament of Fowls* where alliteration also enters:

The shetere ew; the asp for shaftes pleyne.

(PF 180)

The alliterative phrase 'helm tohewen' occurs in the description of the battle-scarred Troilus (*Tr* II, 638); while the verb occurs elsewhere only in the Man of Law's narration of the bloodthirsty Sultaness's butchery (*MLT* 430, 437). The adjective *stierne* is not uncommon but figures twice elsewhere in the alliterative phrase 'stierne and stoute' (*KnT* 2154, *LGW* 1695). The verb *foynen* is readily associated with 'feet', whether it means 'to thrust, lunge' with a weapon, on one's feet, as in 'foyne, if hym list, on foote' (*KnT* 2550), or 'he foyneth on his feet' (*KnT* 2615), or up to one's ankles in blood with 'sharpe speres stronge' as in that memorable duel between Palamon and Arcite earlier in *The Knight's Tale* (1653 ff.), or whether it means 'to kick' as it does in the description of the Green Knight's head rolling along the floor in *Sir Gawain and the Green Knight*, 428:

Þat fele hit foyned wyth her fete, Þere hit forth roled.

Chaucer uses the word only on the three occasions cited, all in
The Knight's Tale. The verb *hurtelen* 'to hurl, cast' is also rare in
Chaucer; it figures in the alliterating 'heterly they hurtelen' in
another vivid Chaucerian battle passage that shows affinities with
the alliterative poetry of his time. Only this time it is a sea fight,
the battle of Actium as described in the legend of Cleopatra, the
first of the stories in *The Legend of Good Women*, better known no
doubt to readers of English literature as the turning point in
Shakespeare's *Antony and Cleopatra*:

> Up goth the trompe, and for to shoute and shete,
> And peynen hem to sette on with the sunne.
> With grysely soun out goth the grete gonne,
> And heterly they hurtelen al atones,
> And from the top doun come the grete stones.
> In goth the grapenel, so ful of crokes;
> Among the ropes renne the sherynge-hokes.
> In with the polax preseth he and he;
> Byhynde the mast begynnyth he to fle,
> And out ageyn, and dryveth hym overbord;
> He styngeth hym upon his speres ord;
> He rent the seyl with hokes lyke a sithe;
> He bryngeth the cuppe, and biddeth hem be blythe;
> He poureth pesen upon the haches slidere;
> With pottes ful of lyme they gon togidere;
> And thus the longe day in fyght they spende,
> Tyl at the laste, as every thyng hath ende,
> Antony is schent, and put hym to the flyghte,
> And al his folk to-go, that best go myghte.
>
> (*LGW* 635-53)

Apart from several technical words in this passage which Chaucer
does not use elsewhere (*crokes* 'hooks', *grapenel* 'grappling iron',
haches 'hatches', *sherynge-hokes* 'shear-hooks', *sithe* 'scythe') and
the word *polax* 'pole-axe, battle-axe' which occurs also in *The
Knight's Tale*, 2544, the two words *heterly* and *ord* are worthy of
note. The first of these is a regular stand-by in the alliterative
poetry, denoting all kinds of physical and emotional violence,
e.g. 'hurtez hem ful heterly' (*SGGK* 1462), 'heterly hated here'
(*Pearl* 402); whereas *ord* 'point' harks back straight to Old English usage in similar battle descriptions, kept alive in the interval

by writers like Laȝamon and the author of *Cursor Mundi*. Neither word occurs elsewhere in Chaucer, nor does *ord* appear to be recorded in this sense in the work of any of Chaucer's close contemporaries.

Both of the descriptions quoted above rely upon devices other than alliteration and unusual diction for their effect. Inversion of normal word order mirrors the thrust and parry of close combat in several vivid instances: 'up spryngen speres', 'out goon the swerdes', 'out brest the blood', 'up goth the trompe', 'in goth the grapenel', 'in with the polax preseth he and he'. There is a good deal of rhetorical patterning, as in 'he styngeth . . .; he rent [i.e. *rendeth*] . . .; he bryngeth . . .; he poureth', and a restless alternation between the third person singular and plural pronouns, between the anonymous *he* or 'he and he' or *hym* and the no less anonymous *they* or *hem*. The mêlée of battle is skilfully realized by such means, although such means are hardly 'bare and pleyn'.

Battle scenes are comparatively rare in Chaucer; he prefers to refer his readers or listeners to others for such matter, to Dares for Troilus's heroic exploits (*Tr* V, 1770–1), for example, or to Petrarch for Queen Zenobia's (*MkT* 2319 ff.). When he does embark upon some martial scene, however, he does so clearly with one eye upon the alliterative poets.

The same cannot be said of that other kind of description in which the alliterative poets excelled, that of landscape. Chaucer's poetry abounds in pleasant arbours, gardens, groves, daisy-meadows, but they are for the most part insipid and uninteresting, because the poet prefers the superlatives of advertisers' English to the eclectic diction of the alliterative masters. The garden in *The Franklin's Tale* is a typical specimen; it is

> ful of leves and of floures;
> And craft of mannes hand so curiously
> Arrayed hadde this gardyn, trewely,
> That nevere was ther gardyn of swich prys,
> But if it were the verray paradys.

> (*FranklT* 908–12)

In *The Parliament of Fowls* the description is made longer by the enumeration of conventional detail, of birds, beasts, spices, and the rest; but the poet's heart is not really in it, hence the effect is pleasing but undistinguished. Flowers are simply 'white, blewe,

yelwe, and rede' (*PF* 186), the streams are *colde* and 'nothyng
dede' (187), the birds sing

> With voys of aungel in here armonye,
> (*PF* 191)

and the air is as *attempre* as in a deodorant advertisement. In the
Prologue to *The Legend of Good Women* it is the sun that is *atempre*
'mild, pleasant', while in the F version the words *swote* 'sweet'
and *swetenesse* are rather overworked (an excess which is corrected
in the G version):

> Upon the smale, softe, swote gras,
> That was with floures swote enbrouded al,
> Of swich swetnesse and swich odour overal,
> That, for to speke of gomme, or herbe, or tree,
> Comparisoun may noon ymaked bee.
> (*LGW* Prol F, 118–22)

Comparisons, as Dogberry says, are indeed odorous.

But some comparisons simply ask to be 'ymaked'. Chaucer himself recalls the garden of Guillaume de Lorris when he remarks
that 'he that wroot the Romance of the Rose' (*MerchT* 2032) could
not have adequately described the beauty of Januarie's garden,
'walled al with stoon' (*ibid.* 2029), so that nothing but another
superlative will do:

> So fair a gardyn woot I nowher noon.
> (*MerchT* 2030)

By contrast, one recalls Criseyde's less luxuriant *yerd* (*Tr* II, 820–2)
or the subdued description of the *Pearl*-poet's 'erber grene', also
rich in perfume and 'powdered' (the word occurs in a similar
context in the *Romaunt*, 1436) with peonies and other plants, but
free from extravagant claims to uniqueness.

Wild and forbidding natural features hardly enter into Chaucer's verse, and when they do, they lack the authenticity, the
'sensuous vividness'[30] of the northern landscapes in *Sir Gawain
and the Green Knight*, for example, or *The Wars of Alexander*.
Chaucer is able to capture something of the 'muscular' diction, as

---

30. The phrase is Derek A. Pearsall's in 'Rhetorical "Descriptio" in "Sir Gawain
and the Green Knight"', *Modern Language Review* L (1955), 130.

it has been called, of the alliterative poets in such descriptive lines as these:

> . . . a forest,
> In which ther dwelleth neither man ne best,
> With knotty, knarry, bareyne trees olde,
> Of stubbes sharpe and hidouse to biholde,
> In which ther ran a rumbel in a swough,
> As though a storm sholde bresten every bough.
>
> (*KnT* 1975–80)

One recalls the rush of the boar hunt as the hunters in *Sir Gawain* 'vmbekesten þe knarre and þe knot boþe' (1434), but in the latter context *knarre* and *knot*, with several other unusual topographical words, depict landmarks in a northwest midland landscape familiar to the poet, whereas Chaucer is talking about trees in a wall-painting. It is an impressive painting, to be sure, and Chaucer is sparing no effort to bring it to life. Thus, in the next sentence, he follows the line of vision 'dounward from an hille, under a bente' (*KnT* 1981), and a few lines later produces a unique noise with 'a rage and swich a veze' (1985), where *veze*, 'a blast, a rush', as the *MED* glosses it (*s.v. fēse*), may well make us wonder with Masui 'why such a word flashed upon the poet'.[31] It represents a substantival equivalent of the Old English verb *fȳsan*, Anglian *fēsan*, 'to impel', but according to the *MED* only one other instance of the noun appears to be recorded in Middle English, in the form *bewese* 'in haste', in a medicinal poem of the mid-fifteenth century. And as a rhyme for it Chaucer selects another uncommon word, *rese* 'to shake, tremble', derived from O.E. *hrisian*, and used nowhere else in his work. Not content with such alliterative echoes and rare native words, Chaucer lifts bodily from Boccaccio's *Teseida* the word *armypotente* 'mighty in arms' (1982, Italian *armipotente*), invariably associated in its few Middle English occurrences with Mars, probably because of Chaucer's usage; he takes over in the same way the phrase 'adamant eterne' (1990, Italian *eterno adamante*).

The whole passage repays study as an example of Chaucer's method of depicting a 'grisly place', as he calls it (1971), an epithet which he associates elsewhere with the temple of Mars, in *Anelida and Arcite*, 3, and which in *The Franklin's Tale* sums up for

31. Masui, p. 43.

Dorigen all the uncanny horror of the rocks of Brittany: 'the grisly rokkes blake' (*FranklT* 859) and, worse still,

> 'thise grisly feendly rokkes blake,
> That semen rather a foul confusion
> Of werk than any fair creacion
> Of swich a parfit wys God and a stable'.
>
> (*FranklT* 868–71)

For Chaucer, as for Dorigen, rough, rugged, craggy scenery was not aesthetically pleasing for its own sake, although it could prove linguistically stimulating; it was something frightening, 'grisly', the direct opposite of the snug familiarity of

> a lytel herber [arbour] that I have,
> Ybenched newe with turves, fresshe ygrave.
>
> (*LGW* Prol G, 97–8)

Where the *Gawain*-poet describes a genuine English landscape as an integral part of the texture of his story, Chaucer paints a Gothic picture to evoke a mood:

> 'But wolde God that alle thise rokkes blake
> Were sonken into helle for his sake!
> Thise rokkes sleen myn herte for the feere.'
>
> (*FranklT* 891–3)

The passage just discussed, despite Chaucer's avowal –

> To clerkes lete I al disputison
>
> (*FranklT* 890)

– is anything but 'bare and pleyn'. Yet Chaucer does of course use many bare and plain words, of which the barest and plainest is undoubtedly the word *thyng* itself, used by Chaucer more than 1,800 times. By far the largest number of occurrences, about 800, is in *Boece*, a point to which further reference will be made in the next chapter. The other prose works are also lengthy and make fairly frequent use of the word *thyng* or its inflected plural *thynges*, except the *Astrolabe*, where the word occurs only about a dozen times, compared with about eighty-five in *Melibee* and twice as many in *The Parson's Tale*. The very ubiquitousness of *thyng* precluded its frequent use in a work of 'science' in which Chaucer endeavoured conscientiously to call 'things' by their proper names, while explaining them in as 'naked' English words as possible.

The occurrence of a common word like *thyng* is presumably related to the length of particular poems; yet it is instructive to note that, the two prose tales apart, the two extremes in *The Canterbury Tales* are *The Prioress's Tale* and *The Wife of Bath's Prologue* and *Tale*, the former with only two instances and the latter with about forty. Yet the latter is only six times, not twenty times, as long as the former. The discrepancy reflects the difference between the Wife's rambling, wordy, highly colloquial mode of speaking and the Prioress's carefully, *fetisly* controlled diction. Other contrasts are equally instructive: the Man of Law, for example, whose 'wordes weren so wise' (*Gen Prol* 313) uses *thyng* and *thynges* considerably (about a third) less often than the Canon's Yeoman, although his tale is about half as long again as the latter's. In this case, also, the difference mirrors the different speech habits of the two pilgrims and of the characters of their tales.

The form *thyng*, which can be singular or plural,[32] occurs much more frequently than the inflected plural form *thynges*, perhaps because of its indefinite function in combinations like 'every thyng', 'any thyng', or 'alle thyng' which occurs alongside 'alle thynges'.[33] In the prose works the inflected plural form is relatively much more common; in both *Boece* and *The Parson's Tale* there are more plural occurrences than singulars. In rhyme, too, *thyng* and *thynges* are useful to Chaucer. According to Masui's calculations, about twelve per cent of the occurrences of the word in either form in the verse tales of *The Canterbury Tales* are in rhyme; but only about five per cent in *Troilus and Criseyde*. In *The Reeve's Tale*, 4129, *thynges* rhymes with clerk John's distinctive northern third person singular present indicative 'he brynges'.

The meanings Chaucer attaches to *thyng* vary considerably. The word is used with an indefinite pronoun in such instances as 'nat that I chalange any thyng of right' (*FranklT* 1324), or 'this Chanoun drough hym neer, and herde al thyng' (*CYT* 685); it can serve as an indefinite pronoun by itself, as in 'he nolde answere for thyng that myghte falle' (*MillT* 3418), where modern English would use 'anything'; it can function as an adverb of

32. Cp. ten Brink, p. 144.
33. On Chaucer's distinction between singular *al(l)* and plural *alle*, see Mustanoja, p. 213.

negation in such a case as 'no thyng ne knew he that it was Arcite' (*KnT* 1519); and 'no thyng' or 'nothyng' often occurs where modern English prefers 'not' or 'not at all', as in 'and made hir bed ful hard and nothyng softe' (*CLT* 228). Other uses are much the same as in other periods of English, as a few examples will illustrate:

By sleighte, or force, or by som maner thyng.
(*WBT* 405)

'Telle us som moral thyng, that we may leere'.
(*CT* VI 325)

He bad his servant fecchen hym this thyng.
(*CYT* 1108)

For al that thyng which I desyre I mis.
(*Lady* 43)

Such colloquial shorthand is evident also in the Chaucerian use of one's *thynges* to mean one's business, the particular concerns of the moment. Thus the divine office in the Breviary which the Shipman's monk had to recite privately while absent from his convent, is simply 'his thynges' (*ShipT* 91); similarly the Wife of Bath speaks of a friar saying 'his matyns and his hooly thynges' (*WBT* 876), not without a hint of irony, surely, in the context. The doomed traveller in Chauntecleer's *exemplum* refuses to let his friend's dream prevent him from carrying on with his business:

'That I wol lette for to do my thynges';
(*NPT* 3089)

and similarly the merchant's commercial activities in *The Shipman's Tale* are summed up by his wife as

'Youre sommes, and youre bookes, and youre thynges'.
(*ShipT* 217)

Chaucer's own poems are referred to as his *thynges* by the goddess of Love in the F version of the Prologue to *The Legend of Good Women* (364) where the G version substitutes *bokes* (342). Both the Squire and the Wife of Bath have appropriate connotations for the word: to the former *thynges* in a particular context are pieces of music:

Herknynge his mynstralles hir thynges pleye,
(*SqT* 78)

whereas for the Wife 'oure bothe thynges smale' (*WBT* 121) are the male and female genitals. No less characteristically, a *thyng* for the Man of Law is a legal document (*Gen Prol* 325), a reminder of the early legal connotations of the word.

At the opposite end of the lexical scale from *thyng* is a group of related words which were most precious to Chaucer, words which contribute to, or sum up, his ideal of a 'verray, parfit' gentil' person. The portrait of the Knight contains several of them:

Trouthe and honour, fredom and curteisie,
> (*Gen Prol* 46)

and so does Pandarus's flattering description of Troilus:

'In whom that alle vertu list habounde,
As alle trouth and alle gentilesse,
Wisdom, honour, fredom, and worthinesse,'
> (*Tr* II, 159–61)

later summed up in the line

'The goode, wise, worthi, fresshe, and free'.
> (*Tr* II, 317)

Most of these words present no difficulties to the modern reader; they have managed to retain much of their Chaucerian value despite the debasing of so much linguistic currency in the intervening centuries. Even *fresshe*, a favourite in contemporary advertising English,[34] still combines with other meanings, as in the phrase 'to get fresh with someone', the pristine connotations of, say, Chaucer's 'yonge, fresshe folkes' (*Tr* V, 1835) with the colloquial implications of husbands who are 'fressh abedde' (*WBT* 1259, *ShipT* 177). On the other hand, *free* (another favourite among advertisers) and its noun *fredom* have lost the Chaucerian senses of nobility and graciousness and impeccable manners, although we can still be 'free', that is magnanimous, generous, or lavish, with our money and possessions, just as some of Chaucer's characters are 'free of dispence', among them that remarkable specimen of young manhood, Perkyn Revelour (*CkT* 4387–8). If to be 'free of dispence' was a virtue, as the Shipman implies (*ShipT* 43 ff., and *cp.* *CLT* 1209), then to be 'esy of dispence',

34. Cp. Geoffrey N. Leech, *English in Advertising: A Linguistic Study of Advertising in Great Britain* (London, 1966), pp. 152 f.

tight-fisted, as the Physician was (*Gen Prol* 441), was presumably a vice. From such 'nygrades of dispence', as Alys of Bath so fervently prays (*WBT* 1263–4), may the good Lord deliver us!

Trouthe has implications for Chaucer and his contemporaries far beyond mere veracity. In *Piers Plowman* C VI, 199 'Saint Truth' becomes the symbol of salvation; and even though Chaucer, his concerns being different, does not elevate the word to such theological heights, he can yet make the Franklin's Arveragus exclaim with passionate sincerity in his moment of agony that

> 'Trouthe is the hyeste thyng that man may kepe'.
>
> (*FranklT* 1479)

'Truth' in the sense of fidelity, integrity, trustworthiness is fundamental to the medieval ideal of chivalry. It is Sir Gawain's most distinctive characteristic, and in the portrait of his Knight Chaucer links *trouthe* and the other virtues cited earlier with *chivalrie*. *Trouthe* is the cornerstone of the Chaucerian ideal of *gentillesse*, 'the quality that Chaucer most deeply admired', as Nevil Coghill says,[35] but it is incomplete without that specifically Christian virtue of compassion, variously called *routhe*, *pite*, *compassioun*, and (mainly in *The Parson's Tale*) *misericorde*. These words are occasionally linked in pairs, as in 'such pittee and such rowthe' (*BD* 97) or 'to have pite or compassioun' (*Bo* I, pr. 4, 234–5), but Chaucer does not treat them strictly as synonyms. Of these words *misericorde* is clearly the most technical as well as the least used. It is appropriate to the Parson, and suits the Summoner's friar's choice diction along with such other Chaucerian rarities as *persecucioun* and *executour* and *potestat* and *penyble*. In *An A B C*, 25 the Virgin is addressed as 'queen of misericorde', and the word recurs ten lines later. It also occurs once in *The Tale of Melibee*, once in *Boece* (in the plural), and once, rather unexpectedly, from the mouth of Criseyde who takes immediate pains, however, to explain what it means:

> And she answerde, 'Of gilt misericorde!
> That is to seyn, that I foryeve al this.'
>
> (*Tr* III, 1177–8)

The word *compassioun* is almost as infrequent as *misericorde*, but is distributed a little more widely among the Canterbury pilgrims,

35. Nevill Coghill, *Chaucer's Idea of What is Noble* (Presidential Address to the English Association, London, 1971), p. 7.

although confined to some of the more respectable, or at least more learned, pilgrims like the Knight, Squire, Parson, Franklin, Man of Law, and Monk. For Troilus, the word has connotations both of *amor*, courtly love, of Criseyde having *compassioun* on him (*Tr* I, 467), and of *amicitia*:

'And this that thow [Pandarus] doost, calle it gentilesse,
Compassioun, and felawship, and trist.'
(*Tr* III, 402-3)

The other two words, *routhe* and *pite*, are more common and up to a point more readily interchangeable. The former provided Chaucer with a handy rhyme for *trouthe*: although there are a few instances of triple rhyme involving *routhe*, *trouthe*, and *slouthe* 'sloth' in *Troilus and Criseyde* and one in *The Man of Law's Tale*, there are only two couplets in which *routhe* rhymes with *slouthe* as against twenty-one couplets rhyming *routhe* with *trouthe*, or, in a few cases, *untrouthe*. This is no mere mechanical convenience, however, for the two concepts had close psychological association for Chaucer, as Criseyde makes clear when she tells Troilus what it was that first attracted her to him:

'But moral vertu, grounded upon trouthe,
That was the cause I first hadde on yow routhe!
Eke gentil herte and manhod that ye hadde. . . .'
(*Tr* IV, 1672-4)

And as with *routhe*, so with *pitee*, except that Chaucer couples the former several times with *synne*, with a meaning probably close to something pathetic or even tragic, as when Criseyde exclaims:

'Ne though I lyved unto the werldes ende,
My name sholde I nevere ayeynward wynne.
Thus were I lost, and that were routhe and synne.'
(*Tr* IV, 1580-2)

On the other hand, it is the word *pitee* that is chosen in preference to *routhe* or the others, for Chaucer's favourite line,

For *pitee* renneth soone in gentil herte,
(*KnT* 1761)

found with slight variations in *The Merchant's Tale* (1986), *The Squire's Tale* (479), and in both versions of the Prologue to *The*

Legend of Good Women (F 503, G 491).[36] An interesting variant
juxtaposes *compassioun* and *pitee* in *The Man of Law's Tale*, 659-60:

> This Alla kyng hath swich compassioun,
> As gentil herte is fulfild of pitee.

Chaucer's variations on this theme seem almost endless, yet *pitee*
clearly occupies the highest place in this subtle scale of words of
compassion, probably for etymological reasons: *pitee* still possessed in the fourteenth-century the two senses of O.Fr. *pite* and
piete, both derived from Latin *pietās*, of 'piety' as well as 'pity,
clemency, compassion'. In English *piety* was not fully differen-
tiated from *pity* until the late sixteenth century.[37] Hence the
obvious religious connotations of Chaucer's *pitee*. Even in those
cases where Robinson and Root print *pietee* (*Tr* III, 1033; IV,
246; V, 1598), presumably for metrical reasons, the majority of
manuscripts of *Troilus and Criseyde* read *pite* or *pete*. For Chaucer
pitee embodies the Christian's duty both to God, *pietās*, and to his
fellow creatures, hence the ready coupling of *pitee* with words of
related import: mercy and pity several times in *Melibee*, 'mercy,
goodnesse, and . . . pitee' in *The Second Nun's Tale*, 51, 'innocence
. . . pite . . . trouthe, and conscience' in *The Legend of Good Women*,
1254-5, and Constance's prayerful 'Lambes blood ful of pitee'
(*MLT* 452).

All these words were obviously precious to Chaucer. To offend
against *trouthe* or to lack *pitee* were grievous failings, summed up by
Criseyde as

> 'Every thyng that souned [tended] into badde,
> As rudenesse and poeplissh [vulgar] appetit'.
> (*Tr* IV, 1676-7)

and even more forcefully by Aurelius as

> so heigh a cherlyssh wrecchednesse
> Agayns franchise and alle gentillesse.
> (*FranklT* 1523-4)

And yet even such precious linguistic material is twisted by the
poet into ironic shapes, perhaps nowhere more obviously so

36. Cp. Raymond Preston, 'Chaucer and the *Ballades Notées* of Guillaume de Ma-
chaut', *Speculum* XXVI (1951), 617.
37. See *The Oxford Dictionary of English Etymology* (Oxford, 1966), *s.v.v. piety, pity*.

than when the Merchant comments upon the dubious morality of his 'fresshe May' with the devastating force of that very same line

> Lo, pitee renneth soone in gentil herte!
> > (*MerchT* 1986)

coupled with such ironic thrusts as

> Heere may ye se how excellent franchise
> In wommen is,
> > (*ibid.* 1987–8)

and

> This gentil May, fulfilled of pitee.
> > (*ibid.* 1995)

Compared with such poignant irony, even the Wife of Bath's efforts pale. She never talks of *pitee* or *routhe*, though she manages to attach a bawdy note to the derivative *pitously* in her reference to her first three husbands' nocturnal labours (*WBT* 202), and although her tale is of course much concerned with *gentillesse*. Even the seemingly innocuous *trewely* is given an ironic twist when in its frequent occurrences in the last two books of *Troilus and Criseyde* it means almost the opposite of 'truly', something like, as Donaldson suggests, '"despite all evidence to the contrary" or "despite what you are thinking", like the *surely* that scholars sometimes employ to support statements which they suspect their readers will feel to be most unsure'.[38]

Chaucer's 'art poetical' abounds in instances of such linguistic tension between literal and ironic uses of words resulting in often highly complex patterns of meaning beneath the seemingly bare and plain surface. Chaucer may not have known our word 'irony' (the *OED* does not record it before the sixteenth century), but he certainly knew the figure, just as he knew other techniques of his art, 'recovered', as Robert O. Payne puts it, 'from the past',[39] without in every case putting a name to them. And yet there are enough literary terms scattered throughout Chaucer's writings to

---

38. Donaldson, *Speaking*, p. 74.
39. Robert O. Payne, *The Key of Remembrance: A Study of Chaucer's Poetics* (New Haven and London, 1963), p. 83.

create an impression of theoretical as well as practical interest in his craft and its terminology. He refers several times to rhetoric, to its *termes*, *colours*, and *figures* (cp. *CT* IV, 16); he speaks of the rhetoricians' *amplificatio* and *abbreviatio* as

> To encresse or maken dymynucioun
> Of my langage,
>
> (*Tr* III, 1335–6)

with the help of a word, *dymynucioun*, that carries the stamp of novelty in the thirteen-eighties. (For Gower (*Conf Am* VII, 160) the word carries the mathematical meaning of 'subtraction'.) There is reference also to 'figures of poetrie' in the learned Eagle's disclaimer of 'hard langage and hard matere':

> 'Have y not preved thus symply,
> Withoute any subtilite
> Of speche, or gret prolixite
> Of termes of philosophie,
> Of figures of poetrie,
> Or colours of rethorike?'
>
> (*HF* 854–9)

The *prolixite* here referred to was another literary term for Chaucer; he uses it only twice elsewhere: in a short critical excursus on the art of story-telling in *The Squire's Tale*, where reference is made to 'fulsomnesse [abundance] of . . . prolixitee' (405), and in *Troilus and Criseyde* II, 1564, where the narrator advocates its avoidance, at least at this point in the narrative.

The business of story-telling is obviously central to Chaucer's literary concern, and a number of words refer to it. Curiously, Chaucer never refers to himself as a *poete*, although he applies the word to Dante and Petrarch, and to Virgil and some other classical writers, as well as using it generally to refer to 'other poets' (*BD* 54) or to 'the fables of the poetis' (*Bo* III, pr. 12, 133). It is not a frequent word with Chaucer (less than a dozen occurrences); nor are the cognate words *poetrie* (used six times, twice in the plural with the sense of 'poems'), *poetical* (used twice), and *poesye* (once). The word *writeris* 'writers' occurs once in *Boece* II, pr. 7, 86, rendering the Latin *scriptorum*; the word *makere* figures two or three times in the sense of 'maker, poet', as in the heading to the Retraction to *The Canterbury Tales*: 'Heere taketh the makere of this book his leve', or in the gloss on the word *tragedien* in *Boece* III, pr. 6, 3–4: '*that is to seyn, a makere of dytees that highten tragedies*'.

To compose a poem or a book, a letter or a song, or to tell a story, is frequently to *endite* in Chaucer's English, as in that of his contemporaries. The *Pearl*-poet uses it thus (*Pearl* 1126). Gower distinguishes neatly between the act of composing a letter (*endite*) and writing it down (*wryte*):

> 'I wole a lettre unto mi brother,
> So as my fieble hand may wryte,
> With al my wofull herte endite.'
>
> (*Conf Am* III, 268–70)

Chaucer makes the same distinction when he says of Philomela,

> She coude eek rede, and wel ynow endyte,
> But with a penne coude she nat wryte.
> But letters can she weve to and fro.
>
> (*LGW* 2356–8)

Again, in the shortest of all his poems, here quoted in full, Chaucer instructs Adam, 'his owne scriveyn' (scribe) to copy out carefully (*wryte*) what the poet has composed ('my makyng'):

> Adam scriveyn, if ever it thee bifalle
> Boece or Troylus for to wryten newe,
> Under thy long lokkes thou most have the scalle,
> But after my makyng thou wryte more trewe;
> So ofte a-daye I mot thy werk renewe,
> It to correcte and eek to rubbe and scrape;
> And al is thorugh thy negligence and rape [haste].
>
> (*Adam* 1–7)

Langland similarly juxtaposes three words of related import in one passage in *Piers Plowman* (C XVIII, 108–10):

> For ther is nouthe non who so nymeth hede,
> That can *versifie* fayre other formeliche *endite*,
> Ne that can construen kyndeliche that poetes *maden*.

The word *endite* derives from O.Fr. *enditer* which developed in Anglo-Norman and in Middle English the legal sense of the modern 'to indict', which existed in fourteenth-century English alongside the sense of 'to compose'. It is used by Chaucer, speaking of his Man of Law, in a sense that combines the legal and literary meanings, 'to draft or compose a legal document', in yet another passage in which several related words are brought together:

> Therto he koude *endite*, and make a thyng,
> Ther koude no wight pynche at his *writyng*.
>
> *(Gen Prol* 325–6)

Although Chaucer frequently uses *write* as synonymous with *endite*, the former verb carries (as in modern English) more obvious connotations of the physical activity than does the latter. Pandarus, urging Toilus to write a letter to Criseyde, suggests that, were he in the latter's place, he

> 'wolde outrely,
> Of myn owen hond, write hire right now
> A lettre',
>
> *(Tr* II, 1004–6)

and goes on to emphasize the manner of the 'writing' as well as its import:

> 'Ne scryvenyssh[40] or craftily thow it write;
> Biblotte it with thi teris ek a lite;
> And if thow write a goodly word al softe,
> Though it be good, reherce it nought to ofte.'
>
> *(Tr* II, 1026–9)

'Enditing', on the other hand, is associated with different critical epithets, as when Pandarus, in the above context, advises Troilus not to 'dygneliche endite' (1024), which the *MED* glosses 'proudly, pretentiously'. Elsewhere, Chaucer couples 'subtilly to endite' (*SecNT* 80), 'kan nat wel endite' (this of himself, in the Prologue to *The Legend of Good Women*, F 414), 'my rude endityng' (also referring to himself, in the Introduction to the *Astrolabe*, 43), Philomela's 'wel ynow endyte' (*LGW* 2356), Harry Bailly's aversion to 'endite / Heigh style' (*CT* IV, 17–18), and so on.

Among other literary words, *make* in the sense of 'compose' is common, and so is *telle* associated with *tale* or *storie*. By contrast, Chaucer only once uses *versified*, in the Monk's introductory

---

40. That is, in the way Adam might have written it. While Chaucer obviously had some unhappy experiences with his secretary, he was nonetheless able to appreciate the professional expertise implied by this word. It occurs nowhere else in Chaucer.

remarks on what *tragedie* is (*MkT* 1978), a recently anglicized verb which, as we saw above, was also known to Langland. The substantive *versifiour* also occurs once, in *Melibee*, 1593, where it renders the French *versifieur*. Equally rare in Chaucer is the verb *compilen* which had in the fourteenth and fifteenth centuries much the same meaning as *endite*, as well as its modern English sense. Gower speaks of 'in a bok compiled' (*Conf Am* VI, 1382), and in Chaucer the only use of the verb is in the colophon to *The Canterbury Tales*, 'compiled by Geffrey Chaucer, of whos soule Jhesu Crist have mercy'. In the Introduction to the *Astrolabe* occurs the only instance of the noun, 'I n'am but a lewd *compilator* of the labour of olde astrologiens' (61–2), glossed 'plagiarist' by the *MED*, somewhat unkindly in view of the generally pejorative connotations of the word in modern English.

A technical literary word to which J. A. Burrow has recently drawn attention,[41] is *poynte* 'to point, to describe in detail'. Chaucer uses the word in this sense in *Troilus and Criseyde* III, 497:

His wordes alle, or every look, to poynte,

and it occurs in *Sir Gawain and the Green Knight*, 1009. Elsewhere, Chaucer prefers to use *discryve* which probably has much the same connotations as *poynte*; for example,

Who koude telle aright or ful discryve
His wo, his pleynt, his langour, and his pyne?
(*Tr* V, 267–8)

Among literary genres, Chaucer distinguishes several types. He refers only once in passing to *comedye* (*Tr* V, 1788) as a contrast to the *tragedye* of *Troilus and Criseyde*, but there are several mentions of *tragedye*, notably in the Monk's collection of such stories. The Monk's definition deserves quoting in full as an illustration of Chaucer's literary criticism in action:

'Tragedie is to seyn a certeyn storie,
As olde bookes maken us memorie,
Of hym that stood in greet prosperitee,
And is yfallen out of heigh degree
Into myserie, and endeth wrecchedly.
And they ben versified communely
Of six feet, which men clepen *exametron*.

41. J. A. Burrow, *Ricardian Poetry* (London, 1971), pp. 69 ff.

In prose eek been endited many oon,
And eek in meetre, in many a sondry wyse.
Lo, this declaryng oghte ynogh suffise.'
                    (*CT* VII, 1973–82)

A more succinct definition, lacking the technical details of the
Monk's *declaryng*, is given in a gloss in *Boece*: '*Tragedye is to seyn a
dite of a prosperite for a tyme, that endeth in wrecchidnesse*' (*Bo* II, pr. 2,
70–2), and a *tragedien*, we are told in a later gloss, is '*a makere of
dytees that highten tragedies*' (III, pr. 6, 3–4). Most of the technical
terminology in these passages will be familiar to the modern
reader. The distinction between prose and verse, the Monk's
prose and *meetre*, is made in other contexts also, usually as 'ryme
or prose' (*LGW* Prol F, 66), or more fully by the Man of Law:

'I speke in prose, and lat him rymes make.'
                    (*CT* II, 96)

In the plural, *meetres* can mean simply verses or poems, as in the
injunction to Chaucer to write poems (*metres*) about 'good women'
in the Prologue (F 562) to the *Legend*, or it can approach rather
more closely to the modern meaning of 'any specific form of
poetic rhythm' (*OED*). The Man of Law appears to be using it
thus in his snide reference to his maker's lack of poetic skill:

'Chaucer, thogh he kan but lewedly
On metres and on rymyng craftily'.
                    (*CT* II, 47–8)

Similarly, the word *vers* (singular and plural are identical) can
mean specifically a line of poetry, as in the endearing admission
that 'som vers fayle in a sillable' (*HF* 1098), or more generally a
division of a poem, a stanza, or even a whole poem. *Troilus and
Criseyde* opens with a reference to 'thise woful vers, that wepen as I
write' (*Tr* I, 7), and *Boece* likewise begins with 'vers [the Latin
carmina, French *chançonnetez*] of sorwful matere. . . . and drery
vers of wretchidnesse' (*Bo* I, m. 1, 2–6). Not all uses of the word
are as lugubrious, however.

A technical word which Chaucer uses only once is *cadence*.
Once again the allusion is to Chaucer's own 'art poetical', this
time from the Eagle's mouth (or beak):

'To make bookys, songes, dytees,
In ryme, or elles in cadence'.

(*HF* 622–3)

Cadence is rhythm, rhythmical construction, the flow of verse or,
for that matter, prose, and may here be intended to contrast with
ryme 'verse, poetry' and refer to some of Chaucer's prose *bookys*.
There is certainly a remarkably sustained rhythm in some of his
prose writing, notably the beginning of Melibee and certain passages in *Boece*, to which further reference will be made in the next
chapter. Yet, despite the contrast implied by the Eagle's 'or elles',
cadence may of course be just another way of referring to Chaucer's
poetry. Gower's line 'of metre, of rime and of cadence' (*Conf Am*
IV, 2414) seems to suggest three aspects of poetry, thus rather
supporting the latter interpretation.

'Tragedie', says the Monk, 'is to seyn a certeyn storie', and
storie is a common generic term in Chaucer, along with *tale*, *fable*,
lay, *song*, and some less frequent ones. Sometimes, Chaucer seems
to be using these words quite indiscriminately, guided perhaps by
sound rather than by any semantic distinctions, as in this instance:

Thanne telle I hem ensamples many oon
Of *olde stories* longe tyme agoon.
For lewed peple loven *tales olde*.

(*PardT* 435–7)

Yet the suggestion has recently been made that Chaucer does
recognize distinctions, namely that *storie* refers to a narrative
purporting to relate actual events, whereas *tale* implies an invented
plot, and similarly *fable* implies lack of historical truth.[42] The case
for *fable* is certainly strong. The Physician makes the point that

this is no fable,
But knowen for historial thyng notable;
The sentence of it sooth is, out of doute,

(*PhysT* 155–7)

and the same distinction is made at the end of the Legend of
Cleopatra:

And this is storyal soth, it is no fable.

(*LGW* 702)

42. See Paul Strohm, 'Some Generic Distinctions in the *Canterbury Tales*', *Modern
Philology* LXVIII (1971), 321–8.

That *fable* is fiction, not to say untruth,[43] is borne out by the fourteenth-century idiom 'withouten any fable', used by Chaucer's Squire (*SqT* 180), and found several times in the *Romaunt* and in other contemporary works. The Parson clinches the point when he responds to Harry Bailly's call for 'a fable anon' with a clerical dignity appropriate to the approaching end of the pilgrimage:

'Thou getest fable noon ytold for me;
For Paul, that writeth unto Thymothee,
Repreveth hem that weyven [abandon] soothfastnesse,
And tellen fables and swich wrecchednesse.
Why sholde I sowen draf out of my fest [fist],
Whan I may sowen whete, if that me lest?'
(*CT* X, 31–6)

Tale, on the other hand, is used much more loosely by Chaucer. Common in phrases like 'telle a tale', 'make a tale', it can also mean simply a speech, an account, something that has just been said, as in *The Knight's Tale*, 1597, or *The Legend of Good Women*, Prologue F, 507. In *Melibee* the phrase 'telle trewely thy tale' (1203), an elaboration of what has gone before, not in the French original, means again, simply ,'say truly what you have to say'. By contrast, the Parson links 'a jape or a tale' (*ParsT* 1024), implying lack of serious substance, something that people 'tellen ... lightly' (*ibid.*), and by far the greatest number of occurrences of the word refers to the stories told by the Canterbury pilgrims, but without much stress on their *soothfastnesse* or lack of it.

The word *storie* is also used loosely at times: Pandarus can quote 'a thousand olde stories' if necessary (*Tr* III, 297), and they are hardly likely to be all 'storyal soth'; yet the word certainly carries the frequent stamp of *auctorite*, particularly in phrases like 'as seith the storie', 'as the story telleth us', 'thise stories beren witnesse', especially when applied to biblical narrative (cp. *MerchT* 1366) or historical events like the murder of Julius Caesar (cp. *MkT* 2710, 2719). In one place Chaucer even introduces what may well have been a new word to the language in 1369 – a word he uses nowhere else – to stress the authenticity of the stories referred to: 'thogh hir stories be *autentyk* '(*BD* 1086).

A *song* to Chaucer is very much what a 'song' still is to us,

43. 'Fables and lesynges' are coupled in the second line of the *Romaunt of the Rose*, rendering the French 'fables ... et mençonges' of the *Roman*.

usually a metrical composition meant to be sung, with or without instrumental accompaniment. But occasionally the substitution of 'saying' rather than 'singing' a song indicates the more general sense of 'a poem' without any specific musical connotation. Thus the Clerk's Envoy is introduced with the announcement

> I wol with lusty herte, fressh and grene,
> *Seyn yow a song* to glade yow, I wene,
>
> (*CLT* 1173-4)

and there are other instances of the same usage. This is true also of the word *lay*, generally, 'a short narrative poem of love, adventure, etc., to be sung and accompanied on instruments, especially the harp' (*MED*). In *The Book of the Duchess* the Black Knight's *compleynte* is spoken:

> He *sayd* a lay, a maner song,
> Withoute noote, withoute song,
>
> (*BD* 471-2)

where the first *song* is meant to be roughly synonymous with *lay*, and the second with *noote* 'tune'. Chaucer several times uses *lay* of birds' song, where modern English would normally prefer 'song': of the nightingale, for example, who sings 'a lay / Of love' in *Troilus and Criseyde* II, 918 ff.; of the swallow, earlier in the same book (64 ff.), whose 'sorowful lay' becomes an insistent *cheterynge* 'twittering' that wakes up the sleeping Pandarus; of the thrush who 'made eek his lay' in Sir Thopas's fair forest (*Thop* 769). In the concert of small birds in the Prologue to *The Legend of Good Women* we hear the *song* of birds (as in *PF* 203) as well as their 'layes of love' (Prol F, 130 ff.). An indirect reference to the swallow's *song* is made by the Miller in describing his Alisoun:

> But of hir song, it was as loude and yerne
> As any swalwe sittynge on a berne.
>
> (*MillT* 3257-8)

Chaucer's usage in these instances is not very different from our own; if anything, it is a little more flexible.

There are other references to 'lays' besides those just cited. The Franklin begins his tale with a reference to old Breton *layes*, generally assumed to be short narrative poems, 'with a strong love interest, often of a pathetic kind':[44]

> Thise olde gentil Britouns in hir dayes
> Of diverse aventures maden layes,
> Rymeyed in hir firste Briton tonge;
> Whiche layes with hir instrumentz they songe,
> Or elles redden hem for hir plesaunce.
>
> (*FranklT* 709–13)

The Franklin's Tale purports to be an example of 'oon of hem' (714), although it is of course not sung, but told to the assembled pilgrims. That Chaucer thought of songs and lays as 'enditynges of worldly vanitees' is plain from his reference in the Retraction to *The Canterbury Tales* to 'many a song and many a leccherous lay' (1087) on the debit side of his literary balance sheet.

In addition to *bookys* and *songes*, Chaucer is also credited (at least before the final balance sheet was drawn up) with *dytees*, as the Eagle calls them in *The House of Fame*, 622, referring to Chaucer, and there is an almost exact parallel in the first recension of *Confessio Amantis* (to which the asterisk refers in Macaulay's edition) when Gower refers to Chaucer as the maker 'of Ditees and of songes glade' (VIII, 2945*). A *ditee* could be almost any literary composition in Middle English, prose or verse, read or recited or sung, a wide semantic range acquired from its Old French etymon *dité* 'composition, treatise'. Apart from the reference to *A Balade of Complaint* as 'this litel pore dyte' (*Bal Compl* 16), only the Eagle uses the word in Chaucer's verse, and in his prose it is confined to a handful of occurrences, half of them in glosses, in *Boece* where it refers to poems generally, to those of Homer in particular ('*Homer with the swete ditees*', V, m. 2, 2), to the songs of Orpheus ('his faire song and his ditee', III, m. 12, 47–8), and, as we noted earlier, to tragedies. Except in the glosses, which are not in Boethius, the word invariably corresponds to the Latin *carmen* of the original, and the French *chançon* or *chançonnetez* of Jean de Meun.

Another literary term of fairly wide meaning but relatively rare occurrence in Chaucer is *geste*. Mostly he uses it of old heroic

44. S. S. Hussey, *Chaucer: An Introduction* (London, 1971), p. 136. Cp. the examples in Bryan and Dempster, pp. 385 ff. and *Lays of Marie de France and Other French Legends*, trans. by E. Mason (London, 1911, repr. 1966).

tales: 'Troian gestes' (*Tr* I, 145), or 'olde Romayn geestes' (*WBT* 642, *MLT* 1126), or 'the geste / Of the siege of Thebes' which the maiden reads to Criseyde and her ladies (*Tr* II, 83–4). But the word can mean simply a story or a tale, a history or any book, as well as the event or exploit described therein. Hence such a general idiom as 'as writen is in geeste' (*Tr* III, 450), or the loose juxtaposition of *story* and *geste* in this passage:

> For myn entent is, or I fro you fare,
> The naked text in English to declare
> Of many a story, or elles of many a geste,
> As autours seyn; leveth hem if you leste!
> (*LGW* Prol G, 85–8)

I call this a 'loose' juxtaposition because it does not appear that Chaucer is here drawing the distinction between fact and fiction, between 'storyal soth' and 'fable', which we noted earlier. He may of course have deemed some *gestes* more credible than others – no doubt he did – but as long as *gestes* could be applied to biblical narratives, like Langland's reference to Job's *gestes* in *Piers Plowman* C XII, 23, complete suspension of belief as in the case of 'fables and swich wrecchednesse' was hardly possible. The sense of 'deed, exploit' also occurs in Chaucer, though more rarely still than the literary one. An example is the reference to those 'that han doon noble gestes' in *The House of Fame*, 1737.

Finally, there are two literary references involving *geeste* in *The Canterbury Tales* worthy of special note. Both involve a tripartite contrast between *prose*, *rym(e)* 'rhymed verse', and *geeste*. The Parson elaborates the latter, 'geeste "rum, ram, ruf"', by lettre' (*CT* X, 43), sufficiently to make it clear that he is referring to alliterative verse, and it is likely that in the interlude between *Sir Thopas* and *The Tale of Melibee* the same meaning is attached to *geeste*.[45] Says Harry Bailly to pilgrim Chaucer:

> 'Sire, at o word, thou shalt no lenger ryme.
> Lat se wher thou kanst tellen aught in geeste,
> Or telle in prose somwhat, at the leeste,
> In which ther be som murthe or som doctryne.'
> (*CT* VII, 932–5)

---

45. G. D. Bone makes the same point briefly in a review in *Medium Aevum* VII (1938), 226.

That there is a distinction between the three terms is obvious, and that it is between rhymed verse, alliterative verse, and prose is highly probable. What is of interest also is that in the Host's scale of literary values prose is the *leeste*, and *ryme* presumably at the top; hence his violent reaction to the 'drasty rymyng' Chaucer has just perpetrated in *Sir Thopas*. The Parson, however, reverses this order. He cannot alliterate, *rym* is to him 'but litel bettre', and thus the choice falls naturally enough on prose. There is delightful irony in the contrast between the Parson's deliberate choice and pilgrim Chaucer's enforced one in *Melibee*; presumably pilgrim Chaucer implies that since *Sir Thopas* 'is the beste rym I kan', and he cannot alliterate either, 'a litel thyng in prose' is all that is left for his second attempt. Whether this excursus into Chaucerian prose conceals any deeper ironic intention we shall consider further in the next chapter.

The list of generic words is not exhausted yet. There is the word *legende*, primarily but by no means exclusively associated with the stories of saints, as in Chauntecleer's reference to the legend of St Kenelm, which he was so anxious for his wife to read that he would gladly give up his shirt (*NPT* 3120–1), or the Second Nun's reference to the legend of St Cecilia which forms the subject matter of her tale (*SecNT* 25, 83). 'Bookes of legendes of seintes' figure on the credit side of Chaucer's literary balance sheet (*CT* X, 1088), but 'the book of the XXV. Ladies' does not, despite the fact that *The Legend of Good Women* is intended to be a highly moral work,

> a glorious legende
> Of goode wymmen, maydenes and wyves,
> That weren trewe in lovyng al hie lyves.
> (*LGW* Prol F, 483–5)

The word *legende* was certainly used in secular contexts, but the hagiographical connotations persisted, and so did the biographical ones. The words *legende* and *lyf* are almost inseparable for Chaucer and some of his contemporaries. Langland speaks of Rechelenesse seeing his name entered 'in the legende of lif', the book of life (*PP* C XII, 206), an extension of the primary meaning of the story of a saint's life to that of anybody's life as recorded in a book or roll or catalogue. The Clerk's life-story of Griselda is a *legende* as far as Harry Bailly is concerned (*CT* IV, 1212d), and the longsuffering wife of the merchant of St Denis in *The Shipman's Tale*, given one chance, could 'telle a legende of my lyf' (*ShipT* 145). The Miller promises to 'telle a legende and a lyf' about a carpenter and his wife (*CT* I, 3141–2), and proceeds to do so. The Wife of Bath similarly links 'legendes and lyves' (*WBT* 686). The conclusion thus appears justified that for Chaucer *legende* either by itself or coupled with *lyf* means something like our word biography. It is interesting to note that the word does not occur outside *The Legend of Good Women* and *The Canterbury Tales*.

Linked with *fables* in the Summoner's description of what his fraudulent friar served out to his gullible victims are *nyfles* (*SumT* 1760), a Chaucerian nonce-word for which the *OED* records no earlier example. It is usually glossed simply 'trifles', a meaning common in the sixteenth and seventeenth centuries (Heywood links fables and *nyfyls*, as Chaucer does). The word 'trifles' itself occurs once in Chaucer, as *trufles* in *The Parson's Tale*, 715, linked with 'wikked and vileyns thoghtes' and with *jangles* and 'alle ordure', that is with idle chatter and all manner of filth – all of them the by-products of idleness. The Summoner's language is not as strong as that, although *fables* connotes the abandoning of truth, as we have seen, so that *nyfles* may be more damning than merely trifles or even 'silly stories' (Robinson's gloss). Skeat suggests 'mockeries, pretences', deriving the word from O.Fr. *nifler* 'to sniff, mock at', and something like pretence or falsehood, deceitful stories or *lesynges* is probably intended; the pairing of *lesynges* with *fables* in the *Romaunt* (2, 4835) suggests a possible parallel.

Another generic literary term which Chaucer uses once is *ympne*, literally 'hymn', of which he enumerates three species:

> 'And many an ympne for your halydayes,
> That highten balades, roundels, virelayes'.
>
> (*LGW* Prol F, 422–3)

An *ympne* is thus some form of lyric poem or song of which the three kinds mentioned were all familiar in the fourteenth century. Several of Chaucer's short poems are called *balades*: *To Rosemounde, Womanly Noblesse, Fortune, Truth, Gentilesse, Lak of Stedfastnesse*, and two of the doubtful poems, *Against Women Unconstant* and *A Balade of Complaint*. Five of these poems employ the seven-line stanza, or rhyme royal, most of them carrying the same rhymes right through. Two of them use an eight-line stanza, and one, *Womanly Noblesse*, a poem of thirty-two lines, employs an unusual rhyme scheme and does not conform to Chaucer's other *balades* in structure. It has an envoy of six lines, whereas in *Fortune*, *Truth*, and *Lak of Stedfastnesse* the envoy has seven lines. The other poems have no envoys. Another *balade* 'Hyd, Absolon, thy gilte tresses clere', identical in structure with *Gentilesse*, occurs in the Prologue to *The Legend of Good Women*, in the F version recited by the poet-dreamer himself, in the G version danced and sung 'in carole-wyse' by the ladies accompanying the god of Love (F 249 ff., G 203 ff.). Like most of Chaucer's other *balades*, 'Hyd, Absolon' repeats the last line of each stanza.

The *roundel* was a country song deriving its name from the fact that the words return again and again to the opening lines. There is a pretty example at the end of *The Parliament of Fowls*, as the birds sing in praise of approaching summer. The tune, says Chaucer, was probably composed in France, but the words are 'swiche as ye may heer fynde':

'Now welcome, somer, with thy sonne softe,
That hast this wintres wedres overshake,
And driven away the longe nyghtes blake!

'Saynt Valentyn, that art ful hy on-lofte,
Thus syngen smale foules for thy sake:
Now welcome, somer, with thy sonne softe,
That hast this wintres wedres overshake.

'Wel han they cause for to gladen ofte,
Sith ech of hem recovered hath hys make,
Ful blissful mowe they synge when they wake:
Now welcome, somer, with thy sonne softe,
That hast this wintres wedres overshake,
And driven away the longe nyghtes blake!'
(PF 680–92)

In *The Knight's Tale*, 1510 ff. Arcite sings the opening lines of a roundel, 'lustily', we are told (1529), in front of the eavesdropping Palamon, but among Chaucer's own short poems the only specimen is the doubtful *Merciles Beaute*, a triple roundel, in which the above pattern is repeated three times over.

The *virelaye* was named after Vire in Normandy (a small town some fifty kilometres south-west of Caen) according to Grove's

Dictionary[46] although the *Oxford Dictionary of English Etymology*
goes no further than citing O.Fr. *virelai*, an altered form of the
obsolete *vireli*, 'perhaps originally a refrain', influenced by *lai* 'lay'.
Chaucer mentions the word only twice, both times in lists: the
one in *The Legend of Good Women* which we are discussing, and
the other in the Franklin's reference to Aurelius's lyric outpour-
ings in 'layes, / Songes, compleintes, roundels, e virelays'
(*FranklT* 947–8). A characteristic of the *virelaye* was the linking of
stanzas by using the end rhyme of one stanza as the principal
rhyme in the next one.

The *compleynt*, in its literary sense, is a poem of lamentation,
a lyrical utterance of personal grief, religious sorrow, or amorous
disappointment. The word is used repeatedly by Chaucer, and
many of his characters utter *compleyntes*, like love-sick Damyan:

> in a lettre wroot he al his sorwe,
> In manere of a compleynt or a lay,
> Unto his faire, fresshe lady May,
>
> (*MerchT* 1880–2)

or Dorigen in *The Franklin's Tale*, 1352 ff. Chaucer's own poems
include several *compleyntes* which have been admirably discussed
by Clemen,[47] particularly the longest and most interesting of them,
The Complaint of Mars. Chaucer uses the word also in the general
senses of lamentation, grief, anguish, complaining, and this is at
times difficult to distinguish from the literary meaning. When
Criseyde gives expression to her grief, 'sobbyng in hire compleynte' (*Tr* IV, 742), there is a fusion of the general and the
literary meanings: the lines she utters make up seven stanzas,
which contain some of the elements of the traditional 'complainte
d'amour' but are not formally distinguished from the surrounding
narrative. Chaucer's best-known *compleynt* is probably the little
song addressed to his purse, written in dire pecuniary straits
towards the end of his life. The poem may be a *compleynt* in kind,
but its envoy makes it in spirit a *supplicacion* – its final word and
one which Chaucer saved up, after its one occurrence in *Boece*,
for this last appeal to royal generosity. It is some comfort to know
even after the lapse of nearly 600 years that the appeal was not
made in vain.

46. Grove's *Dictionary of Music and Musicians*, 5th edn, ed. Eric Blom (London,
1954), Vol. IX, p. 2.
47. Clemen, pp. 179 ff.

Along with the literary vocabulary of which we have been examining a variety of terms go occasional passages of a distinctively critical kind, like the Monk's *declaryng* about *tragedie* quoted earlier. *The Manciple's Tale* concludes with some sound advice on restraining one's tongue and shaping one's speech accordingly which may serve as an immediate moral to the tale of the crow but has obvious wider stylistic implications. Chaucer's own 'litel tonge', as the narrator of *Troilus and Criseyde* calls his (IV, 801), is patently a highly skilled organ which knows when to plump for 'heigh style' and when to speak things in a manner 'bare and pleyn', 'withouten vice of silable or of lettre', as the Squire puts it in one such little stylistic aside (*SqT* 101). Chaucer often pretends to be incompetent, to be merely a rehearser of other people's art (*LGW* Prol F, 73 ff.), to be too busy, or too dull, or too ignorant to tell his tales properly, whether in his own person or in those of his characters, and in consequence makes every possible use of *occupatio*, that invaluable rhetorical device which allowed him either to cut short whatever he was narrating or else to spin it out to sometimes inordinate lengths:

> Myn Englissh eek is insufficient.
> It moste been a rethor excellent,
> That koude his colours longynge for that art,
> If he sholde hire discryven every part.
> I am noon swich, I moot speke as I kan.
>
> (*SqT* 37–41)

This is the Squire speaking with the unmistakable voice of Geoffrey Chaucer, 'rethor excellent' who knew so much about his 'subtyl art' (*Tr* II, 257); who knew that 'th' ende is every tales strengthe' (*ibid.* 260); who knew when to speak 'lewedly to a lewed man' to make things 'palpable' (*HF* 865 ff.); who knew that

> Whoso shal telle a tale after a man,
> He moot reherce as ny as evere he kan
> Everich a word, if it be in his charge,
> Al speke he never so rudeliche and large,
> Or ellis he moot telle his tale untrewe,
> Or feyne thyng, or fynde wordes newe.
>
> (*Gen Prol* 731–6)

Here, in epitome, is the key to Chaucer's art as a poet, as a storyteller, and as a creator of character, and here also is a key to his

English, its richness and variety of register ranging from the
colourful slang of the streets of London to the elaborate formality of the poetic diction cultivated on 'The Mount of Pernaso
[Parnassus]' (*FranklT* 721), and, not least, the venturesome
originality of so much of his vocabulary. These are the themes
which the remaining chapters of this book seek mainly to explore.

CHAPTER 3

I Speke in Prose

𝕤𝕤𝕤𝕤𝕤𝕤

CHAUCER, presumably, like other Englishmen of his age, spoke in prose when he was not actually reciting verses to an audience, a pastime that could not have figured very prominently in his busy life as public servant and as writer. Of his surviving work somewhere between a quarter and a fifth is in prose, yet his prose has been much neglected. What comments there are range from inadequate appraisal to curt, often derogatory, dismissal. A hundred years ago Henry Morley remarked that Chaucer's translation of Boethius's *De Consolatione Philosophiae* 'reads like a student's exercise';[1] while among the most recent comments is S. S. Hussey's appreciative but passing reference to 'the clarity of Chaucer's expository prose'.[2]

The neglect suffered by Chaucer's prose is hardly surprising, standing as it does in the shadow of his poetic achievement; yet any study whether of his literary output in general, or of his handling of the English language in particular, is patently incomplete without paying attention to his prose. What Chaucer himself thought of his prose writings as contributions to edifying literature we know from the Retraction at the conclusion of *The Parson's Tale*, where his *Boece* and 'othere bookes of legendes of seintes, and omelies, and moralitee, and devocioun' (*CT* X, 1088) are placed on the credit side of his literary balance sheet. *The Parson's Tale* undoubtedly belongs here, and, for all its ironic intention, *The Tale of Melibee* probably also. Whether the *Astrolabe* and the *Equatorie of the Planetis* (if it is indeed Chaucer's) also belong to this sober group, or whether they should be classed among his 'translacions and enditynges of worldly vanitees'

---

1. Henry Morley, *English Writers*, Vol. II, Part 1: *From Chaucer to Dunbar* (London, 1867), p. 180.

2. S. S. Hussey, 'The Minor Poems and the Prose', in Vol. I of the Sphere Library *History of Literature in the English Language*, ed. W. F. Bolton (London, 1970), p. 251.

(*ibid.* 1085), may perhaps remain a moot point. The modern reader will detect nothing conducive to spiritual harm in 'lyte Lowyss" astronomical primer, for any suggestion of astrological hocus-pocus is curtly dismissed by Chaucer as 'observaunces of judicial matere and rytes of payens, in whiche my spirit hath no feith' (*Astr* II, 4, 57–9).

But what Chaucer thought of his prose writings *qua* prose is more difficult to determine except in the case of the *Astrolabe*. The pose of modesty and incompetence so familiar from the poems reappears in the Introduction to the *Astrolabe* where Chaucer speaks in his own person, if not as 'the innocent and artless spectator' of the early poems, in Wolfgang Clemen's phrase,[3] yet as the self-styled 'lewd compilator' whose *endityng* is *rude*, and whose English is *light*. *Lewd* Chaucer certainly was not; certainly not in 1391 or thereabouts when the *Astrolabe* was being written at the same time as some of *The Canterbury Tales*, but the two epithets are not inappropriate. Chaucer had set himself a tricky task, as anyone must know who has attempted responsible popularizing of scientific matters. Little Lewis was only ten years old and had about as much Latin as Shakespeare. That he had some previous astronomical instruction is hinted at in Chaucer's passing comment 'as I have shewed the in the speer solide' (*Astr* I, 17, 19–20), a reference either to a globe used by Chaucer to explain the motions of the heavenly bodies or to an earlier treatise on spherical trigonometry. Nonetheless the task of describing an astrolabe and its uses to a child of ten was no easy one, and Chaucer shaped his prose accordingly. *Rude* can mean 'forthright, impolite', even 'crude', as when the Host addressed the Nun's Priest 'with rude speche and boold' (*CT* VII, 280), or when the Merchant, at the height of Damyan's assault, turned to the ladies in his company with a disarming

I kan nat glose, I am a rude man.

(*MerchT* 2351)

In the *Astrolabe* it means above all 'artless', for this, as Chaucer realized, was no place for ornament, for 'curious endityng', or rhetorical flourishes, If there was to be amplification it took the form of 'superfluite of wordes', of deliberate repetition for the sake of easier learning: 'sothly me semith better to writen unto a

3. Clemen, p. 6.

child twyes a god sentence, than he forgete it onys' (*Astr* Introd. 47–9). And the English is intended to be *light*, easy, straight-forward, consisting of 'naked wordes' (*ibid.* 26). The *Astrolabe* must be judged in the light of the occasion and of Chaucer's de-clared intention, as a piece of elementary expositional prose tailored to the understanding of a ten-year-old. As such it largely succeeds.

The sentences vary in length but less so in structure; they tend to be co-ordinated rather than subordinated. What Ian Gordon has described as 'the stop-and-start movement' of 'this snake-like prose'[4] relies heavily on recurring patterns of clauses beginning with *and*, *but*, *tho*, relative pronouns, or simple imperatives like *set*, *loke*, *understond*. Much of this is no doubt due to the Latin version of Messahala's *Compositio et Operatio Astrolabii* which forms the basis and is the principal source of Chaucer's treatise, as the following comparison will illustrate:

Amplius scito quod circulus signorum diuiditur in .2. semicirculos, quorum vnus est a capite capricorni in caput cancri, et alius a capite cancri in caput capricorni; et caput capricorni est solsticium hyemale, caput cancri estiuale. Scito et quod omnis duo equidistantes gradus ab aliquo horum solsticiorum sunt vnius declinacionis versus septentrionalem vel meridiem; et dies eorum vel noctes sunt equales, et umbre et altitudines in media die sunt equales.[5]

Chaucer's version, according to the most reliable manuscript punctuation, makes three sentences of Messahala's two and uses nearly twice as many words. The translator's aim to be as ex-plicit and lucid as possible certainly leads to some 'superfluite of wordes', as 'caput capricorni est solsticium hyemale', for instance, becomes 'the heved of Capricorne is the lowest point where as the sonne goth in wynter', but the Latin prose is none-theless fairly reflected in the albeit much more analytic English of Chaucer's version:

Understond wel that thy zodiak is departed in two halve circles, as fro the heved of Capricorne unto the heved of Cancer, and ageyn-ward fro the heved of Cancer unto the heved of Capricorne. The heved of Capricorne is the lowest point where as the sonne goth in

4. Ian A. Gordon, *The Movement of English Prose* (London, 1966), p. 54.
5. Printed in *A Treatise on the Astrolabe by Geoffrey Chaucer*, ed. Walter W. Skeat (London, 1872), pp. 92 f.

wynter, and the heved of Cancer is the heighist point in which the
sonne goth in somer. And therfore understond wel that eny two
degrees that ben ylike fer fro eny of these two hevedes, truste wel
that thilke two degrees ben of ilike declinacioun, be it southward
or northward, and the daies of hem ben ilike of lengthe and the
nyghtes also, and the shadewes ilyke, and the altitudes ylike atte
midday for evere.

(Astr II, 16, 1–16)

The passage is typical of much of the *Astrolabe* in its avoidance,
as much as possible, of difficult words. Although Chaucer had
used and defined *solsticium* in Part I, 17, 8 and 51, he avoids the
term here. The same is true of *septemtrional* and *meridional*, which
occur elsewhere in the work. The remaining technical terms,
declinacioun and *altitude*, occur frequently in the *Astrolabe*, the
latter indeed nowhere else in Chaucer's work. A fair amount of
technical jargon was, however, inevitable in a treatise of this
nature, and it is interesting to see how Chaucer coped. The temptation to import words straight from the Latin version of
Messahala is more firmly resisted in the *Astrolabe* than it is in the
case of the texts used for Chaucer's other prose translations.
Instead, Chaucer is more inclined to make do with English, or at
least with partly English, equivalents. The word *distant* is an
interesting case in point. It occurs twice in the *Astrolabe*, once
with the French plural ending retained in the form *distantz*, and
nowhere else in Chaucer – or, according to the *OED*, before
Chaucer – except in the *Equatorie*. But Chaucer stopped short of
adopting the Latin *equidistantes* which occurs in a passage quoted
earlier and is there rendered by 'ylike fer', although previously he
had compromised with 'evene distantz' (I, 17, 43). In the *Equatorie*,
however, which, even if it is Chaucer's work, was not specially
tailored to a child's understanding, *equidistant* occurs several times.

Words which the *OED* lists as first recorded by Chaucer have
received their fair share of attention from linguistic historians,
even though Chaucer may not have actually introduced them
into the language;[6] there are about two dozen in the *Astrolabe*,
compared with about seventy in *Boece*. But more attention deserves

---

6. Cp. for example R. M. Wilson's Linguistic Analysis, especially p. 137, in *The
Equatorie of the Planetis*, ed. Derek J. Price (Cambridge, 1955), and the cautious note
by J. R. Hulbert in *Philological Quarterly* XXVI (1947), 302–6.

to be paid to the role played by particular words within the canon of Chaucer's work, and this aspect of his language will occupy us in various contexts of this book, because it has a bearing upon several aspects of Chaucer's art, notably in *Troilus and Criseyde* and in *The Canterbury Tales*. That certain technical terms should occur only in the specific contexts of the prose works is to be expected, but that some of these words should figure in perhaps unexpected places in Chaucer's poems is a matter of critical interest.

Among the words Chaucer uses only in the *Astrolabe* are *clymat* 'one of the regions dominated by certain zodiacal signs' (*MED*); *elevat*; *embelif* 'oblique'; *portatif* 'portable'; *unstraunge*; and, oddly enough, *loppe* 'spider', an Old English word used by King Alfred and Aelfric, and *lopwebbe* 'cobweb'. Some of these, according to the *OED*, were first used by Chaucer: *elevat*, *embelif*, and that happy coinage *unstraunge*, so useful in the phrase 'straunge or unstraunge' (II, 17, rubric) but never apparently used by any other English writer. Some other words remain rare in Middle English, like *portatif* which Langland uses once in a series of images describing love:

Tho was it portatyf and pershaunt as the poynt of a nelde;
(*PP* C II, 154)

or *theorike* 'theory, subject matter', which occurs once in the *Equatorie* and several times in Book VII of Gower's *Confessio Amantis*.

Of particular lexical interest are the passages in the *Astrolabe* which, like the Introduction, are entirely Chaucer's, and those not based on Messahala for which no source has been found. In these, as far as we know, Chaucer's linguistic fecundity is thus, as it were, self-engendered. The opening flourish of the *Astrolabe*, for example, contains two words not found anywhere else in Chaucer, *evydences* and *abilite*, the second of which appears to have been Chaucer's contribution to English literature:

Lyte Lowys my sone, I aperceyve wel by certeyne evydences thyn abilite to lerne sciences touching nombres and proporciouns; and as wel considere I thy besy praier in special to lerne the tretys of the Astrelabie.

(Intr. 1–5)

Throughout the Introduction, indeed, Chaucer taxes 'lyte Lowy's' verbal understanding quite severely, while the modern reader's familiarity with most of the words Chaucer employs may blind him to the fact that many of them were so new or so rarely used that the whole passage takes on a much more exotic flavour than may at first be supposed. Among such words are *usurpe* and *introductorie*, both unique to this passage, the latter a noun apparently adopted by Chaucer from the French. The adjective 'introductory' is not recorded in Middle English at all. A number of technical terms is used here without definition, which suggests that they may have been explained to the pupil beforehand; and again several of these do not occur elsewhere in Chaucer's writings, for example *fraccions* (74), *longitudes* (81), *meridian* (83), *almenak* (93), *ecliptik* (99). Several other words occur so rarely elsewhere that they must have created the same problems of understanding for the medieval reader, unless he had met them previously, words like *latitude* (10), for example, and *mediacioun* (11), *practik* (70), *calculed* (76), *orizonte* (96), *equaciouns* (105), *notefull* (107). Even so familiar-looking a word as *compilator* (61) is not found elsewhere in Chaucer, nor recorded before this occurrence.

Another passage not derived from Messahala that contains further interesting words as well as illustrating something of the syntax and style of the *Astrolabe* is provided by II, 4:

> But thei wol caste that thei have a fortunat planete in hir ascendent, and yit in his felicite; and than sey thei that it is wel. Further over thei seyn that the infortunyng of an ascendent is the contrarie of these forseide thinges. The lord of the ascendent, sey thei that he is fortunat whan he is in god place fro the ascendent, as in an angle, or in a succident where as he is in hys dignite and comfortid with frendly aspectes of planetes and wel resceyved; and eke that he may seen the ascendent; and that he be not retrograd, ne combust, ne joyned with no shrewe in the same signe; ne that he be not in his discencioun, ne joyned with no planete in his descencioun, ne have upon him noon aspect infortunat; and than sey thei that he is well.
>
> Natheles these ben observaunces of judicial matere and rytes of payens, in whiche my spirit hath no feith, ne knowing of her *horoscopum*.

(II, 4, 39–60)

Like the Introduction, this passage contains several neologisms: *succident* (46) 'a succedent house' in the technical astrological sense; *retrograd* (50), probably suggested by *retrogradus* in the Latin version of Messahala in a later paragraph (II, 35, cp. Messahala 361 ff. in Skeat) and here anticipated; and the unique noun *infortunyng* (42) which was perhaps prompted by Chaucer's own earlier use of the participial adjective *infortuned*, uttered by Criseyde in an astrological context:

> 'I, woful wrecche and infortuned wight,
> And born in corsed constellacioun.'
>
> (*Tr* IV, 744–5)

The noun, the verb, and possibly also the adjective *infortunat* (55), as well as the astrological sense of *fortunat* (45), all appear to be Chaucer's adoptions. The word *judicial* occurs in the Wyclifite Old Testament with its modern meaning, but the sense 'having to do with the rules of astrology' (*MED*) is Chaucer's and is unique to this passage. Also in this passage Chaucer employs his neologism *felicite* in the astrological sense of a planet's favourable position, a sense paralleled about the same time in Gower's

> And upon such felicite
> Stant Jupiter in his degre;
>
> (*Conf Am* VII, 933–4)

and similarly *dignite* is used in a technical sense defined by the *MED* as 'the situation of a planet in which its influence is heightened, either by its position in the zodiac or by its aspects with other planets'. 'Tables of dignitees of planetes' are mentioned in the Introduction (106). Furthermore, there are in this passage, as elsewhere in the *Astrolabe*, words of such rare occurrence that something of an exotic flavour inevitably clings to them. Of this kind is *combust* (51), and the later *tortuose* 'oblique' (II, 28, 27), to give just two examples. The former is used once by the Canon's Yeoman (*CYT* 811) in a long and highly technical passage, and once in an astrological context in *Troilus and Criseyde* (III, 717) – clearly a 'scientific' word; the latter, *tortuose*, is used once, and glossed, in the *Astrolabe* (*loc. cit.*) – 'and these same signes fro the heved of Capricorne unto the ende of Geminis ben cleped tortuose signes, or croked signes' – and once in *The Canterbury Tales* in the line

> Infortunat ascendent tortuous,
>
> (*MLT* 302)

spoken by the Man of Law who has something of a penchant for exotic words.

Finally, we must not overlook straight Latinisms like *horoscopum* (II, 4, 60) or the oblique *in horoscopo* which occurs three times in the *Astrolabe*, nor Arabic words lifted straight out of Messahala – *almycanteras* (I, 18, 2, etc.), *almury* (I, 21, 89, etc.), *azimutz* (I, 19, 6, etc.) – which Chaucer takes care to define.

The foregoing excursus on the vocabulary of the *Astrolabe* will have cast some doubt on the genuineness of Chaucer's claim to have relied on 'naked wordes in Englissh', but when it came to technicalities requiring technical terms he obviously could not help using them. On the other hand, the main features of his syntax and his easy, often conversational prose style make the *Astrolabe*, certainly for the modern reader and perhaps for little Lewis also, the most engaging and readable of Chaucer's prose works.

The two parts of the *Astrolabe*, which are all we have of the planned five, apart from the brief Introduction, differ in content, hence in syntax and style. Part I is a description of the instrument and relies heavily on enumerative adverbs like *than* and *next*, and simple connectives like *and* and *but*, to introduce and link series of sentences and clauses. Passive constructions are frequent, as are demonstrative pronouns: 'This zodiak is dividid in 12 principale divisiouns that departen the 12 signes, and, for the streitnesse of thin Astrolabie, than is every smal divisioun in a signe departed by two degrees and two, I mene degrees contenyng 60 mynutes' (I, 21, 44–9). A personal note enters with the frequent use in the whole work, as in 'thin Astrolabie' above, of the second person singular possessive pronoun, applied even, as P. Pintelon notes,[7] to such words as 'thy sonne' (II, 3, 9, etc.), 'thy zodiak' (II, 14, 6, etc.), or 'Now is thin orisonte departed in 24 parties by thin azimutes . . .' (II, 31, 6–7).

Part II offers a number of practical applications, or *conclusiouns*, of the astrolabe, and its chief syntactic feature is the recurrent use of imperatives. Of the forty sections that make up what we have of Part II (omitting the Supplementary Propositions 41–6) thirty-two begin with one or other of the following imperatives: *considere*, *know*, *loke*, *put*, *rekene*, *sek*, *set*, *tak*, *understond*, while others occur

---

7. P. Pintelon, *Chaucer's Treatise on the Astrolabe* (Antwerp, 1940), p. 77.

within the text. But the resulting sentences are not as uniformly dreary as this may suggest, for Chaucer achieves variety by modifying his imperative constructions in a number of ways. Adverbs may be added: 'understond wel', 'sek besily'; two imperatives may be conjoined to begin a sentence: 'Rekne and knowe'; the object of the imperative may be expressed as a simple noun: 'tak the altitude', 'set the degre', or by a clause: 'understond wel that thy zodiak is departed', 'rekene how many degrees . . . ben', 'loke whan that a planete is in the lyne meridional'.

The *conclusiouns* of Part II of the *Astrolabe* vary in length from one short compound sentence ('Know the nombre of the degrees in the houres inequales, and depart hem by 15, and tak there thin houres equales', II, 8) to over eighty lines in Robinson's edition; yet the method leading from an initial 'Understond wel', say, to a concluding 'And thus have I this conclusyoun' (II, 12, 1 and 43) tends to mirror in its syntax the several steps of each argument. Separate sentences, dependent clauses, as well as loosely co-ordinate clauses, tend to be connected by *than* and equivalent adverbs or adverbial phrases, often with a resultant inversion of the normal subject-verb order:[8]

> *And now* is my sonne gon to reste as for that Saturday. *Than* shewith the verrey degre of the sonne the houre of Mercurie entring under my west orisonte at eve; and next him succedith the mone, and so furth by ordir, planete after planete in houre after houre, all the nyght longe til the sonne arise. *Now* risith the sonne that Sonday by the morwe, and the nadir of the sonne upon the west orisonte shewith me the entring of the houre of the forseide sonne. *And in this manere* succedith planete under planete fro Saturne unto the mone, and fro the mone up ageyn to Saturne, houre after houre generaly. *And thus* have I this conclusyoun.
>
> (II, 12, 29–43)

Occasionally the structure becomes so loose that the syntax breaks down, as in II, 4, 44 ff. in a sentence, quoted earlier, in which Chaucer departs from his normal patterns and begins with a

8. Ruta Nagucka, *The Syntactic Component of Chaucer's Astrolabe* (Krakow, 1968), p. 48, puts it like this: 'This transformation changes the order of some segments, which have been postulated for the base structure. It is called the *than* permutation, because *than* is the most frequently encountered element that accounts for this change. . . . There are a great number of instances in the data and a great variety of *than* equivalents which, if shifted to the beginning of a sentence, permute the verb and the subject.'

nominal phrase, 'The lord of the ascendent', and then seems unable quite to retrieve the situation until the concluding 'and than sey thei that he is well', which is really something of a paradigm of the syntax of this part of the *Astrolabe*.

One characteristic feature of Chaucer's syntax, of his prose as well as his verse, is the flexibility in the positioning of adjectives. Normal Middle English prose usage is for adjectives to precede their nouns,[9] and in general Chaucer's practice conforms to this usage. In *The Parson's Tale*, for example, according to the statistics adduced by Michio Masui the proportion of preposed to postposed adjectives is about twenty to one.[10] In Chaucer's poetry the positioning of adjectives is often dictated by aesthetic or prosodic considerations which hardly apply in so prosaic and *rude* a work as the *Astrolabe*, but the fact that the latter is a relatively late work (1391) suggests that Chaucer's usage remained flexible throughout his writings.[11] Sometimes Chaucer simply follows the text he is translating and a number of French-derived adjectives tend to remain postposed, occasionally even retaining French plural endings. Thus *The Tale of Melibee* has, for example, 'oure othere goodes temporels' for the French 'noz autres biens temporelz' (*Mel* 998), and in the *Astrolabe* occur 'sterres fixes' (I, 21, 5), 'lettres capitals' (II, 3, 52), 'partyes evene distantz' (I, 17, 43), although Chaucer was just as ready to put even a French plural adjective before the noun where, as in 'the foure principales plages or quarters of the firmament' (I, 5, 11), stylistic considerations prompted it. In his prose usage then, and certainly in the *Astrolabe*, we find a seemingly random diversity: 'the speer solide' (I, 17, 19); 'the embelif cercle' (II, 26, 29); 'the day vulgar' (II, 9, rubric); 'the vulgar nyght'(II, 9, 6); 'eny sterre fix' (II, 7, 16); 'eny fix sterre' (II, 17, 30). Nor is it much help to look at Chaucer's Latin model, for where Messahala (237) has 'linea meridiana' Chaucer perversely writes 'the meridionall lyne' (II, 21, 2); but where Messahala (260) has 'in meridiana linea' Chaucer

9. Cp. for example Fernand Mossé, *A Handbook of Middle English*, trans. by James A. Walker (Baltimore, 1952), p. 123.

10. Masui, pp. 62 f.

11. This flexibility is not unique to Chaucer and certainly does not constitute 'any stylistic innovation' on his part, as Margaret Schlauch reminds us ('The Art of Chaucer's Prose' in D. S. Brewer, ed., *Chaucer and Chaucerians: Critical Studies in Middle English Literature* (London, 1966), p. 147), but it is nonetheless a noteworthy feature of Chaucer's syntax and style.

equally perversely writes 'the lyne meridional' (II, 14, 4). Very probably Chaucer hardly noticed these discrepancies.[12]

Ian Gordon confesses to 'a certain sympathy' with little Lewis having to cope with his father's prose.[13] One can understand the sentiment in a writer surveying in a grand sweep the entire landscape of English prose, in which Chaucer's *Astrolabe* is obviously but a very minor protuberance; but in its own right, as a piece of straightforward medieval English textbook exposition, it is no mean achievement. At its best, and for the most part, the prose flows artlessly through uncomplicated sentences; at its worst, and not often, the prose is overwhelmed by technicalities inadequately marshalled, the syntax also sometimes, as we have seen, creaking at the joints. But on the whole we may well agree with Pintelon when he speaks of the 'unhampered natural run and quick variety'[14] of the Introduction, and extend at least the first part of this comment to much of the remainder of the *Astrolabe* as well. For right through the work there runs one peculiarly Chaucerian note, a conversational, at times magisterial, current of tags and phrases and endearing hortatory mumblings which the lover of Chaucerian verse cannot help recognizing as familiar linguistic gestures. 'Nota!' and 'nota also!' he enjoins half a dozen times in schoolmasterly Latin as a change from the flood of English imperatives; and 'now have I told the twyes' (an unmistakable echo of *The General Prologue's* 'now have I toold you soothly', 715); and 'that is to seyn'; and 'as it semeth'; and 'by experience I wot wel'; and 'as I have seaid'; and so on from the 'as I suppose' of the opening paragraph to the 'as I first seide' of the last *conclusioun*. And there are other Chaucerian touches besides. There is a slip of the pen into a proper Gallicism, 'par consequens' in II, 38, 30, such as usually is reserved for the colloquial affectations of rogues like Miller, Reeve, and Pardoner. Indeed, it is the Summoner alone who exactly parallels Chaucer's 'par consequens' within the entire corpus of Chaucer's work. There is also, in the *Astrolabe*, an occasional glimpse of Chaucer the maker playing with words, not for the sake of technical exposition, but

12. Chaucer writes 'thys lyne meridional' also when drawing upon John de Sacrobosco's *De Sphaera*, as in II, 39, where Sacrobosco has *meridianus*. Cp. S. W. Harvey, 'Chaucer's Debt to Sacrobosco', *Journal of English and Germanic Philology* XXXIV (1935), 34–8.
13. Gordon, *op. cit.*, o. 54.
14. Pintelon, *op. cit.*, p. 76.

for the sheer poetic love of it: 'And evere as the sonne clymbith upper and upper, so goth his nadir downer and downer . . .' (II, 12, 18–20). The happy *upper* figures only twice elsewhere, in the heavenward soaring of the second book of *The House of Fame*; the no less happy *downer* occurs only here in the *Astrolabe*. Chaucer certainly did not lack inventiveness in his prose, nor is his poetic note invariably subdued, even in so technical a work as the *Astrolabe*: 'In som wynters nyght whan the firmament is cler and thikke sterred . . .' (II, 23, 1–2); 'And preie God save the king, that is lord of this langage, and alle that him feith berith and obeieth, everich in his degre, the more and the lasse' (Intr. 56–9); '*To knowe the verrey degre of eny maner sterre, straunge or unstraunge, after his longitude; though he be indetermynat in thin Astralabye, sothly to the trouthe thus he shal be knowe*' (II, 17, rubric).

The *Astrolabe* occupies quite a distinct place in Chaucer's work as his only certain piece of expository 'scientific' prose. Similarly, the translation of Boethius's *Consolatio* is unique, a labour of love, perhaps, involving rendering Latin verse as well as prose, which sends its echoes into all of Chaucer's subsequent poetry. *The Parson's Tale* and *The Tale of Melibee* are akin in both forming part of *The Canterbury Tales*, but their functions within this work are quite different, hence their diction and syntax, although showing certain affinities, and certainly their prose style, should be judged in the respective context of each tale. It is likely that in the case of both these tales Chaucer was translating from the French. In the case of *Melibee* his source is generally acknowledged to have been *Le Livre de Mellibée et Prudence* of the fourteenth-century French Dominican friar Renaud de Louens, but the immediate source of *The Parson's Tale* is not known. Ultimately the latter derives from two extensive thirteenth-century Latin works, the *Summa* of Raymund of Pennaforte and the *Summa de vitiis et virtutibus* of Guilielmus Peraldus, but a number of syntactical and morphological features in the tale have suggested to earlier scholars that Chaucer's immediate source was more probably French than Latin.[15] A close look at some of the words which are peculiar to *The Parson's Tale* within the body of Chaucer's writing

15. This was the conclusion of H. G. Pfander, 'Some Medieval Manuals of Religious Instruction in England and Observations on Chaucer's Parson's Tale', *Journal of English and Germanic Philology* XXXV (1936), 257. Cp. also Robinson, p. 766.

also points to an immediate French, rather than a Latin, model. For example, the French word *deslavé* 'unwashed, unclean' occurs twice in the tale as *deslavee* with the meaning of 'immoderate': 'a deslavee tonge' (629 where the Latin has *immoderata*) and 'the deslavee appetit' (834). The word *immoderate* occurs in Trevisa's prose, but it is not used by Chaucer who renders its modern meaning elsewhere in *The Parson's Tale* by *unmesurable*, twice (in 818) associated with *appetit*. Among other words of French derivation used by Chaucer only in this tale are *essoyne* 'excuse' (164, a legal term), *lachesse* 'lack of zeal, laziness' (720), *amercimentz* 'penalties' (twice in 752), *nigromanciens* 'necromancers' (603), *divynailes* 'acts of divination' (605). In *The Parson's Tale*, 692, occurs the phrase 'so grevouse and so chargeaunt for to suffre' which closely parallels *Melibee*, 1243, 'ful chargeant and ful anoyous for to heere', which in its turn renders the French 'chargeuse et ennuyeuse'.[16] Chaucer does not use *chargeaunt* anywhere else, and among contemporary works its use is almost wholly confined to cookery recipes and one very French-sounding line in *Sir Gawain and the Green Knight* (1604):

Of þat chargeaunt chace þat were chef huntes.

But it is not only words which are unique to *The Parson's Tale* which point to a French source; others do likewise. The word *poynaunt*, used twice in *The Canterbury Tales* in connection with sauce, occurs in *The Parson's Tale*, 130, where Pennaforte has *acer*; the word *certes* is used lavishly, as it is in *Melibee* where it echoes the French of Renaud; *creat* occurs as a past participle in *The Parson's Tale*, 218, and in *Melibee*, 1103, rendering *crée*; *disobeisaunt* (338), derived from Fr. *desobëissant*, occurs also in *The Parliament of Fowls*, 429; *malisoun* (619), another French adoption, is uttered by the priest in *The Canon's Yeoman's Tale*, 1245; and so on.

Other linguistic features shared by *The Parson's Tale* and *The Tale of Melibee* which point to an immediate French source for the former are the occurrence of French adjectival plural endings and syntactical patterns based on French rather than on Latin usage. Thus 'othere goodes temporels' in *Melibee*, 998, for example,

16. All quotations from *Le Livre de Mellibée et Prudence* are from the text printed by J. Burke Severs in Bryan and Dempster, pp. 568 ff., and from the *Summa* of Pennaforte as printed by Germaine Dempster, *ibid.*, pp. 729 ff.

which renders the French 'autres biens temporelz' is paralleled by 'alle goodes temporeles' and by 'alle goodes espirituels' in *The Parson's Tale*, 685 and 312. Sentences leaning towards French rather than Latin syntax are frequent in *The Parson's Tale*; as an example we may compare line 144 – 'though I wiste that neither God ne man ne sholde nevere knowe it, yet wolde I have desdayn for to do synne' – with Pennaforte's 'si scirem Deos ignoscituros, homines autem ignoraturos, tamen abhorrerem peccatum'. Here there is the typical Chaucerian preference for phrases of the type 'have desdayn', 'do synne', which in *Melibee* are frequently modelled on similar patterns in French: 'for if thou do hem boun-tee' (*Mel* 1189) – 'car ce que tu feras de bien' (*Livre* 366); 'thou shalt also have in suspect' (*Mel* 1197) – 'tu dois avoir en suspect' (*Livre* 374). All these instances, and others more which could be adduced, lend support to the contention that in *The Parson's Tale* as well as in *Melibee* Chaucer was working on a French text.

But the aims and the results were radically different in these two tales. In *The Parson's Tale* the grand design of *The Canterbury Tales* is drawn to its close as attention is switched from the temporal pilgrimage to

> 'thilke parfit glorious pilgrymage
> That highte Jerusalem celestial.'
>
> (*CT* X, 50–1)

Numerous echoes, thematic and verbal, recall earlier tales and their tellers as the Parson places their many and varied concerns into the spiritual perspective of the Seven Deadly Sins and their opposing virtues. Bernard F. Huppé notes how 'the psychology of sin and penance as developed in the *Parson's Tale* provides the most pertinent means for observing the real tension in the Wife's confession'[17] and draws attention to the 'perspective' which the tale provides for the Wife of Bath's marital theory and practice, or for that of Januarie in *The Merchant's Tale*.[18] Numerous other links could be added: with the Monk (*ParsT* 432), the Host (440, 587 ff.), *The Tale of Melibee* (522 ff.), *The Pardoner's Tale* (587 ff., 793 ff.), *The Summoner's Tale* (617), *The Clerk's Tale* (663 ff.), *The Man of Law's Tale* (737), *The Shipman's Tale* (901 ff.).

That this final and climactic 'vertuous sentence' should be of-

17. Huppé, p. 123.
18. *Ibid.*, pp. 147 ff.

fered in prose is not surprising. As a broad generalization it is true that to the audience of the later fourteenth century verse meant entertainment and prose edification, a generalization no less true because there are exceptions, like the popular *Travels of Sir John Mandeville*, or religious meditations and devotions in verse. Nor must we forget that even within one work the boundaries were often hard to draw: the most hypocritical of preaching pardoners could convey a profound spiritual truth in verse, and the most accomplished of mock-heroic verse fables could offer a *moralite*. But there can be no ambiguity about *The Parson's Tale*: the modern reader's boredom and the modern critic's embarrassment pay singular, if paradoxical, tribute to Chaucer's success. Of all the Canterbury tales that of the Parson had to be in prose in order to be securely apart from those 'that sownen into synne' (*CT* X, 1086), in order to rouse the pilgrims from their 'worldly vanitees' (1085) and bring them face to face with the stark truths of eternity. If much earlier in the work Chaucer decided upon another 'litel thyng in prose' it was because nothing else would do as well to cap the inane *rime* of *Sir Thopas*, for that, as we shall see, is what *The Tale of Melibee* does, and does very effectively.

In keeping with the serious aim of *The Parson's Tale*, language and style are carefully controlled. It is a very even work. Like the *Astrolabe* it relies much upon enumerative method and appropriate syntactic structures. Two favourite co-ordinating adverbs are 'forther' and 'forther over', and there are the other familiar co-ordinating conjunctions and adverbs: *and, thanne, now, and therfore, for, for certes*. Inversion of subject-verb order is common after these: 'and therfore seith Salomon' (*ParsT* 227); 'now comth the remedie' (915); 'thanne shal men understonde' (1076). Sentences are mostly kept short: 'Somtyme it comth of Ire or prive hate, that norisseth rancour in herte, as afterward I shal declare. / Thanne cometh eek bitternesse of herte, thurgh which bitternesse every good dede of his neighebor semeth to hym bitter and unsavory. / Thanne cometh discord, that unbyndeth alle manere of freendshipe' (509–11). Where sentences are longer, they are found easily controlled when read aloud. The same applies where Chaucer varies or complicates normal prose syntax in order to be rhetorically effective. *The Parson's Tale* opens with a complex subject, 'Oure sweete Lord God of hevene, that . . . wole . . . but wole . . .' at some remove from its verb, *amonesteth*, but the listener is carried along without difficulty. This is true even where the syntax is, strictly, ungrammatical: 'A man that hath trespased to a lord, and comth for to axe mercy and maken his accord, and set him doun anon by the lord, men wolde holden hym outrageous, and nat worthy so soone for to have remissioun ne mercy' (992).

Syntactic variation takes many forms. A multiple subject may be expressed by noun plus infinitive plus infinitive:

> For certes, *the repentaunce* of a synguler synne, *and nat repente* of alle his othere synnes, *or elles repenten* hym of alle his othere synnes, and nat of a synguler synne, may nat availle. (300)

The normal order subject-verb-object is inverted:

> For soothly oure sweete Lord Jhesu Crist hath spared us so debonairly in oure folies, that if he ne hadde pitee of mannes soule, *a sory song we myghten alle synge.* (315)

A subject separated by intervening phrases or clauses from its verb is repeated by the appropriate pronoun:

> *The same Seint Paul,* after his grete penaunce in water and in lond ... yet seyde *he.* .... (343–4)

> And *Seint Jerome,* whan he longe tyme hadde woned in desert ... yet seyde *he.* .... (345–6)

A predicate expressed by a phrase based on a noun is juxtaposed with another expressed by a phrase based on an infinitive:

> Avarice, after the descripcioun of Seint Augustyn, *is a likerousnesse* in herte to have erthely thynges. / Som oother folk seyn that Avarice *is for to purchacen* manye erthely thynges. (741–2)

Positioning of adjectives remains flexible:

> Espiritueel marchandise is proprely symonye, that is, ententif desir to byen thyng espiritueel. (781)

Infinitives may be preceded by *for to* or *to* or neither:[19]

> The speces of misericorde been, as *for to lene* and *for to yeve,* and *to foryeven* and *relesse,* and *for to han* pitee in herte and compassioun

19. In verse the use of *to* or *for to* seems to be largely determined by metrical reasons. Cp. Masui, p. 138. See also Jan Svartvik and Randolph Quirk, 'Types and Uses of Non-finite Clause in Chaucer', *English Studies* LI (1970), 393–411.

of the meschief of his evene-Cristene, and eek *to chastise*, there as nede is (810).

A preposition may end a sentence, a practice Chaucer has recourse to occasionally in rhyme, although not in the case of *of*:[20]

And right as a marchant deliteth hym moost in chaffare that he hath moost avantage of, right so deliteth the fend in this ordure. (851)

A pleonastic *that* may be inserted to achieve greater clarity:

Of thilke bodily marchandise that is leveful and honest is this: *that*, there as God hath ordeyned that a regne or a contree is suffisaunt to hymself, thanne is it honest and leveful that of habundaunce of this contree, that men helpe another contree that is moore nedy. (778)

– or to achieve some rhetorical effect:

For it is resoun that he that trespaseth by his free wyl, *that* by his free wyl he confesse his trespas. (1012)

These and similar devices show that Chaucer was not translating mechanically but was rather trying to breathe some life and artistic character into the Parson's long treatise. His rhetorical training and his good ear served him well even in such unpromising surroundings. There are some striking similes, like 'the buttokes of hem faren as it were the hyndre part of a she-ape in the fulle of the moone' (424) with its echoes of Isidore of Seville and the later medieval encyclopaedists;[21] and some more homely similes: 'but natheles that oon of thise speces of Pride is signe of that oother, right as the gaye leefsel atte taverne is signe of the wyn that is in the celer' (411), which illustrates the tendency in *The Parson's Tale* to illustrate the subtleties of theological thought from familiar experience. *Leefsel* 'a shady arbour or leafy bower' is a rare word in Chaucer; its only other occurrence is in *The Reeve's Tale*, 4061, 'bihynde the mille, under a levesel'; but it occurs elsewhere in Middle English, and the arbour in front of an inn-door, as described by the Parson, must have been a familiar

20. Sometimes the final preposition is pleonastic, both in prose and in verse. For example: 'yif ther be any thing to which that alle thinges tenden and hyen to' (*Bo* III, pr. 11, 212–14); or:

Unto which place every thyng,
Thorgh his kyndely enclynyng,
Moveth for to come to.

(HF 733–5)

21. Cp. D. Biggins's note on this passage in *Medium Aevum* XXXIII (1964), 200–3.

sight to the Canterbury pilgrims or, for that matter, to Chaucer's own listeners or readers. An even more commonplace simile – 'and passen as a shadwe on the wal' (1068) – occurs with slight variations in both *The Shipman's Tale*, 9, and *The Merchant's Tale*, 1315.

The Parson's Tale has its share of rhetorical figures, among them *anaphora, distributio, exclamatio, repetitio*. Amid the more sober exposition of doctrine, a sudden rhetorical effulgence becomes all the more memorable:

> For certes, outrageous wratthe dooth al that evere the devel hym comaundeth; for he ne spareth neither Crist ne his sweete Mooder. / And in his outrageous anger and ire, allas! allas! ful many oon at that tyme feeleth in his herte ful wikkedly, bothe of Crist and eek of alle his halwes. / Is nat this a cursed vice? Yis, certes. Allas! it bynymeth from man his wit and his resoun, and al his debonaire lif espiritueel that sholde kepen his soule. (558–60)

Sometimes a rhetorical repetition is balanced by a more colloquial one, as in the juxtaposed 'or elles' with '(as) he seith' in this torrent of brief, pithy sentences:

> Whan a man is sharply amonested in his shrifte to forleten his synne, / thanne wole he be angry, and answeren hokerly and angrily, and deffenden or excusen his synne by unstedefastnesse of his flessh; or elles he dide it for to holde compaignye with his felawes; or elles, he seith, the feend enticed hym; / or elles he dide it for his youthe; or elles his compleccioun is so corageous that he may nat forbere; or elles it is his destinee, as he seith, unto a certein age; or elles, he seith, it cometh hym of gentillesse of his auncestres; and semblable thynges. (583–5)

Chaucer had made his Parson, in *The General Prologue*, 'a lerned man, a clerk' (480) and his tale certainly confirms this, even though he shares with some of his fellow pilgrims, the Knight, for example, and the Franklin (cp. *KnT* 1323; *FranklT* 890), the occasional tendency to leave knotty problems to others: 'But so heigh a doctrine I lete to divines' he says in one place (*ParsT* 957); and 'The exposicioun of this hooly preyere, that is so excellent and digne, I bitake to thise maistres of theologie' in another (1043). But the Parson's learning is not solely theological. He knows a good deal about current fashions in clothing, for example, of 'embrowdynge, the degise endentynge or barrynge, owndynge, palynge, wyndynge or bendynge', of 'costlewe furrynge' of gowns, of *maxis* 'trailynge in the dong and in the mire', as well as of the *minis* which he calls 'kutted sloppes, or haynselyns, that thurgh hire shortnesse ne covere nat the shameful membres' (416 ff.). He is as much at home in the colloquial idiom of his day as in the erudite diction of the religious manuals. He can be gentle, even lyrical, but is just as capable of 'snybben sharply for the nonys' (*Gen Prol* 523). And throughout the tale Chaucer matches the Parson's stylistic range with an appropriate range of vocabulary.

There are a good many words in the tale not found elsewhere in Chaucer's writing, a few of which we have already noted. Some of these words Chaucer uses without definition or proper explanation, presumably expecting them to be familiar or at least intelligible to his audience or readers. A few of these are not recorded before Chaucer, technical words like *haynselyns*, just mentioned, 'short jackets' (422) or *hirnia* 'hernia' (423), but the context makes their meaning clear enough: 'thise kutted sloppes, or haynselyns',[22] or at least gives a general hint of their meaning: 'the horrible swollen membres, that semeth lik the maladie of hirnia'. Indeed, Chaucer is at pains not to fox the Parson's audience with unfamiliar words, while not forgoing the maker's privilege to use, adopt, or coin words that seemed to him proper for the context. Words like *damageous, meritorie, undevocioun, unsavory* may not have suggested themselves to Chaucer elsewhere, and may not, like *damageous*, occur anywhere else in Middle English, but the fact that these are all derivatives from familiar words must have made them as readily intelligible to his contemporaries as *lubritorium* would be to a modern motorist seeking to have his car lubricated. Some words like *concupiscence* or *sensualitee* are part of the preacher's stock-in-trade, while others are either explained by appropriate doublets or more painstakingly defined, as in the following examples:[23]

For certes there availleth noon *essoyne* ne excusacioun. (164)

this synne of bakbityng or *detraccion*. (493)

---

22. The opposite of George Borrow's 'long loose tunic or slop', *The Bible in Spain* (London, 18th edn, repr. 1914), ch. XI. Cf. also the Canon's *overslope* 'loose upper garment, cassock' (*CYT* 633). Falstaff's *slops*, however, were baggy breeches (*2 Henry IV*, I, ii. 30).

23. The italicized words are not used by Chaucer outside *The Parson's Tale*.

After bakbityng cometh gruchchyng or *murmuracioun*. (499)

thise false enchauntours or *nigromanciens*. (603)

hire *underlynges* or hire subgetz. (774)

And thus is synne acompliced by temptacioun, by delit, and by consentynge; and thanne is the synne cleped *actueel*. (357)

What seye we of hem that bileeven on *divynailes*, as by flight or by noyse of briddes, or of beestes, or by sort. (605)

The remedie agayns Ire is a vertu that men clepen *Mansuetude*, that is Debonairetee. (654)

Thanne cometh *sompnolence*, that is, sloggy slombrynge, which maketh a man be hevy and dul in body and in soule. (706)

The develes may entre on every syde, or sheten at hym *at discovert*, by temptacion on every syde. (714)

Thanne comth *lachesse*; that is he, that whan he biginneth any good werk, anon he shal forleten it and stynten. (720)

For humble folk been Cristes freendes; they been *contubernyal* with the Lord. (760)

Not the least interesting of the Parson's nonce words, however, are good English words appropriate to one described as

> Ne of his speche daungerous ne digne,
> *(Gen Prol* 517)

unaffected, anxious to get through to his simple *parisshens*, preferring the short word to the long, the Saxon (or Scandinavian) to the Romance, whenever possible; the loyal disciple – were he alive today – of Fowler and Quiller-Couch and Gowers and other high priests of the 'pure English' persuasion. So we have Chaucer placing into his mouth such rarities as *unlust* (680) and *untyme* (1051) and 'this *roten-herted* synne of Accidie' (689) and that very expressive and no less rare pair 'forsleweth and forsluggeth' (685), as well as, from O.E. *drōfig*, '*drovy* or trouble water' (816), or from O.N. *sloppr* those same 'kutted *sloppes*, or haynselyns' (422) previously encountered.

It would be misleading, however, to dwell too long upon the Parson's rare or unique words, for, although they help to illustrate the range of his diction, they are only a relatively small part of his vocabulary. To have produced too ponderously erudite or exotic a sermon would have been out of character and would have missed the declared aim of directing the eyes of all pilgrims, including the most humble and the most 'lewed', up towards 'Jerusalem celestial'. In this respect *The Parson's Tale* is more akin to the pedagogic tone and intent of the *Astrolabe* than to *Boece*, where abstruse thought is often clothed in abstruse language, or to *The Tale of Melibee*, where a pompously inflated style is made the vehicle of a particular satiric intention.

I do not wish to suggest that *The Parson's Tale* is a simple work. As a homily it is of course much longer and more complex in style and diction than, say, the sermons of Wyclif; and as a manual of religious instruction it shares with others of its kind a certain longwindedness of exposition and explanation and conclusion which may have suited medieval leisure but is galling to modern taste. The enumerative method of presentation supplies suitable signposts for listener or reader, as well as for the author, but it is hardly likely to promote such antidotes to 'sompnolence, that is, sloggy slombrynge' as imaginative involvement or even surprise. Where *The Parson's Tale* succeeds in achieving such a response, it does so through the use of colloquial and picturesque diction, whether proverbial or simply idiomatic usage of the day, at times skilfully offset as a relief from doctrinal ponderousness or strings of technicalities. In the following passage, for instance, the weight of 'taylages, custumes, and cariages', of 'amercimentz and raunsonynge' and the learned footnotes to Augustine and Genesis is eased by the familiar Chaucerian use of *certes* and of the demonstrative *thise*, the colloquial 'as they seyn', and idiomatic turns of phrase like 'thynges that they nevere yave hem' and 'sooth is that':

> Of Coveitise comen thise harde lordshipes, thurgh whiche men been distreyned by taylages, custumes, and cariages, moore than hire duetee or resoun is. And eek taken they of hire bonde-men amercimentz, whiche myghten moore resonably ben cleped extorcions than amercimentz. / Of whiche amercimentz and raunsonynge of boonde-men somme lordes stywardes seyn that it is rightful, for as muche as a cherl hath no temporeel thyng that it ne is his lordes, as they seyn. / But certes, thise lordshipes doon wrong that bireven hire bondefolk thynges that they nevere yave hem. *Augustinus, de Civitate, libro nono.* / Sooth is that the condicioun of thraldom

and the firste cause of thraldom is for synne. *Genesis, nono.*
(752–5)

Or again, when enumerating remedies against lechery, for
example, the Parson intersperses colloquial comments or picturesque illustrations to relieve the catalogue:

> Ther neden none ensamples of this; the experience of day by day
> oghte suffise. (927)

> For certes, whan the pot boyleth strongly, the beste remedie is to
> withdrawe the fyr. (951)

> Soothly, a whit wal, although it ne brenne noght fully by stikynge
> of a candele, yet is the wal blak of the leyt. (954)

It matters little whether the hint for such passages came to
Chaucer from his sources or from his own invention; what is of
interest is the language which he employs and its leavening
effect upon *The Parson's Tale* as a whole. The modern reader may
not think that this is, in the modern sense, 'a myrie tale' (*CT* X,
46), but no sympathetic reading of the work can fail to detect a
range of usage, diction and style, which includes many lighter
touches, some of which, *pace* the Parson, are unmistakably and
characteristically Chaucer's own.

In translating Boethius's *De Consolatione Philosophiae* Chaucer
set himself an altogether different task. The close connection
between his *Boece* and *Troilus and Criseyde*, as well as its persistent
influence on *The Canterbury Tales* and the absence of such influence on the earlier poems, have convinced most scholars that
the translation was undertaken soon after 1380, perhaps just
before Chaucer began writing *Troilus and Criseyde*. This probably
makes it Chaucer's first excursion into prose, although the other
prose works, *The Parson's Tale* in particular, are admittedly difficult to date with exactness. *Boece* differs from the others also in
being the translation of a work composed partly in prose, partly
in verse. There are, moreover, a few places in Chaucer's own
poetry where Boethian passages are rendered into verse, thus
affording an occasional comparison between Chaucer's rendering
of the original into both media. Critical opinion prefers the verse
translations, but critical opinion is wrong in dismissing the prose
Boece too readily as second-rate. There is indeed, as Robinson
says (p. 320), 'looseness of structure and diffuseness of language',

and some other patent flaws, but there are also many passages of firm syntactical cohesion, of carefully controlled diction, of active lexical inventiveness, and of genuine poetic sensibility. The dialogue between the narrator and his 'noryce, Philosophie' is often lively in its brisk colloquial give-and-take. There is indeed some evidence to justify Jefferson's conclusion: 'Chaucer, gifted with a sensitive ear, feeling the spirit of his original, has reproduced its enthusiasm, its dignity of expression, and, as best he could, its symmetry of style. His translation is the translation of a poet.'[24]

The weaknesses of *Boece* are certainly not hard to find. The opening *metrum* of the first book has a glaring example of heavy-handed translation in which Chaucer follows neither the Latin of Boethius nor the French version which he also used closely enough to excuse the result, nor does he succeed in writing anything approaching a plain, let alone a poetic, English sentence. The Chaucerian nonce words *unpietous* and *unagreable* do nothing to help. Boethius's lines are:[25]

> Nunc quia fallacem mutauit nubila uultum,
> Protrahit ingratas impia uita moras.
>
> (I, m. 1, 19–20)

Chaucer's version reads:

> But now, for Fortune cloudy hath chaunged hir deceyvable chere to me-ward, myn unpietous lif draweth along unagreable duellynges.
>
> (I, m. 1, 26–9)

Some of the inspiration (if that is the right word) plainly derives from the French translation of Jean de Meun: 'deceyvable chere' from 'decevable voult' (I, m. 1, 17), for example, or 'unagreable duellynges' from 'la desagreable demeure' (17–18), but the general awkwardness is Chaucer's. Not an auspicious launching into prose in mid-career. Nor is such apprentice work as rare as one might wish. The frequent glosses inserted into the text, many of which Chaucer derived from Nicholas Trivet's Latin commentary on Boethius, are not by any means invariable aids to better under-

24. Jefferson, p. 46.

25. All quotations from Boethius are from the Loeb Classical Library edition of *The Theological Tractates* and *The Consolation of Philosophy* (London, 1918, repr. 1968). All references to the French text are to the version edited by V. L. Dedeck-Héry, 'Boethius' *De Consolatione* by Jean de Meun', *Medieval Studies* XIV (1952), 165–275.

standing. A fortunately not typical, somewhat Johnsonian, specimen occurs in Book II:

> . . . for vertu stille sholde nat elden (*that is to seyn that, list that, or he waxe oold, his vertu, that lay now ful stille, ne schulde nat perysshe un-exercised in governaunce of comunes, for which men myghten speken or wryten of his gode governement*).

(II, pr. 7, 6–11)

Chaucer's handling of Boethius's text is often a manhandling. Not infrequently he mistranslates, and editors and commentators have had a busy time pointing out his inaccuracies.[26] More interesting from our immediate point of view, however, is what sort of English Chaucer writes, whether the result of accurate translation or not, although it does of course matter whether the English version makes sense. Other translators of that time, like John Purvey, a close associate of Wyclif's, had firm principles on the art of translation and followed them. The Latin ablative absolute, Purvey suggests, for example,

> may be resolvid into these thre wordis, with convenable verbe, *the while, for, if,* as gramariens seyn. As thus, *the maistir redinge, I stonde* may be resolvid thus: *While the maistir redith, I stonde* either *If the maistir redith* either *For the maistir,* etc. And sumtyme it wolde acorde wel with the sentence to be resolvid into *whanne* either into *aftirward.* Thus, *Whanne the maister red, I stood* either *After the maistir red, I stood.* And sumtyme it may wel be resolvid into a verbe of the same tens, as othere ben in the same resoun, and into this word *et,* that is, *and* in English.[27]

Sometimes Chaucer does resolve Latin ablative absolute constructions into subordinate clauses along the lines suggested in Purvey's prologue; but at other times he retains them as participles, perhaps taking his hint from Jean de Meun (who, in the first quotation below, for example, has 'les nubleces . . . dissolues' for Boethius's 'nebulis dissolutis'):

> Ryght so, and noon other wise, the cloudes of sorwe dissolved and doon away, I took hevene.

(I, pr. 3, 1–3)

26. See the list in Jefferson, pp. 16 ff. Some of Chaucer's mis-readings and mis-translations of the French version are listed by V. L. Dedeck-Héry in 'Jean de Meun et Chaucer, Traducteurs de la Consolation de Boèce', *PMLA* LII (1937), 967–91.

27. Quoted by Basil Cottle, *The Triumph of English 1350–1400* (London, 1969), p. 224, from H. E. Winn, ed., *Wyclif: Select English Writings* (Oxford, 1929), pp. 26 f.

and, the kyng knowynge of it, Y overcom it.

(I, pr. 4, 86–7)

and, the lyght ifounde, graunte hym to fycchen.

(III, m. 9, 41–2)

The results might not have been approved of by Purvey, but they read well enough.

Sometimes a particular Latin construction, for example the participial 'Quorum quidem alii . . . credentes' (III, pr. 2, 15–16), leads Chaucer into an unidiomatic rendering: 'Of the whiche men, some of hem wenen . . .'(III, pr. 2, 25–6), or 'The floury yer yeldeth swote smelles in the first somer sesoun warmynge' (IV, m. 6, 29–31). Sometimes the Latin word-order which permits the object to precede the subject leads Chaucer into a slavish imitation, and the English rendering, when there is no artistic justification for it, becomes unidiomatic, and jarring, particularly when influenced also by the French version: 'Nunc stuporem meum deus rector exaggerat' (IV, pr. 5, 18–19), Jean de Meun's 'Mais ores *me comble et* m'acraist mon esbahissement *et ma merveille* diex gouverneur des chosez' (IV, pr. 5, 18–19), becomes Chaucer's 'But now hepith and encreseth myn astonyenge God, governour of thinges' (IV, pr. 5, 30–1).

Jefferson lists and illustrates a few further syntactical peculiarities of *Boece* which can be ascribed to Chaucer's method, or lack of method, of translation. The most pervasive of these, and one which strongly colours the style of the work, is Chaucer's excessive and often insensitive use of *and* and especially of *that*, because the latter used as a conjunction often rubs shoulder with the pronoun. For example:

> But I have travailed and told yit hiderto for thou scholdest knowe the mowynge of schrewes, which mowynge that semeth to ben unworthy, nis no mowynge; and ek of schrewes, of whiche thou pleynedest that they ne were nat punysschid, that thow woldest seen that thei ne were neveremo withouten the tormentz of hir wikkidnesse; and of the licence of mowynge to don yvel that thou preyedest that it myghte sone ben ended, and that thou woldest fayn lernen that it ne sholde nat longe endure; and that schrewes ben more unsely yif thei were of lengere durynge, and most unsely yif thei weren per-durable.

(IV, pr. 4, 154–68)

On such occasions the reader feels tempted to echo rather wist-
fully Boece's own heartfelt plea: 'I wolde . . . that thow madest
me clerly to undirstonde what thou seist' (III, pr. 10, 168–9).

Certain syntactical features of Chaucer's prose, already encountered in the *Astrolabe* and in *The Parson's Tale*, appear also in
Boece. Negation is frequently expressed, as also in Chaucer's verse,
by several negative particles; and verbs like *doute* and *denye* are
generally followed, as in the French version, by a negative particle:

> For no wight ne douteth that he that mai gon by naturel office of
> feet *ne* be more myghti than he that *ne* may nat.
>
> (IV, pr. 2, 112–14)

> 'Denyestow,' quod sche, 'that alle schrewes *ne* ben worthy to han
> torment?'
>
> (IV, pr. 4, 225–6)

The position of adjectives is flexible, and postposed adjectives,
following the French word-order, occur in *Boece* as in Chaucer's
other prose writings: 'the ordre destynal' (IV, pr. 6, 80–1), 'lif
interminable' (V, pr. 6, 15). Where two adjectives occur, one may,
as also in Chaucer's verse,[28] precede the noun, the other follow it:
'how grete sorwes unsufrable' (III, pr. 7, 4–5), 'con grans dou-
leurs non souffrables' (*ibid.* 3). Once again, direct French influence is apparent, yet further confirmation of the likelihood
that in addition to Boethius's Latin text and Trivet's commentary
Chaucer used Jean de Meun's French prose translation of the
Consolatio. And yet not all French influence in *Boece* can be traced
directly to the French version as edited by Dedeck-Héry. Thus, to
give one example, Chaucer twice uses *ostelementz* 'furniture,
household goods' (II, pr. 5, 119, 131) from O.Fr. (*h*)*ostillement*,
where Jean de Meun has *avoir* (71) and *choses* (79) respectively,
and the Latin *supellectilis* (66, 74). On the other hand, a phrase like
'the abregginge of fortuit hap' (V, pr. 1, 82–3), as Robinson
notes, echoes the French 'l'abregement du cas fortunel' (46) rather than the Latin 'fortuiti causa compendii' (48). Jefferson
(p. 46) cites further examples.

There is some flexibility also in the use of prepositions, in some
cases conforming to idiomatic usage of the time, in others not.

28. Cp. for example the Physician's 'historial thyng notable' (*PhysT* 156).

The verb *loken* 'look' may take a direct object: 'loke nat the ordre of thinges' (IV, pr. 4, 188–9); or it may be followed by *on*: 'loketh nat on these thinges' (*ibid.* 208–9). *Worthy* is normally followed by *of*: 'worthy of torment' (II, pr. 7, 75–6), 'worthy of pite' (IV, pr. 4, 296), as in modern English, but occurs once with *to* plus a noun: 'worthy to the hevene' (IV, m. 7, 72), perhaps modelled on the normal verbal construction, as in 'worthy to ben reverenced' (I, pr. 4, 270). In V, pr. 3, 184–6, 'han hope in God' is followed almost immediately by 'hopen to God', both paralleled elsewhere in Middle English. The omission of any preposition after *maner*, where modern English requires 'of', is normal Chaucerian usage in both prose and verse (although he sometimes uses *of*); for example, in *Boece*: 'a maner fruyt' (III, pr. 7, 5), 'a maner body' (III, pr. 10, 161); in verse: 'every maner wight' (*KnT* 1875), 'som manere jalousie' (*Tr* III, 1030).

The only prose occurrence in Chaucer of the plural *ben* 'bees' occurs in *Boece* III, m. 7, 3: 'thise flyenge flyes that we clepen ben'; just as there is one prose instance of *bees*, in *The Parson's Tale*, 468: 'thise flyes that men clepen bees'. Both forms are attested in rhyme in *The Canterbury Tales*. The word *thing* in Chaucer has both the inflected plural *thinges* and the uninflected plural *thing*,[29] both of which occur in rhyme positions in his verse; but the many cases in *Boece* of 'alle thing' followed by a singular verb (e.g. 'alle thing that profiteth is good', IV, pr. 7, 34–5) should be regarded as indefinite pronouns.[30]

I am not aware whether anyone has ever undertaken a detailed word count of *Boece*, but I would expect the word *thing* to figure high among Chaucer's favourites. A cursory estimate based on Tatlock's and Kennedy's *Concordance* makes the percentage proportion of occurrences of *thing(es)* in *Boece: Canterbury Tales: Troilus and Criseyde* something like 53:36:11. The reason lies largely in the peculiar structural patterns of the Latin language which prompt Jean de Meun to use *chose*, and which prompt Chaucer to make 'thing'-phrases and clauses of many of them. In the following example, Boethius once has 'natura rerum', properly rendered 'the nature of thinges', but Chaucer manages to squeeze a

29. Cp. ch. 2, p. 109. *Yeer* 'year' has the same uninflected plural; cp. ten Brink, p. 144.
30. Kerkhof, pp. 186 ff., distinguishes various functions of the indefinite pronoun *al*. For an example of 'al thyng' occurring close to 'alle thyng', see *CT* VIII, 685–9. Cp. also 'over alle thyng' (*MLT* 277, *Rom* 726) with 'over alle thynges' (*Mel* 1297), etc.

further four *thinges* into the same sentence, one more than in the French version:

Neque enim ab deminutis inconsummatisque natura rerum cepit exordium, sed ab integris absolutisque procedens in haec extrema atque effeta dilabitur.

(III, pr. 10, 16–18)

For the nature of *thinges* ne took nat hir begynnynge of *thinges* amenused and inparfit, but it procedith of *thinges* that ben alle hole and absolut, and descendith so doun into uttereste *thinges* and into *thinges* empty and withouten fruyt.

(*ibid.* 25–30)

This example illustrates the expansion which many Latin sentences inevitably underwent as single parts of speech were turned, often on the analogy of French, into English phrases and clauses, although other words beside *thinges* were of course available to Chaucer, and he did make use of them when it occurred to him to do so. Latin was a synthetic language and Chaucer's English was well on the way to being an analytic one, which, together with the addition of over 400 explanatory glosses, explains why Chaucer's *Boece* is nearly one and a half times the length of Boethius's work. Sometimes the expansion of the Latin becomes needlessly wordy, first in the hands of the French translator, then in Chaucer's, as when Boethius's *celeberrimum* (III, pr. 9, 33–4) becomes 'tres celebrable *par clarté de noblece*' (*ibid.* 33) in the French version, and is then further expanded into Chaucer's 'ryght celebrable by clernesse of renoun and noblesse' (*ibid.* 63–4). The addition of *renoun* was prompted by the French 'celebrité de renommee' a few lines earlier (27), easily rendered as 'celebrete of renoun' (49–50). All this looks like very mechanical translating from the French; and yet Chaucer seems to have been aware of the need to add, occasionally, some further explanatory words in order to clarify some of the Gallicisms he used. For neither *celebrete* nor *celebrable* appears to have been used in English before; neither is used by Chaucer outside *Boece: celebrete* only here, *celebrable* once more in IV, m. 7, 28; and the latter is not, according to the *MED*, used anywhere else in Middle English.

The vocabulary of *Boece* is heavily studded with words like *celebrable* and *celebrete*, specially adopted into Chaucer's English for the occasion and never used again. I have noted around 150 words which Chaucer used only in *Boece*, and this may well be a very conservative estimate; a more exact figure could be arrived at by counting one's way through the *Concordance*, a task which, perhaps understandably, no one appears so far to have undertaken. But even of my estimated 150 words a little less than half appear to be Chaucer's adoptions, both from Latin and from French. They are listed by Jefferson and include such words as *dyffinysshed* 'defined', *fortuit* 'fortuitous', *immoevablete* 'immobility', *presentarie* 'ever-present'. But they are not all derived from Romance sources. The use of *felawschipe* as a verb, for example, which is found in the Wyclifite Bible, recommended itself to Chaucer several times in *Boece*; the noun *henteres* 'grabbers' occurs once in I, pr. 3, 81 in the phrase 'swyche ravyneres and henteres' and nowhere else in Middle English, according to the *MED*. Its origin, M.E. *henten* (from O.E. *hentan*), was common enough in various related meanings, yet *henteres* is clearly a neologism. One wonders which of Chaucer's pair was intended to elucidate the other. The happy coinage *japeworthi* 'ridiculous', half French, half English in origin, is another Middle English nonce word which does excellent service in dismissing 'thilke japeworthi devynynge of Tyresie the divynour' (V, pr. 3, 132–3).

The fact that so many of Chaucer's words in *Boece* were not used by him elsewhere raises an interesting critical question. Jefferson dismisses the suggestion that 'Chaucer was seriously experimenting with the new words for their own sake', because 'he makes very little use of these new words in his subsequent writings, as we might expect if he were interested in the words for themselves'.[31] He goes on to give some examples of careless usage 'hardly consistent with experimentation'. The latter point does not carry much weight, for such instances are few, and other signs of carelessness in *Boece* suggest that Chaucer was certainly nodding at times. This is hardly surprising in a work of such length and complexity. But that Chaucer was experimenting with words seems incontrovertible if we consider the types and morphemic structures involved, the use of certain words for rhetorical or rhythmic effect, alliteration, for example, as well as for the immediate contextual meaning required, and, perhaps most significant, the valuable practice *Boece* afforded for further

[31] Jefferson, p. 26.

lexical inventiveness in *Troilus and Criseyde* and *The Canterbury Tales*.[32]

That quite often Chaucer almost mechanically anglicized a Latin or French word no one would wish to deny; thus we have *adjeccioun* for Latin *adiectio*, *coeterne* for *coaeternum*, *infirme* for *infirma*, *repugnen* for *repugnare*, *entalenten* for French *entalenter*, and so on. The same process was at work in his other translations and has indeed been a common source of new words throughout the history of the English language. Many words thus adopted probably carried something of an exotic air with them, words like *ammonicioun* or *immoevablete*, and therefore remained severely restricted in usage. On the other hand, Chaucer used as well as adopted many words in *Boece* which fitted into familiar Middle English morphemic patterns and had besides a less alien appearance so that they could more readily be used in other contexts or, perhaps more important, as I have suggested, serve as models for further lexical adventures in his later work. Many of Chaucer's common verbs are of the structural type *arise*, *indite*, *repente*, etc.; hence it is natural enough that he should create others of the same type, like *ajust*, *ataste*, *entalenten*, *impetren*, where his source or the context suggested them to him. It so happens that none of the verbs just cited is used elsewhere by Chaucer, but the activity of such word creation in *Boece* undoubtedly facilitated its functioning elsewhere. That is to say, *Boece* was an invaluable linguistic practice ground. One need not look far into Chaucer's subsequent poetry to find evidence: with *ajust*, *ataste*, we may compare the structurally identical *agroted* 'surfeited' in *The Legend of Good Women*, 2454, or *adorneth* in *Troilus and Criseyde* III, 2; with *entalenten* the Pardoner's *envoluped* (*PardT* 942); with *impetren* the Canon's Yeoman's *enbibyng* 'absorbing' (*CYT* 814); and so on. All these verbs occur only in the given passages, and each is a romance adoption by Chaucer of the same type as the verbs listed from *Boece*.

This list could be extended to cover other parts of speech, like adjectives of various types (*celebrable*, *infirme*), or words coined according to certain structural patterns from native English word material, like *henteres*, already discussed, or *forwytere* 'one who

---

[32] For an attempt at a detailed analysis of the structure of Chaucer's words see Jacek Fisiak, *Morphemic Structure of Chaucer's English* (Alabama, 1965), pp. 52 ff.

foreknows' (*Bo* V, pr. 6, 295), the former of which is structurally identical with *swellere*, for example (*Bo* III, pr. 6, 6), and the latter with *pronouncere* (*Bo* II, pr. 3, 56). And these in turn may well have prepared the way for similar neologisms later, like *flemere* 'one who banishes, puts to flight' in the Man of Law's memorable phrase 'flemere of feendes' (*MLT* 460) and the same speaker's *lyvere* 'one who lives' (*ibid.* 1024); or else made it easier for Chaucer to have recourse to rare words of the same pattern, as in a no less memorable phrase in *Troilus and Criseyde* II, 644, 'holder up of Troye', or the Reeve's *market-betere* 'one who loafs around markets' (*RvT* 3936), or in the Wife of Bath's

'A ful greet bryngere out of bisynesse.'

(*WBT* 1196)

This activity is particularly striking in connection with words prefixed with *un-*, of which there is an unusually large number in *Boece*.[33] These are mainly adjectives and past participles, but there are verbs, adverbs, and some nouns as well. Moreover, *Boece* is followed fairly closely by *Troilus and Criseyde*: between them, these two works account for about a hundred nonce *un*-words,[34] compared with less than fifty for all Chaucer's other works. He was obviously experimenting actively with the creation of such words, even where he did not use their antonyms, as in the case of *undepartable*, *unknowable*, *unparigal* 'unequal', *unstaunchable*, or even where no antonym appears to have existed at all in Middle English, as in the case of *uneschuable*. These words range from very short and simple structures like *ungentle*, *unknit*, *unsolemn* to more complex ones like *unmoevablete*, *unrightfully*, *unstablenesse*. A number of these words is common to *Boece* and *Troilus and Criseyde*, underlining the affinity between these two works; for example *unfold*, *unknowyng*,[35] *unworthinesse*. In *Boece* I, m. 5, 31 ff. Boethius asks the recurrent question why righteous and innocent people are allowed to suffer and 'anoyinge folk treden, and that *unrightfully*, on the nekkes of holi men'; a question asked in Book III, 1016 ff. of

33. Other English poets have gone in for this particular activity, e.g. Hardy in *The Dynasts*.

34. By 'nonce *un*-words' I here mean words which occur once or several times in *Boece* or *Troilus and Criseyde* or both, but nowhere else in Chaucer.

35. In the α text of *Troilus and Criseyde* at I, 93. Most editors prefer the reading 'al unwist', but as *unwist* means 'unknown' in Chaucer, *unknowyng* is obviously preferable, quite apart from its parallel in *Boece*.

Troilus and Criseyde by Criseyde, not in exactly the same terms, but introducing two other Chaucerian nonce *un*-words, *ungiltif* and *undeserved*, perhaps suggested by that in *Boece*. Troilus's disquisition on predestination in *Troilus and Criseyde* IV, 958 ff. owes much to *Boece* V, pr. 2, and especially to pr. 3, and it is interesting to note that the rare word *uncerteyn* (*Tr* IV, 989) occurs three times in *Boece* V, pr. 3, together with *unscience*, *uneschewably* and *unjoyned*, all of which Chaucer uses only in *Boece*. Criseyde's exclamation

> O brotel wele of mannes joie unstable!
>
> (*Tr* III, 820)

uses a word, *unstable*, known only to the Prioress, apart from its two occurrences in *Boece*; and presumably it found its way into *Troilus and Criseyde* from *Boece* II, pr. 4, 148, where the noun *unstablenesse* has its only Chaucerian occurrence. Such echoes are not uncommon. But such sober listing can of course not do justice to the sometimes superb poetic effects achieved by Chaucer with the help of these unique words brought into being, as I believe, by the experimenting, in *Boece*. The following examples from *Troilus and Criseyde* will speak for themselves:

> 'Thow mayst allone here wepe and crye and knele,
> But love a womman that she woot it nought,
> And she wol quyte it that thow shalt nat fele;
> *Unknowe*, *unkist*, and lost, that is *unsought*.'
>
> (I, 806–9)

> That for to slen hymself myght he nat wynne,
> But bothe don *unmanhod* and a synne.
>
> (I, 823–4)

> She wente allone, and gan hire herte *unfettre*.
>
> (II, 1216)

> 'O soule, lurkynge in this wo, *unneste*,
> Fle forth out of myn herte.'
>
> (IV, 305–6)

> 'O oold, *unholsom*, and myslyved man,
> Calkas I mene, allas!'
>
> (IV, 330–1)

> 'Thanne shal no mete or drynke come in me
> Til I my soule out of my breste *unshethe*.'
>
> (IV, 775–6)

and ebben gan the welle
Of hire teeris, and the herte *unswelle*.

(IV, 1145–6)

'But humblely, with sorwful sikes sike,
Yow write ich myn *unresty* sorwes soore.'

(V, 1354–5)

Inevitably, the prose of *Boece* cannot compete with the poetry of *Troilus*. Yet there are many passages, particularly in the *metra*, in which Chaucer's use of his language, including the words of his own making, is unmistakably that of a poet, a poet who was just about to embark upon the composition of *Troilus and Criseyde*.

A particularly striking example of the sudden transition from prosy prose to poetic prose occurs at the end of *Boece* III, pr. 11 and the beginning of m. 11:

> And certes that is the thyng that every wyght desireth; and for as mochel as we han gadrid and comprehendid that good is thilke thing that is desired of alle, thanne mote we nedys confessen that good is the fyn of alle thinges.

(III, pr. 11, 225–30)

> Whoso that seketh sooth by a deep thought, and coveyteth not to been disseyvid by no mysweyes, lat hym rollen and trenden withynne hymself the lyght of his ynwarde sighte; and let hym gaderyn ayein, enclynynge into a compas, the longe moevynges of his thoughtes; and let hym techyn his corage that he hath enclosid and hid in his tresors, al that he compasseth or secheth fro withoute. And thanne thilke thing, that the blake cloude of errour whilom hadde ycovered, schal lighte more clerly than Phebus hymself ne schyneth.

(III, m. 11, 1–12)

The opening clause of the *metrum* has an unmistakable poetic rhythm (closely modelled on Boethius's Latin line), and so have several of the succeeding phrases and clauses; the initial alliteration on 'seketh sooth' is echoed by later patterns of alliteration as in 'thanne thilke thing, that' (even the ubiquitous *thing* is drawn into poetic service here) or in the alliteration on [k] which runs through the quoted passage: 'enclynynge . . . compas . . . corage . . . enclosid . . . compasseth . . . cloude . . . ycovered . . . clerly'; the Chaucerian nonce word *trenden*, and the word *mysweyes*, used by Chaucer only here and in the phrase 'makid weery by mysweyes'

(*Bo* V, pr. 1, 20),[36] show how fittingly Chaucer's rare words can be employed. The repetition of 'lat hym ... and let hym ... and let hym' effectively conceals the more commonplace, and in Chaucer's prose all too common, succession of *and* and *and thanne*; unlike the heavier 'gadrid and comprehendid' of the preceding *prosa*, the augmentation in 'rollen and trenden' and in 'enclosid and hid' adds to the smooth, rhythmic flow of the passage while helping to balance the less familiar words with familiar ones. It may be asked how much of all this is due to either Boethius or Jean de Meun. The rhythm of the opening line is certainly suggested by the Latin rather than the French:

> Quisquis profunda mente uestigat uerum,

and so, perhaps, is the alliteration in 'seketh sooth', although there is alliteration also in the opening clause of the French text: 'par pensee parfonde'. The Latin *deuiis*, rather than the French *desvoiabletéz*, probably prompted *mysweyes*, and the prompting was a happy one. Chaucer's 'rollen and trenden' is a clear gain on *reuoluat*; nor does it derive straight from the French. The [k]-alliteration is his own choice, while the flowing clause 'that the blake cloude of errour whilom hadde ycovered' owes its image and its rhythm to Boethius's

> Dudum quod atra texit erroris nubes,
>
> (*ibid.* 7)

although some of the diction is closely modelled on the French, notably 'la noire nue de l'erreur' (*ibid.* 6–7). What all this proves is that, at its best, Chaucer's translation, no matter how close or how minutely indebted to the original or to his French source, can become effective and indeed 'poetic' English prose in its own right. The kinds of excellence which he was able to attain in manipulating the sources of his poems, he can achieve no less, if less often and in a less sustained manner, in manipulating the sources of his prose.

If we are content to accept *Boece* as an uneven work, we are all the more gratified by the many passages of smoothly flowing, idiomatic, and at times poetic, prose. A pleasing balance may be achieved by juxtaposing two simple sentences in which the

36. An adverb *myswey* occurs in the English *Romaunt of the Rose* B, 4766.

familiar conjunctions are made inconspicuous by a controlled
rhythm and regulated word-order:

> For certes swich is the condicioun of alle mankynde, that oonly
> whan it hath knowynge of itself, thanne passeth it in noblesse alle
> othere thynges; and whan it forletith the knowynge of itself thanne
> it is brought bynethen alle beestes.
>
> (II, pr. 5, 149–54)

A small change in the word-order of a repeated phrase may effectively aid the rhythm:

> The see hath eek his ryght *to ben somtyme* calm and blaundysschyng
> with smothe watir, and *somtyme to ben* horrible with wawes and with
> tempestes;
>
> (II, pr. 2, 43–6)

here also, the two contrasting phrases are differently constructed
(two adjectives followed by one noun: one adjective followed by
two nouns), but without disturbing the overall balance. The
basic suggestion for the contrast is in Boethius '(nunc strato
aequore blandiri, nunc procellis ac fluctibus inhorrescere', *ibid.*
25–7), and is developed by Jean de Meun, but the final form is
Chaucer's. Sometimes Chaucer achieves a pithy, proverbial simplicity by combining the meaning of the Latin ('illa fallit, haec
instruit', II, pr. 8, 11) with the diction of the French ('l'amiable
les deçoit; la contraire les enseingne', *ibid.* 11–12), producing
characteristic English rhythms:

> The amyable Fortune desceyveth folk; the contrarie Fortune techeth
>
> (*ibid.* 17–19)

– and sometimes he achieves an almost biblical rhetoric. The
following is the complete *Metrum* 3 of Book III, and, though its
beginning is mistranslated, the whole flows richly on and Chaucer's 'bytynge bysynesse' is a splendid rendering of Boethius's
'cura mordax':

> Al weere it so that a riche coveytous man hadde a ryver or a goter
> fletynge al of gold, yit sholde it nevere staunchen his covetise;
> and though he hadde his nekke charged with precyous stones of the
> Rede See, and though he do ere his feeldes plentevous with an
> hundred oxen, nevere ne schal his bytynge bysynesse forleeten hym
> whil he lyveth, ne the lyghte richesses ne schal nat beren hym
> companye whan he is deed.
>
> (III, m. 3)

The closest to 'bytynge bysynesse' is 'the bytynges of bysynesse' in III, pr. 5, 29, and perhaps the 'swety [i.e. sweaty] bysinesse' of *The Former Age*, 28, but there are numerous other individual phrases in *Boece* which linger in the memory: 'the issues of delices ben sorweful and sorye' (III, pr. 7, 11–12); 'his weeply songes' (III, m. 12, 6); 'and autumpne comith ayein hevy of apples' (IV, m. 6, 32–3);[37] 'God seeth in o strok of thought alle thinges that ben, or weren, or schollen comen' (V, m. 2, 11–13); 'oothre beestis, by the wandrynge lyghtnesse of hir wynges beten the wyndes' (V, m. 5, 5–7).

In his handling of dialogue between Boethius and the Lady Philosophy, Chaucer achieves for the most part an easy, colloquial verisimilitude which owes a good deal, one imagines, to his earlier poems, particularly the conversation between Traveller and Eagle in *The House of Fame*. Brief interrogatives like 'Why so?', 'Why nat?', 'What is that?', 'What elles?' establish a natural tone of voice, as do answers like 'Right so it is' or 'That is sooth' or 'I graunte it' or, simply 'Yis'. The speeches of the two characters are generally long, abstruse, stylised, but their dialogue aptly reminds us that they are conversing, and for all its classical ancestry and occasional Gallicisms, Chaucer's rendering of it has its immediate roots in genuine fourteenth-century English conversation:

'Demestow nat,' quod sche, 'that alle thing that profiteth is good?'
'Yis,' quod I.
'And certes thilke thing that exerciseth or corrigith profitith?'
'I confesse it wel,' quod I.
'Thanne is it good', quod sche.
'Why nat?' quod I.
'But this is the fortune', quod sche, 'of hem that eyther ben put in vertu and batayllen ayein aspre thingis, or elles of hem that eschuen and declynen fro vices and taken the weye of vertu.'
'This ne mai I nat denye,' quod I.
'But what seistow of the merye fortune that is yeven to goode folk in gerdoun? Demeth aught the peple that it is wikkid?'
'Nay forsothe,' quod I; 'but thei demen, as it soth is, that it is ryght good.'

37. Chaucer introduced *autumn* into English in *Boece*, where it occurs four times. Earlier, at *Boece* I, m. 5, 25, he had taken care to define *autumpne* in a gloss as '*that is to seie, in the laste ende of somer*'. He does not use the word anywhere else.

'And what seistow of that othir fortune, ' quod sche, 'that, although it be aspre and restreyneth the schrewes by ryghtful torment, weneth aught the peple that it be good?'

'Nay,' quod I. . . .

(IV, pr. 7, 34–57)

In a sense, the translation of Boethius's *Consolatio* came at a strategic moment in Chaucer's career as a poet. It provided him with a ready-made framework within which he could experiment with words and phrases, rhythms, and sentence patterns quite different from those of the 'early poetry' that lay behind him. It enabled him also to come to grips with Boethius's thought, by laying it bare, examining it at leisure, expanding it, turning it over, as it were, with the help of a flexible style and a growing word power. When he returned in his subsequent poems to render some of Boethius's passages again, this time into verse, the result is all the better for the trial run in prose. It is easy to dismiss the prose as immature, heavy-handed, even ugly, compared with the succinctness and pleasing movement of most of the verse, but it is just as easy, and critically no more helpful, to dismiss the Eagle or the Goose for not being more like Chauntecleer. The point of contrasting passages from *Boece* with corresponding passages in the poems is not to render the former absurd by comparison, but to illustrate Chaucer's growing mastery of English expression; for the prose is not always by any means indifferent, or even bad, nor is the verse invariably a great step forward. The Boethian 'At, omnium mortalium stolidissime, si manere incipit, fors esse desistit' (II, pr. 1, 60–2) is well turned by Chaucer, with some help from the French version, into 'O thow fool of alle mortel foolis! Yif Fortune bygan to duelle stable, she cessede thanne to ben Fortune' (*ibid.* 113–15). When Pandarus picks up the same thought (without actually addressing Troilus as 'O thow fool of alle mortel foolis!') he introduces the image of Fortune's wheel, however much a medieval cliché, but he also has to have recourse to the ubiquitous word *thyng*, which here, in the adverbial phrase 'any thyng' means 'at any time', and in sixteen words of verse does not really improve upon the twelve of the prose:

'For if hire whiel stynte any thyng to torne,
Than cessed she Fortune anon to be.'

(*Tr* I, 848–9)

Nor is the Chaucerian tag always an improvement upon a simple, unencumbered prose sentence, as when 'al this accordaunce of thynges is bounde with love' (II, m. 8, 13–14) becomes

> 'Love, that knetteth lawe of compaignie,
> And couples doth in vertu for to dwelle,
> Bynd this acord, that I have told and telle.'
> *(Tr* III, 1748–50)

But where the change is from prosiness and involute prose syntax to the stark economy of disciplined verse, the uplift is invigorating A wordy sentence, complete with gloss, like 'Thanne, yif it so be that thow art myghty over thyself *(that is to seyn, by tranquillite of thi soule),* than hastow thyng in thi power that thow noldest nevere leesen, ne Fortune may nat bynymen it the' *(Bo* II, pr. 4, 134–8), becomes metamorphosed into a single line in which the central thought is uttered with memorable simplicity:

> And he that hath himself hath suffisaunce.
> *(Fort* 26)

Many other examples of similar transformation could be adduced. Jefferson (p. 67) offers a line by line comparison of *Boece* II, m. 8 with *Troilus and Criseyde* III, 1744–64, in which the most striking juxtaposition is the sentence in lines 16–21 of *Boece*, in Robinson's numbering,

> And yif this love slakede the bridelis, alle thynges that now loven hem togidres wolden make batayle contynuely, and stryven to fordo the fassoun of this world, the which they now leden in accordable feith by fayre moevynges,

with lines 1762–4 of *Troilus and Criseyde*:

> 'And if that Love aught lete his bridel go,
> Al that now loveth asondre sholde lepe,
> And lost were al that Love halt now to-hepe.'

We may prefer Theseus's 'faire cheyne of love', twice repeated in the concluding moments of *The Knight's Tale* (2988, 2991) in a 'Boethian' speech of much power and sonority; yet one cannot deny that the prose too, that same *Metrum* 8 of *Boece* II, has its moments of dignity, its stately turns of phrase, like the corresponding 'al this accordaunce of thynges is bounde with love'

(13–14), which are worthy of our approbation in their own right, and of our close attention as paving the way for the poetry that was to come.

Chaucer's remaining prose work is *The Tale of Melibee*, told by the pilgrim Chaucer as his second contribution to *The Canterbury Tales* after the fiasco of *Sir Thopas*. It thus belongs to *The Canterbury Tales* as *The Parson's Tale* does, and, like the latter, it is full of *sentence*. Both tales are described as *vertuous* and as *murye*; both tales are translations, the Parson's probably from the French, *Melibee* indisputably so. And there the resemblance ends.

In order to understand the functional difference between the two prose tales within the scheme of *The Canterbury Tales* it is worth pausing over their respective introductions. The Parson, in words which have become notorious as a supposedly derogatory comment by Chaucer on contemporary alliterative verse[38] –

> 'But trusteth wel, I am a Southren man,
> I kan nat geeste "rum, ram, ruf," by lettre' –
> > (*CT* X, 42–3)

dismisses such verse, as well as rhyming verse –

> 'Ne, God woot, rym holde I but litel bettre' –
> > (*ibid.* 44)

as inappropriate for the 'vertuous sentence' with which he proposes to end the story-telling. He chooses prose, for reasons which we have already considered, and he adds a disclaimer to absolute literal accuracy:

> 'But nathelees, this meditacioun
> I putte it ay under correccioun
> Of clerkes,'
> > (*ibid.* 55–7)

for the good, if modest, reason (echoed, as we noted earlier, towards the end of the tale) that he is not *textueel*, not well versed in texts. The Manciple, in the tale just ended, had similarly (and indeed, twice over) claimed that he was 'noght textueel' (*MancT* 235, 316), but in the trivial context of a worldly tale, so that the Parson's use of the same word so soon after (a word not used

---

38. S. S. Hussey, for example, in *Chaucer: An Introduction* (London, 1971), p. 118, writes that the Parson 'cannot compose alliterative poetry which he seems to regard as monotonous and old-fashioned'.

elsewhere by Chaucer) is yet another hint that worldly vanities are now going to be placed into a heavenly perspective. For the Parson's texts are not 'fables and swich wrecchednesse' but 'moralitee and vertuous mateere', the Scriptures and the Fathers, and in their proper interpretation and exposition he 'wol stonde to correccioun' (*CT* X, 60), although he understands their meaning well enough:

> 'I take but the sentence, trusteth weel.'
> (*ibid.* 58)

The Parson is everything we expect him to be from earlier acquaintance, except short-winded, so that there is a final, gently ironic touch in one of the last lines of verse of *The Canterbury Tales*, before the prose takes over, as the Host says to the priest:

> 'Beth fructuous, and that in litel space.'
> (*ibid.* 71)

Chaucer does not use *fructuous* elsewhere so that we cannot measure its exact meaning accurately from his own usage—a common enough difficulty with Chaucer; but the primary meaning of the word elsewhere in Middle English is 'fruitful, prolific, luxuriant, fertile', whence the derived sense of '(spiritually fertile), edifying'. *The Parson's Tale* is certainly edifying, but it is also 'prolific', albeit not 'in litel space'; to almost his last line of poetry Chaucer's sense of humour and his verbal playfulness keep him company. And Harry Bailly's wishful 'and that in litel space' is surely inspired by his, and the other pilgrims', experience earlier in the proceedings when, 'stinted' of his 'beste rym', the pilgrim Chaucer got his own back by asking to be allowed, this time, to 'tellen al my tale' and thereupon treating his audience to 'a litel thyng in prose' in the shape of the prodigious *Tale of Melibee*. Once bitten.

Twice the narrator of *Sir Thopas* refers to his forthcoming prose tale as *litel* (*CT* VII, 937, 957)[39] in a prologue that affords several ironic hints of what is to come. The length of *Melibee* is, however, only one ingredient in a complex ironic pattern. There

39. Huppé's thesis that 'this litel tretys' refers not to *The Tale of Melibee*, which Chaucer is introducing here, but to *The Canterbury Tales* as a whole (pp. 235 f.) seems to me quite untenable. To refer to the whole work, even up to this point, as a 'little' narrative would have been just silly, whereas such a reference to *Melibee* is wholly in keeping with the delightful irony of the dramatic situation.

is even greater emphasis in the prologue to *Melibee* upon the contrast between the manner in which the tale is to be narrated and its moral import, its *sentence*. The latter word is repeated five times in less than twenty lines: clearly, Chaucer was anxious to establish his credentials as a moralist, as far as the significance (*sentence*) of the tale was concerned, while allowing himself unrestricted freedom to shape the narrative as he pleased:

'And though I nat the same wordes seye
As ye han herd, yet to yow alle I preye
Blameth me nat.'

(*CT* VII, 959–61)

The point is made more than once, and the analogy with the four evangelists a few lines earlier, whose substance is the same although their *tellyng* may be different, is perhaps appropriate enough to the virtuous counsels of Melibeus's wife, but must at the same time strike one as delightfully incongruous coming from the pilgrim who had just perpetrated *Sir Thopas*. Chaucer was obviously going to tell this 'litel thyng in prose' in some way different from what his audience, who were probably familiar with the outline of the tale of Melibeus and Prudence, might have been expecting. He gives us one specific hint:

'As thus, though that I telle somwhat moore
Of proverbes than ye han herd bifoore
Comprehended in this litel tretys heere. . . .'

(*CT* VII, 955–7)

Perhaps he had his own Pandarus in mind, who trails as long a string of proverbs through *Troilus and Criseyde* as Prudence does in *Melibee*, so that quite early in the piece Troilus is made to exclaim impatiently:

'Lat be thyne olde ensaumples, I the preye.'

(*Tr* I, 760)

For the rest, the tale itself reveals the full extent of Chaucer's joke. But by now the difference in the tone of the prologue to *Melibee* and that of the prologue to *The Parson's Tale* will be obvious. The Parson modestly points to his limitations as a scholar and accepts full responsibility for any imperfections in his sermon; the pilgrim Chaucer announces that, while the significance of his tale is the same as that of other versions, his version is going to be rather

different in the telling. From the maker of *The Nun's Priest's Tale*
such an announcement should occasion no surprise, and yet
hardly any reader of Chaucer appears to have paid adequate
attention to just what Chaucer the pilgrim is saying and doing
here and in *The Tale of Melibee*. Certainly, the tale is not a hoax in
the sense that Chaucer wished to deny its moral point of view;
nor is it simply the offended pilgrim's 'revenge' for having his
recitation of *Sir Thopas* curtailed. E. Talbot Donaldson comes
close to the truth, as I see it, when he speaks of the tale's 'lack of
literary qualities and of any real imagination' as 'nicely suited to
the demonstrated capabilities of the pilgrim Chaucer'.[40] But it is
possible to go further than that, to hear in *Melibee* the final peal of
that 'laughter in the grand style' which Chesterton heard ringing
through the whole *Sir Thopas* episode,[41] and to augment Chesterton's words – 'among all the types and trades, the coarse miller,
the hard-fisted reeve, the clerk, the cook, the shipman, the poet is
the only man who knows no poetry ' – by adding that the poet
knows no prose either.

The reader of this chapter may have wondered at some point
why I kept my discussion of *The Tale of Melibee* to the last. The
answer is that I wanted to demonstrate that Chaucer was capable
of writing perfectly competent English prose, indeed at times
good and even poetic English prose, before offering my suggestion that the prose of *Melibee* is *deliberately* burlesqued, as deliberately as the verse of *Sir Thopas* is *drasty* doggerel.[42] That this was
indeed Chaucer's intention the elaborate prologue to *Melibee* is
presumably designed to announce.

The chief linguistic characteristics of *The Tale of Melibee* are
a close reliance upon the French original of Renaud de Louens,
coupled with a tendency to make the English increasingly prolix,
diffuse, verbose as the tale proceeds, and a heavy infusion of tags,
clichés, and repetitive phrases – the prose equivalents of the
clichés in *Sir Thopas*. The tale begins, as several critics have noted,
with an almost metrically recurring rhythm, as if pilgrim Chaucer

40. Donaldson, p. 937.

41. G. K. Chesterton, *Chaucer* (London, 1932, repr. 1962), ch. 1.

42. The word *drasty*, used by Chaucer only in the two references to *Sir Thopas* (*CT*
VII, 923, 930) means 'foul, filthy, trashy', and has the same connotations as the
modern English 'crap', on which see *A Supplement to the Oxford English Dictionary*,
ed. R. W. Burchfield (Oxford, 1972), *s.v. crap*.

was determined to prove to his audience that though he could not recite good verse he didn't mind having a go at metrical prose. But this is not sustained for long. Instead, Chaucer concentrates increasingly upon ways of augmenting and elaborating upon his French original, not for purposes of rhetorical amplification, nor to clarify the meaning (which generally becomes more obscure), but presumably in order to create a kind of mock-didactic style which, much as with the mock-heroics of *The Nun's Priest's Tale*, makes fun of the *tellyng* without ridiculing the *moralite*.

The basis for the augmentation is in Renaud who is certainly fond of doublets: 'souffisant et raisonnable' (110),[43] 'chascun brait et crie' (187), 'chargeuse et ennuyeuse' (449), and so on. Chaucer took the hint with a vengeance. Hence the simple 'celui qui est oiseux' (874) becomes 'he that is ydel and casteth hym to no bisynesse ne occupacioun' (*Mel* 1591); 'a bonne fin' (1026) becomes unto a good conclusioun and to a good ende' (1727); 'et reçupt leur obligation par leur serement et sur leurs pleges' (1126-7) becomes 'and receyved hire obligaciouns and hir boondes by hire othes upon hire plegges and borwes' (1828), and so forth. By augmenting much further than Renaud, Chaucer inevitably clogs up the movement of his prose where the French achieves a much smoother flow of language. This trend, apparent throughout the tale, becomes glaringly obvious towards the end; compare, for example, Renaud's

> Quant Mellibee ot oÿ toutes les paroles Dame Prudence et ses sages enseignemens, si fut en grant paix de cuer et loa Dieu, qui lui avoit donné si sage compagnie, (1169-71)

with Chaucer's

> Whanne Melibee hadde herd the grete skiles and resouns of dame Prudence, and hire wise informaciouns and techynges, / his herte gan enclyne to the wil of his wif, considerynge hir trewe entente, / and conformed hym anon, and assented fully to werken after hir conseil; / and thonked God, of whom procedeth al vertu and alle goodnesse, that hym sente a wyf of so greet discrecioun. (1870-3)

Indeed, it is this mode of verbal inflation which is the main instrument of Chaucer's mock-didactic technique. Doublets of

43. For the source of the quotations from Renaud's *Livre de Mellibée et Prudence*, see note 16 above. The line references are to this edition.

the kind favoured by Renaud occur in Chaucer's own *Parson's Tale*, as they do in the sermons of Wyclif or the spiritual writings of Richard Rolle,[44] and their exaggerated over-use in *The Tale of Melibee* is the direct counterpart to the use and misuse of over-worked romance clichés in *Sir Thopas*. But doublets are not the only means of verbal inflation. There is hardly a sentence in Renaud's *Livre* which Chaucer does not expand. Renaud's Mellibee becomes, characteristically, 'this Melibeus' in many instances; and even Renaud's simple 'une fille' (9) in the opening sentence becomes puffed up into 'a doghter which that called was Sophie' (967), which happens to be a proper decasyllabic metrical line. A single French verb, 'et se humilie' (361), becomes 'and maketh thee chiere of humylitee' (1187); a single French pronoun, 'a vous' (1123), becomes, absurdly, 'to the excellence and benignitee of youre gracious lordshipe' (1821). As the process reaches its climax, Chaucer abandons his source almost completely, leaving Renaud, whose style and diction have remained constant throughout, far behind; thus

'. . . et vous prions a genoulz et en lermes que vous ayez de nous pitié et misericorde', (1124–5)

grows into a monstrous

'. . . bisekynge yow that of youre merciable pitee ye wol considere oure grete repentaunce and lowe submyssioun, / and graunten us foryevenesse of oure outrageous trespas and offense. / For wel we knowe that youre liberal grace and mercy strecchen hem ferther into goodnesse than doon oure outrageouse giltes and trespas into wikkednesse, / al be it that cursedly and dampnablely we han agilt agayn youre heigh lordshipe'. (1823–6)

Despite the inflated diction, the syntax of *The Tale of Melibee* remains for the most part well under control. Most of the sentences are surprisingly short, Chaucer preferring, once again, to co-ordinate rather than to subordinate them. The familiar conjunctions, adverbs, and adverbial phrases are used, but even here occasional eccentricities occur, like 'and for as muche as that' (1267), instead of his normal 'and for as muche as', of which there

---

44. Cp., for example, the opening lines of chapter 2 of Rolles' *Form of Living*: 'For þat þou has forsakyn þe solace and þe joy of þis world, and taken þe to solitary lyf, for Gods luf to suffer tribulacion and anguys here . . .' (*English Writings of Richard Rolle*, ed. Hope Emily Allen (Oxford, 1931, repr. 1963), p. 89).

is only one other instance in his work, without *and*, in *Boece* III, pr. 10, 55. In addition the syntax is reinforced by many a *certes*, *soothly*, *God woot*, and one solitary *pardee* (1537, where the French (803) has *certes*) to link the sentences into what one writer has aptly called a 'relentlessly sententious' narrative.[45] But on occasions Chaucer's close adherence to the French causes him to depart from normal English usage and to produce un-English idioms or syntax. As he obviously knew enough English to distinguish idiomatic from unidiomatic usage, one can only conclude that these departures from the norm were as deliberate as the rest of the linguistic and stylistic complexion of *The Tale of Melibee*. This view receives strong support from a relatively late dating of the tale, about 1390, which is currently favoured by several authorities. By this time Chaucer had accomplished his *Boece* in prose and much of his poetry, and was about to embark upon the *Astrolabe* and possibly *The Parson's Tale*. To suppose therefore that he was incapable of producing normal English idioms and syntactical patterns would be as foolish as to imagine that he expected the bloated diction of much of *Melibee* or the mock-heroic 'apparatus' of *The Nun's Priest's Tale* to be taken at their face value. Hence such literal renderings from the French as 'to wepen *in* the deeth of hire child' (977) for 'de plorer en la mort de son enfant' (24), where normal usage is 'wepen for', as in

> Thus for your deth I may wel wepe and pleyne;
> (*Pity* 118)

or 'thou shalt also have in suspect' (1197) for 'tu dois avoir en suspect' (377); or 'hou ye shul have yow' (1575) for 'comment tu te dois avoir' (854).

The vocabulary of *The Tale of Melibee* is simpler than that of the other prose works. Chaucer may have been playing with the *tellyng*, but if the *sentence* was to be as edifying as, say, the Nun's Priest's *moralite*, the meaning must not be lost amid the increasing luxuriance of the diction. Only about a dozen words are used in *Melibee* which do not figure elsewhere in Chaucer's works, and another dozen or two are of very restricted occurrence elsewhere.

---

45. Donald MacDonald, 'Proverbs, *Sententiae*, and *Exempla* in Chaucer's Comic Tales: The Function of Comic Misapplication', *Speculum* XLI (1966), 457. The words are here applied specifically to Prudence, but they may be appropriately extended to the whole tale.

Among the former are: *anoyful* (1032), which here renders Fr.
ennuyeuse (109) and is not recorded elsewhere in Middle English,
although its meaning must have been obvious from cognate
words like *anoyinge* or *anoyouse* 'troublesome'; *artelries* (1333)
'ballistic engines', not recorded before Chaucer, but clear enough
from the context 'armure, and artelries'; *chyncherie* (1600) 'miserli-
ness', not recorded before Chaucer, although the adjective
chynche (1603, 1619) is used by other fourteenth-century writers;
hastifnesse (1122, 1133, 1246) is also found in other fourteenth-
century works, as is the adjective *hastif* 'quick, swift, urgent',
which Chaucer uses in other Canterbury tales and in *Troilus and
Criseyde*, as well as in *Melibee*.

Among the words of very restricted occurrence are: *edifices*,
first used by Chaucer in *Boece* and not previously recorded, whose
meaning in *Melibee* is quite clear from the context 'castelles and
othere manere edifices' (1333) and 'heighe toures, and grete edifices' (1336); the verb *examyne* is used by Chaucer only in *Melibee*
and *Boece*, but is recorded earlier in the century, whereas the noun
examynacion was apparently first used by Chaucer (in *Mel* 1267, in a
context in which the verb also occurred), a fact which I would
gladly hide from the eyes of examination-ridden students; *indulgence* is a word with a technical ecclesiastical meaning in the
fourteenth and fifteenth centuries and occurs in the writings of
Wyclif, in *Piers Plowman*, and elsewhere, but Chaucer uses it only
twice, in *Melibee*, 1774, meaning 'mercy, leniency', and in the
Wife of Bath's

> And for to been a wyf he yaf me leve
> Of indulgence,
>
> *(WBT 83–4)*

'he granted me, as a concession, leave to become a wife'; *renovelled*
'renewed' in *Melibee*, 1846, is translated straight from Renaud's
renouvellee (1146), but the verb had been used once in *Boece* (III,
pr. 11, 124) and is used by Chaucer elsewhere: once in the prose
of *The Parson's Tale* (1027) and once in the verse of *The Complaint
of Mars* (19), while the noun *renovelaunces* occurs once in *The House
of Fame*, 693.

Although for the most part these rare or nonce words in
Chaucer's prose vocabulary are of romance origin, there are
some exceptions. Such a one is the word *honycombes* in *Melibee*,

1113, from O.E. *hunig-camb*, which Chaucer uses only once elsewhere, in the unique sense as a term of endearment in Absolon's
cooing address to his beloved:

> 'What do ye, hony-comb, sweete Alisoun,
> My faire bryd, my sweete cynamome?'
>
> *(MillT* 3698–9)

The use of adjectives as nouns is not uncommon in Middle English, and there is a number of examples in Chaucer's verse, many
of them in rhyme. In the prose there are fewer cases, one of which,
in *Melibee*, 1037—'oon of thise olde wise' (corresponding to the
French 'un des anciens' 123) – is exactly paralleled by 'thise olde
wyse' in rhyme in *The Canon's Yeoman's Tale*, 1067. Pandarus also
talks of 'thise wyse' *(Tr* I, 742).

A literal rendering of the French 'freres ne cousins germains'
(596) into 'bretheren, ne cosyns germayns' (1368) preserves the
French adjectival plural in a combination in which Middle English usage fluctuates somewhat. The *MED* records *inter alia*
'doȝhters and susters german', 'bretheren germain', 'bothe cosin
germains', besides 'breþeren germayns', all from the fourteenth
and fifteenth centuries. The positioning of adjectives in *The Tale
of Melibee* is as flexible as in Chaucer's other prose works: 'youre
trewe frendes olde and wise' (1244), 'sweete temporeel richesses'
(1411); but it is possible to discern occasional method in Chaucer's
practice. In the following passage Chaucer places the adjective
before the noun where the French omits the noun altogether, but
after the noun where the French adjective is similarly placed. The
fact that the three preposed adjectives *fer, almyghty, neer,* are all of
Old English origin, whereas the postposed ones are Romance,
may well be a factor contributing to their positioning. The phrase
'almyghty God' renders simply *Dieu*:

> The fer cause is almyghty God, that is cause of alle thynges. / The
> neer cause is thy thre enemys. / The cause accidental was hate. / The
> cause material been the fyve woundes of thy doghter. / The cause
> formal is the manere of hir werkynge that broghten laddres and
> cloumben in at thy wyndowes. / The cause final was for to sle thy
> doghter. (1396–1401)

Word order not directly involving adjectives is varied occasionally
for rhetorical purposes as in the repeated 'up roos thanne an

advocat' (1021), 'up roos tho oon of thise olde wise' (1037), 'up stirten thanne the yonge folk' (1035), but such cases are rare. For the most part the relentless greyness of the tale is unrelieved by such rhetorical colours.

That *The Tale of Melibee* has bored modern readers and bothered the critics is not surprising. Its unusual combination of sententious counselling and bloated diction puts it in a class by itself, akin only to *Sir Thopas* and *The Nun's Priest's Tale* with which, as well as with the tales of Shipman, Prioress, and Monk, it is linked in Group B, Robinson's VII, of *The Canterbury Tales*. The grouping is presumably not accidental, for the group contains the only two tales cut short by higher authority, as it were, separated from each other by *Melibee*, preceded by the Prioress's with its 'idiom . . . sustained by liturgical reminiscences'.[46] and followed by the Nun's Priest's, in which a moral is presented by means of another familiar story made different in the *tellyng*. To assume that into such a carefully wrought pattern of tales Chaucer placed such a lengthy piece of extravagant prose without some ulterior artistic motive seems to me too naive to be acceptable. To regard the poet as simply revealing himself here as a 'counselor of prudence' is as shortsighted as to regard *Sir Thopas* as mainly a piece of literary criticism.[47] Chaucer is not a straightforward didactic writer, but when he wishes to write straightforward didactic prose, in an unmistakably serious manner, then he does so, and announces it as such, in *The Parson's Tale*. For *The Parson's Tale*, with its range of diction and variety of rhetorical effects is, for all its length and flaws, a not unworthy piece of medieval didactic prose. To attempt to burlesque the style of such a piece without, however, losing its *sentence* was no easy task even for as accomplished a writer as Chaucer was at the beginning of the last decade of his life. Yet this is what I believe he tried to do in *The Tale of Melibee*. There are three possibilities regarding this tale: first, that Chaucer could not do any better; secondly, that he thought this mode of writing it appropriate and effective, perhaps even beautiful; thirdly, that he was being funny. The first is disproved by the amount of much

---

46. G. H. Russell, 'Chaucer: The Prioress's Tale', in *Medieval Literature and Civilization: Studies in Memory of G. N. Garmonsway*, ed. D. A. Pearsall and R. A. Waldron (London, 1969), p. 214. Russell also argues well for the deliberate contrasting of *The Prioress's Tale* with the preceding *Shipman's Tale*.

47. Cp. Paul G. Ruggiers, *The Art of the Canterbury Tales* (Madison, 1965), p. 21.

better prose writing, of various kinds from the simple to the ornate, which Chaucer has left us. The second is the view of many critics who, like Margaret Schlauch, have spoken admiringly of the 'heightened colour' and 'dignified style and high seriousness' of the work.[48] This would be acceptable, even with some reservations, if the style of *Melibee* and particularly its diction were sustained at an acceptably 'heightened' level throughout. But there comes a point beyond which lies not sublimity but bathos, and this point Chaucer reaches well before the end of his tale when bloated circumlocution, which he had been rehearsing all along, is given full play. The third possibility makes the best sense of the grouping of the tales at this point and of the *Sir Thopas-Melibee* episode as a whole. It makes sense also of the close proximity of *Melibee* and *The Nun's Priest's Tale*, and it makes sense of the peculiar linguistic and stylistic complexion of *The Tale of Melibee* in which Chaucer put his ability to manipulate English prose for an original purpose to a severe test indeed. That in the final analysis the mock-didactic prose of *Melibee* is nowhere near as successfully realized as the mock-heroic verse of *The Nun's Priest's Tale* is not so much an indication of Chaucer's failure as a prose writer as a tribute to his greatness as a poet.

48. Margaret Schlauch, 'The Art of Chaucer's Prose' in D. S. Brewer, ed., *Chaucer and Chaucerians: Critical Studies in Middle English Literature* (London, 1966), pp. 155 f.

CHAPTER 4

Cherles Termes

🔊🔊🔊🔊🔊🔊

The Miller's Tale and *The Reeve's Tale* are probably Chaucer's most ingenious linguistic *jeux d'esprit*, the one allowing full play to what Donaldson has called his 'genius for devaluation',[1] the other a unique medieval exercise in the use of dialect for literary purposes. Both tales are fabliaux, rollicking bawdy stories about very earthy characters doing very earthy things like petting and pissing, fighting and farting, stealing and 'swyving'. And common to both is the colloquial, idiomatic English of the village street, and smithy, of mill and cottage, of labourers and petty officials and wenches – what the Reeve himself in determining to outdo the Miller's tale calls 'his cherles termes' (*RvT* 3917). I propose in this chapter to interpret this phrase very widely, to include Chaucer's colloquial English as it appears in vocabulary, idiom, syntax, and figurative usage, as well as his use of vulgarisms and their attendant euphemisms, of various modes of address, and of the interjections and exclamations, except for oaths and asseverations, which are scattered so lavishly throughout all his poetry. Chaucer's swearing deserves a chapter to itself.

Relatively little close attention has been paid to Chaucer's colloquial English. Twenty years ago Margaret Schlauch wrote a short pioneering article[2] which followed close upon Donaldson's on *The Miller's Tale* just cited; H. S. Bennett, Wolfgang Clemen and some other critics have commented on colloquial elements in the poems;[3] hence it is upon these and a few other small, if solid, foundations that the present chapter must be constructed. One of the difficulties, of course, is to recognize the popular idiom of

1. Donaldson, *Speaking*, p. 28.

2. Margaret Schlauch, 'Chaucer's Colloquial English: Its Structural Traits', *PMLA* LXXVII (1952), 1103–16. There are also some scattered remarks in Gösta Langenfelt's work of forty years ago, *Select Studies in Colloquial English of the Late Middle Ages* (Lund, 1933), especially pp. 36 ff.

3. H. S. Bennett, *Chaucer and the Fifteenth Century* (Oxford, 1947), pp. 78, 84–6; Clemen, pp. 62–3, 119–20, 152, 160–1.

Chaucer's day without such modern aids as dictionaries of Middle English slang and unconventional English, recordings of uneducated speech, and the like. In such circumstances conjecture becomes unavoidable, particularly because Chaucer does not make our task any easier by mingling what appears to be genuinely colloquial fourteenth-century English with moments of much more stylized utterance. Often this may well be deliberate characterization. The Reeve, for example, is crude enough when describing the nocturnal activities at Trumpington mill, but he is also rather given to *sermonyng* (*RvT* 3899), which explains his occasional leaning towards words like *esement* (4179, 4186), often found in legal contexts, which he uses with a meaning, 'redress', apparently all his own in the fourteenth century, or *disparage* (4271) in which he combines the two senses of 'to degrade socially' (in which sense the Wife of Bath once uses the word, *WBT* 1069) and 'to defile a woman' (in which the Clerk once uses it, as a noun, *CLT* 908).

A further difficulty is provided by Chaucer's own irrepressibly colloquial tone. No other English poet is so thoroughly addicted to conversational comments, tags, interjections, asides, expletives like *parde*, and all the rest of them, even in his most serious moments, as when the Legend of Cleopatra closes with

> I preye God let oure hedes nevere ake!
> (*LGW* 705)

or as when yet another 'dar I seye' creeps into one of the last, devout stanzas of *Troilus and Criseyde* (V, 1845). Chaucer is not alone among his contemporaries in being able to reproduce colloquial registers of speech; even so unlikely a poem as *Pearl* has instances.[4] But Chaucer is unique in having made an unmistakably colloquial tone the characteristic mode of all his major poetry, and of much of his prose as well. This is no artlessness, however, no native woodnote wild; for Chaucer's most seemingly artless (it used to be customary to call them 'naive') verses are often wrought with particular skill. Even Harry Bailly's 'spontaneous' outbursts throughout *The Canterbury Tales* are most skilfully contrived. When *The Shipman's Tale* is concluded, the Host launches into a typically colloquial piece:

4. Cp. A. C. Spearing, *The Gawain-Poet: A Critical Study* (Cambridge, 1970), p. 158.

'Wel seyd, by *corpus dominus*', quod oure Hoost,
'Now longe moote thou saille by the cost,
Sie gentil maister, gentil maryneer!
God yeve the monk a thousand last quade yeer!
A ha! felawes! beth ware of swich a jape!
The monk putte in the mannes hood an ape,
And in his wyves eek, by Seint Austyn!
Draweth no monkes moore unto youre in.'

(CT VII, 435–42)

Harry Bailly is one of a select few who use *corpus* in their swearing and the 'vulgar' Latin *corpus dominus* is uniquely his. On the other hand, the reference to 'Seint Austyn' in the context of the Ship-man's monk is a well-contrived echo of the latter's own

'God and seint Austyn spede yow and gyde!'

(ShipT 259)

and further back still of the two allusions to 'Austyn' in the pilgrim Monk's portrait (*Gen Prol* 187–8). The Shipman's knowledge of the coast 'fro Gootlond to the cape of Fynystere' (*ibid.* 408), and the fact that he was 'a good felawe' (395) are similarly recalled. The familiarity with things Flemish which he shares with his maker may be alluded to in the Host's use of the Flemish word *quade* 'bad, evil', which elsewhere the Cook quotes in a Flemish proverb:

But 'sooth pley, quaad pley,' as the Flemyng seith,

(CT I, 4357)

while the idiom itself, 'a thousand last quade yeer', which means literally 'a thousand loads of bad years' is appropriate enough, addressed to the Shipman, as well as unmistakably colloquial. So also is the phrase 'to put an ape in someone's hood', that is to make a fool of them, which plays on the common use of *ape* in the sense of 'dupe', as well as reminding the audience that the Shipman himself was as adept at duping merchants as was the 'daun John' of his tale.[5] The approbatory 'wel seyd' and 'sie gentil maister, gentil maryneer' are as much in character as the exclamatory 'a ha! felawes!', so that the whole passage is revealed as a most skilfully wrought texture of subtle allusions, echoes, ironies, colloquial

5. Pandarus has a similar expression: 'Loke alwey that ye fynde / Game in myn hood', i.e. make fun of me (*Tr* II, 1109–10).

idioms, and unique traits of character. And yet it reads as easily and appears as artless as any piece of natural English speech.

Clearly, such close verbal analysis of Chaucer's verse is only possible in gobbets, and all we can hope to achieve in this chapter is to point to some characteristics of Chaucer's colloquial style and language in the expectation that this will help to illumine for the reader one aspect of Chaucer's art not much discussed hitherto. Although all Chaucer's poetry rings with his colloquial tone, the richest notes are of course heard in the mouths of his *cherles*, and of characters like the Host, the Wife of Bath, and Pandarus, together with an occasional *kakelynge* from goose and duck and eagle and cock and hen. Hence, many of the best illustrations will come from these.

Harry Bailly does not tell a story, he just talks, and so does the Wife of Bath in her long preamble; and it is in their talking, however artfully contrived, that many aspects of colloquial Middle English are exemplified. The irregular syntax of spoken English is mirrored in the concatenation of clauses and phrases not always co-ordinated according to any strict grammatical patterns, as one thought leads rapidly to the next:

'For, and I sholde rekenen every vice
Which that she hath, ywis I were to nyce;
And cause why, it sholde reported be
And toold to hire of somme of this meynee, –
Of whom, it nedeth nat for to declare,
Syn wommen konnen outen swich chaffare;
And eek my wit suffiseth nat therto,
To tellen al, wherfore my tale is do.'
(*CT* IV, 2433–40)

Other speakers use a similarly breathless syntax, as in this sentence from the Cook with its repeated *that*, each referring to a different antecedent:

And for ther is no theef withoute a lowke,
That helpeth hym to wasten and to sowke
Of that he brybe kan or borwe may,
Anon he sente his bed and his array
Unto a compeer of his owene sort,
That lovede dys, and revel, and disport,

And hadde a wyf that heeld for contenance
A shoppe, and swyved for hir sustenance.

(CkT 4415–22)

A complete break in syntactic structure is achieved by introducing
a subject, leaving it without a predicate, and finishing the sentence with a different subject and predicate:

For sikerly a prentys revelour
That haunteth dys, riot, or paramour,
His maister shal it in his shoppe abye,
Al have he no part of the mynstralcye.

(CkT 4391–4)

On the other hand, such a construction could be justified as an extended possessive, indicated by the complex noun-phrase 'a
prentys revelour . . . paramour' with a following possessive
pronoun *his*, equivalent to the not unusual, though normally less
complex, use of compound relatives of the type 'that . . . his'
(meaning 'whose'), or 'that . . . him' ('whom'):

That day by day to scole was *his* wone.

(PrT 504)

That now, on Monday last, I saugh *hym* wirche.

(MillT 3430)

Pronouns are often used carelessly in colloquial English, and
Chaucer mirrors this in several ways. A pronoun may be inserted
between a noun and its verb where the two are separated by
several intervening clauses and phrases:

Metellius, the foule cherl, the swyn,
That with a staf birafte his wyf hir lyf,
For she drank wyn, thogh I hadde been his wyf,
He sholde nat han daunted me fro drynke!

(WBT 460–3)

Similarly, the Wife of Bath repeats the object by a pronoun
where the normal word order is inverted, a complex noun phrase
being followed by a single substantive acting as subject:

And olde and angry nygardes of dispence,
God sende *hem* soone verray pestilence!

(WBT 1263–4)

A pronoun may have no immediate antecedent, as in the following instance where the repeated *he* refers not to the antecedent *God*, but to an understood *man*, last expressed as 'a good felawe' two sentences earlier:

> For God so wys be my savacioun,
> I ne loved nevere by no discrecioun,
> But evere folwede myn appetit,
> Al were *he* short, or long, or blak, or whit;
> I took no kep, so that *he* liked me,
> How poore *he* was, ne eek of what degree.
>
> *(WBT* 621–6)

Or a pronoun may be omitted altogether, whether in idiomatic turns of speech like 'bifel that' or 'nedeth namoore to', or in sudden conversational transition from one subject to another:

> And so I dide ful often, God it woot,
> That made his face often reed and hoot
> For verray shame, and blamed hymself for he
> Had toold to me so greet a pryvetee.
>
> *(WBT* 539–42)

Typical also of colloquial usage is the amplification of a preceding pronoun by an explanatory phrase, as in

> Til trewely we hadde swich daliance,
> This clerk and I,
>
> *(WBT* 565–6)

or the use of a pronoun to refer inaccurately not to the whole noun-phrase preceding it, but only to part of it, in this case *mouses*:

> I holde a mouses herte nat worth a leek
> That hath but oon hole for to sterte to.
>
> *(WBT* 572–3)

More typical perhaps of the Wife's somewhat wayward manner of speaking than of colloquial usage generally is the topsy-turvy use of *thee* for the plural and of *oure* for the singular as she resumes her personal history after a brief astrological excursus:

> But now to purpos, why I tolde *thee*
> That I was beten for a book, pardee!
> Upon a nyght Jankyn, that was *oure* sire,
> Redde on his book.
>
> *(WBT* 711–14)

A few lines further on (722), she uses *it* to refer to Samson's *heres*, and a few lines further on still, another colloquial *it* is allowed to intrude:

Of Clitermystra, for hire lecherye,
That falsly made hire housbonde for to dye,
He redde *it* with ful good devocioun.
(*WBT* 737–9)

Chaucer's use of *this* in a sense much weaker than the demonstrative, almost exactly that of the definite article (except that it can be used, unlike the article, before proper names) is a familiar feature of his language. It corresponds to a similar use in modern colloquial English. Examples abound: 'this monk', 'this gentil monk', 'this goode wyf', 'this chapman', from *The Shipman's Tale*; 'this hende Nicholas', 'this Absolon', 'this carpenter', 'this Alisoun', from *The Miller's Tale*;

In this meene while
This yeman gan a litel for to smyle;
(*FrT* 1445–6)

and so forth. The plural *thise* is used similarly: 'thise curatz', 'thise wykes two', from *The Summoner's Tale*; as well as in what Robinson has called (p. 674) 'a generalizing sense', as in the Wife of Bath's 'thise olde folk' (*WBT* 1004), or

Thise wormes, ne thise motthes, ne thise mytes,
(*WBT* 560)

or in the Knight's

As doon thise loveres in hir queynte geres.
(*KnT* 1531)

Conjunctions are sometimes used as carelessly as pronouns in colloquial English, but again it is only when we read rather than hear a sentence like the following that we detect faulty syntax:

And Absolon, hym fil no bet ne wers,
But with his mouth he kiste hir naked ers
Ful savourly, er he were war of this.
(*MillT* 3733–5)

Conjunctions may of course be omitted altogether, two sentences being asyndetically juxtaposed:

> Thou seyst men may nat kepe a castel wal,
> It may so longe assailled been over al.
>
> *(WBT* 263–4)

> 'I am adrad, by Seint Thomas,
> It stondeth nat aright with Nicholas.'
>
> *(MillT* 3425–6)

> And on a day it happed, in a stounde,
> Sik lay the maunciple on a maladye.
>
> *(RvT* 3992–3)

Prepositional usage sometimes differs from that of modern English, as in the Reeve's perhaps idiomatic 'this person . . . / In purpos was' *(RvT* 3977–8); the Summoner's 'parfourne up' *(SumT* 2261) and Troilus's 'perfourme it out' *(Tr* III, 417); the Summoner's 'I have be shryven . . . at my curat' *(SumT* 2095); or his variants 'fro this world bireve' and 'bireve out of this world' *(SumT* 2111, 2113). The Manciple *(CT* IX, 86) and the Franklin's Arveragus *(FranklT* 1481) both use the phrase 'up peyne of deeth', paralleled by the herald's 'up peyne of los of lyf' in *The Knight's Tale*, 2543. The Wife of Bath's odd use of *upon* in 'and wered upon my gaye scarlet gytes' *(WBT* 559) and *on* in 'that wereth on a coverchief or a calle' (1018) is probably a somewhat idiosyncratic variant of the common Middle English usage 'haven upon', to wear, found, for example, in the Friar's 'he hadde upon a courtepy of grene' *(FrT* 1382).

Although here illustrated largely from Chaucer's more vulgar characters, such usages are of course not confined to them. Many of them will be found elsewhere in Chaucer's poetry. The same applies to other aspects of Chaucer's colloquial English, his frequent use of idiomatic turns of phrase, for example, often in dialogue, of which Harry Bailly furnishes some characteristic instances: 'lat se now' *(CT* I, 831); 'so moot I gon, / This gooth aright' (I, 3114–5); 'a devel way' (I, 3134); 'pees, namoore of this' (III, 1298); 'therof no fors! lat alle swiche thynges go. / But wyte ye what?' (IV, 2430–1); 'straw for youre gentillesse!' (V, 695): 'of hym make I no fors' (IX, 68).

It may be instructive to list some other colloquialisms from some other speakers, to illustrate their richness and variety:

The Miller: 'why, lat be . . . lat be' (*MillT* 3285); 'he shal out of his studiyng' (3467); 'what! Nicholay! what, how! what, looke adoun!' (3477); 'Jakke fool' (3708); 'have do . . . com of' (3728); 'this goth faire and weel' (3743).

The Reeve: 'and somdeel sette his howve' (*RvT* 3911, to make a fool of him); 'and straunge he made it of hir mariage' (3980); 'made fare' (3999, made a fuss); 'he craketh boost' (4001, he makes threatening noises); 'and hardily they dorste leye hir nekke' (4009); 'step on thy feet! Com of, man, al atanes!' (4074); 'make a clerkes berd' (4096, cheat him, a phrase used also by the Wife of Bath in *WBT* 361); 'so was hir joly whistle wel ywet' (4155).

The Wife of Bath: 'say ye no? . . . I sey this . . . this is to seye' (*WBT* 123 ff.); 'the bacon was nat fet for hem, I trowe, / That som men han in Essex at Dunmowe' (217–18); the unique 'goon a-caterwawed' (354); 'yet tikled I his herte' (395) and 'it tikleth me aboute myn herte roote' (471); 'but now, sire, lat me se, what I shal seyn? / A ha! by God, I have my tale ageyn' (585–6); 'what sholde I seye?' (627); 'tel me who?' (692); 'wol ye heere the tale?' (951).

The Friar: 'a! . . . *benedicite*! what sey ye?' (*FrT* 1456); 'I do no fors' (1512); 'wel twight' (1563); 'com of' (1602).

The Summoner: 'ey, maister, welcome be ye . . . / how fare ye, hertely?' (1800–1); 'that swymmen in possessioun' (1926); 'no fors . . . but tel me' (2189); and a particularly lively piece of dialogue:

'Ey, Goddes mooder,' quod she, 'Blisful mayde!
Is ther oght elles? telle me feithfully.'
    'Madame,' quod he, 'how thynke ye herby?'
'How that me thynketh?' quod she, 'so God me speede,
I seye, a cherl hath doon a cherles dede.'
                              (2202–6)

The Pardoner: 'it shal be doon' (*PardT* 320); 'alle and some' (336); the unique, punning

I rekke nevere, whan that they been beryed,
Though that hir soules goon a-blakeberyed!
                              (405–6)

'of this mateere it oghte ynogh suffise' (434); 'what, trowe ye . . . / That' (439 ff.); 'nay, nay, I thoghte it nevere, trewely!' (442); 'now hoold youre pees!' (462); 'I wol thee telle al plat' (648); 'go bet'

(667, hurry up, be gone! which is also used in a similar way by Juno in *The Book of the Duchess*, 136, talking to her messenger, and in the lively calls of the hunters in the Legend of Dido: 'Hay! go bet! pryke thow! lat gon, lat gon!' in *The Legend of Good Women*, 1213); 'it nedeth never-a-deel' (670); 'herkneth, felawes, we thre been al ones' (696); 'what, carl, with sory grace!' (717); 'in lasse while / Than thou wolt goon a paas nat but a mile' (865–6); 'what nedeth it to sermone of it moore?' (879).

The Eagle in *The House of Fame*: 'let see! darst thou yet loke now?' (*HF* 580); 'now wel . . . / First, I . . .' (605 f.); 'now herke, be thy trouthe! / Certeyn . . .' (613 ff.); 'wherfore, as I seyde, ywys, (641); 'Geffrey, thou wost ryght wel this' (729); 'thus wost thou wel' (781), and so on; 'I preve hyt thus – take hede now –' (787); 'now have I told, yf thou have mynde' (823); 'pardee, hit oughte the to lyke!' (860); and:

> 'A ha!' quod he, 'lo, so I can
> Lewedly to a lewed man
> Speke, and shewe hym swyche skiles
> That he may shake hem be the biles,
> So palpable they shulden be',
>
> (865–9)

where 'shake hem be the biles' is a colloquial idiom meaning, literally, 'shake or grasp by the beaks', i.e. to get hold of, to understand; 'top and tayl, and everydel' (880); 'lat be . . . thy fantasye!' (992); 'yis, pardee . . . wostow why?' (1000); and:

> 'Nay, dred the not therof,' quod he;
> 'Hyt is nothing will byten the;
> Thou shalt non harm have trewely.'
>
> (1043–5)

Chaucer places into his own mouth many similar colloquial utterances, particularly in his exchanges with the Knight in *The Book of the Duchess* and with the Eagle in *The House of Fame*. The shorter octosyllabic line, as well as his own pose as the artless, rather naive spectator tend to produce brief idiomatic exclamations and questions heavily buttressed, as they often are in actual conversation, by mild expletives: 'say, felowe, who shal hunte here?' (*BD* 366); 'a Goddes half, in good tyme!' (*BD* 370); 'but, sir, oo thyng wol ye here?' (*BD* 546); ' "y trowe hyt, sir," quod I, "parde!" ' (*BD* 1046); ' "no fors," quod y, "hyt is no nede" '

(*HF* 1011); ' "yis, parde!" quod y, "wel ynogh" ' (*HF* 1032); and
a few longer examples which it would be a pity not to quote in full:

'Loo, [sey] how that may be?' quod y;
'Good sir, telle me al hooly
In what wyse, how, why, and wherfore
That ye have thus youre blysse lore.'

(*BD* 745–8)

   'What los ys that?' quod I thoo;
'Nyl she not love yow? ys hyt soo?
Or have ye oght doon amys,
That she hath left yow? ys hyt this?
For Goddes love, telle me al.'

(*BD* 1139–43)

'Nay, for sothe, frend,' quod y;
'I cam noght hyder, graunt mercy,
For no such cause, by my hed!
Sufficeth me, as I were ded,
That no wight have my name in honde.
I wot myself best how y stonde;
For what I drye, or what I thynke,
I wil myselven al hyt drynke,
Certeyn, for the more part,
As fer forth as I kan myn art.'

(*HF* 1873–82)

The chief characteristics of such colloquial turns of speech are
their monosyllabic quality and their heavy reliance upon stock
phrases, clichés, tags, oaths, and sententious commonplaces, often
dressed up as proverbs. Modern conversational English has
much the same features: one need think only of the frequent
recurrence of such phrases as 'sort of' or 'you know'; of the worn-
out figures and dead metaphors and stale formulas fulminated
against by the advocates of plain words and pure English; and of
the meaningless hummings, hawings, interjections, and ejacula-
tions which constantly assault our ears – one need think only of
these to acknowledge how well Chaucer captured the same tones
six hundred years ago. In syntactical terms, as already noted, the
main features are loose, irregular, or distorted sentence structure,
incomplete sentences, careless use of parts of speech, lack of
proper agreement between mutually dependent parts of speech,

like nouns and pronouns or nouns and verbs, ellipsis, and repetitiveness.

The monosyllabic quality of colloquial speech is well exploited by Chaucer in the lively exchanges between characters that occur in almost all his poems. In moments of excitement, whether caused by surprise, or fear, or anger, most English people utter short words, generally words of Anglo-Saxon origin; so do English hens:

> 'Avoy!' quod she, 'fy on yow, hertelees!
> Allas!' quod she, 'for, by that God above,
> Now han ye lost myn herte and al my love.
> I kan nat love a coward, by my feith!'
>
> *(NPT* 2908–11)

The length of the words is not an invariable indicator of the 'tone' of a passage of Chaucerian verse, but it often helps to distinguish a more colloquial passage from one of more learned, expository, or speculative import. When Pertelote continues in the following strain a few lines further on, the difference is obvious:

> 'Nothyng, God woot, but vanitee in sweven is.
> Swevenes engendren of replecciouns,
> And ofte of fume and of complecciouns,
> Whan humours been to habundant in a wight.'
>
> *(NPT* 2922–5)

The stock phrases and tags which fill out so many Chaucerian lines, and which contribute so much to the total conversational effect of a great deal of Chaucer's poetry, are also generally made up of short, familiar words. Often they are cast in the first person singular: 'I dar nat seyn', 'I can na moore', 'as I yow tolde', 'as I shal telle', 'as shortly as I can it trete', 'I wol yow seyn' – all from the first five stanzas of *The Parliament of Fowls*. Others are simply tags, verbal appendages that help the metre along or complete a line without furthering the meaning nor as a rule, for that matter, hindering it. The reader of Chaucer soon learns to distinguish between the meaningless tag and some similar, though functionally important, phrase:

> She was not cause of myn adversite,
> But he that wroghte her, *also mot I the*,
> That putte such a beaute in her face,
>
> *(Mars* 266–8)

where the italicized phrase, 'so may I thrive', but for the rhyme, might just as well, and a little more aptly, have been 'also dar I seyn', or 'as I shal yow telle', or any one of a dozen other choices. On the other hand, the following italicized phrase, which belongs to the same family of idioms, has a clearer semantic function:

> If thou lovest thyself, thou lovest thy wyf;
> No man hateth his flessh, but in his lyf
> He fostreth it, and therfore bidde I thee,
> Cherisse thy wyf, *or thou shalt nevere thee.*
>
> (*MerchT* 1385-8)

Some of the colloquial stock idioms are alliterative jingles, like 'thurgh thikke and thurgh thenne' (*RvT* 4066), 'by stokkes and by stones' (*Tr* III, 589), 'as fayn as fowel' (*KnT* 2437; cf. *ShipT* 51); many of them are proverbs or proverbial phrases or sententious remarks,[6] expressed directly or as similes or woven more unobtrusively into narrative or dialogue. Chaucer's poetry is studded with proverbs as is much of his prose. He singled out 'somwhat moore / Of proverbes' as one of the peculiarities of his version of the story of Melibeus and Prudence, although in substance the proverbial material of *The Tale of Melibee* derives closely from the French original. Of the poems *Troilus and Criseyde* has the greatest proportion of proverbs and sententious remarks, very few of which Chaucer derived from Boccaccio's *Filostrato*, and of the three major characters in the poem Pandarus is most addicted to them. In fact, he utters more proverbial sayings in one form or another than the other characters taken together, excepting the narrator, that is, for much of the latter's comments upon characters and events are also couched in sententious form. This is of course in the best medieval rhetorical tradition, for the theorists had recommended proverbs, especially as suitable beginnings and endings of poems, and some of the poets, like Deschamps, upon whom Chaucer had modelled himself, knew such precepts and followed them in their own work. But Chaucer was never a slavish follower, whether of other poets or of rhetorical theory, and the use to which he put his numerous proverbs and sententious remarks was generally very much his own. Mrs Gordon has recently argued, for example, that Chaucer's frequent

6. This tripartite classification is that of Bartlett Jere Whiting, *Chaucer's Use of Proverbs* (Cambridge, Mass., 1934). As Whiting admits (p. viii), it is sometimes hard to uphold.

use of the *prosecutio cum proverbiis* adds not a little to the ambiguities of *Troilus and Criseyde* by giving 'specious plausibility to an
argument by the use of sayings in common use, held to express
truths generally accepted and hence of value as "proof" of the
argument'[7]. The Wife of Bath is also furnished with numerous
proverbs and sententious sayings as well as with much relevant
learning, some of which she turns most skilfully to support her
often specious reasoning.

The fact that proverbial material is generally very much 'of the
folk', simple and colloquial in form and diction, is of immediate
relevance to our present discussion, for it provided much of the
raw material for Chaucer's representation of colloquial English.
As in living speech, so are proverbial sayings embedded in the
speech of Chaucerian narrators and characters, embodying figures
and phrases and words familiar from long usage. At the most
obvious level are proverbs which are cited as such, and duly
announced as such by phrases like 'men seyn' or 'it is seyd':

> 'Men seyn, "to wrecche is consolacioun
> To have another felawe in hys peyne".'
>
> (*Tr* I, 708–9)

> For it is seyd, 'man maketh ofte a yerde
> With which the maker is hymself ybeten
> In sondry manere,' as thise wyse treten.
>
> (*Tr* I, 740–2)

The announcement may be more forthright still:

> 'Lat this proverbe a loore unto yow be:
> "To late ywar, quod beaute, whan it paste".'
>
> (*Tr* II, 397–8)

> And therfore this proverbe is seyd ful sooth,
> 'Hym thar nat wene wel that yvele dooth'.
>
> (*RvT* 4319–20)

Other proverbs are inserted into the verse without such patent
identification. They may be the narrator's comments:

> For kaught is proud, and kaught is debonaire.
> This Troilus is clomben on the staire,

7. Gordon, p. 73.

And litel weneth that he moot descenden;
But alday faileth thing that fooles wenden;
(Tr I, 214–17)

or they may be spoken by one of the characters:

'Ye, wyf', quod he [Arveragus], 'lat slepen that is stille'.
(FranklT 1472)

Criseyde and, much later in the poem, Diomede, utter the same
proverb, both using the masculine pronoun, which in Criseyde's
case, although it makes the proverbial character of the comment
obvious, may be thought a trifle inappropriate:

[Criseyde] seide, 'He which that nothing undertaketh,
Nothyng n'acheveth, be hym looth or deere.'
(Tr II, 807–8)

'But for t'asay,' he [Diomede] seyde, 'it naught ne greveth;
For he that naught n'asaieth, naught n'acheveth.'
(Tr V, 783–4)

Much proverbial material is incorporated into figurative usage,
either in the form of straight similes:

As any pecok he was proud and gay,
(RvT 3926)

or in more complex patterns in which proverbial matter may be
combined with a colloquial idiom to produce a pointed contextual
innuendo:

And yet as proud a pekok kan he pulle.
(Tr I, 210)

The phrase 'to pull a peacock', that is to pull out its feathers, may
be taken to mean, in this case, to deflate Troilus's pride by proving
him as vulnerable to Love as other proud men; but it also recalls
for the reader of *The Canterbury Tales* the narrator's description of
the Summoner,

Ful prively a fynch eek koude he pulle,
(Gen Prol 652)

in which a colloquial idiom, *pullen a finch*, glossed by the *MED* as
'to do something with cunning, to pull a clever trick', not only
suggests the Summoner's fraudulent practices, but also has sexual

195

overtones.[8] The association with fornication is made clear by the preceding lines –

> He wolde suffre for a quart of wyn
> A good felawe to have his concubyn
> A twelf month, and excuse hym atte fulle –
>
> *(Gen Prol* 649–51)

and appears to persist in later English colloquial idiom.[9] In the *Troilus* passage the god of Love has just scored a direct hit on Troilus, thereby tumbling him from his proud position, but the line also connotes the further deception inherent in Troilus's falling in love, the inevitability of an even further descent into ill fortune, an idea more fully developed by the narrator in the neat stanza (211 ff., part of which is quoted above). And the presence of the sexual overtones attested in the lines about the Summoner may well be suspected here also if we accept the claim that in the following stanza (218 ff.) the figure of Bayard the horse represents the flesh.[10] As so often in Chaucer's mature poetry, a wealth of meaning lies beneath the seemingly simple colloquial surface.

Among Chaucer's proverbial figures is one group which adds particularly to the impression of colloquial naturalism: the group of devaluating phrases of the type 'naught worth a beene'. The implied similes are of the most homely sort; daily experience, after all, is crowded with trivialities. The Host nicely covers the range from pretty to ugly worthlessness, from his reference to *The Monk's Tale* as 'nat worth a boterflye' (*CT* VII, 2790), to his dismissal of pilgrim Chaucer's 'drasty rymyng' of *Sir Thopas* as 'nat worth a toord' (*CT* VII, 930), a word, incidentally, which only he uses, here and in his angry retort to the Pardoner at the end of the latter's tale (*PardT* 955). The items which figure in the Middle English scale of unimportance vary as much as the idioms

8. Pointed out by G. L. Kittredge in a paper of 'Chauceriana', *Modern Philology* VII (1909–10), 475–7.

9. Cp. Dekker's phrase in *The Guls Hornbook and the Bel-man of London,* 'what a woodcocke they puld', quoted in context by Eston Everett Ericson in *English Studies* XLII (1961), 306. No doubt Chaucer was aware of similar idioms involving birds in contemporary Italian. Readers of Boccaccio will recall Caterina asleep with Ricciardo's 'nightingale' (*usignuolo*) in her hand, as well as the general reference to the young couple 'hunting birds' together (*ucello agli usignuoli*; cp. the German *vögeln,* to copulate) in the fourth tale of the fifth day of the *Decameron.*

10. Cp. D. W. Robertson, Jr., *A Preface to Chaucer: Studies in Medieval Perspective* (Princeton, 1963), pp. 253–5, 476.

which enclose them (one recalls, for example, Langland's picturesque 'ich sette by pardon nat a peese nother a pye-hele!' (piecrust) *PP* C X, 345), and Chaucer does not by any means exhaust all possibilities. *Straw* and *mite* are his favourites, both of respectable biblical ancestry, while beans, butterflies, flies, gnats, haws, hens, leeks, and tares all occur more than once. So far it is certainly a conservative list, except that hens, even the 'pulled hen' of *The General Prologue*, 177, must have been worth more than gnats and flies, especially before the days of mass-produced poultry. As is to be expected, the Wife of Bath is expert at derogation as well as mistress of the appropriate vocabulary. She 'wol nat wirche as muchel as a gnat' (*WBT* 347); she holds 'a mouses herte nat worth a leek' (572); of her fifth husband's proverbs she 'sette noght an hawe' (659); and coming rather closer to her own domestic economy she adduces an 'olde sho' (708) and a *rake-stele* (rake-handle, 949) as equally worthless. And it is the old woman in *The Wife of Bath's Tale* who dismisses 'swich arrogance' as 'nat worth an hen' (1112), just as Chaucer's Monk dismisses his texts as worth neither 'a pulled hen' nor 'an oystre' (*Gen Prol* 177, 182). Pandarus's language has much in common with the Wife of Bath's, not least the tendency to lard it with proverbial wisdom, and in one conversation with Criseyde in Book III of *Troilus and Criseyde* he manages to refer to the worthlessness of 'an hawe' (854), 'a myte' (900), and the particularly effective, because multiplied, 'two fecches' (936), the vetch (*vicia*) being a familiar enough genus of cultivated vegetable of the bean variety, as well as of wild plants, in medieval England. If Pandarus does not give 'a straw for alle swevenes signifiaunce' (*Tr* V, 362), the Merchant's Januarie does not give a 'straw for thy Senek, and for thy proverbes' (*MerchT* 1567) and follows this up with a rather more original

'I counte nat a panyer ful of herbes
Of scole-termes.'

(*MerchT* 1568–9)

Are 'two fecches' worth just a little more than one? And what of Criseyde's '*thre* hawes' (*Tr* IV, 1398)? Is a basket full of herbs slightly more complimentary than a straw? Is the Host's 'botel hey' (bundle of hay), which he anticipates the Cook's tale will be worth (*CT* I X, 14,) a trifle more appreciative than the butterfly and the turd with which he dismissed Monk and *Thopas*? Probably not, but these are nice speculations.

Most of these idioms, as will have been noted, are similarly structured: I count, hold, reckon, set, something as worth or not worth a bean, fly, mite, or whatever it is. One slight variation is provided by the use of the word *montance* 'amount', hence 'value', as in Arcite's 'ne sette I nat the montance of a tare' (*KnT* 1570), or in the crow's

> 'Noght worth to thee, as in comparisoun,
> The montance of a gnat'.
>
> (*MancT* 254-5)

Another variation is provided by the phrasal type 'deere ynough a . . .', dear enough at the price of something, the 'something' being again a familiar item of little or no value, a *myte* (*Tr* IV, 684; *LGW* 741), a *leek* (*CYT* 795), a *rysshe* (rush, *Tr* III, 1161), a *jane* (a small Genoese coin, worth about a halfpenny, *CLT* 999).

If the proverbs and proverbial figures which we have been discussing add their share to what Clemen has called a 'note of sturdy realism and the racy speech of every day',[11] so do the many words and images in Chaucer's work drawn from medieval domestic and rustic life. Not all of them, by any means, are of Chaucer's own invention and some may also have proverbial affinities. The Wife of Bath's catalogue of domestic animals and appliances, for example, is taken almost word for word from the Latin of Theophrastus quoted in Jerome's *Epistola adversus Jovinianum* ('A cardinal, that highte Seint Jerome, / That made a book agayn Jovinian', *WBT* 674-5), yet it suits admirably, and reinforces, the Wife's constant reference to details of everyday life:

> Thou seist that oxen, asses, hors, and houndes,
> They been assayed at diverse stoundes;
> Bacyns, lavours, er that men hem bye,
> Spoones and stooles, and al swich housbondrye,
> And so been pottes, clothes, and array.
>
> (*WBT* 285-9)

Her animal images are similarly drawn from familiar surroundings: 'dronken as a mous' (246), 'as a spaynel' (spaniel, 267), 'noon so grey goos' (269), 'lyk a cat' (348), 'right as wormes shende a tree'

11. Clemen, p. 63.

(376), 'as an hors I koude byte and whyne' (386), 'and al day after hidde hym as an owle' (1081). In line 602 the Wife of Bath says of herself: 'but yet I hadde alwey a coltes tooth', a homely enough expression on the surface, but one that is made all the more suggestive of lasciviousness by having been used of himself by the Reeve (*CT* I, 3888) and by the description of wanton old Januarie as 'al coltissh, ful of ragerye' (*MerchT* 1847). (The Wife, it should be remembered, was similarly 'ful of ragerye' (wantonness, *WBT* 455), a word not used elsewhere by Chaucer.) The Miller's Alisoun is also like 'a joly colt' and 'sproong as a colt dooth in the trave' (sprang as a colt does in a restraining frame, *MillT* 3263, 3282).

These are only a few of the animals that figure in Chaucer's more domestic imagery. Ants, bees, cattle, fish, hares, lambs, moths, fawns, swine, wasps, could be added to the list, not to mention birds. Chaucer has about fifteen words for 'horse',[12] ranging from the *jade* ridden by the Nun's Priest (*CT* VII, 2812), through words like *amblere, hakeney, rouncy,* to more aristocratic terms, such as the *courser* of the Knight's and Squire's tales, or the 'steedes and palfreys' of the lords in *The Knight's Tale* 2495. Sir Thopas, fittingly, rides upon a 'steede gray' (*Thop* 751), also referred to as a *dextrer* (913), more commonly M.E. *destrer* from O.Fr. *destr(i)er*. From O.N. *kapall* derives *capel*, a word common in fourteenth-century alliterative poetry, for example in *Sir Gawain and the Green Knight,* 2175:

Þe knyȝt kachez his caple, and com to þe lawe.

Chaucer's indebtedness to the 'alliterative vocabulary' of his contemporaries is not great, and it is interesting that for him *capel, capul* was a vulgarism rather than a 'poetic' word, for he puts it squarely among the 'cherles termes', while yet retaining something of its alliterating contexts: Harry Bailly uses it twice in quick succession:

'To kepen hym and his capul out of the slough;
And if he falle from his capul eftsoone'.
(*CT* IX, 64–5)

The Reeve uses it twice, once in his own narration in the alliterating jingle 'hir capul cacche' (*RvT* 4105), and once in a speech by

12. See A. A. Dent, 'Chaucer and the Horse', *Proceedings of the Leeds Philosophical and Literary Society* IX (1959), 1–12.

clerk John, in whose northern idiom the word seems especially appropriate (*RvT* 4088). Friar and Summoner each use the word once alongside the alliterating *cart* (*FrT* 1554, *SumT* 2150). Beyond these six occurrences Chaucer had no use for the word. But he himself must have spent a good portion of his life on horseback, *coursers* rather than *capels*, one hopes, whether on missions abroad, or going about his official business around London from Woolwich to Windsor, or attending to his duties as deputy forester of the royal forest of North Petherton in Somerset. He knew all about a horse's harness, fodder, and movements, and there is an authentic note about the 'hayt, Brok! hayt, Scot!' of the angry carter in *The Friar's Tale* (1543) trying to get his hay wain moving again, or the shouts of the two clerks in *The Reeve's Tale* (4101) chasing their runaway horse with 'keep! keep! stand! stand! jossa, warderere. . . .'

Apart from domestic animals, the catalogue of 'swich housbondrye' quoted above from the Wife of Bath's Prologue refers to domestic utensils, clothing, and, by implication, to other aspects and articles of domestic life, like food and drink. *The General Prologue* to *The Canterbury Tales* is full of picturesque details of medieval English life, particularly among the less exalted classes, and similar details are scattered through many of the tales. By themselves, in narrative or description, these details do not of course constitute, although they do contribute to, the impression of colloquial idiom which so much of Chaucer's poetry creates. It is their use in colloquial sayings and figurative expressions that adds considerably to the Chaucerian naturalism of speech and narration. The Wife of Bath frying her fourth husband 'in his owene grece' (*WBT* 487), Pandarus vowing that

> 'this nyght shal I make it weel,
> Or casten al the gruwel in the fire',
>
> (*Tr* III, 710–11)

the Host referring to the Cook's twice-cooked food colloquially as 'many a Jakke of Dovere' (*CT* I, 4347) – these and numerous other examples help to illustrate the picturesque robustness of Chaucerian colloquial English.[13]

But the diction of colloquial English does not rely exclusively

13. For other examples, arranged by subject matter, see Friedrich Klaeber, *Das Bild bei Chaucer* (Berlin, 1893), pp. 89–99.

upon close reference to domestic commonplaces. Many colloquial words and phrases occur in Chaucer which are simply
part of the vocabulary of contemporary everyday speech, and
among these we must reckon the vulgarisms of the *cherles* and, as
far as we think we can recognize it as such, fourteenth-century
slang.

Some of Chaucer's colloquial words have remained thus in
later English. We still speak colloquially of 'the gift of the gab',
retaining something at least of the meaning of M.E. *gabben* which
Chaucer uses several times with such meanings as 'to prate,
speak idly, boast, lie'. There is a little group of words like *gabben*,
all conveniently rhyming with one another and all three having a
colloquial ring about them. In *The Miller's Tale* John the carpenter
says:

> 'I am no labbe;
> Ne, though I seye, I nam nat lief to gabbe',
> > (*MillT* 3509–10)

and the same rhyme is used by Pandarus, *labbe* having much the
same meaning ,'idle talker, blabbermouth', in both passages:

> 'Proverbes kanst thiself ynowe and woost,
> Ayeins that vice, for to ben a labbe,
> Al seyde men soth as often as thei gabbe.'
> > (*Tr* III, 299–301)

That some of the scribes of *Troilus and Criseyde* found these words
confusing (all three exist as verbs and as nouns) is not really surprising, and thus we find several manuscripts reading *blabbe* at
line 300, which means yet again 'one who talks idly, foolishly'.
Pandarus *is* rather given to all three of these activities, gabbing,
labbing, and blabbing, and it is wholly appropriate that at one
crucial point in the poem his lengthy *unthrift* (nonsense, foolish
talk) should provoke Troilus into retorting 'Whi gabbestow?'
(*Tr* IV, 481). Equally appropriate, as far as we can judge from
Harry Bailly's marital revelations, is his reference to his wife as
'of hir tonge, a labbyng shrewe is she' (*CT* IV, 2428).

Another word that retains something of its medieval flavour
today is *jangle*, which Chaucer's Parson defines succinctly: 'Janglynge is whan a man speketh to muche biforn folk, and clappeth
as a mille, and taketh no keep what he seith' (*ParsT* 406), an

accomplishment which the Wife of Bath aptly applies to herself,

> And of my tonge a verray jangleresse,
> *(WBT* 638)

and which in *The Parliament of Fowls* is equally appropriately applied to 'the janglynge pye' (magpie, 345). The Miller is described as having an enormous mouth, 'as greet ... as a greet forneys', and as being 'a janglere' (*Gen Prol* 559–60), Criseyde is willing to endure 'of wikked tonges janglerie' (*Tr* V, 755), and the summoner of *The Friar's Tale* was 'ful of jangles' (*FrT* 1407).

The word *clap* exists in several senses in modern English as it did in Middle English, but perhaps it is only the phrases 'to clap eyes on' and 'to clap someone in gaol' which are in current colloquial use. For Chaucer the word means primarily a loud noise (e.g. 'the clappe of a thundringe', *HF* 1040) or, as a verb, the action of producing a loud noise, like the Parson's 'clappeth as a mille', just quoted, which has its equivalent in the German folksong 'Es klappert die Mühle am rauschenden Bach', or the Miller's description of Alisoun's

> 'Tehee!' quod she, and clapte the wyndow to.
> *(MillT* 3740)

Gower, in *Confessio Amantis* I, 2390–1, comes closer to the colloquial Middle English sense of *clappen* as 'to chatter' or 'to talk noisily or too much', when he makes the Confessor say:

> Ther mai nothing his tunge daunte,
> That he ne clappeth as a Belle,

a figure repeated later in the same poem (V, 4640). Chaucer uses the term either derogatorily, as when the Clerk refers to a fickle mob as 'ay ful of clappyng' (*ClT* 999), or almost slangily:

> The Reve answerde and seyde, 'Stynt thy clappe!
> Lat be thy lewed dronken harlotrye.'
> *(CT* I, 3144–5)

> 'Ye,' quod oure Hooste, 'by seint Poules belle!
> Ye seye right sooth; this Monk he clappeth lowde.'
> *(CT* VII, 2780–1)

A nice touch of ambiguity enters into the second occurrence of the word *clappeth* in the following passage, which refers both to the summoner's knocking and to his slangy words:

This somonour clappeth at the wydwes gate.
'Com out,' quod he, 'thou olde virytrate!
I trowe thou hast som frere or preest with thee.'
'Who clappeth?' seyde this wyf, *'benedicitee!*
God save you, sire, what is youre sweete wille?'

(FrT 1581–5)

Harry Bailly's language abounds in words of a colloquial character, some of which Chaucer uses nowhere else. Some of them may
well represent contemporary slang. The Priest's reproachful
'What eyleth the man, so synfully to swere?' (*CT* II, 1171), for
example, draws forth this retort:

'O Jankin, be ye there?
I smelle a Lollere in the wynd',

(CT II, 1172–3)

where *Jankin* is a derisive diminutive of 'Sir John', a common
appellation of priests, and *Lollere* carries connotations of lollers
or vagabonds, as well as of mumbling priests, hence Lollards or
Wyclifites. Harry Bailly, who makes no secret of his interest in
the sexual prowess of priests and monks, may be playing even
further on the meaning of *Jankin*, for Jankin is the typical rustic
lover of several Middle English songs, and it is probably no
accident that there is a curly-haired apprentice in the Wife of
Bath's entourage called Janekyn, as well as 'Jankyn, oure clerk'
whose 'legges . . . faire' qualified him to become the fifth husband
(*WBT* 303 ff., 595 ff.).[14] What Harry Bailly is 'smelling in the
wind' may well be quite a noseful. In a passage already glanced at
(ch. 3, p. 173, n. 42) Harry Bailly's sense of hearing is involved as
well as his sense of smell. The latter is clearly affronted by the
drasty nature of Chaucer's rhyming in *Sir Thopas* which is 'nat
worth a toord', but the 'drasty speche' also makes Harry's 'eres
aken' (*CT* VII, 923 ff.). The words *drasty* and *toord* are very much
Harry Bailly's type of language, and they are his only. He has in
fact quite a few words private to himself within the Chaucer
canon, some of which at least have a strongly colloquial ring,
particularly in passages in which he has a go at one of the pil-

14. Cp. Tauno F. Mustanoja, 'The Suggestive Use of Christian Names in Middle
English Poetry', in *Medieval Literature and Folklore Studies: Essays in Honor of Francis
Lee Utley*, ed. Jerome Mandel and Bruce A. Rosenberg (New Brunswick, 1970), pp.
65–6.

grims, or fulminates against Mrs Goodelief Bailly, or reports the latter's outbursts:

> 'She bryngeth me forth the grete *clobbed* staves.'
>
> (*CT* VII, 1898)

> 'Whan she comth hoom she *rampeth* in my face.'
>
> (*ibid.* 1904)

> ' "To wedden a *milksop*, or a coward ape,
> That wol been *overlad* [browbeaten] with every wight!" '
>
> (*ibid.* 1910–11)

> 'Thou woldest han been a *tredefowel* aright.'
>
> (*ibid.* 1945)

> 'Religioun hath take up al the corn
> Of tredyng, and we borel men been *shrympes*.
> Of fieble trees ther comen wrecched *ympes*.'
>
> (*ibid.* 1954–6)

> 'Why is thy lord so *sluttish*, I the preye?'
>
> (*CT* VIII, 636)

> 'See how he *nappeth* [snoozes, has a nap]! see how, for cokkes bones.
> ...'
>
> (*CT* IX, 9)

> 'And *fneseth* faste, and eek he hath the pose.'
>
> (*ibid.* 62)

All the italicized words are unique to Harry Bailly in Chaucer's work, although most of them are found recorded elsewhere in Middle English. In some cases, the colloquial tone of Harry's usage (generally suggested by the context as much as by the words themselves) is echoed in other works; in the case of *nappen*, for example, by the opening of Passus VIII of the C text of *Piers Plowman*:

> Tho cam Sleuthe al by-slobered with two slymed eyen.
> 'Ich most sitte to be shryuen,' quath he, 'or elles shal ich nappe.'

This is not to deny that the word can be used quite straight, as a synonym for 'sleep' in alliterative poetry, for example:

> And quen hit neʒed to naʒt nappe hym bihoued.
>
> (*Patience* 465)

On the other hand, *fnesen*, which derives like *nappen* from Old English, and has a regular Middle English meaning 'to sneeze', is given a sense 'to wheeze' or better 'to snort' in Harry Bailly's line of which the *MED* quotes no other instance.

Some of Harry's colloquialisms are shared, as one would expect, by other earthy characters. The *pose*, for example, which means a cold in the head, is referred to also by the Reeve, in the very graphic account of the miller's household, complete with guests, 'addressing themselves' – very audibly – to sleep in the mill at Trumpington. The passage is rich in colloquial words, idioms, and images, and is worth quoting at length:

> Wel hath this millere vernysshed his heed;
> Ful pale he was fordronken, and nat reed.
> He yexeth, and he speketh thurgh the nose
> As he were on the quakke, or on the pose.
> To bedde he goth, and with hym goth his wyf.
> As any jay she light was and jolyf,
> So was hir joly whistle wel ywet.
> The cradel at hir beddes feet is set,
> To rokken, and to yeve the child to sowke.
> And whan that dronken al was in the crowke,
> To bedde wente the doghter right anon;
> To bedde goth Aleyn and also John;
> Ther nas na moore, – hem nedede no dwale.
> This millere hath so wisely bibbed ale
> That as an hors he fnorteth in his sleep,
> Ne of his tayl bihynde he took no keep.
> His wyf bar hym a burdon, a ful strong;
> Men myghte hir rowtyng heere two furlong;
> The wenche rowteth eek, *par compaignye.*

$$(RvT\ 4149-67)$$

Closer analysis of this passage reveals the typical colloquial tendency to co-ordinate rather than subordinate sentences, and to construct short sentences on similar patterns. There are some phrases which have a popular idiomatic ring about them: 'vernysshed his heed', had drunk heavily; 'as any jay she light was and jolyf'; 'so was hir joly whistle wel ywet'; 'ne of his tayl bihynde he took no keep', probably a bawdy innuendo in view of the Reeve's earlier reference to 'an hoor heed and a grene tayl' (*RvT* 3878). The expressions '*on* the quakke', '*on* the pose', meaning respectively afflicted with respiratory congestion and with a cold in the head, also have an idiomatic sound: one would expect *in* as in the Miller's 'in some woodnesse or in som agonye' (*MillT* 3452) or the similar 'in frenesye' (in a frenzy) of *The Summoner's Tale*, 2209, and *Troilus and Criseyde* I, 727. The phrase 'bar hym a burdon', i.e. provided him an accompaniment, echoes the familiar line from *The General Prologue*,

> This Somonour bar to hym a stif burdoun,
> (*Gen Prol* 673)

where there is a sexual connotation which may be ironically present also in the Reeve's line.[15] There are the naturalistic domestic touches of the passage: the baby's cradle, rocking, and suckling; the now empty *crowke* 'jug', a word derived from O.E. *crūce* but not apparently recorded anywhere else in Middle English, though presumably cognate with *crokke* 'jar', O.E. *crocca*, used once by Chaucer in *Truth*, 12; the absence of any need for a sleeping-draught (*dwale*); the simile of the horse; the familiar and colloquially exaggerated measure of 'two furlong', without plural -s as is normal in nouns of measurement (although not invariable: cp. 'fully fyve mile' and 'miles three', *CYT* 555, 561). And finally there are several individual words adding their share to the total colloquial effect: *fordronken* 'very drunk', which I prefer to read as one word, as in *The Pardoner's Tale*, 674, although in the Reeve's passage Robinson and some other editors read 'for dronken' or 'for dronke' ('because of drunkenness');[16] *yexeth* 'hiccups'; *quakke* 'respiratory congestion'; *pose* 'cold in the head'; *bibbed*; *fnorteth* 'snores, snorts', a word used only here and, no less aptly, of the messenger in *The Man of Law's Tale*, 790 who 'drank, and wel his girdel underpighte', that is drank and stuffed himself full of food; *rowtyng*, *rowteth* 'snores', like the Miller's carpenter who also *routeth* (*MillT* 3647) in 'dede sleep'. The final touch, the aping of the Miller's *par compaignye* (cp. *MillT* 3839), is in keeping with the Reeve's avowed intention to *quite* the Miller; it is also in keeping with the affectation of several of the *cherles* to parade an occasional French idiom: the Summoner, the Shipman, and the Pardoner do it too.

The word *wenche* deserves fuller comment. Its use in Chaucer is

15. See the note by B. D. H. Miller in *Notes and Queries* N.S. VII (1960), 404–6, and cp. Ann S. Haskell's comment in *Chaucer Review* I (1966–67), 86.
16. For a discussion of words with the *for-*prefix, see ch. 2, pp. 92 ff.

confined to the lower orders, except in the three instances in which its social implications are deliberately spelt out: by the narrator in a line which Muscatine, following Clemen, character-izes as 'the idiom of popular balladry, with its fillers and tags':[17]

Lord and lady, grom and wenche;
(*HF* 206)

by 'this fresshe May':

'I am a gentil womman and no wenche;'
(*MerchT* 2202)

and by the Monk in his tale of Balthasar:

'Thy wyf eek, and thy wenches. . . .'
(*MkT* 2227)

For the rest, the colloquial nature of the word[18] is demonstrated by the people who use it and by the females to whom it is applied: the Miller's Alisoun is no doubt Chaucer's wench *par excellence* aptly characterized as 'so gay a popelote or swich a wenche' (*MillT* 3254), fit to be debauched by a lord, or married to 'any good yeman' (*ibid.* 3269–70), and the Miller clearly thinks of her and her serving-woman in the same terms (cp. *ibid.* 3631). A close second, however, is the Malyne of *The Reeve's Tale*, a 'wenche thikke and wel ygrowen',

With kamus nose, and eyen greye as glas,
With buttokes brode, and brestes rounde and hye.
(*RvT* 3974–5)

Her ready acquiescence in Aleyn's amorous assaults may be due to previous acquaintance with the young man (cp. 4022–3), or to the fact that she has inherited her father's *kamus* nose, which may have had libidinous connotations for Chaucer's more learned listeners.[19] But it suggests above all that she is kin to the wenches alluded to by the Wife of Bath in almost the same breath as she utters the, in the context highly ambiguous, proverb, 'Whoso that first to mille comth, first grynt' (*WBT* 389, 393); and kin also

17. Muscatine, p. 109.

18. 'Not a respectable word in Chaucer's eyes' comments Donaldson correctly, *Speaking*, p. 25, n. 1. Cp. also Katherine T. Emerson's note in *Notes and Queries* N.S. IV (1957), 277–8.

19. Cp. the note by W. Arthur Turner in *Notes and Queries* N.S. I (1954), 232, and Curry, p. 85.

to the *retenue* of wenches at the disposal of such men as the summoner in *The Friar's Tale* (1355), the Pardoner (*PardT* 453), Perkyn Revelour (*CkT* 4374), or, for that matter, the hermits *en route* to Walsingham in *Piers Plowman* (C I, 51–2). Gower neatly defines the term by adding an appropriate epithet, 'the comun wenche' (*Conf Am* II, 3097), but in the alliterative poetry, as so often, the semantic distinctions are blurred for prosodic reasons. Thus Langland uses the term as readily of Couetise-of-eyen as of Mercy (C XIII, 12; C XXI, 118), and even of the Virgin (C XIX, 134). Chaucer, on the other hand, untrammelled by alliterative requirements, is consistent, and even allows one of his lesser creatures, the Manciple, to expatiate upon the social and moral implications of the word. The Manciple's tale of the crow is such a short one that he is given every opportunity to spin it out with appropriate observations and rhetorical amplifications, including a final moral which takes up a fifth of the whole tale. Although the speaker twice claims to be 'a man noght textueel' (*MancT* 235–6, 316), he is yet able for the sake of linguistic propriety in his narrative to offer a neat semantic analysis of two sets of words: lady / wench, and tyrant / outlaw, of which the first concerns us here. In view of the hypocritical May's protestations in *The Merchant's Tale*, the Manciple's excursus is particularly relevant:

> If men shal telle proprely a thyng,
> The word moot cosyn be to the werkyng.
> I am a boystous man, right thus seye I,
> Ther nys no difference, trewely,
> Bitwixe a wyf that is of heigh degree,
> If of her body dishonest she bee,
> And a povre wench, oother than this –
> If it so be they werke bothe amys –
> But that the gentile, in estaat above,
> She shal be cleped his lady, as in love;
> And for that oother is a povre womman,
> She shal be cleped his wenche or his lemman.
> And, God it woot, myn owene deere brother,
> Men leyn that oon as lowe as lith that oother.
>
> (*MancT* 209–22)

It is a measure of Chaucer's artistic achievement that, although the naturalistic, often racy, speech of many of his characters appears to be much of a kind, the methods employed differ between different characters. This is an important aspect of his characterization and will occupy us further in a later chapter. For the moment, it will be enough to draw attention to a few of the differences. Unlike the Host, the Wife of Bath, for example, uses few colloquial words, except vulgarisms and their attendant euphemisms, not used by other speakers in Chaucer. On the other hand, her talking is strongly characterized by colloquial syntax, made up of strings of co-ordinated clauses, lax use of pronouns, syntactical *non-sequiturs*, tags, frequent oaths and asseverations, though rather milder ones than Harry Bailly's, and is rich in proverbs and other sententious utterances. The Miller's skill at devaluing courtly romantic diction has already been referred to and has been admirably discussed by Donaldson. No hearer or reader of *The Miller's Tale* could have missed the delicious irony of having, within a dozen lines of the opening of the tale, such words as the following applied to 'a poure scoler' lodging with 'a riche gnof' at Oxford:

> This clerk was clepte *hende* Nicholas.
> Of *deerne love* he koude and of *solas*.
> > (*MillT* 3199–200)

The Reeve's strongly idiomatic narrative is individualized by his tendency to *sermonyng* as well as, and much more strongly so, by his use of dialectal forms and words both in his own person, and in the speech of his two northern clerks. The speech of Pandarus is a unique medley of almost all the colloquial, naturalistic devices known to Chaucer, syntactical and lexical: only he and the Pardoner *affile* their *tonges* in Chaucer, a word of much stronger connotation in its fourteenth-century occurrences than the *MED*'s 'polish, improve' suggests. Gower uses it aptly enough of Ypocrisie,

> Which with deceipte and flaterie
> Hath many a worthi wif beguiled.
> For whanne he hath his tunge affiled,
> With softe speche and with lesinge . . .
> > (*Conf Am* I, 676–9)

and Chaucer clearly had similar connotations in mind when applying the word to the Pardoner (*Gen Prol* 712) and to Pandarus's particular blend of 'softe speche and . . . lesinge' (*Tr* II, 1681).

Much of Pandarus's talk is strongly sententious, and in addition he often uses a hearty conversational tone to prod or persuade his listeners, mainly Troilus or Criseyde. Like the Host, he has his own 'private' colloquialisms: 'ye, haselwodes shaken!' (*Tr* III, 890); 'ye, haselwode!' (V, 505); 'from haselwode, there joly Robyn pleyde' (V, 1174), for which there appear to be no exact parallels recorded anywhere in the fourteenth century. The sense generally attached to these phrases is something in the nature of derision or incredulity; the *OED* glosses 'of course', presumably to be pronounced with appropriate contextual intonation, while the *MED* equates *haselwode* in these instances with 'foolishness, nonsense'. Perhaps that is all there is to Pandarus's exclamations, perhaps one can speculate a little further knowing the speaker's generally colloquial, sometimes bawdy, propensities. Hazelwood, because of its soft and elastic nature, was in common use for the manufacture of tally sticks,[20] and a tally stick in Chaucer's English was *taille* (*Gen Prol* 570), a word sufficiently close in pronunciation to *tayl* 'tail' (and its slang sense 'penis') to afford Chaucer opportunity for some bawdy puns elsewhere (cp. p. 220 below). Perhaps Pandarus's 'ye, haselwode!' and 'ye, haselwodes shaken!' are thus rather more bawdy than one might at first have supposed; the context of these two idioms certainly supports this view. The third occurrence may be a more literal, and possibly literary, reference to the hazel wood of some medieval *pastourelle*, as Root suggests (pp. 550 f.), but the bawdy connotation is possibly here also. Pandarus also has his own domestic or rustic idioms, using some words, like the three '-stone' words following, which are not, surprisingly enough, found anywhere else in Chaucer: 'a *wheston* [whetstone] is no kervyng instrument' (I, 631); 'with *slynge-stones*' (II, 941); 'as don thise rokkes or thise *milnestones*' (II, 1384).

A few of Chaucer's characters use words which are best described as slang; expressive, picturesque words, avoided by more respectable people, which add a good deal of force and pungency

20. Cp. Maurice Hussey, *Chaucer's World: A Pictorial Companion* (Cambridge, 1967), p. 93. There is an illustration of a tally stick on p. 94. See also the two studies by Hilary Jenkinson, both richly illustrated, in which reference is made to the regular use of hazel for tallies: 'Exchequer Tallies', *Archaeologia* LXII (1911), 367–380 (see especially 373), and 'Medieval Tallies, Public and Private', *Archaeologia* LXXIV (1924), 289–351 (especially 314).

to some churl's utterance. The Friar, for example, refers to an old
widow as a *ribibe* (*FrT* 1377), literally a musical instrument of the
fiddle family, or, more correctly, 'a bowed fiddle related to the
rebeck, but larger, consisting of an oval-shaped sound-box with
a separable neck, having two pairs of strings tuned in fifths'.[21]
It is probably the same instrument as that referred to as a *rubible* in
The Miller's Tale, 3331, on which Absolon the parish clerk –
among his many other accomplishments – was able to 'pleyen
songes' and as a *ribible* in *The Cook's Tale*, 4396, where Perkyn
Revelour is the virtuoso. Its slang usage referring to an old
woman may have been suggested by its shape or, more vulgarly,
by the fact that it could be played either at the shoulder or supported between the knees. This latter mode of playing does not,
however, apply to the rebeck, 'a small fiddle with three strings,
consisting essentially of a pear-shaped sound box with a short
neck', which has a similar shape to the *ribibe*, but 'was played at
the shoulder with a bow'.[22] This word is used later in *The Friar's
Tale*, 1573, by the summoner of the story, but whereas *ribibe* in
line 1377 is preceded by the explanatory 'an old wydwe', *rebekke*
is used by itself. The latter in its slang sense probably owes something also to Fr. *rebéquer* 'to answer impertinently or sulkily'.
Skeat assumed that *rebekke* in the sense of 'old woman' derived
originally from a pun on *Rebekke*, the biblical Rebecca, who is
twice referred to in *The Merchant's Tale* (1363, 1704), both times
rhyming with *nekke*, as *rebekke* is in *The Friar's Tale*; but the
association with the shape of both musical instruments, possibly
with the sounds they produced, with the mode of playing the
ribibe between the knees, and the general bawdy suggestion of
'playing' on a woman as on a fiddle, all point to the kind of
transference common in slang usage. The word *ribibe* is similarly
used by both Skelton and Ben Jonson. Both words probably
came into Middle English from Old French in their musical
senses. It is interesting to compare with these Middle English
slang terms the Vulgar Latin *vitula* 'fiddle', *vetula* 'old woman', and
vidula 'woman'.

The Friar's summoner uses another pair of slang words, both
addressed to the same old woman: 'thou olde virytrate' (1582)

21. Henry Holland Carter, *A Dictionary of Middle English Musical Terms* (Blooming-
ton, 1961), p. 407.
22. *Ibid.*, p. 400.

and 'olde stot' (1630). Of these the second is more easily explained, as its normal meaning is either a stallion, as in the description of the Reeve in *The General Prologue*, 615:

This Reve sat upon a ful good stot,

from O.E. *stot*, cognate with German *Stute* 'mare'; or a bullock, as in O.N. *stútr*, which is the probable meaning in Langland's

And sutthe Grace of hus goodnesse gaf Peers foure stottes.
(*PP* C XXII, 267)

Translated into slang, applied to an old woman with appropriate shift of gender, *stot* could thus mean either 'old nag' or 'old cow'. A similar transference of an animal word to a human being is the slang sense of 'blynde bosarde', blind buzzard, meaning a stupid, worthless person in *Piers Plowman* B X, 266.

The word *virytrate* appears to contain a second element *trot* or *trat* found in later Middle English and in Middle Scots with the meaning of 'old woman'. Its slang usage may have been aided by association with the verb *trotten* 'to move or ride at a trot', which in its turn may have shared the bawdy overtones of some other 'riding' words, such as the common Middle English word *prikken* 'to ride' which is used by the Reeve of John's amorous endeavours:

He priketh harde and depe as he were mad.
(*RvT* 4231)

What the element *viry-* might mean is not known, but it is probably the same as in the equally enigmatic *viritoot* which has the same ring of slang about it in the context of the blacksmith's playful words in *The Miller's Tale*:

'Som gay gerl, God it woot,
Hath broght yow thus upon the viritoot.
By seinte Note, ye moot wel what I mene.'
(*MillT* 3769–71)

Skeat conjectured that *viri-* might derive from O.Fr. *virer* 'to turn' and that *toot* represents O.Fr. *tot*, Fr. *tout* 'all', the general sense of the line being 'has brought you thus so early astir'. In view of the smith's sexual innuendo, a more vulgar meaning is more likely, and one is tempted to read the slang word *toute*, *towte* 'hole' into *viritoot*, as this plays such an important part in the denouement of *The Miller's Tale* (cp. 3812, 3853), but the rhyme with the long open [ɔ:] of *woot* is an impossible one. Chaucer uses *woot* only thirteen times in rhyme in all his poetry, and all the rhyming words have the same vowel sound, as in *hoot* 'hot' which occurs in nine of the thirteen couplets. More attractive, because it fits in with our suggestion that *virytrate* may have connotations of 'riding a woman' and mean something like a 'gay gerl' who is rather past it, is the conjecture of Leo Spitzer that *viritoot*, from Fr. *virevoulte*, may be a slangy equivalent of riding, gambolling, capering, with the particular sense of fornication[23] – but conjecture it remains.

In his description of the Miller in *The General Prologue* Chaucer uses a word, *knarre*, which, unless it is a particularly audacious poetic figure, may perhaps be considered as a slang word. Having characterized the Miller as

> a stout carl for the nones;
> Ful byg he was of brawn, and eek of bones,
> *(Gen Prol* 545–6)

Chaucer goes on to describe him as 'short-sholdred, brood, a thikke knarre' (549) and continues with further physical details which make up almost the whole of the portrait. The word *knarre* has several meanings in Middle English: 'a crag, or twisted rock', as in its three occurrences in *Sir Gawain and the Green Knight*; 'a swelling or protuberance in the flesh'; and 'a knot in wood or trees' (*MED*). The latter sense is contained in the adjective *knarry* which Chaucer uses once in *The Knight's Tale*, 1977: 'with knotty, knarry, bareyne trees olde'. But of the sense in which it is applied to the Miller, a sturdy, thick-set fellow, perhaps even with the moral overtones of Donaldson's gloss 'bully', the *MED* knows no other instance.

The Miller starts his tale with a reference to John the carpenter as 'a riche *gnof*' (3188), another picturesque slang word, meaning 'churl, lout, boor', of which the *MED* cites no other instance. Skeat derived *gnof* from Hebrew *ganāv* 'thief', whereas the *MED* relates it to East Frisian *gnuffig* 'ill-mannered, coarse'. Nares's *Glossary* quotes a colourful occurrence of the word in the sixteenth-century *Mirror for Magistrates*:

23. Leo Spitzer, 'A Chaucerian Hapax Legomenon: *upon the viritoot*', *Language* XXVI (1950), 389–93.

There on a blocke my head was stricken off,
As Baptist's head for Herod, bloudy gnoffe.

Whether the constable's 'as obstinate a young gonoph as I know'
in Dickens's *Bleak House* (ch. 19) takes its form and meaning
straight from the Hebrew *ganāv* or derives from M.E. *gnof*, it is
impossible to say. G. L. Brook simply lists it as part of Dickens's
'substandard vocabulary'.[24]

Also in *The Miller's Tale* occurs the comic threefold *clom* 'shut
up!' which illustrates the difficulty of distinguishing neatly between Middle English colloquial usage and genuine slang:

'Now, *Pater-noster*, clom!' seyde Nicholay,
And 'clom', quod John, and 'clom' seyde Alisoun.
(*MillT* 3638–9)

The *MED* records no other instance of the word used apparently
as an interjection or possibly as an imperative, only two examples
of the noun, meaning 'silence', found close together in one mid-
fourteenth-century source.[25] The more obviously colloquial
idioms meaning 'be quiet'! sound rather different from *clom*, like
Nature's 'hold youre tonges there!' (*PF* 521), or Troilus's

'I am nat deef. Now pees, and crye namore',
(*Tr* I, 753)

one of many examples of this use of 'peace' in Chaucer, a favourite
device, incidentally, of Harry Bailly's for asserting his right as
master of ceremonies.

The Cook's fragment holds out promise, regrettably left un-
fulfilled, of what might have become a highly colourful tale, in
manner as well as in matter. His lively description of Perkyn
Revelour delights in phrases like 'hoppe and synge' (*CkT* 4382),
'this joly prentys' (4399, 4413), 'a compeer of his owene sort'
(4419), where *compeer* is just as pejorative as it is in Chaucer's
only other use of the word, applied to the Pardoner:

With hym ther rood a gentil Pardoner
Of Rouncivale, his freend and his compeer.
(*Gen Prol* 669–70)

24. G. L. Brook, *The Language of Dickens* (London, 1970), p. 252.
25. In Richard Morris's edition of Dan Michel's *Ayenbite of Inwyt*, E.E.T.S. 23
(1866, reissued 1965), pp. 264, 266.

The Cook uses two words which have all the appearance of slang:

> And for ther is no theef withoute a *lowke*,
> That helpeth hym to wasten and to *sowke*
> Of that he brybe kan or borwe may.
>
> *(CkT* 4415–17)

Skeat conjectured, probably correctly, that *lowke* is 'an accomplice', ultimately derived from the Old English verb *lūcan* in its rarer meaning of 'to pluck out, pull out', whence the development into the slang sense of someone who helps to 'pluck' people; and to *sowke* 'suck' them, that is to cheat them, is another slang term derived from a standard word. The word *brybe* in the above passage carries the normal Middle English meaning of 'to steal, pilfer, purloin', whether by 'sucking' or, as in *The Friar's Tale*, 1378, by practising extortion.

Chaucer's Reeve, or rather his clerk John, appears to have been the first Englishman to use the word 'cockney', in the phrase 'I sal been halde a daf, a cokenay' *(RvT* 4208), presumably a slang development of the M.E. *coken-ei*, facetiously a 'cock's egg', therefore an imperfect egg, comparable to the modern colloquialism 'a bad egg' applied to a worthless person. The accompanying *daf* 'fool, half-wit' points to the likely meaning of *cokenay*; Langland uses *daffe* with appropriate epithets like 'dotede daffe' *(PP* C II, 139) and 'dronken daffe' (C XIV, 236). A *cokenay* was thus presumably something of a fool, and a weakling fool at that, the sort of person Mrs Goodelief Bailly described so vividly as 'a milksop, or a coward ape' *(CT* VII, 1910).

An especially interesting piece of slang, or perhaps better cant, that is the jargon of a particular group of people, in this case the London dock workers, is the Manciple's reference to the Cook:

> 'I trowe that ye dronken han wyn ape,
> And that is whan men pleyen with a straw',
>
> *(MancT* 44–5)

which refers to the practice of 'drilling a tiny hole in a cask of wine and sucking out the liquor *through a straw*'.[26]

The bawdy connotations of some of Chaucer's slang words and phrases may not be easily demonstrable today, but in some

---

26. See Nevill Coghill's note on monkey wine in his translation of *The Canterbury Tales* (Harmondsworth, rev. edn, 1963), pp. 520f.

cases they are unmistakable. Both the Wife of Bath and the Reeve, for example, use the phrase 'a myrie fit' to describe particularly lively amorous encounters (*WBT* 42, *RvT* 4230), whereas the word *fit* is normally applied in Middle English to unfortunate occurrences. In *The Reeve's Tale* Chaucer exploits the contrast between the straight and the bawdy use of the word *fit* in a passage rich in *double-entendre*:

> 'For, John,' seyde he, 'als evere moot I thryve,
> If that I may, yon wenche wil I swyve.
> Som esement has lawe yshapen us;
> For, John, ther is a lawe that says thus,
> That gif a man in a point be agreved,
> That in another he sal be releved.
> Oure corn is stoln, sothly, it is na nay,
> And we han had an il fit al this day;
> And syn I sal have neen amendement
> Agayn my los, I will have esement.'
>   (*RvT* 4177–86)

The 'il fit' is soon turned into Aleyn's 'swynking' with the girl and into John's 'myrie fit' with her mother, and the bawdiness of the transformation is helped along by the play upon the word *esement* in its legal sense and in the sense of 'relief of the body by evacuation' (*MED*), and the similar ambiguity in the line 'that in another [point] he sal be releved'.

Chaucer's 'bawdy tongue' has been the object of some scholarly attention,[27] and merits proper notice in a discussion of his 'cherles termes'. The most striking feature of Chaucer's bawdy is its wholesomeness. With what Braddy calls 'unreserved frankness and stark honesty' Chaucer uses many quadriliterals or the so-called four-letter words like *cunt*, *arse*, *piss*, *fart*, and *shit*: Chaucerian *queynte*, *ers*, *pissen*, *fartyng*, and *shiten*. Such words have now re-established themselves in the more robust vocabulary of daily intercourse, and Chaucer's current popularity in various contemporary media – radio, television, musical comedy – owes something to this fact. A few other words belong to the same group, like *coillons* 'testicles', from the French, not recorded elsewhere in Middle English except in Lydgate's *Secrees of Old Philisoffres*,

27. Cp. for example Haldeen Braddy, 'Chaucer's Bawdy Tongue', *Southern Folklore Quarterly* XXX (1966), 214–22.

and Lydgate took much of his more esoteric vocabulary from
Chaucer. The word is used by Harry Bailly in a forthright outburst typical of the man (*PardT* (952). But Chaucer's bawdy is not
always so straightforward: some of it is dressed up in figurative
language, mostly slang, like Harry Bailly's use of *fundement* in the
slang sense of 'anus' (*PardT* 950), or turned into euphemisms,
which may be used, as in the case of the Wife of Bath, for purposes of characterization; and there is also a good deal of word-
play, innuendo, and punning, in which Chaucer exploits vulgar
situations or episodes for more subtle artistic aims.

Some of these modes are illustrated in the passage from *The
Reeve's Tale* quoted above: alongside the robust 'yon wenche wil I
swyve' is the playing upon *fit* and *esement* and *releved* and perhaps
upon *point*. The Miller refers to Absolon's misplaced kiss as
having been bestowed on Alisoun's 'nether ye', a figure that
contrasts vividly with the directness of Nicholas's *towte* in the
next line (*MillT* 3852–3), and there is a similar contrast in the
Wife of Bath's crude *queynte* and elegant '*bele chose*' within three
lines of each other (*WBT* 444, 447). Chaucer clearly enjoyed the
verbal dexterity such contrasts entail as well as exploiting the
different attitudes and points of view they suggest. The Merchant's
ambivalent attitude to marriage, part romantic, part sorely
disillusioned, finds expression in much of the complex pattern
of irony which makes up his tale; one instance, here relevant, is
the contrast between his avowedly *rude* ('I kan nat glose') description of Damyan's assault on May up on the pear tree:

> And sodeynly anon this Damyan
> Gan pullen up the smok, and in he throng,
> $\qquad$ (*MerchT* 2352–3)

and the strikingly modest view seen, through Januarie's new-
found sight, of the same picture a few lines further on:

> Up to the tree he caste his eyen two,
> And saugh that Damyan his wyf had dressed
> In swich manere it may nat been expressed,
> But if I wolde speke uncurteisly.
> $\qquad$ (*ibid.* 2360–3)

The language of love-making is generally robust in Chaucer,
though it may be tempered, as in *Troilus and Criseyde*, with a good

deal of courtliness and delicacy of touch. The Merchant tells of Januarie's desire for May, 'that he that nyght in armes wolde hire streyne' (*MerchT* 1753), in the same terms used by the narrator in *Troilus and Criseyde*, 'this Troilus in armes gan hire streyne' (*Tr* III, 1205). But there the resemblance ends, although some other verbal echoes persist, like Januarie's *paradys* and Troilus's *hevene*, for however much the actions may be similar, the circumstances are as different as the characters involved. One need only think of Troilus's

> And therwithal a thousand tyme hire kiste,
> (*Tr* III, 1252)

at the same time as recalling Januarie's

> He lulleth hire, he kisseth hire ful ofte;
> With thikke brustles of his berd unsofte,
> Lyk to the skyn of houndfyssh, sharp as brere –
> For he was shave al newe in his manere –
> He rubbeth hire aboute hir tendre face,
> (*MerchT* 1823–7)

to see the gulf that separates these so similar situations. Other speakers describing love-making in Chaucer's poetry inevitably reveal something about themselves in doing so. The *trede-foul* Nun's Priest neatly maintains the fiction of the farmyard:

> He fethered Pertelote twenty tyme,
> And trad hire eke as ofte, er it was pryme.
> (*NPT* 3177–8)

Rather more delicately, we are told of the 'blisse and joye' of the paired birds in *The Parliament of Fowls*, as

> ech of hem gan other in wynges take,
> And with here nekkes ech gan other wynde.
> (*PF* 670–1)

The Miller's Tale is particularly robust in its outspoken references to *queynte* and *haunchebones* and 'thakking' wenches 'about the lendes', yet it manages to be much less crude than *The Reeve's Tale*, for example, in describing sexual intercourse, because the mock-courtly tone is allowed to take over again, and 'hende' Nicholas who knew about 'deerne love . . . and . . . solas' is allowed to enjoy his beloved 'in bisynesse of myrthe and of solas' (*MillT*

3654). A typical Chaucerian touch is added as the Miller provides a musical accompaniment to the adulterous union in the carpenter's bed, and then leads on from 'the revel and the melodye' of the lovers' busyness to 'the belle of laudes' ringing as 'freres in the chauncel gonne synge' (3652–6). The echo, moreover, of the wedding of Palamon and Emelye 'with alle blisse and melodye' (*KnT* 3097) shows how consistently the Miller's exercise in devaluation is carried on throughout the tale. The Reeve, on the other hand, grinds no literary axes; he just wants to *quite* the Miller. Hence the plain bawdy of such lines as these:

> And on this goode wyf he leith on soore.
> So myrie a fit ne hadde she nat ful yoore;
> He priketh harde and depe as he were mad.
> *(RvT* 4229–31)

> 'As I have thries in this shorte nyght
> Swyved the milleres doghter bolt upright'.
> *(ibid.* 4265–6)

When we are told of the Shipman that 'of nyce conscience took he no keep' (*Gen Prol* 398), we are to some extent prepared for the tale that Chaucer finally assigned to him, even if, as some critics believe, it may have been intended originally for a female pilgrim. The moral framework of *The Shipman's Tale* is a strictly mercenary one, so that all its values and activities are assessed in simple monetary terms of gain and loss. This applies as much to the relationship between the merchant and his wife as to the affair between the latter and the monk 'daun John'. There is no emotional involvement, not even the lively animal energy of the Reeve's two clerks, in the monk's calculated amorousness:

> 'For I wol brynge yow an hundred frankes.'
> And with that word he caughte hire by the flankes,
> And hire embraceth harde, and kiste hire ofte.
> *(ShipT* 201–3)

When the business agreement is finally consummated, the hundred francs are mentioned again and at the end 'daun John' departs with as little ceremony as if he had simply called to make a purchase at a shop:

> And shortly to the point right for to gon,
> This faire wyf acorded with daun John

That for thise hundred frankes he sholde al nyght
Have hire in his armes bolt upright;
And this acord parfourned was in dede.
In myrthe al nyght a bisy lyf they lede
Til it was day, that daun John wente his way,
And bad the meynee 'farewel, have good day!'

(ibid. 313–20)

The love-making between the wife and her husband is placed in the same mercantile context:

And al that nyght in myrthe they bisette;
For he was riche and cleerly out of dette,

(ibid. 375–6)

and no attempt is made to soften the crude reporting in such coarse phrases as 'up he gooth and maketh it ful tough' (379) by letting any emotions play upon the scene except the over-riding preoccupation of the participants with money. Right to the final bawdy pun on *tale, taille* 'penis',[28] and *taillynge* 'tally, reckoning' the narrator of *The Shipman's Tale* succeeds in reducing, with what Donaldson aptly calls 'almost mathematical precision',[29] a human situation to an exercise in book-keeping.

The pun just referred to is one of a group of bawdy puns in Chaucer, some of which are more obvious than others. The words *swynk* 'work' and *swynken* 'to work, toil, labour', for example, have an unmistakably obscene sense in phrases like 'myn heed is toty of my swynk to-nyght' (*RvT* 4253) or 'how pitously a-nyght I made hem swynke' (*WBT* 202), which Chaucer is ready enough to exploit in a passage like this one:

How myghte a man han any adversitee
That hath a wyf? Certes, I kan nat seye.
The blisse which that is bitwixe hem tweye
Ther may no tonge telle, or herte thynke.
If he be povre, she helpeth hym to swynke;
She kepeth his good, and wasteth never a deel;
Al that hir housbonde lust, hire liketh weel.

(MerchT 1338–44)

28. Cp. the Reeve's 'to have an hoor heed and a grene tayl' (*RvT* 3878), and *WBT* 466. It is interesting to note that the wood of tallies was used green. See Hilary Jenkinson, 'Medieval Tallies, Public and Private', *Archaeologia* LXXIV (1924), 313.
29. Donaldson, p. 931.

The Summoner's language is made distinctive by a number of idiosyncrasies, his penchant for bits of Latin and French, for example, or his use of several words rare or unique in Chaucer, and he also displays a notable tendency to pun. Not all his puns are bawdy, however:

> Fro Paradys first, if I shal nat lye,
> Was man out *chaced* for his glotonye;
> And *chaast* was man in Paradys, certeyn.
>
> (*SumT* 1915–17)

Others, on the other hand, clearly are bawdy: the punning on *ers* 'arse', for example, in *ars-metrike* (2222), and in the contrast between 'the develes ers' (1694) and 'Goddes eres' (1941) and perhaps there is word-play also on the slang sense of *fundement* (2103); or the pun on 'what is a ferthyng worth parted in twelve' as it is described in the rubric after line 2242. A somewhat more learned play on a word is that on the literal meaning of the Latin word *eructare* 'to belch' in the words from the psalter quoted by the Summoner's friar, '*cor meum eructavit*', which the King James Version renders 'my heart is inditing a good matter' (Psalm 45 : 1), but which the speaker in *The Summoner's Tale* (1934) accompanies by an onomatopoeic 'buf!' which, as Skeat politely puts it, 'is probably intended to represent the sound of eructation'. The lewd pun on *burdoun* 'staff, stick, hence phallus' as well as 'bass accompaniment' in *The General Prologue*, 673, we have already noted.

Chaucer's favourite obscene pun is undoubtedly that on *queynte*, common enough as an adjective with meanings like 'strange, curious, skilful, elaborate', which as a noun was a vulgarism for the female genitals. The ambiguity is certainly present in the Miller's 'al this queynte cast' (*MillT* 3605), and in the Wife of Bath's 'a queynte fantasye' (*WBT* 516); whether it is also present in Troilus's apostrophe to Criseyde's empty house, which contains the line

> O thow lanterne of which queynt is the light,
>
> (*Tr* V, 543)

where the literal meaning of *queynt* is 'extinguished', from the verb *quenchen*, is debatable.[30] The same must be said of several other

30. Cp. Gordon, pp. 133 ff.

occurrences of the word in *Troilus and Criseyde*. There may be a pun on *queynte* in the Reeve's 'queynte crekes' (*RvT* 4051) where *crekes* adds further to the possible ambiguity, for the word apparently carried the rare meaning of 'anal cleft', derived from its primary meaning 'inlet, creek', as well as the apparently unique sense here of 'tricks, wiles'. For each of these senses the *MED* can cite only one example. If there is punning here, irony demands that the pun is the narrator's, not the miller's who is speaking in the tale. Yet another possible pun on *queynte* is in the Merchant's outburst against fickle Fortune on the occasion of Januarie's going blind. 'O sodeyn hap!' he rails, 'o thou Fortune unstable!' and goes on to 'O brotil joye! o sweete venym queynte!' (*MerchT* 2057 ff.) where the ambiguity would derive naturally enough from the description less than a dozen lines earlier of Januarie's amorous performances with his wife in their secluded garden.

As a straightforward vulgarism *queynte* is used only by the Miller and the Wife of Bath. The latter's complex character ('I am al Venerien / in feelynge, and myn herte is Marcien', *WBT* 609–10), however, demanded something more linguistically subtle than mere coarseness. For the Wife's sexual urges were not only tempered by a strong, controlling mercenary instinct, they were also to some extent at loggerheads with aspirations to gentility, as the long excursus on *gentillesse* in her Tale suggests, as does her insistence that

> In al the parisshe wif ne was ther noon
> That to the offrynge bifore hire sholde goon.
> *(Gen Prol 449–50)*

Hence the tug-of-war in the Wife's marital autobiography between coarseness and gentility, between bawdy and slang at one extreme and euphemism and rhetorical flourishes at the other. She affects bawdy puns like some of her fellow pilgrims, as in the proverbial 'a likerous mouth moste han a likerous tayl' (*WBT* 466), or in the somewhat more genteel playing on *heed* and *maydenheed* in her tale (887 f.). Her euphemisms for the female genitals show considerable linguistic inventiveness. They come in various languages:

Latin — I hadde the beste *quoniam* myghte be.
(WBT 608)

French – For if I wolde selle my *bele chose.*

(*ibid.* 447)

Whan that he wolde han my *bele chose.*

(*ibid.* 510)

English – That made me I koude noght withdrawe
My *chambre of Venus* from a good felawe,

(*ibid.* 617–18)

which last phrase anticipates the Host's, 'Venus paiementz' later in *The Canterbury Tales* (VII, 1961). The male genitals are described by the Wife with no less euphemistic skill: 'nether purs' (*WBT* 44b); 'sely instrument' (132); 'swich harneys' (136), which latter term appears to have come into more general literary use in the thirteen-eighties, for it is found in the Wyclifite Bible (Genesis 9:23) as the equivalent of the King James Version's 'nakedness', as well as in Trevisa's translation of Higden's *Polychronicon.* Collectively, the genitals are referred to as 'membres . . . of generacion' (116) and as 'oure bothe thynges smale' (121). The Wife's frequent references to sexual intercourse show the same vacillation between coarseness and euphemism:

Ye shul have queynte right ynogh at eve.

(*WBT* 332)

How pitously a-nyght I made hem swynke!

(*ibid.* 202)

Thanne wolde I suffre hym do his nycetee.

(*ibid.* 412)

The common Middle English verb *dighten*, whose basic meanings were 'to prepare, arrange, appoint', much as for the O.E. *dihtan*, appears to have developed a slang sense of 'to have sexual inter-course' in the later fourteenth century. In *Piers Plowman* C II, 27–8

In hus dronkenesse a day hus douhtres he dighte,
And lay by hem bothe as the bok telleth –

the word takes the place of the idiomatic 'dude / dede [did] bi' his daughters, that is, dealt with or treated them, of the earlier A and B versions. Chaucer gives the word in its obscene sense once to the Manciple:

How that another man hath dight his wyf,

(*MancT* 312)

and, characteristically, twice to the Wife of Bath:

> Was for t'espye wenches that he dighte.
> (*WBT* 398)

> And lete hir lecchour dighte hire al the nyght.
> (*ibid.* 767)

That the Wife of Bath is well aware of her tendency towards circumlocution is clear from an occasional remark like

> Ye moot wel what I meene of this, pardee!
> (*ibid.* 200)

Most of the time, however, her garrulous performance simply bubbles on, presumably on the assumption that the audience is able to grasp all the innuendoes, the euphemisms, slang terms like the picturesque *bacon* for 'old meat', hence 'old men' (418), baby language like 'lat me ba [kiss] thy cheke!' (433), and, for that matter, the often tortuous thought expressed in no less tortuous syntax. It is a virtuouso performance played simultaneously on several registers of language, from coarse slang to phrases of assured poetry –

> For joye he hente hire in his armes two,
> His herte bathed in a bath of blisse,
> A thousand tyme a-rewe he gan hire kisse –
> (*WBT* 1252–4)

unsurpassed anywhere in Chaucer's work. Even Pandarus, whose language has some strong affinities with the Wife's, is not her equal; even the Pardoner, who plays upon the English language, like the Wife, as on a musical instrument, may rival but cannot surpass the Wife's unique performance. It is no wonder that critics have long spoken of the Wife of Bath, as of Falstaff, as one of the few truly great comic figures in English literature.

There is hardly a word she utters that does not reveal something about her, and not the least revealing part of her performance is the long querulous harangue of lines 235–378, in which we hear some of the authentic tones of medieval English domestic bliss, at least from 'biside Bathe'. The reiterated 'thou seyst . . .' sets the reproachful tone, varied every now and then by an inverted 'seistow', as the catalogue unfolds. But particularly telling are the abusive epithets flung at the pitiful old husbands, endearments of a kind presumably to be expected from one who was easily 'out of alle charitee': 'sire olde kaynard' (235) is the first, where *kaynard* is probably of French origin, ultimately possibly from Latin *canis* 'dog', and means something like 'sluggard, dotard'. It is a rare word of which the *MED* cites only three other instances, the earliest from *Havelok the Dane*. The list continues with 'sire olde lecchour' (242); 'thou verray knave' (253); then side-steps to allow the inclusion of the strong word *holour* 'fornicator' (254), common enough in religious literature, and used to some effect by Chaucer's Parson (*ParsT* 626, 857, 878), once in a phrase 'thise olde dotardes holours' (857), which would certainly qualify as one of the Wife's uxorial endearments. Her catalogue goes on with *lorel* (273), a word Chaucer used once, in *Boece* I, pr. 4, 308, to render the Latin *perditissimum* 'one who is utterly lost', but nowhere else. Langland is quite partial to the word and places it into contexts which help to determine the Wife of Bath's likely meaning, like 'loreles that lecherie haunten' (*PP* C I, 75), and 'lewed lorel!' (B VII, 136), so that a sense of 'worthless, abandoned wretch' is probable. Next in the Wife's list is 'olde dotard shrewe' (291), watered down to 'olde dotard' in 331, a word which, as we noted, the Wife shares with the Parson. It is not used elsewhere by Chaucer, who may have been the first to use it in literary English, although Gower also uses it once in *Confessio Amantis* VI, 2307, accompanied, as in Chaucer's three instances, by the adjective *olde*. The Wife's next epithet is a particularly rich one: 'olde barel-ful of lyes!' (302), unique to the Wife of Bath and to her creator, and even in its literal sense 'barrel-ful' is not apparently recorded before Chaucer invented this effective figure. In line 355 occurs 'sire shrewe' and in 357 'sire olde fool', followed by the more elaborate 'o leeve sire shrewe' coupled with the pious 'Jhesu shorte thy lyf!' (365) to conclude this extraordinary exercise in wifely affection. Compared with this list, the mere 'theef' and 'false theef' bestowed later upon the fifth husband (809, 800) are tame indeed.

There is a rich give and take in the robust terms of abuse which several of Chaucer's *cherles* fling at each other, not always intended to be as insulting as they sound, as when Aleyn, fresh from his amorous 'noble game', mistakenly addresses the miller playfully as 'thou John, thou swynes-heed' (*RvT* 4262). The miller's response is heartfelt, however: 'false harlot . . . / false, traitour! false clerk!' (4268–9), *harlot* 'scoundrel, rogue, lecher' being a common Middle English term of abuse, as the Parson makes clear ('thou dronkelewe harlot', *ParsT* 626) or as Langland suggests by the company *harlotes* keep (*PP* C VII, 362 ff.). There is rich irony in the paradox 'a gentil harlot' which Chaucer applies to the Summoner in *The General Prologue*, 647. The word *traitour* is generally used appropriately, as when 'this Phebus' thus addresses the crow in *The Manciple's Tale*, 271, but *theef* is used more indiscriminately, as in the same tale: 'o false theef!' (292; cp. 295), or in the Wife of Bath's abuse of her fifth husband, noted earlier, or in Pandarus's 'thef, thow shalt hyre name telle' (*Tr* I, 870). The Manciple, both in his tale and out of it, displays some competence at abusive language. Addressing the Cook, whom he has just described, as 'this dronken wight' (*CT* IX, 35), curtly as 'man' (37), he continues with a vividly alliterating line:

'Fy, stynkyng swyn! fy, foule moote thee falle!'
(*CT* IX, 40)

to be followed at once by a sugary 'now, sweete sir' (42), for irony is as powerful a weapon as direct abuse. Harry Bailly's 'o Jankin' to the Parson (*CT* II, 1172) is as uniquely his within the Chaucer canon as is his 'thou beel amy' to the Pardoner (*CT* VI, 318). In the latter's tale the three ruffians address each other with varying degrees of irony as 'felawes', 'bretheren', 'my deere freend', but keep their abuse for the old man: 'carl', 'olde cherl', 'thou false theef' (*PardT* 717, 750, 759). The cognate words *cherl* and *carl* are both terms of abuse in Middle English, the former rather more frequently: 'false cherl' (*SumT* 2153), 'ye proude cherles alle' (*NPT* 3409), 'Metellius, the foule cherl, the swyn' (*WBT* 460), 'the fouleste cherl or the fouleste womman that lyveth'(*ParsT* 147), 'thou lyest, false cherl' (Gower, *Conf Am* III, 1252). It is often difficult to be certain whether *cherl* is free from such connotations, even where its basic meaning of 'any person not belonging to the nobility or clergy' (*MED*) is intended; for example, in the reponse of 'the gentil tercelet' to the duck's contribution to the discussion in *The Parliament of Fowls*:

'Now fy, cherl!' quod the gentil tercelet,
'Out of the donghil cam that word ful right!'
(*PF* 596–7)

Usually the word *cherl*, and the word *carl* no less, is loaded with derivative meanings, most of them contemptuous or abusive:

> The Millere is a cherl, ye knowe wel this.
>> (*CT* I, 3182)

> The Millere was a stout carl for the nones.
>> (*Gen Prol* 545)

But when this latter line is repeated almost *verbatim* by the Miller himself in his tale, the primary meaning of *carl* 'a man (usually of low estate)' seems to be all that is intended:

> His knave was a strong carl for the nones.
>> (*MillT* 3469)

Here Chaucer is not manipulating the word so much as the situation: the irony of the repetition lies in the Miller's unconscious echo of the poet's earlier loaded comment upon himself.

The 'cherles termes' which they use to each other and of each other may vary, but they are generally very much in character and they constitute an important element in the racy naturalism of much of Chaucer's poetry. The use of personal names in address adds a further colloquial touch: 'abyd, Robyn' (*CT* I, 3129); 'leve brother Osewold' (*CT* I, 3151); 'now telle on, Roger' (*CT* I, 4345); 'and therfore, Herry Bailly, by thy feith' (*CT* I, 4358); 'deere suster Alisoun' (*WBT* 804); the constant iteration of the friar's 'Thomas' in *The Summoner's Tale*; 'ye, Troilus, now herke' (*Tr* I, 624); 'lo Pandare, I am ded' (*Tr* IV, 376); 'Geffrey, thou wost ryght wel this' (*HF* 729); and so on. The informal use of professional names or words defining rank has much the same effect, and as a rule it is a person's mode of addressing those whom he considers his inferiors or at best his equals. Not surprisingly, the speaker is often Harry Bailly:

> 'Now elles, Frere, I bishrewe thy face,'
> Quod this Somonour.
>> (*CT* III, 844–5)

> 'In feith, Squier, thow has thee wel yquit'.
>> (*CT* V, 673)

> 'What, Frankeleyn! pardee, sire, wel thou woost'.
>> (*ibid.* 696)

'Thou beel amy, thou Pardoner', he sayde.

(*CT* VI, 318)

'Ther-of no fors, good Yeman', quod oure Hoost;
'Syn of the konnyng of thy lord thow woost'.

(*CT* VIII, 652–3)

'But yet, Manciple, in feith thou art to nyce'.

(*CT* IX, 69)

In all the quotations just given the speakers employ the second person singular of the personal pronoun, the mode used to address equals or inferiors.[31] The pronoun and the informality of address by name or profession or rank reinforce one another. 'Thow fol', says Pandarus to Troilus (*Tr* I, 618), in a phrase in which the plural pronoun would be highly improbable in an age in which social distinctions were carefully observed in appropriate language. A good many people call each other 'fool' or 'olde fool' (*WBT* 357) or 'verray fool' (*KnT* 1606) or 'Jakke fool' (*MillT* 3708) in Chaucer's poetry, but none of them shouts the word up the social ladder with the aid of the plural *ye*. The word *sir*, on the other hand, can be used with either the singular or the plural of the personal pronoun, although the singular generally has an ironic ring about it, as when the Eagle addresses his passenger as 'beau sir' (*HF* 643), or the Host addresses the pilgrim Chaucer with 'Sire, at o word, thou shalt no lenger ryme' (*CT* VII, 932). The Wife of Bath's use of *sire* with *thou* and *thee* is similarly ironic in her harangue to the three old husbands, and perhaps also in the *Tale* itself when the knight is reminded, in full court, of his promise to marry the old hag:

'Bifore the court thanne preye I thee, sir knyght,'
Quod she, 'that thou me take unto thy wyf'.

(*WBT* 1054–5)

When later in the story the old woman has become his wife, she addresses the knight in the formal mode customary for a lady to her lord, calling him 'sir' and using the plural pronoun, much as Dorigen does to Arveragus:

'Sire, I wol be youre humble trewe wyf'.

(*FranklT* 758)

The word *dame* is used in Middle English to describe or address a woman of rank, the head of a convent, the mistress of a household,

31. On the use of the personal pronoun in Chaucer, see below, ch. 7, pp. 382 ff.

or the mother of young children. The word is usually employed in quite straightforward fashion, and its social implications are unmistakable: 'ther dorste no wight clepen hire but "dame"' (*RvT* 3956), 'and clepe me "faire dame" in every place' (*WBT* 296); yet it was apparently possible to go one step higher: 'it is ful fair to been ycleped "madame"' (*Gen Prol* 376), and it is interesting to note Chaucer's usage. The word *dame* figures in the speech of the lower orders: Miller, Reeve, Shipman, Pardoner, Summoner, Friar, Wife of Bath, and Manciple; Harry Bailly addresses the Wife of Bath as 'dame'; apart from these the Merchant uses it three times as a form of address, the Man of Law only in the form 'dame Custance' and 'dame Hermengyld', as does the Nun's Priest in 'dame Pertelote', and the word occurs frequently in *The Tale of Melibee* to render the identical French word. Outside *The Canterbury Tales* the word occurs twice in *The Book of the Duchess* ('dame Juno', 'dame Nature'), twice in *The Parliament of Fowls* ('dame Pees', 'dame Pacience'), and once in *The House of Fame* ('dame Fortune'). It also occurs in all three parts of *The Romaunt of the Rose*. In other words, *dame* is not found in the courtly contexts of the Knight's or Squire's tales, nor in *Troilus and Criseyde*, nor in *The Legend of Good Women*. In these poems *madame* is used, albeit sparingly, alongside the much more common *lady*. The Franklin's Aurelius obviously favours *madame*, for he uses it seven times, and so does Chauntecleer who uses it five times, and the Prioress is not *dame*, but 'madame Eglentyne' (*Gen Prol* 121). The modern reader of Chaucer is thus justified in suspecting irony in some of the uses of both words, and although the *MED* does not draw attention to the possibility, it appears from his usage that for Chaucer at least *dame* may have been a genteel rather than a *gentil* word. Such subtle distinctions are less common among his contemporaries, however. The other Ricardian poets, to use J. A. Burrow's convenient term, use *dame* and *madame* with less obvious discrimination. In *Confessio Amantis* Albinus addresses his wife as *dame* with the singular pronoun (I, 2551), but the Lover addresses Venus as *ma dame* with both singular and plural pronouns (e.g. I, 168; VIII, 2882); so also, but only with the plural pronoun, does the 'wofull womman' to Rosiphelee in Book IV, 1374 ff., though the latter responds with *suster*. Langland's Dreamer uses *ma dame* to address the various ladies encountered in the course of his pilgrimage. King Arthur addresses Guinevere as 'dere dame' and with the plural pronoun in *Sir Gawain and the Green Knight*, 470, whereas Gawain addresses his hostess once as *madame* (1263) also with the plural pronoun, and both the ladies of Hautdesert are referred to as 'two so dyngne dame' by the poet (1316). The normal courtly word here, as in Chaucer, is *lady*. All the poets agree, however, in using *dame* as a label; for example, 'dame Heleine' (*Conf Am* V, 3073), 'dame Studye' (*PP* B X, 135), 'dame Pouert, dame Pitee, dame Penaunce' (*Patience* 31).

In direct address Chaucer normally uses the plural pronoun with both *dame* and *madame*, as when the Pardoner addresses the Wife of Bath:

> 'Dame, I wolde praye yow, if youre wyl it were',
> (*WBT* 184)

or when, in his affected mixture of French and English, the Summoner's friar orders his dinner:

> 'Now dame,' quod he, 'now *je vous dy sanz doute*,
> Have I nat of a capon but the lyvere,
> And of youre softe breed nat but a shyvere'.
> (*SumT* 1838–40)

Pandarus addresses Criseyde:

> Quod Pandarus, 'Madame, God yow see,
> With al youre fayre book and compaignie!'
> (*Tr* II, 85–6)

But there are exceptions:

> 'Madame,' seyde they, 'we be
> Folk that here besechen the
> That thou graunte us now good fame',
> (*HF* 1553–5)

yet within a few lines the speakers revert, as one might have expected all along, to the plural:

> 'Telle us what may your cause be'.
> (*ibid.* 1563)

Whereas in the formal language of courtly love the plural pronoun is customary, the singular is more common in the more earthy atmosphere of village love-making. And along with it come appropriately colloquial endearments. Aleyn and Malyne address each other as 'thou' and use such terms as 'sweete wight', 'deere lemman', 'goode lemman' (*RvT* 4236 ff.). But Chaucer does not adhere strictly to whatever linguistic conventions may have existed in these matters, if indeed there were any. He makes Januarie address his wife in the elevated poetic language of the Song of Solomon, yet uses the singular pronoun:

> 'Rys up, my wyf, my love, my lady free!
> The turtles voys is herd, my dowve sweete;
> The wynter is goon with alle his reynes weete.
> Com forth now, with thyne eyen columbyn!'
>
> (*MerchT* 2138–41)

Similarly the Wife of Bath's Jankyn addresses 'myn owene trewe wyf' in the singular, although he is at that very moment handing the reigns of *soveraynetee* over to her (*WBT* 819 ff.). By contrast, the lovesick Absolon addresses his beloved politely in the plural, but employs terms of endearment plainly designed to parody the more courtly language and conventions of *fine amour*:

> 'What do ye, hony-comb, sweete Alisoun,
> My faire bryd, my sweete cynamome?
> Awaketh, lemman myn, and speketh to me!
> Wel litel thynken ye upon my wo,
> That for youre love I swete ther I go.'
>
> (*MillT* 3698–702)

The Miller had already extolled Alisoun vividly in terms not used elsewhere by Chaucer as a *popelote* (*MillT* 3254, literally 'little doll, poppet'), a *prymerole* (3268, 'primrose'), and a *piggesnye* (3268, literally 'pig's eye', perhaps also a popular name of a flower), so that Absolon's tasty, if esoteric, endearments come as no surprise. The word 'honey-comb' occurs elsewhere in Chaucer only in its literal sense in *Melibee*, 1113, 'cinnamon' nowhere else, and as terms of endearment the *MED* knows no other examples of either word. Chaucer is turning the conventions of romantic diction, with its indebtedness to flowery meads and herb gardens and fanciful wild-life reserves, to his own happy use. The 'faire bryd', probably 'bird', possibly 'bride', perhaps even the alliterative word *birde* 'lady', returns as 'sweete bryd' a few lines further

231

on (*MillT* 3726), Absolon having by this time overcome the temptation to pun further on *sweete* 'sweet' and *swete* 'sweat'.

The word *lemman* appears half a dozen times in *The Miller's Tale*. The Manciple links it with *wenche*, neither of them respectable words, neither of them fit for more refined erotic contexts. It suggests adulterous lust, treacherous love, and rape, in Chaucer's usage, as in the references to Delilah as Samson's *lemman* (*WBT* 722, *MkT* 2063), to Deianira as Hercules's *lemman* (*MkT* 2119), and to Lucretia as the *lemman* Tarquin is about to rape (*LGW* 1772). In *The Man of Law's Tale* it occurs once (917) in a similar context of what the narrator calls 'foule lust of luxurie' (925). The ironic force of the word in *Sir Thopas* is made obvious by the innuendo of the following line:

> 'An elf-queene shal my lemman be
>   And slepe under my goore',
>
> (*Thop* 788–9)

where 'under my goore', literally under my robe or coat, has the bawdy connotations which this phrase occasionally has in Middle English. Elsewhere in Chaucer only the Reeve uses *lemman* in the two instances cited earlier, hence there can be no doubt about the semantic standing of the word in Chaucer's usage. To Gower *lemman* meant 'concubine' (*Conf Am* VII, 1899), while in the alliterative poetry, the use of *lemman* is similar to that of *wenche*: both words cover much wider ranges of meaning than in Chaucer, and the convenient alliteration of *lemman* with *love* made it, for Langland, a suitable word for serious theological and allegorical purposes (cp. *PP* C XI, 132; XXI, 186). At the same time, the debasement evident in Chaucer's usage is also found in alliterative poems, as in *Purity*, 1370, or in *Piers Plowman* C VIII, 26, where Sleuthe confesses:

> 'Ich ligge a bedde in Lente, my lemman in myn armes'.

Absolon's language of love is not yet exhausted. In addition to calling Alisoun 'my sweete leef' (*MillT* 3792), she is his *deerelyng* 'darling' (3793), a word Chaucer does not use elsewhere, surprisingly perhaps, as it has a perfectly respectable distribution in Middle English sacred as well as secular writings.

Alisoun's response to the blandishments of 'this joly lovere Absolon' is justly famous, for it provides one of those uniquely

Chaucerian moments when high comedy (or in this case perhaps, more aptly, low comedy) finds its perfect expression:

> 'Tehee!' quod she, and clapte the wyndow to,
> And Absolon gooth forth a sory pas.
> *(MillT* 3740–1)

The 'sory pas' soon turns into 'a softe paas' (3760) as Absolon plots his revenge, but the heroine's suggestive 'tehee!' goes on ringing in the reader's (and presumably Absolon's) ear. There are many other interjections in Chaucer's poetry, but none of them is as uniquely appropriate as Alisoun's giggle. Interjections and exclamations are very much part of ordinary colloquial English speech and Chaucer uses them freely, sometimes no doubt for purely metrical reasons, but often to express or emphasize some particular emotion. Exclamations are also rhetorically important, whether in the simple figure of *exclamatio* or as part of another figure, like *repetitio* or *anaphora* or *apostrophe*. Simple interjections like 'a' or 'ey' are often combined with oaths, either for metrical reasons, or to add force: 'ey, Cristes foo!' *(MillT* 3782); 'ey! Goddes precious dignitee!' *(PardT* 782); 'ey, Goddes mooder' *(SumT* 2202); 'a, Seinte Marie, *benedicite!' (MerchT* 1337); but more often they serve a variety of other purposes.

The most common interjections and exclamations in Chaucer are 'a', 'allas', 'ey' (which Robinson, in *Troilus and Criseyde*, mostly prints as 'I'), 'fy', 'ha', 'harrow', 'lat be', 'lo', 'o', 'weylaway', 'what', and 'why'. Looked at like this it seems a dull enough catalogue, but Chaucer manages to rouse them all into lively action to express every shade of emotion from wonder to scorn, from disgust to delight, from doubt to cocksureness, and for the most part their inclusion adds yet again to the colloquial tone of his dialogue and to the naturalism of his narrative.

There is what Bernard F. Huppé calls the 'physical grunt'[32] of shock or surprise as Palamon spies Emelye:

> And therwithal he bleynte and cride, 'A!'
> *(KnT* 1078)

Rather more pleasant, presumably, than the mixture of consternation and disgust which Absolon packs into his 'fy! allas! what have I do ?' *(MillT* 3739) which calls forth Alisoun's memorable giggle.

32. Huppé, p. 51.

Alisoun herself, however accommodating she eventually turns out to be, has her moment of indignation as she tries to repulse 'hende' Nicholas's frontal assault:

> 'Why, lat be,' quod she, 'lat be, Nicholas,
> Or I wol crie "out, harrow" and "allas"!'
>
> (*MillT* 3285–6)

She doesn't actually do so, but in *The Nun's Priest's Tale* the shock of discovering the abduction of Chauntecleer makes the widow and her daughters rush out with 'out! harrow! and weylaway! / Ha! ha! the fox!' (*NPT* 3380–1), which suggests that for Chaucer the assaults of a subtle clerk and a sly col-fox produce much the same noises. There is wrath in the miller's monosyllabic 'ye' and 'a' as he learns of Aleyn's 'noble game' with his daughter (*RvT* 4268–9), as there is in the friar's 'a! false cherl' (*SumT* 2153) on receipt of his unexpected windfall.

For the Pardoner exclamatory language is part of his rhetorical virtuosity. He throws out an emphatic 'what' to launch a rhetorical question, and answers it with an appropriate 'nay, nay' a moment later (*PardT* 439 ff.). His disquisition upon gluttony, gambling, and swearing is punctuated by numerous rhetorical 'o's' and 'allas's', which he takes up again at the conclusion of his tale proper. The Summoner's friar indulges in a similar piece of rhetorical *exclamatio* with his reiterated 'a!' in *The Summoner's Tale*, 1963–5, and somewhat more elaborately the Canon's Yeoman, who is fond of interjections like 'a! nay! lat be' (*CYT* 862), utters a series of them in *The Canon's Yeoman's Tale*, 923 ff., including the expressive

> 'Straw!' quod the thridde. . . .
>
> (*CYT* 925)

Sometimes a Chaucerian 'a!' is simply a shout, as when Criseyde's domestics rush out to see Troilus pass by:

> 'A, go we se! cast up the yates wyde!'
>
> (*Tr* II, 615)

Often 'a' or 'ey' are used with a word of address serving as the equivalent for modern English words and phrases like 'well', 'now', 'oh dear', 'look here', 'never mind':

> 'A, goode sir, no fors,' quod y.
>
> (*BD* 522)

'A! sire, ye sholde be hende'.

(*CT* III, 1286)

'A! goode sire Hoost, I have ywedded bee'.

(*CT* IV, 1233)

'Ey, uncle myn, welcome iwys,' quod she.

(*Tr* II, 87)

In an argument, a retort may be similarly introduced, in prose as well as in verse:

'A', quod Melibee, 'now se I wel that ye loven nat myn honour ne my worshipe.'

(*Mel* 1681)

'A! wel bithought! for love of God,' quod she.

(*Tr* II, 225)

'A! may it be no bet?' quod Pandarus.

(*Tr* II, 429)

A suggestion of one-upmanship may be conveyed by a judiciously placed interjection:

'A!' thoghte this frere, 'that shal go with me!'

(*SumT* 2144)

'A ha! felawes! beth ware of swich a jape!'

(*CT* VII, 439)

'A ha!' quod he, 'lo, so I can
Lewedly to a lewed man
Speke, and shewe hym swyche skiles. . . .'

(*HF* 865–7)

'A ha!' quod Pandare, 'here bygynneth game.'

(*Tr* I, 868)

'Nay, therof spak I nought, ha, ha!' quod she.

(*Tr* II, 589)

Criseyde's 'ha, ha!' may be no more than a jolly giggle, of course, less mischievous than Alisoun's 'tehee!', and more like the Cook's merry laugh 'ha! ha!' which is the first sound he utters (*CT* I, 4327).

There is contrition in Troilus's 'a, lord! I me consente' (*Tr* I,

936), and in Pandarus's apologetic 'o, mercy, dere nece' (*Tr* II,
591); incredulity in Criseyde's

> 'Ye, holy God,' quod she, 'what thyng is that?
> What! bet than swyche fyve? I! nay, ywys!'
>> (*Tr* II, 127-8)

and sorrow in Alcyone's 'a! mercy! swete lady dere!' (*BD* 108),
and Dido's 'o, wel-awey that I was born!' (*HF* 345). There is a
whole series of emphatic monosyllables punctuating the meeting
of Troilus and Criseyde at the opening of Book III of *Troilus and
Criseyde*, expressing a variety of confused emotions:

> 'Ha, a,' quod Troilus so reufully.
> . . . .
> 'O, for the love of God, do ye nought so
> To me,' quod she, 'I! what is this to seye?'
> . . . .
> 'I! what?' quod she, 'by God and by my trouthe,
> I not nat what ye wilne that I seye.'
> 'I! what?' quod he [Pandarus], 'that ye han on hym routhe.'
>> (*Tr* III, 65 ff.)

Particularly effective in reflecting colloquial speech are the inter-
jected hummings and hawings and paddings of informal dialogue:

> 'And there I saugh oure dame, – a! where is she?'
> 'Yond in the yerd I trowe that she be,'
> Seyde this man, 'and she wol come anon.'
> 'Ey, maister, welcome be ye, by Seint John!'
> Seyde this wyf, 'how fare ye, hertely?'
> . . . .
> 'Ye, God amende defautes, sire,' quod she.
> 'Algates, welcome be ye, by my fey!'
>> (*SumT* 1797 ff.)

Or in monologue, as when the Wife of Bath tries to recapture the
gist of her narrative:

> But now, sire, lat me se, what I shal seyn?
> A ha! by God, I have my tale ageyn.
>> (*WBT* 585-6)

One interjection Chaucer did not use is the contemptuous *baw*
'bah!', used twice to great effect by Langland: 'ye, baw for bookes!'

(*PP* C XIII, 74), and '"ʒe, bawe!" quaþ a brewere' (C XXII, 398). The word is hardly the same as the Summoner's belch 'buf!' (*SumT* 1934), as Skeat asserts.

One of the characteristics shared by many of Chaucer's characters, gentles and churls, is their love of song, but presumably Chaucer distinguished, as would his audience, between what would nowadays be called 'serious' and 'pop' music. The little boy's devout *O Alma redemptoris*[33] in *The Prioress's Tale* is fit accompaniment to the unfolding of his pathetic martyrdom, while at the other extreme is the lewd duet 'Com hider, love, to me!' of Pardoner and Summoner (*Gen Prol* 672-3). In *The Nun's Priest's Tale* cock and hen are depicted in joyful domestic accord singing what was evidently another popular song of the age, 'My lief is faren in londe' (*NPT* 2879). The Squire 'syngynge . . . was, or floytynge, al the day.' (*Gen Prol* 91) and was capable of composing his own songs, though we are not told what they were. The Parson refers to 'thilke newe Frenshe song, "*Jay tout perdu mon temps et mon labour*"' (*ParsT* 248), possibly, as Skeat suggests, the refrain of a French *ballade*, used again as a complete line of verse in *Fortune*, 7. Another snatch of song is quoted in the *Complaynt D'Amours*, a poem doubtfully assigned to Chaucer:

> I may wel singe, 'In sory tyme I spende
> My lyf;' that song may have confusioun!
> (*Compl d'Am* 24-5)

Examples of 'songes, compleintes, roundels, virelayes' (*FranklT* 948) are scattered throughout Chaucer's work, as separate poems or incorporated in others. Some are elaborately wrought poems, like Anelida's *compleynt* in *Anelida and Arcite*, others are modest pieces of a few lines, like the little encomium in praise of the daisy sung by the group of ladies in the Prologue to *The Legend of Good Women*:

> And songen with o vois, 'Heel and honour
> To trouthe of womanhede, and to this flour
> That bereth our alder pris in figurynge!
> Hire white corowne bereth the witnessynge.'
> (*LGW* Prol F 296-9)

---

33. He refers to it as an *anthem*, a word not used by Chaucer elsewhere, in *PrT* 660, although mostly it is simply called a *song*.

Many a Chaucerian character may be found singing 'with vois memorial in the shade' (*Anel* 18), but a colloquial, or a humorous, or an ironic note often enters into the singing. The crow's 'cokkow! cokkow! cokkow!' in *The Manciple's Tale*, 243, the duck's 'ye quek' and the goose's *kakelynge* in *The Parliament of Fowls*, 594, 562, demonstrate that not all bird song in Chaucer is melodious; nor is all human song, witness Januarie's nuptial

> Whil that he sang, so chaunteth he and craketh,
> (*MerchT* 1850)

where *craketh* presumably carries all the obnoxious connotations of unpleasant noises suggested by the Parson's use of the word: 'by chirkynge [creaking] of dores, or crakkynge of houses, by gnawynge of rattes' (*ParsT* 605). The snoring of the assembled household at Trumpington is ironically referred to as 'slyk a sang' by Aleyn listening to 'this melodye' (*RvT* 4168–70), and there is irony of a different sort in Nicholas's singing, of an evening, *Angelus ad virginem*, followed by 'the Kynges Noote', whatever that was,[34] 'so swetely that all the chambre rong' (*MillT* 3215). There are several references to sacred hymns like the *Angelus ad virginem*, an Annunciation conductus the text of which happens to be preserved; for example, the worldly friar's claim in *The Summoner's Tale* that '*Te Deum* was oure song, and nothyng elles' (1866), or his mention of the *Placebo* (2075), from the opening of the antiphon *Placebo Domino in regione vivorum* which began the vespers of the Office of the Dead. That to sing *Placebo* had acquired an ironic connotation by Chaucer's time is likely from the Summoner's usage, as well as from the Parson's comment: 'flatereres been the develes chapelleyns, that syngen evere *Placebo*' (*ParsT* 617).[35]

There is a fair amount of singing in *Troilus and Criseyde*, songs of love and joy and *compleyntes*, Antigone's song in II, 827–75, but Pandarus's voice is uniquely his, whether 'he song; she pleyde' (III, 614) as he entertains Criseyde at his house, or skips into

---

34. Cp. Fletcher Collins, 'The Kinges Note', *Speculum* VIII (1933), 195–7, and George L. Frost, 'The Music of *The Kinges Note*', *ibid.*, 526–8. For a recent suggestion that 'Kynges Noote' is a continuation of the English lyrics of *Angelus ad virginem* see Jesse M. Gellrich, 'Nicholas' "Kynges Noote" and "Melodye"', *English Language Notes* VIII (1971), 249–52.

35. See further Beverly Boyd, *Chaucer and the Liturgy* (Philadelphia, 1967), *passim*.

Troilus's bedroom, and

> right at his in-comynge,
> He song, as who seyth, 'Somwhat I brynge',
> > (*Tr* II, 1308–9)

perhaps another allusion to some popular song. The Miller's
Absolon is more of a virtuoso, blessed with a high voice, so that
'he song som tyme a loud quynyble' (*MillT* 3332), a part sung by a
voice a fifth above the treble,[36] later referred to as a 'voys gentil
and smal' (3360), but audible enough to wake the carpenter with
his little serenade:

> 'Now, deere lady, if thy wille be,
> I praye yow that ye wole rewe on me.'
> > (*MillT* 3361–2)

Alisoun's accomplishments are mainly of a lower order, but she
seems to be at least quoting, if not like the Prioress actually
'entuning', a bit of some popular song in 'com pa me', that is
'come kiss me' (*MillT* 3709), where the reading of several manuscripts suggests that *pa* is probably the same word as the Wife
of Bath's *ba* 'kiss' (*WBT* 433). There may well be other snatches of
fourteenth-century pop music embedded in Chaucer's work –
some verses certainly read like it – but they are practically impossible to identify today. What may be asserted with some
assurance, however, is that the lusty singing of some of Chaucer's
characters, the few fragments of popular songs which we can
recognize, as well as the ironic references to sacred hymns, are yet
further devices employed by the poet to reflect the language of his
day, and more especially the colloquial registers of so many of his
characters, whether or not they actually 'tolden harlotrie'.

36. Not an octave, as stated by Robinson and others, including the *OED*. Cp.
Grove's *Dictionary of Music and Musicians*, 5th edn, ed. Eric Blom (London, 1954),
Vol. VI, p. 1036. I am grateful to Mr G. A. Anderson for pointing this out to me.

CHAPTER 5

Many a Grisly Ooth

𝕊𝕊𝕊𝕊𝕊𝕊

T HERE is a charming little domestic scene in Part 1 of Shake-speare's *King Henry IV* (III. i.) in which Hotspur asks his wife to sing a song:

> Hotspur: Come Kate, I'll have your song too.
> Lady Percy: Not mine, in good sooth.
> Hotspur: Not yours, in good sooth? Heart, you swear like a
>   comfit-maker's wife. 'Not you, in good sooth!'
>   and 'as true as I live!' and 'as God shall mend me!'
>   and 'as sure as day!'
>   And givest such sarcenet surety for thy oaths
>   As if thou never walk'st further than Finsbury.
>   Swear me, Kate, like a lady as thou art,
>   A good mouth-filling oath, and leave 'in sooth'
>   And such protest of pepper gingerbread
>   To velvet guards and Sunday citizens.
>   Come, sing.

Lady Percy, as it happens, does neither to oblige her husband: she 'will not sing', nor does she spice the air of the Archdeacon's house in Bangor, where some editors place this scene, with 'a good mouth-filling oath' or two. Other ladies of that time, and of earlier and later ages no less, were less fastidious. Queen Elizabeth I had some particularly mouth-filling favourites, like 'Jesus!', 'God's death!' 'God's wounds!' 'by God's son!', 'God's blessign of thine heart!', which make one wish that our own sovereign lady might now and again lard her ceremonial orations with some similar expletive fit for royalty, perhaps Henry II's favourite, 'by the very eyes of God!'

Actually, the swearing of Shakespeare's characters – even his more impetuous or vulgar ones – is surprisingly mild and un-differentiated, certainly after the passing of the Act to Restrain Abuses of Players, 1606. In the main they content themselves with swearing by God in some uncomplicated way, and even

Falstaff is content with an occasional 'zounds' or ''sblood' or 'by the Lord'. In this respect he would have cut a decidedly virtuous figure had he been among Chaucer's Canterbury pilgrims. Harry Bailly would have been more to Hotspur's taste than Lady Kate or Falstaff; he is substantial proof that in the later fourteenth century good mouth-filling oaths were very much in the air. That most of them were religious in character is not surprising, for it was a religious age. All swearing has something dare-devil about it; that is why in our own age the strongest expletives are sexual or scatological. Nowadays to tear Christ's body to pieces, as the revellers do in *The Pardoner's Tale* –

> And many a grisly ooth thanne han they sworn,
> And Cristes blessed body al torente –
> *(PardT* 708–9)

would fall rather flat. By contrast, sexual oaths are non-existent in Chaucer, and this despite the robust, earthy diction of his *cherles* and of forthright characters like Pandarus or the Wife of Bath. The same holds for Chaucer's contemporaries, of whom Gower, averse to swearing in the *Confessio Amantis* at least, is by far the most virtuous. The *Gawain*-poet has a modest 'in faye' and 'par ma fay' in *Pearl*, and a few similarly mild oaths in *Sir Gawain and the Green Knight*: 'ma fay', 'in fayth', 'in god fayth', 'bi Kryst' (reserved for Sir Bertilak), 'bi þe rode', 'bi God' (Sir Gawain's favourite), 'for Gode', the Green Knight's 'bigog', and towards the end of the poem (2122) Sir Gawain is even prepared to promise that

> I schal swere bi God and alle his gode halȝez.

Langland's characters are a little more inclined to swear 'grete othes', but they do so without any of the discrimination that makes Chaucer's oaths and imprecations so interesting. In *Piers Plowman* the Dreamer, Conscience, the king, Clergy, a common woman, and others all swear 'bi Crist', or in more elaborate terms, 'by Cryst that me made', 'by hym that rauhte on rode', 'by Crist and by his corone bothe'. Others swear 'by this light', 'by Marye of heuene' or simply 'by Marie', 'by verrai God', 'by seynt Poule', and so on. Mostly the alliteration rather than the speaker's character or social class determines the oath. In Chaucer, prosodic reasons also play their part, particularly when oaths occur as rhyme words,[1] but even here the poet is more discriminating than his contemporaries, for example in the choice of the names of saints, like 'Seint Austyn' (*CT* VII, 441), or 'seint Martyn' (*ShipT* 148), or 'Seynte Clare' (*HF* 1066). Chaucer had a good ear for oaths and used them, as we shall see, not only to add definition to character and class, but to add irony, to provide a touch of local colour, and to create atmosphere and background.

Not surprisingly, it is the more vulgar characters who swear most, in *The Canterbury Tales* at least. *Troilus and Criseyde* with its numerous asseverations of good faith is, as we shall see, somewhat different, and in *The Legend of Good Women* there are no vulgar characters. Of the earlier poems, *The Parliament of Fowls* is distinguished by the duck's picturesquely inappropriate 'by myn hat!' (*PF* 589), and by one of the eagles swearing not incongruously 'by seint John' (451). The saint here invoked may have been chosen because the eagle was the symbol of St John the Evangelist, or possibly simply for rhyme, but 'the sturdy tone' of the bird's speech, oath included, is, as Clemen points out,[2] appropriate enough for one who was 'of lower kynde' than the first eagle. Apart from these, there are in *The Parliament of Fowls* a couple of those ubiquitous *parde's* (509, from the turtle; 571, from the sparrow-hawk), a 'God wot' from Nature (663), and twice the Dreamer utters a somewhat half-hearted 'Lord' (171, 669). This is not a rich harvest, considering the liveliness of the debate and the possibilities of differentiating further between the debaters.

On the other hand, there is rather more swearing in Chaucer's two other early poems, *The Book of the Duchess* and *The House of Fame*, although the characters are not really vulgar. But both these poems employ the shorter octosyllabic line in which the temptation to fill out with a tag is greater than in the longer line of the heroic couplet or the rhyme royal stanza. This is probably due both to the more frequent occurrence of rhyme and to the difficulty of fitting more complex sentence patterns into the rhyme. Thus one may well wonder whether in *The Book of the Duchess* the use of 'by my trouthe' in four of its eight occurrences (*BD* 98, 466, 591, 1309) is not simply dictated by the need to rhyme with *routhe*, an important word in the story of the Black Knight's

1. Cp. Masui, ch. XXI.
2. Clemen, p. 159.

love-suit, and whether, similarly, other oaths, like 'a Goddes
half' (370, 758), 'by oure Lord' (544, 651, 690, 1042), 'before God'
(677), 'so God me save' (755), 'as helpe me God' (838), and their
variants, are not introduced to help the metre along rather than to
add anything of importance to the sense. Occasionally, a whole
line or almost a whole line is given over to some such oath:

> 'For, also wys God yive me reste.'
> *(BD 683)*

> 'By God, and by his halwes twelve.'
> *(ibid. 831)*

> 'And eke, as helpe me God withal.'
> *(ibid. 1205)*

Sometimes, particularly in the Dreamer's contributions to the
dialogue, the oaths come thick and fast, and together with more
commonplace tags, combine to form a picture of well-intentioned
but somewhat incompetent, not to say incoherent, outpouring
of counsel or comfort indicative of the Dreamer's role in the
poem. The conversational tone of such passages depends as
much upon the inclusion of these tags and oaths, as upon the
monosyllabic character of much of the diction and the co-ordinated clauses with their repetitive *and* and *but* and *for*:

> 'By oure Lord,' quod I, 'y trow yow wel;
> Ryght so me thinketh by youre chere.
> But, sir, oo thyng wol ye here?
> Me thynketh in gret sorowe I yow see.
> But certes, sire, yif that yee
> Wolde ought discure me youre woo,
> I wolde, as wys God helpe me soo,
> Amende hyt, yif I kan or may.
> Ye mowe preve hyt be assay;
> For, by my trouthe, to make yow hool,
> I wol do al my power hool.
> And telleth me of your sorwes smerte;
> Paraunter hyt may ese youre herte,
> That semeth ful sek under your syde.'
> *(BD 544–57)*

Hence it would be too facile to dismiss the use of oaths in *The
Book of the Duchess* as merely mechanical. Already in his first
long poem Chaucer was clearly responding to characteristic

elements in contemporary English speech, at least to the extent
of recognizing them and incorporating them in dialogue.

In *The House of Fame* this tendency is carried further. Both the
Dreamer and his learned guide, the Eagle, pepper their talk with a
good many oaths of the sort encountered already in *The Book of
the Duchess*, but now, surprisingly, 'be Cryste' (*HF* 271) is ad-
mitted into the repertoire, perhaps to stress the topicality of the
narrator's comments upon the story of Dido and Aeneas, although Chaucer's later usage brands this as definitely a vulgar
oath; and more saints are invoked than in the earlier poem. In
The Book of the Duchess occurs only one such invocation, 'be seynt
Johan!', uttered by the narrator towards the end of the poem in a
couplet generally regarded as containing thinly veiled allusions to
Blanche, *white*, duchess of Lancaster (Lune-caster 'Roman fort
on the River Lune' but taken as Long-caster, *long castel*), and
John of Gaunt, *Johan*, created Earl of Richmond at the age of two,
when Richmond in Yorkshire (Rich-mount, *ryche hil*) came into
his possession:

> A long castel with walles white,
> Be syent Johan! on a ryche hil.
>
> (*BD* 1318–19)

In *The House of Fame* allusions involving saints are of different
kinds. There is an interesting cluster of invocations to saints at
the end of Book II and the beginning of Book III, most of which
can be, with some degree of probability, contextually justified.
The Eagle's reference to 'Seynt Julyan, loo, bon hostel!' (*HF*
1022) as he arrives with his passenger at the house of Fame is
appropriate, for St Julian was patron saint of hospitality, and
there is an added ironic note in thus welcoming to the seat of
Fame one earlier identified as 'Geffrey' (729). The play on *Peter*
and on *roches*, based on St Matthew's 'Thou art Peter, and upon
this rock I will build my church' (XVI: 18), follows a few lines
later:

> 'And what soun is it lyk? 'quod hee.
> 'Peter! lyk betynge of the see,'
> Quod y, 'ayen the roches holowe'.
>
> (*HF* 1033–5)

Equally emphatically at the beginning of the line is the other occurrence of *Peter* in the poem (2000). Admittedly, the Eagle is here sitting 'hye upon a stoon', but it would be too far-fetched to see in this a play on words comparable to that on *Peter* and *roches* in lines 1034–5. 'Peter!' is a common enough exclamation, but its use by the merchant's wife in *The Shipman's Tale* (214), as well as by the Summoner, Canon's Yeoman and Wife of Bath alone among Chaucer's characters, and by the castle porter alone in *Sir Gawain and the Green Knight*, makes one inclined to view the Eagle in *The House of Fame* as rather more akin to his cousin 'of lower kynde' in *The Parliament of Fowls* than might at first have been suspected. In *Piers Plowman*, 'Peter!' is the first word uttered by Piers in the poem in all three versions (C VIII, 182), and in the B text the 'lewed lorel' of a priest twice exclaims it in the Pardon scene (B VII, 112, 130). 'Peter' is presumably a colloquial shortening of the fuller 'by seynt Peter of Rome' (C IX, 1) or 'bi Peter the apostel' (A VII, 3), and Chaucer's usage, as well as that of the *Gawain*-poet and possibly Langland, suggests that it is something of a class indicator.

The third saint to be invoked is 'Seynte Clare' (1066) whose name, admittedly, provides a useful rhyme for 'al this loude fare' of the preceding line, but who may well have been introduced here, as Marie Neville has argued, for more cogent reasons.[3] Known to Chaucer and presumably his audience as co-founder and patron of an order of nuns, the Minoresses, who had a convent close to Aldgate where the poet lived from 1374 to 1386, St Clare, a disciple of St Francis, was particularly associated with the rule of silence which the nuns of her order were strictly bound to observe. The bull of her canonization speaks of her, as Marie Neville records, 'in a sentence that might serve as an ironic comment on the *House of Fame*: "Silebat Clara, sed sua fama clamabat"', and the conclusion seems warranted that 'for Chaucer and his audience mention of St Clare, and the inevitable association with her order, would, in a passage descriptive of strident clamor, suggest a contrasting silence'. Whatever one may think of H. S. Bennett's claim that Chaucer 'could not get from his words those "peripheral overtones" which have meant

3. Marie Neville, 'Chaucer and St Clare', *Journal of English and Germanic Philology* LV (1956), 423–30. In addition to arguing for the contextual aptness of 'Seynte Clare', this paper draws attention to some interesting links between Chaucer and the convent of the Minoresses at Aldgate.

so much to later writers',[4] this is certainly not true of his use of saints' names, Here it is simply that the modern reader of Chaucer is deaf to the 'overtones'.

That the fourteenth-century Englishman sometimes swore by his local saint is evident from several instances in *The Canterbury Tales*; in *The House of Fame* it is Chaucer's *alter ego*, the dreaming Geffrey, who does so appropriately enough early in Book III: 'by seynt Thomas of Kent!' (1131). And it is the Dreamer also who invokes 'seynt Gyle', Saint Giles or Aegidius (1183), perhaps simply to enhance the exotic description of the castle of Fame for which he claims that 'my wit ne may me not suffise'. In *The Canon's Yeoman's Tale*, 1185, St Giles is invoked by the rascally canon and in *Sir Gawain and the Green Knight*, 1644, by Sir Bertilak, in both cases simply as a convenient rhyme for *while*. This simple explanation is probably also true of the Eagle's 'be seynt Jame' (*HF* 885), for neither St James the apostle, whose shrine at Compostella, 'in Galice at Seint-Jame', the Wife of Bath had visited, nor St Giles, patron of cripples, beggars, and blacksmiths, is contextually particularly appropriate.

Saints apart, however, Eagle, Dreamer, and the other speakers swear very much alike in *The House of Fame*, and even such rarer Chaucerian oaths as 'by my thrift' (1847), and 'by my hed' (1875) within thirty lines of each other near the end of the poem add little more than a certain novelty to the swearing, yet well in keeping with the colloquial character of the dialogue. The expression 'by my thrift' is akin to the common tag 'so moot I thryve' and its variants, with a literal meaning 'by my prosperity'. Pandarus uses it twice (*Tr* II, 1483; III, 871) and Criseyde once (*Tr* IV, 1630); apart from these only the thieving miller of Trumpington utters it, but with a meaning made ironically appropriate by the short shrift he eventually receives for his own *sleighte*:

> 'They wene that no man may hem bigyle,
> But by my thrift, yet shal I blere hir ye,
> For al the sleighte in hir philosophye.'
>> (*RvT* 4048–50)

It does not seem to have been a common oath at any time. In Shakespeare only King Henry uses a similar expression in *Henry*

4. H. S. Bennett, *Chaucer and the Fifteenth Century* (Oxford, 1947), p. 83.

VIII, III, ii. 109–10: 'How, i' the name of thrift, /Does he rake this together?'

Much the same holds for swearing by one's head, which the Dreamer does once in *The House of Fame* in a succession of lines packed with tags:

'Nay, for sothe, frend,' quod y;
'I cam noght hyder, graunt mercy,
For no such cause, by my hed!
Sufficeth me, as I were ded,
That no wight have my name in honde.'

(*HF* 1873–7)

Saturn swears by his head in *The Knight's Tale* (2670) and Pandarus is said to have done so in *Troilus and Criseyde* (V, 283). He does so openly in Book IV, 593, and if he intends to imply that he is prepared to lose his head he means it, for only a few lines further on, in the same speech, he avers:

'I wol myself ben with the at this dede,
Theigh ich and al my kyn, upon a stownde,
Shulle in a strete as dogges liggen dede,
Thorugh-girt with many a wid and blody wownde'.

(*Tr* IV, 624–7)

There are some interesting parallels between Pandarus's speech and Arcite's speech in *The Knight's Tale*, 1153 ff., which suggests that Chaucer may have been recalling his own words, notably Pandarus's 'thorough love is broken al day every lawe' (618) and Arcite's

'And therfore positif lawe and swich decree
Is broken al day for love in ech degree',

(*KnT* 1167–8)

and Pandarus's 'by myn hed' echoing Arcite's 'by my pan' (*KnT* 1165). Such borrowings or echoes from within his own work are not uncommon in Chaucer. The word *pan* means strictly the upper part of the skull, and by itself or in the compound *braynpanne* 'cranium', which goes back to O.E. *brægenpanne*, is found in various Middle English writings. Gower distinguishes neatly between the whole head and the *pan*:

> ... he ... smot his hed of thanne,
> Wherof he tok awey the Panne,
> Of which he seide he wolde make
> A Cuppe. ...
>
> (*Conf Am* I, 2471–4)

And Langland clearly intends the same distinction:

> ȝut Pees putte forth hus hefd and hus panne blody.
> (*PP* C V, 74)

That Arcite's 'by my pan' is meant to be as subtle is highly improbable, but the Host presumably intends it when, in addressing the Monk, he says

> '... and I were a pope,
> Nat oonly thou, but every myghty man,
> Though he were shorn ful hye upon his pan,
> Sholde have a wyf. ...'
>
> (*CT* VII, 1950–3)

Swearing by one's crown, 'the top of the head in a contemptuous sense', as Dr Johnson puts it, is yet another variant. Aleyn swears 'by my croun' (*RvT* 4041) and some fifty lines later the miller of Trumpington ironically echoes the oath (4099); apart from these two no one else swears by his crown in Chaucer. The remaining variants of this type of oath refer not to the head but to headgear, namely the duck's 'by myn hat' (*PF* 589) already mentioned, and the oath 'by myn hood' which the distraught Troilus utters as he awaits the promised return of Criseyde (*Tr* V, 1151), and which the god of Love once exclaims for emphasis, buttressed by a further *pardee*, in the Prologue to *The Legend of Good Women* (F 507). The rascally canon of *The Canon's Yeoman's Tale* varies 'by myn hood' in a good mouth-filling line:

> 'For, by my feith, I nolde, for myn hood'.
> (*CYT* 1334)

The group of oaths just discussed are all colloquial, but are not confined to any particular class of speakers. 'By my pan' is the only one which can be regarded as a slang expression. That Arcite should be the only person in Chaucer to use it is perhaps surprising, but the context of the quarrel between him and Palamon called for strong language and some stronger oath than the handful of mild exclamations which the Knight permits himself and his other characters in the telling of his tale. As we shall see later, Arcite's swearing tends to be rather more forceful than anyone else's in *The Knight's Tale*. The restraint is broken soon enough, however, when Harry Bailly 'lough and swoor' at the conclusion of the Knight's tale and the Miller launches on his. It is worth noting that Chaucer makes very little use of the *head* oaths compared with religious oaths, although they were common in French popular poetry.

In *Troilus and Criseyde* there are numerous oaths, but the incidence of swearing is uneven: there is least in Books I and V, most in Books II and III. The oaths themselves fall into a large group of *God* oaths, mainly of the type 'for Goddes love', a smaller group of the type 'by my trouthe', and a still smaller group invoking classical deities. All the major characters in the poem swear, Pandarus most of all, and there appears to be more design in the oaths, their nature, distribution, and their speakers, in *Troilus and Criseyde*, than in any of Chaucer's previous poems. The almost constant invocations of God add an unmistakable religious dimension to narrative and dialogue which may seem out of keeping with the classical setting and the poignant love story, but which prepares the reader or listener at least to some extent for the overtly Christian attitude adopted by the narrator in the poem's concluding stanzas. After an unceasing succession of upward glances to God throughout the poem, it comes as no real surprise to be urged thus:

> up casteth the visage
> To thilke God that after his ymage
> Yow made.
>
> (*Tr* V, 1838–40)

The tragedy of Troilus and Criseyde was that for all their invoking of God's grace and aid and blessing they did not, indeed could not, avert their fate. But the 'yonge, fresshe folkes' of Chaucer's time can repudiate 'feynede loves' and turn to

> hym, the which that right for love
> Upon a crois, oure soules for to beye,
> First starf, and roos, and sit in hevene above.
>
> (*Tr* V, 1842–4)

This direct reference to Christ would have been out of place

earlier in the poem, yet the numerous *God* oaths are unmistakably
Christian, as are, *par contraire*, the imprecations calling upon the
devil, as well as other religious allusions:

> And Pandarus, in ernestful manere,
> Seyde, 'Alle folk, for Godes love, I preye,
> Stynteth right here, and softely yow pleye.
>
> Aviseth yow what folk ben hire withinne,
> And in what plit oon is, God hym amende!'
> And inward thus, 'Ful softely bygynne,
> Nece, I conjure and heighly yow defende,
> On his half which that soule us alle sende,
> And in the vertu of corones tweyne,
> Sle naught this man, that hath for yow this peyne!
>
> Fy on the devel!. . . .'
>
> (*Tr* II, 1727–37)

Whatever one wishes to make of the enigmatic 'corones tweyne'
of line 1735, the reference in the preceding line to 'Him who sent
us all our souls' certainly supports a Christian interpretation, like
E. Talbot Donaldson's crowns of martyrdom and purity, or R. K.
Root's justice and mercy, with reference to Christ and the Virgin
Mary, and the tone of the whole passage favours some such reading. To regard this as a 'glaring anachronism' on Chaucer's part
is to ignore the strong Christian colouring imparted to the whole
poem by the frequent invocations of God. Here are some further
examples:

> 'And, God so wys be my savacioun,
> As I have seyd, youre beste is to do soo.'
>
> (*Tr* II, 381–2)

> 'Depardieux,' quod she, 'God leve al be wel!
> God help me so. . . .'
>
> (*Tr* II, 1212–13)

> 'For, by that God that bought us bothe two'.
>
> (*Tr* III, 1165)

> 'Ye ben so depe in-with myn herte grave,
> That, though I wolde it torne out of my thought,
> As wisly verray God my soule save,
> To dyen in the peyne, I koude nought.

And, for the love of God that us hath wrought,
Lat in youre brayn non other fantasie
So crepe, that it cause me to dye!'

(*Tr* III, 1499–1505)

'Thus seyde I nevere er now to womman born;
For, God myn herte as wisly glade so,
I loved never womman here-biforn
As paramours, ne nevere shal no mo.
And, for the love of God, beth nat my fo'.

(*Tr* V, 155–9)

Occasionally, the *God* oaths are particularly crowded. In Book II, for example, in just twenty lines of dialogue with Pandarus, Criseyde utters the following: 'God forbede', 'so God yow save', 'by God', 'for Goddes love', 'ye, holy God', 'as help me God', as well as the orthodox Catholic sentiment,

'It sate me wel bet ay in a cave
To bidde and rede on holy seyntes lyves'.

(*Tr* II, 117–18)

If Pandarus swears most of all in *Troilus and Criseyde*, over eighty times, Criseyde is not far behind with more than sixty oaths. Troilus utters about forty oaths and the narrator about twenty more. Together with a handful from the minor characters, this adds up to more than 200 oaths, the majority of which invoke the name of God, without taking into account the frequent use of *pardee*, *benedicitee* and 'God woot'. The narrator's favourite exclamation is 'Lord!' The theme of fidelity and trustworthiness is underlined both by the frequent occurrence in the poem of the adverb *trewely* and by a number of oaths of the type 'by my trouthe', emanating ironically enough mainly from Pandarus and from Criseyde, while the oaths invoking classical deities reinforce the classical background of the story. There are about twenty of the latter in the poem, most of them coming from Pandarus, with Criseyde again close behind. Outside *Troilus and Criseyde* 'classical' oaths are few. The god of Love swears by his mother, 'by Seynt Venus', in the Prologue (F 338) to *The Legend of Good Women*. In the Legend of Lucretia occurs:

'As wisly Jupiter my soule save',

(*LGW* 1806)

and in that of Ariadne:

'By Mars, that is the chef of my beleve'.
(*LGW* 2109)

Mars also figures in *The Knight's Tale*: 'by myghty Mars' (1708), 'by myghty Mars the rede' (1747), and the dying Arcite twice invokes Jupiter in words which resemble a prayer more than an oath *KnT* 2786, 2792).

As Herbert Starr observed in his essay on Chaucer's oaths,[5] oaths invoking classical deities were unlikely to have been common in actual life in Chaucer's day, particularly among the 'lewed' people. Pandarus's 'for Joves name in hevene' (*Tr* I, 878) would have been as much a class indicator in late fourteenth-century London as would be the 'by Jove' of a nineteenth-century Englishman, but it is unlikely that Chaucer used these oaths for such a purpose. They add a classical tint to a classical tale but add nothing to our knowledge of the characters using them. This is less true of the large number of religious oaths in *Troilus and Criseyde*, however. It is significant that Troilus swears less than Pandarus and Criseyde and that on the whole his oaths are less intense and less colloquial than those of the other speakers. His language throughout the poem is courtly, 'his is the voice of the "highest" style in the poem',[6] and Chaucer certainly extends this distinction to Troilus's swearing. He is the only one in the poem to use the French 'mafay' (III, 52) and shares two other French oaths with Criseyde who 'in terms of style', as Muscatine says, 'speaks in both idioms'; 'pardieux' and 'depardieux' are used by both of them. Pandarus uses none of these. Troilus, like the narrator, is fond of the simple 'Lord', and this together with modest oaths of the type 'for the love of God' makes up the bulk of his swearing. He swears, in short, like a knight:

'Frend, as I am trewe knyght,
And by that feyth I shal to God and yow'.
(*Tr* III, 1648-9)

Criseyde frequently invokes God, shares some French oaths with Troilus, some classical ones with Pandarus, and tends to use

5. Herbert W. Starr, 'Oaths in Chaucer's Poems', *West Virginia University Bulletin*: *Philological Studies* IV (1943), 44-63. I am indebted to this paper for several valuable suggestions.
6. Muscatine, p. 135.

more mouth-filling oaths like 'for his love, which that us bothe made' (II, 500) or 'by that God that bought us bothe two' (III, 1165). Pandarus is the most colloquial swearer of the three and apart from French oaths (always excepting the ubiquitous 'pardee' which everyone uses) utilizes the whole range of oaths in *Troilus and Criseyde*. He frequently avers his trustworthiness with a 'by my trouthe', as often as not ironic enough in the circumstances, swears by his thrift and by his head, utters strong imprecations like 'to dethe mot I smyten be with thondre' (II, 1145), calls upon God's help at least a dozen times, fills his mouth occasionally with a phrase like 'by God and yonder sonne' (II, 1237), and generally plays upon the name of God as on an organ. In short, we do learn something about the characters in *Troilus and Criseyde* from their swearing. Chaucer may not have weighed up every single utterance in the poem before assigning it to its speaker, but he certainly created three distinct personal idioms, and in these the oaths play their part.

In *The Canterbury Tales* it is the vulgar characters who swear most and most profanely, with Harry Bailly well out in front, the Wife of Bath some way behind, followed by Pardoner and Miller. Within the tales, too, it is the lower orders who swear most commonly, though there are some interesting exceptions. Dorigen, for example, in *The Franklin's Tale*, has some oaths that might have satisfied Hotspur:

'By thilke God that yaf me soule and lyf'.
> (*FranklT* 983)

'No, by that Lord,' quod she, 'that maked me!'
> (*ibid.* 1000)

'Nay, nay,' quod she, 'God helpe me so as wys!'
> (*ibid.* 1470)

And another female heroine, the hen Pertelote, however 'curteys she was, discreet, and debonaire', spices her discourse with a handful of oaths that would not have disgraced a less *discreet* damsel. So, for that matter, does her lordly husband, and we can see in this yet another strand added by Chaucer to the complex mock-heroic texture of *The Nun's Priest's Tale*: farmyard fowl that pepper their conversation with 'by God', and 'for Goddes love', and 'by that God above', and 'as wys God helpe me', while they peck around the yard, and 'feather' each other, and talk of *Catoun* and medicinal herbs and the meaning of dreams, are surely in a class by themselves. Distant cousins they may be of the garrulous Eagle of *The House of Fame* and the quacking duck of *The Parliament of Fowls*, but Chaucer's art has made great strides since then: beneath the royal exterior of Chauntecleer and the romantic beauty of his paramour there lies, God wot, something decidedly vulgar.

There are many reasons why people swear. Dorigen swears to emphasize the firm conviction of her own fidelity and of the impossibility of the task she imposes by calling upon God as witness. Pertelote punctuates her shocked lecture with ungallinaceous exclamations that fit neatly into the metre. The rioters in *The Pardoner's Tale* swear mightily because they are a trio of drunken, gambling, swearing revellers embodying these very same 'sins of the tavern' which the Pardoner has just been preaching against. The false canon in *The Canon's Yeoman's Tale* betrays himself as the churl he is because he swears as the other *cherles* do, by the 'devel of helle!', for instance (*CYT* 1238). So do Harry Bailly and the Wife of Bath and the Manciple and the various purveyors of *harlotrie*. Shock, fear, anger, surprise, incredulity, are some of the emotional states that find outlets in swearing. Chaucer knew enough about human psychology, however, to know that people do not swear only in moments of emotional stress. He knew that some people swear from habit, and that some never swear at all; hence the contrast, for example, between the Host and the Second Nun, both of whom directly invoke the name of God about the same number of times, the latter with all due piety, the former invariably 'in vain'. Many oaths are of course little more than meaningless exclamations of no particular intensity, especially the common 'God woot' and 'pardee' scattered freely throughout Chaucer's poetry and some of the prose. They serve the same purpose as other mild interjections and innocuous tags, adding a colloquial touch or simply making the line scan.

Apart from profane exclamations, oaths may serve as vows, 'to intensify or confirm a promise or statement', in Herbert Starr's words, but the distinction is not always easy to draw. Dorigen's 'God helpe me so as wys!', quoted above, is perhaps of this kind, as is Canacee's

'I wolde amenden it er that it were nyght,
As wisly helpe me grete God of kynde!'
                              (*SqT* 468–9)

But when Alisoun utters 'as help me God' followed almost at
once by a forceful 'by Jhesu' (*MillT* 3709–11), the profanity of the
exclamation is obvious. Oaths intended as vows may of course
be plainly declared as such, whether playfully,

And finally he [Pandarus] swor and gan hire seye,
By this and that, she sholde hym nought escape,
                              (*Tr* III, 556–7)

or seriously, as when Criseyde comforts Troilus,

And therwithal she swor hym in his ere,
'Iwys, my deere herte, I am nought wroth,
Have here my trouthe!' and many an other oth.
                              (*Tr* III, 1109–11)

Such confirmatory oaths were sworn for all manner of things.
The pilgrims assenting to the Host's proposals for the Canterbury
pilgrimage swore oaths 'with ful glad herte' (*Gen Prol* 810–11);
the three revellers of *The Pardoner's Tale* swear

To lyve and dyen ech of hem for oother,
As though he were his owene ybore brother,
                              (*PardT* 703–4)

just as Palamon and Arcite are brothers 'ysworn ful depe' (*KnT*
1132), and the summoner and the devil of *The Friar's Tale* with an
ironic 'by my feith'

Everych in ootheres hand his trouthe leith,
For to be sworne bretheren til they deye.
                              (*FrT* 1404–5)

Pandarus, who swears rather glibly, on one occasion reminds
Criseyde of 'alle the othes that I have yow sworn' (*Tr* II, 299);
and many a Chaucerian lover, male and female, swears fidelity,
whether like Aeneas simply with his 'ryght hond' (*HF* 322), or
like Criseyde with a flood of solemn asseverations:

'And this on every god celestial
I swere it yow, and ek on ech goddesse,
On every nymphe and deite infernal,
On satiry and fawny more and lesse,

255

That halve goddes ben of wildernesse;
And Attropos my thred of lif tobreste
If I be fals! now trowe me if yow leste!'
                    (*Tr* IV, 1541–7)

Admittedly, the lady doth protest too much, as if mere quantity
of oaths could ensure *trouthe*. One is reminded of the guide in
Sir Gawain and the Green Knight, 2120 ff., tempting Gawain and
swearing concealment

        'bi God and alle his gode halȝez,
    As help me God and þe halydam, and oþez innoghe',

or of Theseus taking literally Ariadne's invitation to 'swere it
here, *upon al that may be sworn*' (*LGW* 2102) and filling the next
twenty lines with solemn oaths.

By contrast, a knight's oath was his *seuretee*, to use the Squire's
word (*SqT* 528), and Chaucer does not usually elaborate when
someone 'swoor . . . as a knyght', in this case Arveragus (*FranklT*
745). It was enough to swear, like Duke Theseus, 'upon my
trouthe, and as I am a knyght' (*KnT* 1855) or, for that matter, like
Sir Gawain's 'I swere þe for soþe, and by my seker traweþ' (*SGGK*
403). There was no need to spell out for a medieval audience what
a legitimate oath, as distinct from a profanity, consisted of. Yet
for the benefit of his Canterbury pilgrims Chaucer twice repeated
the familiar words from Jeremiah IV:2; in the verse of the
Pardoner:

    Of sweryng seith the hooly Jeremye,
    'Thou shalt swere sooth thyne othes, and nat lye,
    And swere in doom, and eek in rightwisnesse',
                    (*PardT* 635–7)

and in the prose of the Parson:

    And if so be that the lawe compelle yow to swere, thanne rule yow
    after the lawe of God in youre swerying, as seith Jeremye, *quarto
    capitulo*: 'Thou shalt kepe three condicions: thou shalt swere in
    trouthe, in doom, and in rightwisnesse.' / This is to seyn, thou shalt
    swere sooth; for every lesynge is agayns Crist.
                    (*ParsT* 592–3)

Pardoner and Parson have more to say about, or rather against,
swearing, although their motives for doing so are poles apart.
Both men are reacting to the stream of vigorous profanities

issuing from the mouth of Harry Bailly who, even in an age of hearty religious swearing, must have been something of an extremist. Bailly opens the proceedings, as it were, by his dead father's soul (*Gen Prol* 781) and ends them with his invitation to the Parson to tell 'a fable anon, for cokkes bones!' (*CT* X, 29), having in the meanwhile explored every nuance of vulgarity and profanity known to him. He becomes, in a manner of speaking, Chaucer's prime exemplum both of the art of swearing and of its immorality. There is no doubt that the Parson has him in mind when he condemns the habitual affectation of strong oaths: 'What seye we eek of hem that deliten hem in sweryng, and holden it a gentrie or a manly dede to swere grete othes? And what of hem that of verray usage ne cesse nat to swere grete othes, al be the cause nat worth a straw? Certes, this is horrible synne' (*ParsT* 601). To no one else among the pilgrims do these words apply as aptly as to the Host, whose swearing had once before stung the Parson into a rebuke. As the Man of Law's tale of Constance comes to an end, Harry Bailly addresses the Parson:

'Sir Parisshe Prest,' quod he, 'for Goddes bones,
Telle us a tale, as was thi forward yore.
I se wel that ye lerned men in lore
Can moche good, by Goddes dignitee!'
(*CT* II, 1166–9)

The Parson's rebuke is a gentle one, with its mild *benedicite*, the equivalent of many a later English country vicar's 'bless my soul!':

The Parson hem answerde, '*Benedicite!*
What eyleth the man, so synfully to swere?'
(*ibid.* 1170–1)

But Harry Bailly is not so easily silenced and retorts in no contrite or conciliatory manner:

Oure Host answerde, 'O Jankin, be ye there?
I smelle a Lollere in the wynd,' quod he.
'Now! goode men,' quod oure Hoste, 'herkeneth me;
Abydeth, for Goddes digne passioun,
For we schal han a predicacioun;
This Lollere heer wil prechen us somwhat'.
(*ibid.* 1172–7)

In the end, however, the Parson, as we have seen, has the last word. Perhaps he looked straight into the sinful pilgrims' eyes as he paraded the deadly sins before them in his concluding sermon, much as the B.B.C. producer made his Parson do in the televised *Canterbury Tales*. There can be no doubt whose eyes he would look into when he came to denounce the habitual swearer in the words of Ecclesiasticus XXIII:11: 'And thynk wel this, that every greet swerere, nat compelled lawefully to swere, the wounde shal nat departe from his hous whil he useth swich unleveful swerying' (*ParsT* 593).

The Pardoner responds to the Host's swearing rather differently. As the Physician's tale ends, 'oure Hooste gan to swere as he were wood' (*CT* VI, 287), uttering amid other profanities the particularly blasphemous 'by nayles and by blood!' (288) and the exotic 'by Seint Ronyan!' (310). Both these oaths are echoed by the Pardoner, the former in his harangue against swearing (*PardT* 651–2), the latter almost immediately after the Host had said it (*CT* VI, 320). Saint Ronyan or Ronyon is sufficiently distinctive to attract attention; he does not occur anywhere else in Chaucer. It is possible that the name is a variant of St Ninian, the Scottish missionary saint who died *ca.* 432, and whose tomb in the church at Whithorn, known as 'Candida Casa' (White House), in Wigtownshire, became a favourite pilgrimage shrine in the Middle Ages. But it is not only possible but probable that the Host was also punning on the words *ronian* 'a mangy animal', *ronyon* 'kidney', from Fr. *rognon*, and English *runnion* 'the male organ'. The M.E. adjective *roynous* 'scabby' may also have been drawn into the punning, as the medical context of the passage with its *urynals* and *cardynacle* and the rest suggests. The Host's smug 'seyde I nat wel?' (311) hints at rather more than a straightforward reference to a saint. The Pardoner's subsequent performance includes a highly rhetorical condemnation of swearing in which he suddenly addresses some person directly in the singular, 'I wol *thee* telle al plat' (*PardT* 648), and the next person to be thus addressed, at the end of the tale, is 'sire Hoost' (943). It is a superbly ironic situation as the Pardoner, unquestionably the most depraved of all the Canterbury pilgrims, charges Harry Bailly with being 'moost envoluped in synne' (942), hence most in need of the relics and pardons which the Pardoner is offering for sale – a confrontation between a sexually abnormal confidence trickster and a loud, crude, profane publican. Its resolution is a masterpiece: the enraged Host turns the tables on the Pardoner by making, in one and the same breath, a thoroughly vulgar allusion to the latter's questionable virility and, with the aid of an oath by the holiest of all Christian symbols, to his fraudulent tricks and phoney relics:

> 'Thou woldest make me kisse thyn olde breech,
> And swere it were a relyk of a seint,
> Though it were with thy fundement depeint!
> But, by the croys which that Seint Eleyne fond,
> I wolde I hadde thy coillons in myn hond
> In stide of relikes or of seintuarie.
> Lat kutte hem of, I wol thee helpe hem carie;
> They shul be shryned in an hogges toord!'[7]
>
> (PardT 948–55)

It is clear from our discussion so far that Chaucer distributed his oaths with a good deal of discernment among the characters of his later poems, and that the oaths themselves varied considerably in type and intensity. Only the 'classical' oaths are much of a kind and severely restricted in occurrence to appropriate poems and speakers. In structure the classical oaths are patterned upon the common religious oaths used by Chaucer, with appropriate substitutions; classical names appear in place of God or Christ or a saint, whether in short, simple oaths of the type 'by God', 'holy God', 'as help me Crist', 'for love of God', or in longer, more complex oaths like 'by thilke God that yaf me soule and lyf', or 'by God and by seint John'. Some examples of the corresponding classical oaths follow:

From *The Knight's Tale*: 'by myghty Mars' (1708); 'by myghty Mars the rede' (1747); 'and Juppiter so wys my soule gye' (2786).

From *The Legend of Good Women*: 'by Seynt Venus, that my moder ys' (F 338); 'as wisly Jupiter my soule save' (1806); 'by Mars, that is the chef of my beleve' (2109).

From *Troilus and Criseyde*: 'for Joves name in hevene' (I, 878);

> 'by the goddesse Mynerve,
> And Jupiter, that maketh the thondre rynge,
> And by the blisful Venus that I serve';
>
> (II, 232–4)

'by Neptunus, that god is of the see' (II, 443); 'by Mars, the god

---

7. See further Ralph W. V. Elliott, 'Our Host's "Triacle": some Observations on Chaucer's "Pardoner's Tale"', *A Review of English Literature* VII, 4 (1966), 61–73.

that helmed is of steel' (II, 593); 'for the love of Marte' (II, 988); 'nay, help me so the moone' (II, 1312); 'by natal Joves feste' (III, 150); 'by the goddes that in hevene dwelle' (III, 590); 'as wolde blisful Jove, for his joie' (IV, 335); 'as helpe me Juno, hevenes quene' (IV, 1594); 'for the love of Cinthia the sheene' (IV, 1608); 'as help me now Pallas' (V, 977).

Many Chaucerian oaths are imprecatory, that is, they call down some misfortune or punishment upon the person addressed, quite often the speaker himself. Here classical substitution is exceptional, as in Helen of Troy's 'Joves lat hym nevere thryve' (*Tr* II, 1607). Normally, the speaker utters a good Christian curse whatever the context. It may take the form of a simple sentence with the verb *shrewen* or *bishrewen* 'to curse': 'I bishrewe thy face' (*CT* III, 844);

> 'Nay thanne,' quod he, 'I shrewe us bothe two.
> And first I shrewe myself, bothe blood and bones'.
>
> (*NPT* 3426–7)

It may even take the form of a prayer: 'I bidde God I nevere mote have joie' (*Tr* III, 875), or 'I pray to God, so yeve me sorwe and care' (*CT* I, 4335). The curse may be expressed by an auxiliary verb or as a simple optative: 'to dethe mot I smyten be with thondre' (*Tr* II, 1145); 'the devel quyte hym his while' (*LGW* 2227). The latter is the most common pattern, whether the agent invoked is the devil or, more commonly, God. Chaucer manages to introduce considerable variation into this simple structure, as these examples will illustrate: 'God yeve hem meschaunce' (*Tr* III, 1385); 'God yeve youre herte kare' (*Tr* III, 1565); 'the devel spede hym that it recche' (*Tr* IV, 630); 'Jhesu shorte thy lyf' (*WBT* 365); 'the devel go therwith' (*WBT* 476); 'the feend . . . yow fecche, body and bones' (*FrT* 1544); 'God lat hym nevere thee' (*SumT* 2207); 'ther God his bones corse' (*MerchT* 1308); 'God yeve it harde grace' (*CT* VIII, 665); 'the foule feend hym quelle' (*CT* VIII, 705); 'the devel out of his skyn / Hym terve' (i.e. flay; *CYT* 1273–4).

The curse becomes even more effective with the omission of the verb, as in this prize specimen from *The Shipman's Tale* (405):

> 'What! yvel thedam on his monkes snowte!'

Of the religious oaths proper a few derive directly from the French: 'pardee', 'parfay', 'pardieux', 'depardieux', 'mafay'. Of

these, 'pardee' is by far the most common and is scattered pretty
haphazardly throughout all Chaucer's poems, from the earliest to
the latest. It even creeps into the highly moral *Tale of Melibee*
(1537). It is no respecter of sex or class: Chaucer himself as narrator uses it, so do the Host and the Knight and the Miller; so do
Dorigen and Constance and the Wife of Bath and Criseyde; so do
Pandarus and Troilus, and the Eagle and the hen. Clearly, this was
a mild expletive, little more than a tag, and even its original
Christian meaning was probably hidden from many of its fourteenth-century users, much as the original meaning of modern
'gosh' is unknown to many English speakers today.

'Parfay' is much rarer. It occurs once with beautiful incongruity
in Absolon's nocturnal fantasy:

> 'Som maner confort shal I have, parfay.
> My mouth hath icched al this longe day;
> That is a signe of kissyng atte leeste',
>   (*MillT* 3681–3)

once as a rhyming tag in *The House of Fame* (938), and three times
each in *The Man of Law's Tale* and *The Parson's Tale*. In the verse of
The Man of Law's Tale 'parfay' once serves as a rhyme word (849),
twice as an emphatic opening to the line (110, 1037). In *The
Parson's Tale* 'parfay' is used in one passage, presumably for
stylistic reasons, as a variant of *soothly* and *certes*: 'For *soothly*,
nature dryveth us to loven oure freendes, and *parfey*, oure enemys
han moore nede to love than oure freendes; and they that moore
nede have, *certes* to hem shal men doon goodnesse' (*ParsT* 527).
In the other two instances (497, 867) the use of 'parfay' seems
fortuitous; indeed some manuscripts read *pardee* in line 497. All
we can say is that 'parfay' was for Chaucer probably more intense,
and certainly much more exclusive, than 'pardee', which dis-
guises the sacred meaning of its second element more effectively.

This is even more true of 'pardieux' and 'depardieux'. The Man
of Law adds to his predilection for 'parfay' one 'depardieux'. It is
the second word he utters in *The Canterbury Tales*:

> 'Hooste,' quod he, '*depardieux*, ich assente;
> To breke forward is nat myn entente.'
>   (*CT* II, 39–40)

His penchant for more exotic words, more fully revealed in his tale, is thereby established from the start. Although he introduces his tale with the words 'I speke in prose' (96) and then tells the story of Constance in verse, there is no reason to doubt, as I hope to demonstrate in a later chapter (ch. 7), that this tale is the one Chaucer intended for him. It is clear that even so modest a pointer as the solitary 'depardieux' fits in with the diction of *The Man of Law's Tale* as we have it. Apart from this occurrence, there are three others, two in *Troilus and Criseyde*: Troilus uses exactly the same words as the Man of Law: 'depardieux, ich assente!' (*Tr* II, 1058) and in both cases the emphatic nature of the utterance clearly derives from the French mouthful. Criseyde utters her 'depardieux' soon after (II, 1212); it is also emphatic, also addressed to Pandarus, also connected with writing a letter. Chaucer's linking of the two parallel episodes with the aid of this rare oath is typical of his 'art poetical'. The fourth occurrence of 'depardieux' (*FrT* 1395) has Chaucer perhaps playing ironically with the meaning of the oath, 'by God', for it is the disguised devil of *The Friar's Tale* who says it in a speech of veiled allusion to his own identity and the *shire* he hails from. The unsuspecting summoner, perhaps impressed by the devil's French, promptly responds with 'Grantmercy'. The shorter 'pardieux' is used once by Troilus (*Tr* I, 197) and once by Criseyde (II, 759). Both are passages in which the lovers soliloquize about love, but the parallels are certainly less striking and the two occurrences more widely separated than in the case of 'depardieux' in Book II. In any case, manuscript readings vary, and it would be foolish to indulge in critical subtleties depending heavily on single words. Although Robinson and Root and Donaldson and Skeat print 'pardieux' or 'pardeux' at II, 759, the Globe *Chaucer*, for example, has the much less distinctive 'parde'.

The remaining French oath, 'ma fay', suits Troilus's courtly diction (*Tr* III, 52) as it suits the mocking tone of *Sir Thopas* in its fuller form 'par ma fay' (*Thop* 820). The courtly associations of the phrase are well exploited by the poet of *Pearl*:

> Of countes, damysel, par ma fay,
> Wer fayr in heuen to halde asstate,
> Oþer elleȝ a lady of lasse aray. . . .
>
> (Pearl 489–91)

And in *Sir Gawain and the Green Knight* it is a courtly lady who

alone uses the phrase (1495). There are of course English equivalents of these oaths ,'by my fey', 'upon my feith', as there are of the
others, 'by God', 'before God' and so on, but their functions are
clearly different for Chaucer. Whereas 'par ma fay' has courtly
connotations, the anglicized 'by my fey' is used almost exclusively
by Chaucer's lower orders: the Host, the Wife of Bath, the Cook,
Alisoun in *The Miller's Tale*, Symkyn in *The Reeve's Tale*, and others.
Arveragus's emphatic 'by my fay' (*FranklT* 1474) at a crucial
moment in the story is a noteworthy exception, as is Arcite's 'by
my fey' (*KnT* 1126). The latter fits into the pattern of Arcite's
diction, alongside his 'by my pan', 'God helpe me so', 'by God
that sit above', 'for love of God', and the invocations of Jupiter,
as rather more vigorous, if a little less courtly, than the diction of
Palamon or Theseus. It is worth recalling that Chaucer's Knight
himself 'nevere yet no vileynye ne sayde' (*Gen Prol* 70), and that
his own swearing was minimal. His opening 'a Goddes name'
(*ibid.* 854) is a pious rather than a profane exclamation in the
context, and he does not swear when he stills the quarrel between
Host and Pardoner, nor when he *stynteth* the Monk of his tale with
no more than a mild 'hoo!'

Yet another non-English exclamation is 'benedicite', which,
though not strictly an oath, may be briefly considered here. It
means something like 'bless us, bless my soul, my goodness, etc.'
(*MED*) and was metrically useful, as it could be pronounced with
anything from two to five syllables. It occurs as 'bendiste' in
Troilus and Criseyde I, 780. Its use ranges from the Parson's gentle
rebuke to Harry Bailly to the Wife of Bath's much more forceful:

'What rowne ye with oure mayde? *Benedicite!*
Sire olde lecchour, lat thy japes be!'
(*WBT* 241–2)

Several times 'benedicite' is preceded by 'a' or 'ey', and most of
Chaucer's uses of the word are in rhyme.

Starr has estimated, conservatively, I think, that there are some
two hundred different oaths in Chaucer, God's plenty indeed, a
veritable paradise of profanity, and all we can hope to do in what
remains of this chapter is to attempt to put into some semblance
of order those which we have not yet properly discussed. It is
easy to tackle the remaining non-religious oaths, for they are few:
Pandarus's innocuous 'by stokkes and by stones' (*Tr* III, 589) is

used by no one else; 'by my fader kyn' and its variants (*youre, thy*)
occur half a dozen times in the speech of lower characters, if one
may include Pertelote here and the Merchant's Placebo, who has
already revealed something of himself by his use of 'by my fay'.
'By my lyf' has several variants: 'upon my lyf', 'on peril of my lyf',
'up peril of my lyf'; none of them is common and their use is confined (if we may draw yet another social distinction) mainly to the
Chaucerian middle class: the merchant in *The Shipman's Tale*, the
squire in *The Summoner's Tale*, the old woman who turns out so
agreeably in *The Wife of Bath's Tale*, Calchas in *Troilus and Criseyde*,
and a few others. In such phrases as 'up peril of my lyf' and 'up
peyne of deeth' it is difficult to draw a clear distinction between a
genuine oath and an asseveration. It is only in context that the full
force of such exclamations can be felt.

Among Chaucer's religious oaths the most common, and the
mildest, is 'God woot'. Indeed, it is often so weak as to be hardly
an oath at all, little more than a mild interjection. Everyone uses it,
in much the same way as 'pardee', its intensity varying a little
according to position and context. It occasionally appears as 'God
it woot' for purely metrical reasons. The intensity of 'by God'
varies rather more and, as in later English, its positioning and
intonation can turn it into an emphatic oath of considerable force.
Compare, for example, the playful use of 'by God' as no more
emphatic than, say, 'indeed' in Theseus's speech about Arcite's
and Palamon's love for Emelye:

> 'But this is yet the beste game of alle,
> That she for whom they han this jolitee
> Kan hem therfore as muche thank as me.
> She woot namoore of al this hoote fare,
> By God, than woot a cokkow or an hare!'
>
> *(KnT* 1806–10)

with the much more forceful use by the Summoner threatening
to get his own back on the Friar:

> 'Nay,' quod the Somonour, 'lat hym seye to me
> What so hym list; whan it comth to my lot,
> By God! I shal hym quiten every grot.'
>
> *(CT* III, 1290–2)

The Wife of Bath, whose talent at swearing is second only to
Harry Bailly's, is particularly adept at playing variations on

simple oaths like 'by God', 'God woot', and even 'pardee', for Chaucer has succeeded admirably in creating for her an individuality of voice to which even these brief oaths add an important distinctive element:

By God! he smoot me ones on the lyst.
(*WBT* 634)

For, God it woot, I chidde hem spitously.
(*ibid.* 223)

It is my good as wel as thyn, pardee!
(*ibid.* 310)

'By God', like most Chaucerian oaths, has simple variants, such as 'before God' or the uncommon 'God toforn' which occurs ten times, all in *Troilus and Criseyde*, but could be varied further by various modes of expansion. As a rule, the more complex the expansion, the more forceful the oath. One common method was to turn the oath into a possessive phrase: 'by Goddes dignitee', 'by Goddes sweete pyne', 'for Goddes herte', 'a Goddes half', 'on Goddes name', 'ey! Goddes mercy', 'for Goddes sake'. Another method was to add an appropriate adjective: 'for verray God', 'ye, holy God'; or an adverb: 'by God above', 'by that God above'; or both: 'by heigh God above'; or a relative clause: 'by God that sit above', 'by God that this world made', 'by God that for us deyde'. The last method afforded particular scope for the swearer's ingenuity and is repeatedly used by Chaucer to elaborate on character or throw into relief the situation that forces the speaker to utter such an intense oath:

'By thilke God that yaf me soule and lyf'.
(*FranklT* 983)

'By thilke God that formed man alyve'.
(*LGW* 1792)

'For, by that God that bought us bothe two'.
(*Tr* III, 1165)

One common variant of the *God* oath was the type 'for Goddes love' or 'for love of God', found mainly among Chaucer's gentlefolk, for whom it may well have been, as Starr suggested, a more intense oath, as they could not stoop to some of the forceful

profanities available to the lower orders. There is certainly a good
deal of intensity in the Dreamer's urgent 'for Goddes love, telle
me al' in *The Book of the Duchess*, 1143, or in the suppliant's 'for
Goddis love, have mercy on my peyne' of *The Complaint unto Pity*,
98, or in Criseyde's impatient

> 'Now, uncle deere,' quod she, 'telle it us
> For Goddes love; is than th' assege aweye?'
> > (*Tr* II, 122–3)

In 'for Goddes love, that sit above' (*HF* 1758) two familiar oaths
are combined to fill a whole line, while a different variant is
provided by Pertelote's 'for Goddes owene love' (*NPT* 2954).
Oaths of the type 'for Goddes love' and 'for love of God' account for nearly one fifth of the oaths in *Troilus and Criseyde*: apart
from the three main characters, the oath is used by the narrator,
by Helen, Diomede, and by Calchas once in the expanded 'for the
love of God and of bounte' (*Tr* IV, 109).

A further group of *God* oaths is the type 'God help me so',
another of Pandarus's favourites which, if it can be assigned to
any social group in Chaucer, was used principally by the middle
classes, and by those of a higher order whose swearing tended that
way, like Arcite. On the other hand, the variant 'as help me God',
apart from several occurrences in *The Book of the Duchess*, was put
by Chaucer mainly into the mouths of several of his more earthy
women, the Wife of Bath, the Miller's Alisoun, the wife of *The
Shipman's Tale*, as well as Criseyde. The Wife of Bath uses it, as
she does so many of her oaths, with much vigour:

> As help me God, I laughe whan I thynke
> How pitously a-nyght I made hem swynke!
> > (*WBT* 201–2)

> As help me God! I was a lusty oon.
> > (*ibid.* 605)

She and the Squire's Canacee and Criseyde play variations on this
theme:

> As helpe me verray God omnipotent.
> > (*WBT* 423)

> 'As wisly helpe me grete God of kynde!'
> > (*SqT* 469)

'As wisly help me God the grete'.
                    (*Tr* II, 1230)

A further set of variations consists of substituting another verb for
help, most commonly, 'so God me save', but these verbs also
occur: 'so God me wisse' (i.e. guide), 'so God me speede', 'so
God yow blesse', as well as elaborations like 'for God so wisly
have mercy upon me' (*FranklT* 1475), 'so wisly God my soule
brynge in blisse' (*MerchT* 2175), 'also wisly God my soule blesse'
(*CT* VII, 922), 'God so my soule save' (*CLT* 505, *Tr* III, 102), 'also
wys God yive me reste' (*BD* 683) ,'God so wys be my savacioun'
(*Tr* II, 381), 'as wisly verray God my soule save' (*Tr* III, 1501),
'as wisly God myn herte brynge at reste' (*Tr* III, 1518), 'as wisly
God my soule rede' (*Tr* IV, 1364).

The religious oaths so far considered have all invoked the
name of God and these are by far the most common. Oaths invoking Christ are less common, those invoking Jesus are rarer
still, and there are no oaths in Chaucer by the Holy Ghost, except
by implication in two oaths invoking the Trinity: the wife in *The
Summoner's Tale* says to the friar

'Chideth him weel, for seinte Trinitee!'
                    (*SumT* 1824)

and the Franklin, speaking in his own person, swears 'by the
Trinitee' (*CT* V, 682). With one exception, oaths by Christ and
by Jesus are restricted to Chaucer's *cherles* and to characters in
their tales. Chaucer is clearly drawing another important class
distinction as well as passing a moral judgment, for these oaths
not only branded the speaker as vulgar, they were also regarded
as particularly reprehensible. Several of them occur in *The Miller's
Tale*: John the carpenter swears 'by Jhesus, hevene kyng' (*MillT*
3464), less blatantly 'by hym that harwed helle' (3512; similarly
the friar in *SumT* 2107), and utters the mouthful: 'nay, Crist
forbede it, for his hooly blood!' (3508). Alisoun swears pointedly
'by Jhesu, (3711), to which Absolon responds with a forceful 'for
Jhesus love, and for the love of me' (3717). Finally, Gerveys the
smith adds his share: 'for Cristes sweete tree' (3767) and 'ey,
Cristes foo!' (3782). The two clerks in *The Reeve's Tale* belong to
the same class: 'for Cristes peyne', says John (*RvT* 4084); 'for
Cristes saule', says Aleyn (4263). The Cook adds 'for Cristes
passion' to the 'Ha! ha!' which is his first contribution to the

Canterbury pilgrimage (*CT* I, 4327), while the Wife of Bath exclaims simply 'Lord Crist!' (*WBT* 469). Thomas in *The Summoner's Tale* vulgarizes 'as help me God' even further by substituting *Crist* (*SumT* 1949), while the Friar introduces into his tale a 'ther Jhesu Crist yow blesse' (*FrT* 1561) and makes the old woman exclaim

> 'Now, Lord,' quod she, 'Crist Jhesu, kyng of kynges,
> So wisly helpe me, as I ne may',
>
> (*FrT* 1590–1)

both of which could be, somewhat dubiously, regarded as prayers rather than as profanities. On the other hand, there can be no doubt about the irony in the Pardoner's 'now, for the love of Crist, that for us dyde' (*PardT* 658), and in the lymytour's 'for Goddes sake' and 'for Cristes sake' at the opening of *The Summoner's Tale* (1717, 1732). One need only compare in context the Physician's pious 'for Cristes sake' (*PhysT* 81) or the blind Briton's 'in name of Crist' in *The Man of Law's Tale*, 561, to hear the difference in tone. Finally, there is the narrator's exceptional 'be Cryste' in *The House of Fame*, 271, introduced into this early poem before Chaucer had started apportioning his oaths more discerningly. It is unlikely that he would have used this expression here ten years later.

The same probably holds true for the introduction of 'Seynte Marye!' into the Eagle's discourse (*HF* 573), for in *The Canterbury Tales* oaths by the Virgin are similarly reserved for the lower orders. Some simply exclaim 'Marie!' (*ShipT* 402, *CYT* 1062); others '(by) seynte Marie' (*PardT* 685, *MerchT* 1899) or 'by oure Lady' (*CYT* 1354); others again swear more elaborately by the queen of heaven:

> 'Help, for hir love that is of hevene queene!'
>
> (*MerchT* 2334)

> Sire hoost, in feith, and by the hevenes queene.
>
> (*CYT* 1089)

The Merchant, obsessed with marital problems and many a 'heigh fantasye' about young women, introduces several oaths by Mary, including the telling 'a wyf! a, Seinte Marie, *benedicite*'! (*MerchT* 1337), and concludes his tale appropriately with 'God blesse us, and his mooder Seinte Marie!' (2418). Sir Thopas, similarly given to erotic day-dreams, utters a similar 'o seinte Marie, *benedicite*!' (*Thop* 784), and in *The Friar's Tale* the old woman utters yet another of those prayerful profanities previously encountered, this time invoking Mary:

> 'Twelf pens!' quod she, 'now lady Seinte Marie
> So wisly help me out of care and synne'.
>
> (*FrT* 1604–5)

A variation, turning this into a classical oath, is Criseyde's 'as helpe me Juno, hevenes quene' (*Tr* IV, 1594), which we noted earlier.

Just as 'God' was occasionally exclaimed by itself (e.g. *Tr* I, 276, 552), so another way of invoking God was to use the word 'Lord', by itself, as is frequently done in *Troilus and Criseyde*; or else in a phrase, 'a, Lord', 'o Lord', 'by oure Lord', with possible further elaboration: 'by that ilke Lord that for us bledde' (*ShipT* 178), 'by that Lord that formede est and west' (*Tr* II, 1053), 'by that ilke Lord that made me' (*Tr* IV, 1236, *FranklT* 1000). And just as Mary is queen of heaven, so is Christ king of heaven in a number of Chaucerian oaths: 'by hevene kyng' (*HF* 1084, *MerchT* 2407), 'by hevene kyng, that for us alle dyde' (*CT* VII, 2796), 'by God, oure hevene kyng' (*ShipT* 393), and so on.

One way of intensifying an oath was by combining it with another, and there are many situations in Chaucer's poetry when oaths of exceptional force appear to have been called for and when they were produced in this manner. The Pardoner's interruption of the Wife of Bath's prologue is of this kind. He does not simply intrude, he barges in head first, as it were, as is suggested by the sudden 'up stirte', the inverted order of subject and verb, and the strategically placed 'and that anon':

> Up stirte the Pardoner, and that anon:
> 'Now, dame,' quod he, 'by God and by seint John!
> Ye been a noble prechour in this cas.'
>
> (*WBT* 163–5)

Such compounding of 'by God' with a 'by a saint' oath was a common device, witness an equally forceful example from *The Shipman's Tale*:

'Nay,' quod this monk, 'by God and seint Martyn,
He is na moore cosyn unto me
Than is this leef that hangeth on the tree!'
(ShipT 148–50)

The Black Knight does even better, at least quantitatively:

'Shortly, what shal y more seye?
By God, and by his halwes twelve,
Hyt was my swete. . . .'
(BD 830–2)

Other versions of the compounded oath are the particularly reprehensible 'by God, and by the hooly sacrement' of one of the rioters in *The Pardoner's Tale*, 757, and the strong oath to secrecy sworn by the wife in *The Shipman's Tale*, 135, 'by God and by this porthors', the *porthors*, O.Fr. *portehors*, literally 'carry-abroad', Latin *portiforium*, being a breviary. In *Troilus and Criseyde*, where compound oaths invoking saints were inadmissible, Chaucer made up others: there are, for example, several instances of 'by God and by my trouthe', some examples of compounded classical oaths, and, from Pandarus, 'by God and yonder sonne' *(Tr* II, 1237).

The nadir of swearing in Chaucer was undoubtedly any oath involving reference to some part of the body of Christ, and it is against such oaths that the indignation of contemporary preachers and writers like Robert of Brunne and Dan Michel of Northgate is specifically directed.[8] Wyclif has this to say: 'Also alle comyn swereris bi Goddis herte, bonys, nailis, and sidis, and oþere membris, and false and veyn swereris, wiþ lecchours, and alle oþere þat comynly don aȝenst ony of Goddis hestis, for þei ben comyn mysdoeris, rennen fully in þis sentence.'[9] Chaucer's Parson adds a familiar parallel to his condemnation: 'For Cristes sake, ne swereth nat so synfully in dismembrynge of Crist by soule, herte, bones, and body. For certes, it semeth that ye thynke that the cursede Jewes ne dismembred nat ynough the preciouse persone of Crist, but ye dismembre hym moore' *(ParsT* 591).

8. For a more detailed treatment of medieval denunciations of such swearing see Rosemary Woolf, *The English Religious Lyric in the Middle Ages* (Oxford, 1968), Appendix G, 'Complaints against Swearers', pp. 395–400.

9. 'The Grete Sentence of Curs Expounded' in *Select English Works of John Wyclif*, ed. Thomas Arnold (Oxford, 1871), Vol. III, p. 332. Starr quotes this and another passage on p. 53 of the article cited.

Already the Pardoner, in setting the scene for his tale in a Flemish
tavern, had made the same point:

Hir othes been so grete and so dampnable
That it is grisly for to heere hem swere.
Oure blissed Lordes body they totere, –
Hem thoughte that Jewes rente hym noght ynough;
And ech of hem at otheres synne lough.
(*PardT* 472–6)

And again, later in the tale:

And many a grisly ooth thanne han they sworn,
And Cristes blessed body al torente.
(*ibid.* 708–9)

The Pardoner himself offers several examples of anatomical oaths
in his discourse on swearing:

'By Goddes precious herte,' and 'By his nayles,'
And 'By the blood of Crist that is in Hayles'
. . . .
'By Goddes armes. . . .'
(*PardT* 651–4)

One of the rioters repeats the last of these (*PardT* 692) and adds
yet another, 'Goddes digne bones' (695), and there are around two
dozen further examples in the language of the Host and the
cherles. Harry Bailly's swearing is particularly rich in anatomical
oaths; nearly half of all these in Chaucer are his. It was his 'for
Goddes bones' coupled with 'by Goddes dignitee' that provoked
the Parson's rebuke (*CT* II, 1166 ff.). God's bones are his favourite
theme (*CT* II, 1166; IV, 1212b; VII, 1897), together with euphemistic or 'vulgar Latin' variations: 'for cokkes bones' (IX, 9; X,
29), 'by corpus bones' (VI, 314; VII, 1906; compare also his 'by
corpus dominus', *CT* VII, 435). God's bones provide material also
for the hero of *The Summoner's Tale* at a moment when only the
strongest expletive could do justice to the disappointed friar's
wrath:

The frere up stirte as dooth a wood leoun, –
'A! false cherl,' quod he, 'for Goddes bones!
This hastow for despit doon for the nones.
Thou shalt abye this fart, if that I may!
(*SumT* 2152–5)

Clerk John in *The Reeve's Tale*, on discovering the horse's escape, shouts a northern version of the oath in a passage full of strident exclamations:

> This John goth out and fynt his hors away,
> And gan to crie 'Harrow!' and 'Weylaway!
> Our hors is lorn, Alayn, for Goddes banes,
> Step on thy feet! Com of, man, al atanes!'
>
> (RvT 4071–4)

And a few lines later he adds a further anatomical oath in a passage richly loaded with oaths:

> 'Allas,' quod John, 'Aleyn, for Cristes peyne,
> Lay doun thy swerd, and I wil myn alswa.
> I is ful wight, God waat, as is a raa;
> By Goddes herte, he sal nat scape us bathe!
> Why ne had thow pit the capul in the lathe?
> Ilhayl! By God, Alayn, thou is a fonne!'
>
> (*ibid.* 4084–9)

The Summoner swears by 'Goddes armes two' (*CT* III, 833), but it is left to the drunken Miller to utter as his first words in *The Canterbury Tales* what is perhaps the most reprehensible oath in all Chaucer, a triple 'dismembrynge of Crist', delivered 'in Pilates voys'. This unique reference to Pilate is usually explained as an allusion to the harsh, ranting voice of the Pilate of the mystery plays, but there is the even more immediate link between Pontius Pilate and the dismembering of Christ which the Miller's oath would have suggested:

> But in Pilates voys he gan to crie,
> And swoor, 'By armes, and by blood and bones,
> I kan a noble tale for the nones'.
>
> (*CT* I, 3124–6)

In his tale, the Miller has a number of vulgar oaths, as we have seen, by Jesus, by Christ, as well as a good many lesser ones. He adds a few anatomical oaths for good measure: the carpenter's 'for his hooly blood' (*MillT* 3508), Nicholas's 'by Goddes corpus' (3743), and the latter's *cri de coeur*, with its ironic echo of John XIX:34:

> 'Help! water! water! help, for Goddes herte!'
>
> (*MillT* 3815)

Even Harry Bailly's dismembering does not reach triple proportions, his 'harrow! . . . by nayles and by blood!' (*CT* VI, 288) being probably his strongest oath. Whether the nails were those of Christ's fingers or those used in the crucifixion has been the subject of some scholarly debate, but Skeat and Robinson are probably right in doubting whether any medieval swearer ever bothered his head about such subtleties. Wyclif includes nails among the *membris* of Christ's body; the Parson includes Christ's soul, so that to swear 'by Goddes soule', as does the Miller (*CT* I, 3132) and the Reeve's Aleyn (*RvT* 4187), or 'for Cristes saule', as Aleyn also does (4263), is just as reprehensible.

In the final analysis, it is the anatomical oath rather than any other aspect of their diction that brands the lowest of Chaucer's low characters, the Host, the Miller, the Summoner, the Reeve, and the Pardoner, whether in their own persons or in their tales. But it is as instructive to note who does not use these oaths, as it is to note who does: the Wife of Bath undoubtedly has a bawdy and a vulgar tongue, but she stops short of tearing Christ to pieces, and so do the Friar and the Shipman and the Cook, in what little we have of him, and the Merchant, who swears a lot but never quite so vulgarly, and the Nun's Priest's farmyard animals. By their oaths ye shall know them.

If it was particularly sinful to swear by God's soul, it was probably somewhat less so to swear by one's father's or mother's soul, as several of Chaucer's characters do. B. J. Whiting writes that 'whatever the implications of the oath [by the soul of a parent] for Chaucer, during the next two centuries it was reserved for comic scenes and was used only by low, vulgar or rustic characters.'[10] The implications for Chaucer are much the same. Harry Bailly, we recall, vulgar as he is, starts his contribution to the Canterbury pilgrimage 'by my fader soule that is deed' (*Gen Prol* 781) and uses the oath elsewhere; and the Shipman, if he is indeed intended to be the speaker at this point, also swears 'by my rader soule' (*CT* II, 1178). Similarly, in *The Merchant's Tale* Januarie swears by his father's soul (2393) while Proserpina swears rather more elaborately and perhaps to comic effect 'by my moodres sires soule' (2265). Her maternal grandfather was Saturn whose

10. B. J. Whiting, 'By my fader soule', *Journal of English and Germanic Philology* XLIV (1945), 8. Whiting cites as the only exception Antonio's oath in Shirley's *Maid's Revenge*.

rare appearances in Chaucer are at least distinguished by his once swearing by his own head (*KnT* 2670)

There remain the devil and the saints. 'My sone', says the Manciple's mother, 'from a feend men may hem blesse' (*MancT* 321), and by implication 'unto the devel blak and rough of hewe' may men curse, as does the old woman in *The Friar's Tale* with such visible results (1622 ff.). There are relatively few oaths by the devil in Chaucer's poetry, and most of them are curses; but a few are straightforward oaths like the simple 'devel' which intrudes as effectively as the modern English equivalent into an occasional sentence, in this case Troilus's:

'Thow koudest nevere in love thiselven wisse:
How devel maistow brynge me to blisse?'
(*Tr* I, 622–3)

Or, from the Legend of Hypermnestra:

'What devel have I with the knyf to do?'
(*LGW* 2694)

Rather stronger is the canon's 'What, devel of helle! sholde it elles be?' (*CYT* 1238), appropriate language from one who was 'feendly bothe in werk and thoght' (*ibid.* 1303), but no worse than a good many of the devilish imprecations Chaucer ascribes to others. There are several instances in Chaucer of what seems to have been a popular medieval oath, which appears in a milder form as 'a devel wey', and in a stronger form as 'a twenty devel wey'. It means something like 'to the devil' or 'in the devil's name' or 'for the devil's sake', appropriately intensified to 'for twenty devils' sake' or 'in the name of twenty devils' in the more forceful version. There is a robust example of the latter in the narrator's 'a twenty devel-wey the wynd hym dryve!' in the Legend of Ariadne (*LGW* 2177) which concludes fifty lines later with an equally outspoken 'the devel quyte hym his while!' (2227). The Reeve, the Miller's Alisoun, the Canon's Yeoman, and the lord in *The Summoner's Tale* also make use of these expressions.

Several of the imprecations calling upon the devil are highly picturesque:

The devil sette here soules bothe afyre!
(*LGW* 2493)

'Hoold cloos thy mouth, man, by thy fader kyn!
The devel of helle sette his foot therin!'
(CT IX, 37–8)

the devel out of his skyn
Hym terve, I pray to God, for his falshede!
(CYT 1273–4)

'The devel have part on alle swiche rekenynges!'
(ShipT 218)

'The feend,' quod he, 'yow fecche, body and bones!'
(FrT 1544)

Others are more commonplace, though effective enough: 'the devel be hys soules bane!' (*HF* 408), 'the devel have his bones!' (*Tr* I, 805), 'the devel spede hym that it recche!' (*Tr* IV, 630), 'the foule feend me fecche!' (*FrT* 1610), 'the devel go therwith!' (*WBT* 476). Chaucer disposes of *The Tale of Sir Thopas* by making Harry Bailly exclaim 'Now swich a rym the devel I biteche!' (*CT* VII, 924), and in very similar terms the treacherous crow is disposed of in *The Manciple's Tale*, 306–7. Troilus curses the unwelcome coming of 'cruel . . . / Envyous . . . / Dispitous day' in a highly rhetorical mode with a 'Thyn be the peyne of helle!' (*Tr* III, 1458), while the Wife of Bath's affection for her fifth husband finds curiously negative expression in words not unlike Troilus's, though the sentiment is different: 'God lete his soule nevere come in helle!' (*WBT* 504).

The point was made earlier in the chapter that in using the names of saints, whether in oaths or not, Chaucer could count upon the connotative force of these names, many, if not all, of which were probably familiar to his audience. The point of making clerk John swear 'by seint Cutberd' (*RvT* 4127) is lost unless the audience recognizes St Cuthbert as a saint with strong north-country associations, more particularly with Lindisfarne, where he was prior and bishop, and with Durham, where his bones eventually found rest. I suggested that already in a poem as early as *The House of Fame* Chaucer made use of such connotations by selecting in several instances saints appropriate to the context. This is certainly true of some later uses of saints' names. At the same time, the modern critic runs the risk of being over-subtle if he attempts to explain every saintly occurrence in Chaucer's poems in this way. This is particularly true of oaths invoking saints, some of which were as common and probably as void of specific connotations as many of the other oaths in colloquial use which this chapter has examined. St John in particular and to a lesser extent St James are repeatedly invoked, whether by themselves or in compound oaths of the type 'by God and by St John'. Many of Chaucer's saints, however, are less commonplace. The carpenter of Oxford invoking 'seinte Frydeswyde' (*MillT* 3449) could not have chosen more appropriately, for St Frideswide's associations are wholly with Oxford, and the fourteenth-century audience knew her shrine as a place of pilgrimage to which such people as Chaucer's own Clerk of Oxenford would pay regular solemn visits. In addition, there is some evidence that St Frideswide was celebrated for her proficiency in the art of healing,[11] hence it is doubly fitting that John should call on her for help when he suspects that Nicholas has fallen 'in some woodnesse or in som agonye' (*MillT* 3452). A similar topical relevance attaches to the 'croys of Bromeholm' emphatically invoked by the miller's wife in *The Reeve's Tale* 4286.

In *The Shipman's Tale*, which takes place in France, 'at Seint-Denys', at least two French saints are invoked with equal appropriateness, and possibly a third. The monk daun John swears 'by Seint Denys of Fraunce' (*ShipT* 151), Denis or Dionysius, patron saint of that country, and a few lines previously (148) 'by God and seint Martyn'. St Martin, the fourth-century bishop of Tours, was another celebrated French saint, also a patron saint of France. Later in the tale the merchant says

> 'also God me save,
> And by that lord that clepid is Seint Yve',
>
> (*ShipT* 226–7)

a name that has provoked some learned speculation. The least likely candidate is the seventh-century British bishop, St Ives of Huntingdonshire, favoured by Skeat. Robinson supports St Yves or Yve, patron saint of Brittany, canonized in 1347, an attractive suggestion in view of the Shipman's knowledge of 'every cryke [creek] in Britaigne and in Spayne' (*Gen Prol* 409). But there is a third candidate, favoured by Miss Cline,[12] a good

11. See Ruth Huff Cline, 'Four Chaucer Saints', *Modern Language Notes* LX (1945), 480 f.
12. *Ibid.*, 482.

deal nearer to Saint-Denis-sur-Seine than Brittany, namely St Ivo, who became bishop of Chartres in 1091. In view of St Denis and St Martin, and also of the specific reference to Genylon 'of France' in line 194, there is every possibility that Chaucer was using here another relatively local saint, local that is to Paris, for the distance from Chartres to St Denis is not much more than fifty miles. While appropriate to *The Shipman's Tale* the oath by 'Seint Yve' does not seem to fit particularly well into *The Summoner's Tale* where exactly the same line occurs: 'And by that lord that clepid is Seint Yve' (*SumT* 1943). As it happens, there is nothing that to my knowledge links any of the three possible candidates with Holderness in Yorkshire, where the Summoner places his tale. Chaucer was probably rhyming more or less mechanically with *thryve*. He does this elsewhere (*RvT* 4264, *WBT* 312) where very similar lines occur, this time demanding a different rhyme, and the choice of saint here ('by that lord that called is seint Jame') appears equally mechanical.

The oaths by St Thomas refer, with one exception, to St Thomas à Becket. The exception is the Merchant's 'by Seint Thomas of Ynde' (*CT* IV, 1230). According to tradition St Thomas the apostle brought the Gospel to India and was martyred there. Miss Cline has pointed out the significance of the Merchant's choice of saint in enforcing the truth of what he was saying – 'that I seye sooth' – by invoking the apostle whose incredulity concerning Christ's resurrection finally gave way to a confession of faith which was the first explicitly to recognize his divinity. In other words, even doubting St Thomas would have to recognize the truth of the Merchant's claim that 'we wedded men lyven in sorwe and care' (*ibid.* 1228). That the other four oaths by St Thomas refer to à Becket is highly probable, as he might be considered the patron of the pilgrimage to his shrine, although actually only the Wife of Bath invokes him in her own person (*WBT* 666). His name is first mentioned casually as the pilgrims depart out of Southwark and are called to a halt at 'the wateryng of Seint Thomas' (*Gen Prol* 826), close to the second mile stone on the road towards Canterbury on what is now the Old Kent Road in London S.E.1.[13] The remaining oaths by St Thomas occur in *The House of Fame*, 1131, and in *The Miller's Tale*, 3291, both poems

13. For details see Francis P. Magoun, Jr, *A Chaucer Gazetteer* (Chicago, 1961), pp. 50, 170.

sharing the specific 'by seint Thomas of Kent'. The carpenter's two oaths by St Thomas (*MillT* 3425, 3461) frame, as it were, the reference to St Frideswide, but more significant probably is the fact that both provide handy rhymes for *Nicholas*.

One other saint figures in an oath in *The Miller's Tale*, St Neot, or in the blacksmith's version, 'by seinte Note' (*MillT* 3771). St Neot was a ninth-century Saxon saint whose doings are known almost exclusively from later medieval legends, including the interpolations made in the eleventh century into Asser's *Life of King Alfred*. One of these interpolations tells of Alfred before his marriage endeavouring to combat his carnal desires by frequently rising at cockcrow to visit the churches and relics of the saints – 'galli cantu et matutinis horis clam consurgens, ecclesias et reliquias sanctorum orandi causa visitabat'. Hence the ironic connection between St Neot, whom Alfred is said to have visited and held in great esteem, and the blacksmith's remarks to Absolon about the latter's unexpectedly early appearance.[14] The smith's artful 'ye woot wel what I mene' in the same line as 'by seinte Note' (which was not chosen for rhyme) points to the audience's likely awareness of the significance of the innuendo:

> 'What, Absolon! for Cristes sweete tree,
> Why rise ye so rathe? ey, *benedicitee*!
> What eyleth yow? Som gay gerl, God it woot,
> Hath broght yow thus upon the viritoot.
> By seinte Note, ye woot wel what I mene.'
>
> (*MillT* 3767–71)

Among the most interesting swearers in *The Canterbury Tales* is the Prioress, whose 'gretteste ooth was but by Seinte Loy' (*Gen Prol* 120). St Éloi or Eligius, a seventh-century Frenchman, occurs elsewhere in Chaucer only in the carter's thankful 'I pray God save thee, and Seinte Loy!' in *The Friar's Tale*, 1564, as his cart is safely pulled out of the mud. The carter's choice of saint is understandable, for St Eligius was patron of carriers as well as of goldsmiths. But why the Prioress's 'Seinte Loy'? After much expenditure of scholarly ink, John M. Steadman has probably summed up most convincingly the several reasons for Chaucer's

14. See further Angus Macdonald, 'Absolon and St Neot', *Neophilologus* XLVIII (1964), 235–7.

choice.[15] That the need to rhyme with the apt word *coy* had something to do with Chaucer's choice is likely, but it is equally likely that, in John Livingston Lowes's words,[16] 'under the happy guidance (very probably) of his rhyme', 'a flash of inspiration' made Chaucer pick on St Loy. There is multiple irony in associating his name with the Prioress: first, because her greatest oath is so mild, especially when compared with the hard swearing going on all around her, as to be almost no oath at all. Such moderate invocation of a celebrated courtier-saint was wholly in keeping with the Prioress's own painstaking affectation of 'cheere / Of court', of courtly manners and deportment. But secondly, it so happens that the Prioress never swears at all in *The Canterbury Tales*, and in picking on St Loy Chaucer was perhaps recalling an incident in the saint's life when his king, Dagobert I of the Franks, demanded an oath of the saint, and the latter refused to swear. So convinced was Dagobert of Eligius's integrity that he accepted 'sa parole seulement', as one source puts it. Hence, to swear by St Loy may have had for Chaucer and his audience the connotation of not swearing at all, appropriate for the Prioress. Thirdly, there is an ironic contrast between the many genuine works of mercy performed by St Eligius, recorded by his biographer, and the *charitable* devotion accorded by the Prioress to mice and little dogs. The saint was particularly active in the relief and ransoming of prisoners, and the Prioress's heart bled 'if that she saugh a mous / Kaught in a trappe' (*Gen Prol* 144–5). That the Prioress was somewhat fastidious about her appearance Chaucer suggests by repeating the words *semely* and *fetis* 'neat, elegant' several times in her portrait; and again there is, despite the superficial elegance in appearance, contrast with St Loy who wore a hair shirt under his courtly garments. Finally, St Eligius was celebrated in the Middle Ages particularly for his skill in working precious metals, another facet which may have played its part in Chaucer's associating him with a lady fond, among other personal ornaments, of a 'brooch of gold ful sheene' (*ibid.* 160). That Chaucer carried all these details, and perhaps others more dug up by modern scholarship, clearly in his head when composing the Prioress's portrait, is impossible; what matters is that he knew

15. John M. Steadman, '"Hir Gretteste Ooth": The Prioress, St Eligius, and St Godebertha', *Neophilologus* XLIII (1959), 49–57.

16. John Livingston Lowes, 'The Prioress's Oath', *Romanic Review* V (1914), 380.

or remembered enough about St Eligius to touch off by mentioning his name a whole grapeshot of connotations, each single shot sufficiently charged with irony to leave its mark upon the recipient.

The aptness of a saint's name may rest in a pun rather than in any direct religious or biographical associations. The Pardoner's iteration of the Host's 'Seint Ronyan' is of this type, as we have seen. More complex still may be the play upon 'Seint Joce' in the Wife of Bath's reference to her fourth husband:

> I seye, I hadde in herte greet despit
> That he of any oother had delit.
> But he was quit, by God and by Seint Joce!
> I made hym of the same wode a croce.
>
> *(WBT* 481–4)

St Joce, or Josse or Judocus, was a seventh-century Breton saint, patron of pilgrims, whose hermitage became the monastery of St Josse-sur-mer, about halfway between Abbeville and Calais, in a part of France which became, as Skeat points out, 'familiar to many Englishmen in the course of the wars of Edward III', as it must be to many tourists today. St Joce's symbol was a pilgrim's staff, a *burdoun*, a word whose obscene connotation, 'phallus', Chaucer exploited elsewhere (*Gen Prol* 673, and possibly in *RvT* 4165). It is upon this double meaning of *burdoun* ,'the same wode', suggested by the reference to St Joce, as well as on the double meaning of *croce*, literally 'staff', figuratively 'cross, hence burden, penance', that the Wife of Bath seems to be playing here. She is paying back, she says, the philanderer among her several husbands by making his marital transgressions a burden, 'I made him of that burdoun a burden'.[17] The wording of line 484 and the ryme *Joce:croce* may well have been suggested to Chaucer by a similar phrase in the Testament of Jean de Meun, as Skeat and Robinson have pointed out, but the transference to *Saint* Joce and the resulting word-play appear to be his own refinement.

Harry Bailly has one mouth-filling oath which has so far eluded any completely satisfactory explanation:

> Oure Hooste seyde, 'As I am feithful man,
> *And by that precious corpus Madrian,*

17. See Ann S. Haskell, 'The St Joce Oath in the Wife of Bath's Prologue', *Chaucer Review* I (1966–7), 85–7.

I hadde levere than a barel ale
That Goodelief, my wyf, hadde herd this tale!'
(*CT* VII, 1891-4)

None of the saintly candidates for *Madrian* so far advanced fits the context particularly well, except possibly the obscure St Mathurin, whose 'precious body' would not stay interred until returned to France, according to the popular *Legenda Aurea*. But it is equally possible that Harry Bailly was not invoking any saint at all, but simply swearing by some exotic word that happened to come into his head. Not by any means all the words unique to him in Chaucer are colloquial ones; he shares a few rare words with others, like *sophyme* 'sophism', and has a few of his own, like *fructuous* 'fruitful, edifying'. The comparatively rare M.E. word *madrian* or *madrean*, recorded from the middle of the fourteenth century on, derives from O.Fr. *madrian* and apparently denotes the product of treating ginger with lye.[18] It appears to have been some kind of delicacy and figures as such in a list in Deschamps's *Miroir de mariage*, a work upon which Chaucer drew for his discussions of marriage in the Wife of Bath's prologue and in *The Merchant's Tale*. The present instance also involves comments on marriage, Harry Bailly's own, hence the possibility of a distant echo of Deschamps's 'Annis, madrïan, noix confites . . . / Et aultres epices assez'. That Harry Bailly should turn *madrian* into yet another 'vulgar' Latinism, like *corpus dominus*, is quite in character. That he should swear ironically by something meaning literally 'that precious body of sweetmeats' as he remembers his wife, is perhaps not untypical either of the man's colourful diction or of his swearing. Chaucer could not have been stumped for a rhyme for *man*; something more subtly appropriate must have suggested so exotic an oath as this involving *madrian*. Nor is it coincidence perhaps that the only 'saints' in Chaucer, not so far identified as such, figure in oaths uttered by Harry Bailly.

There can be no dispute about the aptness of the oath 'by the croys which that Seint Eleyne fond' uttered by the Host in his violent retort to the Pardoner at the end of the latter's performance (*CT* VI, 951). We have already noted the pungent irony

18. This was pointed out by George L. Frost, 'That Precious Corpus Madrian', *Modern Language Notes* LVII (1942), 177-9. Frost transcribes a fourteenth-century recipe, 'To Mak Conserue of Madrian', but does not explore the relevance of the word to Harry Bailly's swearing.

of contrasting the holiest of Christian relics with the Pardoner's collection of fraudulent trash, the mitten and the 'pigges bones' and the pillow case. In a different way, the Host swears appropriately 'by Seint Austyn' in his comments on the Shipman's tale (*CT* VII, 441), echoing the Shipman's monk's earlier reference to St Augustine, and the two allusions to the saint earlier still in the pilgrim Monk's portrait.[19]

There is one oath by St Simon the Apostle in *The Canterbury Tales*, uttered by Thomas in *The Summoner's Tale*, 2094. The importunate friar of the tale has finished his harangue and is now urging Thomas to confess, but patently more eager for the sick man's gold than for his soul. At this point Thomas utters his 'nay . . . by Seint Symoun!' If the choice of saint here is at all meaningful, it presumably plays ironically upon the friar's zeal, for St Simon was called 'the zealous one' by St Luke (VI:15), whether on account of his character or as a member of the Jewish party of Zealots is here immaterial. The friar's zeal for 'gold, to make oure cloystre' (2099) certainly knew no bounds, and it would be characteristic of Chaucer's art to choose an oath which, once again, possessed contextually appropriate connotations.

It has been suggested that the same is true of the summoner's rather unexpected 'by the sweete seinte Anne' in *The Friar's Tale*, 1613, for as the fiend himself addresses the old widow as 'myn owene mooder deere' (1626), the summoner's oath invoking the mother of Mary, the patron saint of mothers, adds its own ironic flavour.[20] But once again the rhyme, this time with *panne*, may have helped to guide Chaucer's choice of saint. The word *panne* is used only once elsewhere in *The Canterbury Tales* in rhyme, with *thanne* in *The Canon's Yeoman's Tale*, 1210.

Chaucer's animals, as we have seen, swear as readily as his people. The Eagle begins his first proper speech with a forceful 'Seynte Marye!' (*HF* 573) and from then swears happily on. In *The Parliament of Fowls* several of the birds swear, more or less vigorously, with the aid of an occasional 'parde', a hat, and a saint, although the incidence of swearing in this poem is exceptionally low. On the other hand, the cock and hen of *The Nun's Priest's Tale* cover a wide range of oaths, from an innocuous 'parde' to Perte-

19. See above, ch. 4, p. 183.
20. See Constance Hieatt, 'Oaths in the "Friar's Tale"', *Notes and Queries* N.S. VII (1960), 6.

lote's mouth-filling, and line-filling 'Up peril of my soule and of my lyf' (*NPT* 2944). Daun Russell the fox, whom we have not so far considered, adds a few suitable oaths and imprecations to his discourse. The prayerful 'God his soule blesse!' (*ibid.* 3295) fits nicely into the oily diction of his flattering address to Chauntecleer, punctuated with its repeated 'sire' and 'certes' and 'trewely'. The speech ends with a fitting 'for seinte charitee' (3320), a rare oath reserved by Chaucer for appropriately humorous or ironic use. Not counting pilgrim Chaucer's own 'par charitee' in *Sir Thopas*, 891, there are only two other instances besides the fox's. Palamon is imploring Theseus in somewhat breathless confusion:

'But sle me first, for seinte charitee!
But sle my felawe eek as wel as me;
Or sle hym first. . . .'

> (*KnT* 1721–3)

And in *The Summoner's Tale* the zealous friar is imploring Thomas in similar breathlessness, and not without some confusion of his own as to who really founded his particular order, whether Elijah or Elisha:

'But syn Elye was, or Elise,
Han freres been, that fynde I of record,
In charitee, ythanked be oure Lord!
Now Thomas, help, for seinte charitee!'

> (*SumT* 2116–19)

With these occasions in mind the fox's unctuous 'now syngeth, sire, for seinte charitee' gains even more ironic force: be charitable, he is in fact saying; and, please, let me catch you 'by the gargat' (throat). The fox's tone remains hypocritical ('in feith', 3414; 'God help me so', 3425) until the final outburst with its forceful, and now heartfelt 'God yeve hym meschaunce' (3433). In their swearing, as in other ways, Chaucer's animals reveal their humanity.

Chaucer himself also swears, whether as narrator of his poems, or as Dreamer, or as pilgrim. He never descends to anatomical oaths, however, nor to any other *grisly* oaths which could be branded as particularly vulgar or particularly reprehensible. His most common oath is the simple 'Lord!', particularly as narrator in *Troilus and Criseyde* and as Dreamer in *The House of Fame*. His most daring oath is probably 'by Goddes sweete pyne' (*CT* VII,

936), uttered in response to Harry Bailly's request for something better than *Sir Thopas*. In between lies the familiar range of conventional medieval English oaths, 'by God', 'God me save', 'help me God so wys', 'for Goddes love', 'by heven kyng', 'by oure Lord', 'by my trouthe', and a few variants, perhaps fifty or sixty or so in all, and all well in keeping with the roles and attitudes Chaucer assumes in his poems. In *Sir Thopas*, where the narrator's role is not a straightforward one, the burlesquing of romantic diction is extended to the oaths. The narrator begins his second fit, or the third, if J. A. Burrow is right,[21] with an affected *'par charitee'* (*Thop* 891), while Sir Thopas himself is credited with 'o seinte Marie, *benedicite*!' (784) and with *'par ma fay'* (820), and in line 872 is made to swear a 'minced' oath, fit for 'a mealy-mouthed hero':

> And there he swoor *on ale and breed*
> How that the geaunt shal be deed,
>   Bityde what bityde!
>
> (*Thop* 872-4)

The 'minced' or 'idle' oath, as Beatrice White has pointed out, substitutes an innocuous euphemism for a blasphemy, in this case 'ale and bread' for the elements of the Sacrament – 'a subtle underlining of the mock-heroic character of Sir Thopas that in undertaking a prodigious adventure against a swashbuckling monster he prepares for the enterprise in so linguistically unadventurous and secure a fashion, for he was not only "faire", but "gente"'.[22] Chaucer contrasts Sir Thopas's oaths in two directions, with the Host's hard swearing as he stops the tale, and, within the tale itself, with Sir Olifaunt's 'by Termagaunt!' (810), a forceful oath by a Saracen idol, popular enough in medieval romances, and chosen here with the same unfailing perspicacity which characterizes Chaucer's swearing through so much of his poetry.

21. J. A. Burrow, '"Sir Thopas": An Agony in Three Fits,' *The Review of English Studies* N.S. XXII (1971), 54-8.

22. Beatrice White, 'Two Chaucer Notes', *Neuphilologische Mitteilungen* LXIV (1963), 175.

CHAPTER 6

In Science so Expert

🔯🔯🔯🔯

SOMETHING of what Chaucer understood by the word *science* may be gleaned from his words about Calchas, father of Criseyde, who is introduced near the beginning of *Troilus and Criseyde*. The words which in this chapter I wish to apply to the poet himself, 'in science so expert' (*Tr* I, 67), Chaucer here applies to Calchas who had arrived at the knowledge 'that Troie sholde destroied be (68) by his scientific expertise and promptly applied this knowledge practically by deserting to the enemy. Calchas, says Chaucer in one of his more blatant puns,

> knew by calkulynge,
> And ek by answer of this Appollo, –
> (*Tr* I, 71–2)

in short, by using the two 'scientific' methods fundamental to an understanding of Chaucerian dialectic and, by implication, of much of his poetry.[1] *Calkulynge*, the computing and calculating of appropriate mathematical and astrological data, is the empirical method of observation and investigation and corresponds to what Chaucer variously calls *assay* 'investigation, test(ing)' (e.g. *LGW* 9) or *experience* (e.g. *KnT* 3001) or *preef*, *preve* 'proof, confirmation, experience', as in 'by preeve which that is demonstratif' (*SumT* 2272). And the consulting of Apollo's oracle at Delphi corresponds to the appeal to higher authority, *auctoritee*, which in Chaucer so often takes the form of referring either to specific authors ('myn auctour', 'Tullyus', 'Boece', etc.) or in more general terms to 'olde bookes' or to 'thise wise clerkes', generally those, as Pandarus adds, 'that ben dede' (*Tr* III, 292). Chaucer clearly recognized both of these as legitimate modes of cognition, and both figure in discussions of various issues and situations in the poems. Several times they are explicitly juxtaposed; for example, in the Wife of Bath's opening words:

1. This aspect is particularly stressed in John Lawlor's *Chaucer* (London, 1968).

'Experience, though noon auctoritee
Were in this world, is right ynogh for me';
(*WBT* 1–2)

or in the opening line of the legend of Phyllis:

By preve as wel as by autorite.
(*LGW* 2394)

In *The Nun's Priest's Tale* the two disputants in the debate about
the significance of dreams represent the two approaches: Pertelote the hen is empirical and practical and recommends a laxative;
Chauntecleer the cock has recourse to what 'men may in olde
bookes rede' (*NPT* 2974) and displays notable erudition as he
cites a whole string of these. *The House of Fame*, itself indebted to
Chaucer's own reading of 'olde bookes', yet offers scope for
'preve by experience' (*HF* 878) as the traveller is enabled to find
things out for himself. It is important amid all the wealth of book
learning paraded by Chaucer and his creatures and amid all the
pseudo-science of the Middle Ages to remember that Chaucer was
not unaware either of the existence or of the importance of personal observation as a mode of cognition. Although for us foremost a poet, Chaucer was also very much an active man of affairs
and, as the *Treatise on the Astrolabe* demonstrates, something of a
man of science in the modern sense.

The parallel with modern science must not, of course, be
carried too far. Calchas may have been employing recognized
cognitive methods, but basically the one depended upon much
astrological mumbo-jumbo, and the other was plain superstition.
He is not called a 'gret devyn' (*Tr* I, 66) for nothing, for a 'divine'
in Middle English is not only a philosopher or theologian, but
also a soothsayer, augur, or astrologer. The word illustrates as
well as Chaucer's word *science* itself the difficulty facing the
twentieth-century reader who is confronted with medieval
'science', 'these monstrosities of error', as W. C. Curry calls them.
And yet, as Curry's book amply demonstrates, a full appreciation
of Chaucer's art is impossible without recognizing both the
richness of his knowledge of 'a well-known body of universally
accepted scientific principles', and the poet's 'admirable restraint
and . . . discriminating judgment in the employment of these
materials'.[2]

2. Curry, pp. xi, xviii.

The present chapter does not aim to duplicate the studies in Chaucer's use of medieval scientific material so ably carried out by Curry and other Chaucerian scholars; its purpose is rather to examine the range and character of Chaucer's scientific and technical vocabulary and some of the uses he makes of it. For this purpose I propose to allow myself some semantic stretching of the term 'scientific' in order to include groups of words relating to certain activities, like commerce or sport, which no self-respecting faculty of science in a modern university could possibly want to have anything to do with.

The two sciences[3] which figure most in Chaucer's work are theology and astronomy. The Catholic Church of the fourteenth century was still very much a primary influence in the lives of European people and hardly any activity was untouched by its doctrines and its rules for the conduct of daily living. Negatively, this found linguistic expression in the oaths medieval people swore by God and all that was holy, for their irreverence and blasphemy presupposed belief. Positively, the language reflected in its rich theological and ecclesiastical vocabulary the central importance of the Christian religion and of the Church and its institutions. Chaucer's poetry, and his prose no less, bear witness to this. Even a classical tale like that of Troilus and Criseyde, removed in time and action into a pre-Christian era, carries throughout its length the stamp of a Christian vocabulary; largely, as has been shown, in the form of oaths and asseverations, but not entirely. References to the creation, to God's governance of the world, to God's saving power, to God's omniscience, to the atonement, to eternal punishment, to holy saints' lives, to the clergy, all reflect the pervasiveness of Christian terminology even in *Troilus and Criseyde*. Troilus's prayer may be addressed to 'the pitouse goddes everichone' (*Tr* IV, 949), but the long soliloquy on fate, predestination and free will that follows (958 ff.) is couched in terms that may have come to Chaucer from Boethius, but which are very much part of the vocabulary of medieval Christian debate: *abusioun*, especially in the sense of 'heresy', *corsednesse*, *divine purveyaunce*, *eterne*, *fre chois*, *predestyne*, *prescience*, *thynges temporel*. The end of the poem allows fuller rein to the language of Christian admonition and adoration, and apart from

---

3. At this point it seems as well to dispense with inverted commas and to use the word science in one of its medieval senses as 'branch of learning'.

the Chaucerian nonce word *uncircumscript* (*Tr* V, 1865), employs a much simpler, less Latinate vocabulary. This division is characteristic of all English religious diction, not only Chaucer's, namely between the often highly abstruse vocabulary of theological debate and the simpler, emotionally charged vocabulary of devotion. The former came into Middle English from Romance sources, the latter is largely Anglo-Saxon in origin; hence the difference between words as in the list just cited and these in the concluding stanzas of *Troilus and Criseyde*:

> And loveth hym, the which that right for love
> Upon a crois, oure soules for to beye,
> First starf, and roos, and sit in hevene above.
> (*Tr* V, 1842–4)

> And to that sothefast Crist, that starf on rode,
> With al myn herte of mercy evere I preye,
> And to the Lord right thus I speke and seye.
> (*ibid.* 1860–2)

To turn from *Troilus and Criseyde*, even its concluding stanzas, to several of the Canterbury Tales is to see Chaucer's theological vocabulary, as it were, switched on to the full. He had clearly absorbed much of the diction and style of devotional and hagiographical writing, as well as of sermons and treatises, and, not least, the liturgy of the Roman Rite and the Scriptures, numerous passages of which he translated himself and incorporated into his own writings.[4] He may have written or translated more than we know of, for he refers in the concluding words to *The Canterbury Tales* to 'the translacion of Boece de Consolacione, and othere bookes of legendes of seintes, and omelies, and moralitee, and devocioun' (X 1088), but even what we have shows his familiarity with, and mastery of, the appropriate idiom. If *The Parson's Tale* falls under 'omelies' and *The Tale of Melibee* under 'moralitee', the tales of Prioress and Second Nun can be classified as 'legendes of seintes', the latter more strictly so, as the word *legende* (as in *SecNT* 25) had come to be associated specifically with the life and death of a saint, whereas *The Prioress's Tale* is strictly a 'miracle of the Virgin'. Both tales, however, depend for their effect upon

---

4. See W. M. Thompson, 'Chaucer's Translation of the Bible', in *English and Medieval Studies Presented to J. R. R. Tolkien*, ed. Norman Davis and C. L. Wrenn (London, 1962), pp. 183–99).

what G. H. Russell has called 'the assured language of a tradition of Christian writing that is venerable and rich'.[5] The vocabulary covers the whole range of Christian experience, and practically every word must have possessed for the medieval listener connotations of various kinds, varying, that is, with his education and the intensity of his own devotional life. One of the fundamental concepts in Christian doctrine is that of 'charity', Chaucer's *charite*, and its use by Chaucer may serve to illustrate something of the rich connotative texture of so central a term, as well as some of the poet's more idiosyncratic uses for ironic purposes.

The word *charite* carries in Middle English primarily the meaning of Christian love, between God and his creatures, and between man and his neighbour. In the Wyclifite Bible, as in the later King James Version, it renders the Greek *agape*, and the word is understandably common in this sense in Middle English religious literature. The derived meaning of an act of kindness or benevolence, of charity in the sense of alms-giving, which is the most common meaning in modern English, is recorded in Middle English as early as *The Peterborough Chronicle*, and is equally common in middle English religious writing. Chaucer expresses the radiant quality of Christian love, with a glance ahead at the saint's martyrdom, in describing St Cecilia as 'brennynge evere in charite ful brighte' (*SecNT* 118), and in the portrait of the Plowman he sums up the ideal of the Christian man:

> A trewe swynkere and a good was he,
> Lyvynge in pees and parfit charitee.
> God loved he best with al his hoole herte
> At alle tymes, thogh him gamed or smerte,
> And thanne his neighebor right as hymselve.
>
> > (*Gen Prol* 531–5)

Other Christian virtues are ranged alongside *charite* in various contexts, whether straight as in *The Parson's Tale* or with ironic overtones as in *The Summoner's Tale*:

> 'Therfore we mendynantz, we sely freres,
> Been wedded to poverte and continence,
> To charite, humblesse, and abstinence,

5. G. H. Russell, 'Chaucer: The Prioress's Tale', in *Medieval Literature and Civilization: Studies in Memory of G. N. Garmonsway*, ed. D. A. Pearsall and R. A. Waldron (London, 1969), p. 225.

> To persecucioun for rightwisnesse,
> To wepynge, misericorde, and clennesse.'
>
> *(SumT* 1906–10)

The Prioress is *charitable* and *pitous* (*Gen Prol* 143), central Christian virtues both and marks of true *gentillesse*, as Chaucer repeatedly avers in his favourite line 'pitee renneth soone in gentil herte' (*KnT* 1761, *MerchT* 1986, *SqT* 479, *LGW* F, 503); what is amiss is the direction of the Prioress's love and compassion. The above passage from *The Summoner's Tale* shows how clearly the senses of 'Christian love' and of 'acts of charity' are interwoven in Chaucer's usage. The latter meaning is often spelt out, as when the Parson repeatedly speaks of 'werkes of charite' or 'charitable werkes', and the word can mean in Middle English simply 'an act of kindness' without any specifically Christian connotations, as when it is applied to Theseus in *The Knight's Tale*, 1433, or by Sir Gawain with reference to the hospitality accorded to him at Hautdesert (*SGGK* 2055). A further step towards directing the word into secular usage is its employment in contexts of *fine amour*, where its religious connotations are deliberately and often ironically shifted from *agape* to *eros*. Thus Troilus expresses the ecstasy of his union with Criseyde thus:

> 'O Love, O Charite!
> Thi moder ek, Citherea the swete,
> After thiself next heried be she,
> Venus mene I',
>
> *(Tr* III, 1254–7)

while later in the poem Criseyde's portrait refers to her as *charitable* and not lacking in *pite* (*Tr* V, 823 f.), the Prioress's virtues, we note, which at this stage in *Troilus and Criseyde* can only underline the fundamental ambiguity in Criseyde's character or what Mrs Gordon has called 'the teasing enigma [of] her behaviour'.[6] Chaucer was not the only one to extend these concepts of *charite* and compassion to what some critics call the 'religion' of courtly love; nor was he the only one to water down the original concept of *agape* into a convenient idiom in which little, if anything, survives of the doctrinal sense of being or not being in a state of grace. In such a line as the narrator's 'I am no bet in charyte' in

6. Gordon, p. 113.

The House of Fame, 108, religious echoes are indeed faint, and the idiom 'out of alle charitee' can be applied as readily to Cupid (*KnT* 1623) as to the Wife of Bath on receiving a social snub (*Gen Prol* 452). On the other hand, the use of 'seinte charitee' in oaths may be regarded not so much as part of the secularization of the word, but rather as a paradoxical tribute to the continuing importance of the concept in Christian thought and doctrine.

Such a modest semantic exercise as the above on *charite* could and no doubt should be carried out for many Chaucerian words of a technical kind, preferably in the more extended and erudite manner of C. S. Lewis, but our aim here is simply to illustrate the way in which some awareness of the character of Chaucer's scientific vocabulary can illuminate his art. In the passage from *The Summoner's Tale* quoted earlier, for example, other technical theological words are used which possess serious religious connotations made ironic in the context of the friar's harangue. Twice in rapid succession the friar refers to his order as 'we mendynantz, we freres' (*SumT* 1906, 1912), a word found nowhere else in Chaucer, perhaps because in no other context but a begging friar's passionate plea for 'gold', could the word 'mendicant' become so fittingly satiric. But the irony goes deeper, for the *misericorde* to which the friar also claims to be wedded is precisely the virtue which should free him from greed, or, as the Parson puts it, 'the releevynge of Avarice is misericorde, ... a vertu by which the corage of a man is stired by the mysese of hym that is mysesed' (*ParsT* 804 ff.). No medieval listener attuned to sermons on the deadly sins and their antidotes could have missed the poignancy of the friar's *misericorde* in the wider context of Christian conduct, any more than he would overlook the reference to *abstinence*, the remedy against gluttony (*ParsT* 831), in view of the friar's earlier ordering of a particularly choice menu from his hostess's larder. At the same time the friar's whole speech depends for its effect, apart from his smooth rhetoric, upon his persuasive familiarity with the appropriate technical vocabulary, whether common words like *clennesse*, *poverte*, *preyeres*, or rare ones like *contemplaunce* (perhaps, as the *MED* suggests, coined by Chaucer for rhyme), *executour* in the line

'Ire is, in sooth, executour of pryde',
(*SumT* 2010)

or *persecucioun*, not used elsewhere in Chaucer, but found in the same phrase 'persecucioun for rightwissnesse' in the Wyclifite rendering of Matthew V:10.

Chaucer's theological vocabulary, in the widest sense, runs into hundreds of words, most of them of Romance origin. In Hans Remus's survey[7] this group accounts for half of Chaucer's total technical vocabulary and, if we add words of Old English origin, the percentage increases even further, as relatively few of Chaucer's technical words in other fields derive from Old English. The differing appeal between words of Germanic and Romance origin we noted briefly in connection with the concluding stanzas of *Troilus and Criseyde*. In the two hagiographical tales, more particularly the Second Nun's, the technicalities of theological diction are softened and rendered emotionally effective by a careful admixture of native English words, sometimes suggested by Chaucer's sources as remembered from scripture or liturgy, sometimes perhaps drawn from the poet's own devotional experience:

> O mooder Mayde! o mayde Mooder free!
> O bussh unbrent, brennynge in Moyses sighte,
> That ravyshedest doun fro the Deitee,
> Thurgh thyn humblesse, the Goost that in th'alighte,
> Of whos vertu, whan he thyn herte lighte,
> Conceyved was the Fadres sapience,
> Help me to telle it in thy reverence!
> $(PrT\ 467–73)$

A richly Romance line, like

> O martir, sowded [i.e. confirmed] to virginitee,
> (*ibid.* 579)

may be followed by one made up of native English words:

> Now maystow syngen, folwynge evere in oon.
> (*ibid.* 580)

Words of emotive appeal and of doctrinal import can effectively combine in a phrase and again it matters little where Chaucer's inspiration came from; what is important is the resulting poetic

7. Hans Remus, *Die kirchlichen und speziell-wissenschaftlichen Romanischen Lehnworte Chaucers* (Halle, 1906).

texture, richly wrought of divers linguistic strands: 'thow welle of mercy, synful soules cure' (*SecNT* 37), 'Virgine wemmelees' (47), 'sonne of excellence' (52), 'sower of chaast conseil' (192), 'corone of lif' (388). Such phrases, of course, occur in other tales as well: in the prayers of Constance, for example, who addresses the Virgin as

'Thow glorie of wommanhede, thow faire may,
Thow haven of refut, brighte sterre of day'.
(*MLT* 851-2)

It is interesting to note how much better a phrase like 'thow haven of refut' (i.e. refuge) serves its purpose in these balanced lines in which devotional fervour finds appropriate expression amid familiar figures, than in the much more abstract diction of Chaucer's *ABC*, based on an episode in Guillaume Deguilleville's *Pèlerinage de la Vie Humaine*, where the same phrase occurs (*ABC* 14) amid a torrent of words of Romance origin. The effect of these words in the latter poem may well be, as Clemen claims,[8] to 'heighten' the language, but they equally effectively remove the poem from the realm of private prayer to that of more patently conscious artistry. Chaucer was able to judge well enough what was linguistically suitable for a highly artificial poetic exercise, and what was proper in a moment of fervent emotional outpouring. This can be illustrated further by his use of some of the words denoting the central figures of the Christian faith, of the Trinity. The words *God, Lord, Jhesu Crist* are ubiquitous; by contrast, *deitee*, used several times in connection with pagan divinities, is used only twice in Christian contexts, once prayerfully by the Prioress (*PrT* 469), and once theologically by the Canon's Yeoman (*CYT* 1469). The word *divinitee* is used only technically, as in St Cecilia's explanatory

'So in o beynge of divinitee,
Thre persones may ther right wel bee',
(*SecNT* 340-1)

or in *Boece*, especially III, pr. 10, where it means the quality of being divine. Chaucer's two remaining uses of the word refer to the science of theology and are both given to the devil (*FrT* 1512, 1638). The word *trinitee* is even more sparingly used and is only

8. Clemen, p. 176.

once prayerfully invoked, by the Prioress's abbot, 'in vertu of the hooly Trinitee' (*PrT* 646). The remaining occurrences, at least in Robinson's edition, are in oaths.

Many words, not strictly theological, refer to the organization and institutions of the medieval Church and were presumably as familiar to fourteenth-century Englishmen as present-day terms of politics and government are to us. Characteristically, there are a good many more words describing people than ecclesiastical buildings or their furnishings in Chaucer. In the General Pro-logue to *The Canterbury Tales*, for example, Friar Hubert is referred to as a *lymytour* (209), a friar licensed to beg within defined limits, his *lymytacioun* (*WBT* 877), as a *licenciat* (220), one licensed to hear confessions, and as one who was not like a *cloysterer* (259), a 'cloistered' monk, a word here and elsewhere readily and perhaps ironically associated with threadbare clothes and poverty (cp. *CT* VII, 1939). Friar Hubert was more privileged than the *curat* (219), the parish priest, to whom the parishioner would normally turn for confession and absolution, as the Summoner's Thomas did:

> 'I have be shryven this day at my curat.'
>
> (*SumT* 2095)

The Monk, like the one in *The Shipman's Tale*, is an *outridere* (166), one who spent a good deal of his time outside his monastery, generally regarded as a technical term for a monastic official charged with the supervision of granges and other outlying pro-perty, ('hir graunges and hire bernes wyde' (*ShipT* 66)), but here given the wider and appropriately ironic sense of one who loved riding abroad, mainly to hunt. For all his self-indulgence a patient man, Chaucer's Monk takes in good part the Host's bantering allusions to his possible standing within his monastery:

> 'Upon my feith, thou art som officer,
> Som worthy sexteyn, or som celerer,
> For by my fader soule, as to my doom,
> Thou art a maister whan thou art at hoom;
> No povre cloysterer, ne no novys,
> But a governour'.
>
> (*CT* VII, 1935–40)

Both the *sexteyn* 'sacristan', and the *celerer* 'cellarer', were officials of some dignity. The Summoner's friar also mentions the *sexteyn* of his house, as well as the *fermerer* (*SumT* 1859), a shortened form of *enfermerer*, the friar in charge of the infirmary. No particular difficulty attaches to such words for the modern reader of Chaucer, except that some of the subtler social distinctions are now less easy to recapture, and such distinctions mattered to those among Chaucer's clerical characters who aimed to 'ben holden digne of reverence' (*Gen Prol* 141).

The Prioress's word *clergeon* (*PrT* 503) normally refers to a young cleric, or one in minor orders, but is used by her of a seven-year-old schoolboy, a not improper usage as the word could also be applied to a chorister or choir-boy, and such a one the Prioress's young martyr clearly hoped to be even though at his age he could only just have begun his schooling.[9] There is thus a peculiar pathos in applying the word *clergeon* to the little boy with his sweet voice ('puer vero clericus erat habens vocem claram', as one of the analogues has it) about to be martyred before he was able to become a *clergeon* proper in any of the senses of the word. This is irony of a different kind from the Prioress's more apparent digs at monastic dignitaries:

> This abbot, which that was an hooly man,
> As monkes been – or elles oghte be,
>> (*PrT* 642–3)

and

> This hooly monk, this abbot, hym meene I.
>> (*ibid.* 670)

Coming from this particular lady, even within the context of a tale so pathetic that it 'sobered' all the Canterbury pilgrims, the poignancy of these remarks is all the more delectable, not least because much earlier in the work Chaucer had cleverly juxtaposed this *fetis* Prioress with her 'cheere of court' and his worldly Monk – 'a manly man, to been an abbot able' (*Gen Prol* 167). It is hard not to believe that for many medieval people words like *abbot* carried unflattering overtones very similar to those evoked today by such words as 'politician' or 'policeman'. In Guillaume de Lorris's *Roman de la Rose*, for instance, is the origin ('plus gras que abez ou prieurs') of the English *Romaunt's* satiric

9. See Carleton Brown's comments in Bryan and Dempster, p. 465.

For oft I see suche losengours
Fatter than abbatis or priours,

(*Rom* 2693–4)

and there are other examples of an almost inevitable association of good living or wealth with dignitaries of the Church. Even the ordinary cleric comes in for his share. The simple priest of *The Canon's Yeoman's Tale*, the *annueleer* (*CYT* 1012) whose job it was to sing anniversary masses in memory of the dead, was happily supplied with ample 'spendyng silver', yet not enough apparently to withstand the Canon's blandishments. He might have avoided his subsequent *confusioun* if he had taken to heart what Langland had to say about 'prestes that han *no* spendyng-seluer' (*PP* C XIV, 101 ff.). If words like 'abbot', 'prior', 'priest' possessed some derogatory connotations by Chaucer's time, some other words, like 'friar' or 'pardoner' had probably travelled even further towards becoming almost completely pejorative. A tradition of satire was leaving its mark, particularly when it became embedded in proverbial sayings, like the fifteenth-century proverb 'Thre freris and thre fox maken thre shrewys', quoted in the *MED*, or the Summoner's

'Lo, goode men, a flye and eek a frere
Wol falle in every dyssh and eek mateere.'

(*CT* III, 835–6)

In Langland's field full of folk friars are prominent,

alle the foure ordres,
Prechynge the peple for profit of the wombe,

(*PP* C I, 56–7)

but the pardoners are not far behind and in depravity at least their equals. Wyclif refers to a pardoner 'with stolen bulls and false relics', obviously first cousin to Chaucer's master trickster. As early as *The House of Fame* Chaucer associated pardoners with *lesinges* 'deceits' and 'boystes crammed ful of lyes' (*HF* 2121 ff.) and it is almost impossible to find a Middle English use of the word not packed with satire, dislike, or downright hatred.

That such people could not thrive without a credulous populace bred on superstition is a sad comment on the age, but just as modern Englishmen are often taken in by advertisements couched in specious scientific jargon, so their forebears fell for the no less

296

specious learning of friars and pardoners. Pleasant, we are told, was the Friar's *In principio* (*Gen Prol* 254), the opening words of St John's gospel, which even the poorest widow was happy enough to pay a farthing for, not so much out of reverence for friar or scripture but because she believed in what was widely regarded as a charm, an apotropaic formula against demons and other malignant forces.[10] The Summoner's friar drops an occasional Latin phrase for the same mercenary ends:

> With *qui cum patre* forth his wey he wente,
>
> (*SumT* 1734)

and with '*Deus hic!*' he enters the house where he usually does better than anywhere else, adding a *Te Deum* and a *Placebo* to his snatches of French later on. The Pardoner 'blerede hure eyen', befuddled their eyes, as Langland puts it, as he regales the poor country folk with his monotonously recurrent, albeit imposing, *Radix malorum est Cupiditas* (*PardT* 334, 426), and, slyly, as he says,

> 'in Latyn I speke a wordes fewe,
> To saffron with my predicacioun,
> And for to stire hem to devocioun.'
>
> (*PardT* 344–6)

The Summoner himself, equally unsavoury a creature, also had his snatches of Latin, his 'termes...two or thre' (*Gen Prol* 639), his *Questio quid iuris* (646), for example, and suffered in addition from a peculiar though profitable infirmity which made him 'speke no word but Latyn' (638) when he was inebriated. Chaucer knew all about the art of linguistic hoodwinkery, of 'countrefeted termes.../ To seme wys' (*PhysT* 51 f.), and one suspects that there are moments in his work when he finds it hard to resist the temptation himself.

But like Heine laughing at his own romantic tears, so Chaucer can laugh at his own linguistic flourishes, and even a minor display of astronomical lore offers as good an opportunity as any:

> But sodeynly bigonne revel newe
> Til that the brighte sonne loste his hewe;
> For th'orisonte hath reft the sonne his lyght, –
> This is as muche to seye as it was nyght!
>
> (*FranklT* 1015–18)

10. See Morton W. Bloomfield, 'The Magic of *In Principio*', *Modern Language Notes* LXX (1955), 559–65.

Did he, one wonders, recall his own version of *Boece* I, m. 6, 1 ff. when he wrote this? His rendering of Boethius's compact

> Cum Phoebi radiis graue
> Cancri sidus inaestuat

into a heavy-handed clause with an almost apologetic gloss to follow: 'Whan that the hevy sterre of the Cancre eschaufeth by the bemes of Phebus (*that is to seyn, whan that Phebus the sonne is in the synge of the Cancre*) . . .'? The temptation to show off astronomical knowledge in often abstruse technical language was for Chaucer an ever-present one, and he did not always laugh it off as happily as in *The Franklin's Tale*. The temptation was all the greater because astronomy (in which I include astrology, as the division in the Middle Ages, in so far as there was one, is by no means always clear) was for all its practical usefulness a more esoteric science than theology, and much of its technical vocabulary could not so easily be rendered accessible to the uninitiated by a helpful infusion of familiar words of native origin. It may well be debated whether even the 'light Englissh' of the *Astrolabe* and its 'super-fluite of wordes' are really fit for a young student, as a good many technicalities inevitably remain no matter how hard Chaucer strove to avoid them.

In the poems astronomy serves many purposes, thereby reflecting its various basic functions in a number of medieval sciences; hence astronomical words are found in many different contexts. There is for example the use of appropriate astronomical data for fixing the date or time of an occurrence, like the beginning of the Canterbury pilgrimage in the familiar opening lines of *The General Prologue*, in which astronomical terms like 'the Ram', 'halve cours yronne', are fitted without incongruity into a poetic opening passage containing elements of the spring openings found in many medieval poems. Other examples come to mind in which Chaucer's poetic genius successfully assimilated scientific concepts into richly poetic passages, the description, for instance, of 'the colde, frosty seson of Decembre' in *The Franklin's Tale*:

> Phebus wax old, and hewed lyk laton,
> That in his hoote declynacion
> Shoon as the burned gold with stremes brighte;
> But now in Capricorn adoun he lighte,
> Where as he shoon ful pale, I dar wel seyn.

The bittre frostes, with the sleet and reyn,
Destroyed hath the grene in every yerd.
Janus sit by the fyr, with double berd,
And drynketh of his bugle horn the wyn;
Biforn hym stant brawen of the tusked swyn,
And 'Nowel' crieth every lusty man.

(FranklT 1245–55)

The astronomical element is admittedly slight in the diction of this
passage, but just sufficient to lend an edge to the Franklin's
avowal, a few lines later,

I ne kan no termes of astrologye,

(ibid. 1266)

followed at once by a flood of technical terms which must have
foxed even the more learned members of Chaucer's audience, let
alone the Canterbury pilgrims: *his tables Tolletanes, expans yeeris,
rootes, centris, argumentz, proporcioneles convenientz, equacions, eighte
[or ninthe] speere, Alnath, Aries, firste mansioun, face, terme* (*FranklT*
1273 ff.).

The Squire is fond of indicating time in astronomical terms:

Phebus the sonne ful joly was and cleer;
For he was neigh his exaltacioun
In Martes face, and in his mansioun
In Aries, the colerik hoote signe;

(SqT 48–51)

or, later in the tale:

Phebus hath laft the angle meridional,
And yet ascendynge was the beest roial,
The gentil Leon, with hia Aldiran. . . .

(ibid. 263–5)

Similarly the Merchant's:

The moone, that at noon was thilke day
That Januarie hath wedded fresshe May
In two of Tawr, was into Cancre glyden.

(MerchT 1885–7)

In the days before wrist watches not only cocks who like Chauntecleer knew 'by nature' (*NPT* 2855) but even people of little
learning, like Harry Bailly who was 'nat depe ystert in loore',

299

knew just enough astronomy to calculate the time of day and the day of the month. At least so Chaucer implies by devoting the first fifteen lines of Fragment II of *The Canterbury Tales* to Harry Bailly's discovery that it was 10 a.m. on April the 18th. As the passage is full of boy scout information it is worth quoting at length:

> Oure Hooste saugh wel that the brighte sonne
> The ark of his artificial day hath ronne
> The ferthe part, and half an houre and moore,
> And though he were nat depe ystert in loore,
> He wiste it was the eightetethe day
> Of Aprill, that is messager to May;
> And saugh wel that the shadwe of every tree
> Was as in lengthe the same quantitee
> That was the body erect that caused it.
> And therfore by the shadwe he took his wit
> That Phebus, which that shoon so clere and brighte,
> Degrees was fyve and fourty clombe on highte;
> And for that day, as in that latitude,
> It was ten of the clokke, he gan conclude,
> And sodeynly he plighte his hors aboute.
>
> (*CT* II, 1-15)

Here Chaucer's English succeeds in being truly 'light', and technical terms are reduced to a minimum. The 'artificial day' is explained in the *Astrolabe* II, 7 in a section headed 'To knowe the arch of the day, that some folk callen the day artificiall, fro sonne arisyng tyl it go to reste'; the word *quantitee* was coming into vogue in the fourteenth century and although not common in Chaucer outside the *Astrolabe* was used often enough and in various contexts to suggest that it must have been familiar to his audience; whereas *latitude* was strictly a technical term and seems to have been introduced into written English by Chaucer. It occurs only once elsewhere in his poetry, in an astronomical context in *The Merchant's Tale*, 1797, but is common in the *Astrolabe*. The adjective *erect* is unique to this passage in Chaucer's work and in Middle English generally; presumably he derived it from Latin *erectum* in one of his astronomical source books. His normal word is *upright*, in scientific contexts (e.g. *Astr* II, 38, 8–10) as well as in others.

Although in the above passage it is Harry Bailly who is supposed to be doing the calculating, Chaucer is himself the narrator. In *Troilus and Criseyde* Chaucer, again as narrator, frequently uses astronomical data for determining time. Inevitably, as the preceding quotations illustrate, mythological figures enter into these calculations as astronomical occurrences are turned into human situations or allegorized. Chaucer's early poem *The Complaint of Mars* is at heart a story about the attraction, union and separation of the mythological Mars and Venus told in the manner of a courtly love suit, but it is at the same time an account of the movement of the planets Mars and Venus conceived in a proper astronomical manner and expressed in terms appropriate to both strands in the poem:

> Sojourned hath this Mars, of which I rede,
> In chambre amyd the paleys prively
> A certeyn tyme, til him fel a drede,
> Throgh Phebus, that was comen hastely
> Within the paleys yates sturdely,
> With torche in honde, of which the stremes bryghte
> On Venus chambre knokkeden ful lyghte.
>
> (*Mars* 78–84)

In *Troilus and Criseyde* this blend of astronomy and classical mythology is particularly fitting in reinforcing the background of the story, and Chaucer displays both skill and restraint in weaving technical terms into the texture of the diction:

> Whan Phebus doth his bryghte bemes sprede,
> Right in the white Bole, it so bitidde,
> As I shal synge, on Mayes day the thrydde. . . .
>
> (*Tr* II, 54–6)

> The bente moone with hire hornes pale,
> Saturne, and Jove, in Cancro joyned were,
> That swych a reyn from heven gan avale. . . .
>
> (*ibid.* III, 624–6)

> The brighte Venus folwede and ay taughte
> The wey ther brode Phebus down alighte;
> And Cynthea hire char-hors overraughte
> To whirle out of the Leoun, if she myghte;
> And Signifer his candels sheweth brighte,
> Whan that Criseyde unto hire bedde wente. . . .
>
> (*ibid.* V, 1016–21)

The close connection between medieval astronomy and astrology added a further dimension to such definitions of time as these various quotations illustrate. May the 3rd, for example, seems to have had a specific significance for Chaucer: it not only brought Pandarus his 'teene in love' in *Troilus and Criseyde* II, 50 ff., but also turned out fateful for Chauntecleer in *The Nun's Priest's Tale* where 'on a Friday fil al this meschaunce' (*NPT* 3341),[11] and for Palamon in *The Knight's Tale* whose escape from prison took place on May the 3rd. The conjunction of Juptier, Saturn and the crescent Moon in the sign Cancer described in Book III of *Troilus and Criseyde* is an extremely rare one and Chaucer was no doubt thinking of such an occurrence in May 1385, the first for 600 years, and of its astrological implications of floods and heavy rains when introducing it into this central episode in the poem. Actually, Chaucer disclaims any personal faith in astrological observaunces . . . and rytes of payens' in the *Astrolabe* II, 4, but gives at the same time a concise account of how to set about observing the 'ascendent', the point of the zodiacal circle which is rising above the horizon at a given moment, thus enabling a person's horoscope, his *nativyte*, to be cast, or an *eleccion* to be determined, that is to decide whether the time was propitious for some specific undertaking. In *The Franklin's Tale* the narrator dismisses astrology in even stronger terms as 'swich folye / As in oure dayes is nat worth a flye' (*FranklT* 1131–2), yet Chaucer was not averse to making use of astrological lore when it suited him. Perhaps the poet in him accepted things the scientist rejected, and if Chaucer combined some belief in astrological prognostications with a firm faith in God he was merely behaving like most other medieval men. The *locus classicus* of Chaucer's affirmation of astrological truth is in *The Man of Law's Tale* and has been the subject of a detailed study by W. C. Curry as well as of comments by other scholars and editors.[12] It is a passage in which technical terms are woven into a highly rhetorical texture, thereby assuming for themselves a poetic quality quite absent in comparable passages of scientific prose. It is interesting for this reason to place alongside the relevant stanzas from *The Man of Law's Tale* some extracts from the *Astrolabe* as well as from the more artistic prose of *Boece*, some passages of which Chaucer may have been

11. Thirty-two days since the end of March (*NPT* 3187–90).
12. Curry, ch. 7, and see the note in Robinson, p. 693.

recalling when composing these stanzas for the Man of Law.
Thus the *Astrolabe*: 'And note that the first moevyng is clepid
moevyng of the first moevable of the 8 speer, which moeving is
from est into west, and eft ageyn into est. Also it is clepid girdel
of the first moeving for it departith the first moevable, that is to
seyn the spere, in two like partyes evene distantz fro the poles of
this world' (*Astr* I, 17, 37–44); – businesslike, 'light' English
sentences, a far cry from the Man of Law's fiery rhetoric, crowded
with astronomical terms:

> O firste moevyng! crueel firmament,
> With thy diurnal sweigh that crowdest ay
> And hurlest al from est til occident
> That naturelly wolde holde another way,
> Thy crowdyng set the hevene in swich array
> At the bigynnyng of this fiers viage,
> That crueel Mars hath slayn this mariage.
>
> Infortunat ascendent tortuous,
> Of which the lord is helplees falle, allas,
> Out of his angle into the derkeste hous!
> O Mars, o atazir, as in this cas!
> O fieble moone, unhappy been thy paas!
> Thou knyttest thee ther thou art nat receyved;
> Ther thou were weel, fro thennes artow weyved.
>
> Imprudent Emperour of Rome, allas!
> Was ther no philosophre in al thy toun?
> Is no tyme bet than oother in swich cas?
> Of viage is ther noon eleccioun,
> Namely to folk of heigh condicioun?
> Noght whan a roote is of a burthe yknowe?
> Allas, we been to lewed or to slowe!
>
> (*MLT* 295–315)

The uninitiated among Chaucer's readers, whether the more
'lewed' among his contemporaries, or a modern reader unversed
in astrology, will no doubt respond to the portentous rhetoric of
these lines even if they need help in unravelling Constance's
horoscope. The language is rich in reminiscence as in invective-
ness. The 'diurnal sweigh' recalls phrases from *Boece*, for *sweigh*
occurs only four times in Chaucer, two of them in *Boece*: '. . . and
turnest the hevene with a ravysschynge sweigh' (I, m. 5, 3–4),

and 'the swyftnesse and the sweigh of hir turnynge wheel' (II, pr.
1, 112–18); while *diurnal* itself is unique here, and apparently not
previously recorded in English. The first line quoted above also
has its Boethian echo in 'the swifte moevynge of the firmament'
(IV, m. 1, 8), while *hurlest* is another nonce Chaucerian word,
possibly echoing *Boece* V, m. 4, 52–3, in Robinson: 'soun hurteleth
to the eres and commoeveth hem to herkne', where Chaucer may
have written *hurleth*, the reading in the Harleian manuscript which
both Caxton and Thynne followed.

Several of the words employed are severely technical, even if
they do assume some poetic glamour in the context: *ascendent*,
carefully explained in the *Astrolabe* II, 4, remains a strictly
astronomical term throughout Middle English usage; *tortuous*
occurs only here and in the *Astrolabe* II, 28, 25–8 where Chaucer
explains it in a matter-of-fact sentence that contrasts sharply with
the Man of Law's particularly sonorous line – 'Infortunat ascendent tortuous':

> And these same signes fro the heved of Capricorne unto the ende of
> Geminis ben cleped tortuose signes, or croked signes, for thei arise
> embelyf [i.e. obliquely] on oure orisonte.

The word *atazir* is a nonce Chaucerian Middle Englishing of an
Arabic word, probably through Old French, used in astrological
treatises of a planet exerting influence, or of the influence thus
exerted. Its ringing use in the above stanza demonstrates the
poetic strength of an exotic piece of jargon which probably no
one in Chaucer's audience understood. And it fits in well with
the Man of Law's choice diction. The *eleccioun*, as already noted,
is the choice of a favourable time for some undertaking, in this
case Constance's voyage (*viage*), and to calculate this it was usual,
wherever possible, to refer back to the 'epoch' (*roote*) of the person's nativity (*burthe*).

Chaucer obviously attached considerable importance to these
astronomical and astrological details and sought far afield for the
right words; for both in *The Man of Law's Tale* and in the legend of
Hypermnestra, where another horoscope is given (*LGW* 2576 ff.),
he took pains to be technically accurate. Indeed, he invented these
two passages, neither of which is found in his sources. By referring the events and the outcome of both these stories to the influence of the stars, Chaucer supplied, as Curry suggests, both 'a

semblance of meaning to life' and an explanation of why things happened to the two heroines as they did.[13] The appeal to astrology thus becomes not a personal act of faith but an artistic inspiration, and its success demanded both scientific accuracy and a poetic manipulation of the appropriate vocabulary.

One person skilled in practical astrology was Chaucer's Doctour of Phisik whose portrait in the General Prologue declares him 'grounded in astronomye' and able to treat his patient 'by his magyk natureel' (*Gen Prol* 411 ff.). It is worth pausing over the Doctor's portrait as it illustrates well the close connection between astrology and medieval medicine. Chaucer may not have been himself an expert in medical science but he displays considerable familiarity with medical practices and terminology, both in the description of his Doctor and in reference to medical matters elsewhere in his work. In making the Doctor conversant with astrology Chaucer indicates the importance of this science both for the diagnosis and treatment of disease. The word *roote* may well mean here (423), as it does in the Man of Law's use, the 'epoch' in the astronomical sense, rather than merely the 'cause', for *cause* is twice used in this context distinct from *roote*. Knowledge of the astronomical data relevant to the beginnings of a disease was as important as keeping an eye on the constellations while the disease was in progress. Hence the importance of the *houres* (416), another ambiguous term, which could refer simply to the stages of a disease, equivalent to the Latin *hora*,[14] as well as to the lunar and planetary influences at work during each of the twenty-four hours. Probably Chaucer meant both, for the Doctor not only administered physical remedies, 'drogges and ... letuaries' (426), drugs and electuaries, the latter perhaps simply another general term for 'medicines', but he also employed 'his magyk natureel' (416). In other words, he was able to deal both with the immediate physical disturbance caused by some imbalance in the bodily humours, 'were it of hoot, or coold, or moyste, or drye' (420), and with the primary cause of the illness which lay in the stars and could only be treated by astrological expertise, 'natural magic', as the Franklin also calls it (*FranklT* 1125, 1155). The latter treatment involved what Chaucer calls

13. Curry, p. 170.
14. Cp. Pauline Aiken, 'Vincent of Beauvais and the "houres" of Chaucer's Physician', *Studies in Philology* LIII (1956), 22–4.

'fortunen the ascendent / Of his ymages for his pacient' (417–18), in other words choosing a propitious moment for making talismanic images, which could be either waxen effigies of the patient, or seals of wax or metal, depicting appropriate astrological figures or signs. In *The House of Fame*, where a similar allusion is made, Chaucer makes clear that *ymages* could be made for maleficent purposes as well as to cure the sick and that the term 'natural magic' carried connotations of sorcery and witchcraft which were patently inseparable from discussions of medieval medicine:

> Ther saugh I pleye jugelours,
> Magiciens, and tregetours,
> And Phitonesses, charmeresses,
> Olde wicches, sorceresses,
> That use exorsisacions,
> And eke these fumygacions;
> And clerkes eke, which konne wel
> Al this magik naturel,
> That craftely doon her ententes,
> To make, in certeyn ascendentes,
> Ymages, lo, thrugh which magik
> To make a man ben hool or syk.
>
> (*HF* 1259–70)

The modern reader's reaction to such a welter of technicalities, here and in the Doctor's portrait and in some other passages, like Pertelote's diagnosis of Chauntecleer's malaise (*NPT* 2923 ff.), is probably no different from that of Chaucer's contemporaries, nicely summed up by Gower's Amans when confronted with a similar display of medical-astrological language:

> Min holi fader, be youre leve
> Of al that ye have spoken hiere
> Which toucheth unto this matiere,
> To telle soth riht as I wene,
> I wot noght o word what ye mene.
>
> (*Conf. Am* VI, 1360–4)

What makes Chaucer's medical passages of particular linguistic interest and what must have contributed not a little to his audience's bewilderment is the rarity and novelty of quite a sizable portion of his medical jargon. True, not by any means all the words first ascribed to Chaucer in the *OED* or *MED* were of his own coinage, whether medical terms or others, but even if known orally or from sources lost to us, they are likely to have been rare and largely unfamiliar words. Hence there is here, as in other Chaucerian contexts, something exotic about Chaucer's diction, of which the modern reader, familiar with words like *cordial*, *digestible*, *drogges* 'drugs', is liable to remain unaware. Of these three words the first two are used by Chaucer only in the Doctor's portrait and are not previously recorded, while the third is rare, though known to Langland and Lydgate in the alliterating 'dyas and drogges', remedies and drugs. The word *letuaries* is also rare though Harry Bailly knows it (*CT* VI, 307), and the noun *pacient* in the sense of 'a person receiving medical treatment' does not appear to have been recorded before Chaucer used it in *Troilus and Criseyde* and in *The Canterbury Tales*, and much the same is true of the words *exorsisacion* 'act of incantation' and *fumygacion* 'use of fumigation as part of an incantation' in *The House of Fame*.

This mixture of astrological and medical lore, so well summed up in the Knight's line,

> Somme hadden salves, and somme hadden charmes,
> (*KnT* 2712)

does not prevent Chaucer from displaying his knowledge of more strictly medical treatment when it suits him: *salve* itself, 'ointment', is a word of venerable Germanic antiquity, and although it already possessed for Chaucer something of its later figurative sense (as in *Tr* IV, 944) it is still essentially a medical term. Thus Canacee is described as making 'salves newe of herbes preciouse' (*SqT* 639–40) with which to treat the injured hawk. Among other medicinal remedies mentioned by Chaucer is the Canon's Yeoman's *boole armonyak* 'Armenian bole', used as a styptic and antitoxin (*CYT* 790), which heads a lengthy catalogue of substances and other items, rather haphazardly assembled, as the speaker admits; further, the various remedies proved incapable of curing the Summoner's *whelkes* and *knobbes*:

> Ther nas quyk-silver, lytarge [lead ointment] ne brymstoon,
> Boras, ceruce [white lead], ne oille of tartre noon;
> Ne oynement that wolde clense and byte . . . ,
> (*Gen Prol* 629–31)

a list which, like the Canon's Yeoman's, is made exotic by a number of words of foreign origin, previously unrecorded in English. There are other linguistic novelties (italicized) in Pertelote's list of '*digestyves* / Of wormes' followed by *laxatyves* (*NPT* 2961 ff.), and the Knight's '*fermacies* of herbes' (*KnT* 2713), where *fermacie*, Old French *farmacie* derived ultimately from Greek, denotes a purgative medicine, as well as in the Knight's

> That neither *veyne-blood*, ne *ventusynge*,
> Ne drynke of herbes may ben his helpynge.
> The vertu *expulsif*, or animal,
> Fro thilke vertu cleped natural
> Ne may the venym voyden ne *expelle*.
>
> (*KnT* 2747–51)

Here *veyne-blood* and *ventusynge* both denote blood-letting, the latter by means of a cupping-glass or 'ventose'. The apothecary in *The Pardoner's Tale* refers to his concoction of drugs as a *confiture* (*PardT* 862), a word not otherwise recorded in Middle English, and among other medicines intended to be imbibed, though, one hopes, with less fatal consequences, are the Knight's *save* (*KnT* 2713), probably from Latin *salvia* 'sage', referring to a medicinal drink of herbs, the Reeve's narcotic *dwale* (*RvT* 4161), and Harry Bailly's characteristic *galiones* (*CT* VI, 306), a name probably invented on the spot, after Galen, on analogy with *ypocras* (*ibid.*). The latter represents the name Hippocrates and denotes a drink of wine with sugar and spices strained through a cloth; that it had other than strictly medical uses is obvious from Januarie's reliance on it to fortify his *corage* as he prepares for his bridal bed (*MerchT* 1807).

Apart from such mainly rare and novel words describing modes of treatment Chaucer was familiar with the names of a number of diseases, some of which he probably derived straight from his sources, as in *Boece* and *The Parson's Tale*, others possibly from his knowledge of medical treatises, like the work of Vincent of Beauvais whom he mentions once in *The Legend of Good Women* (Prol G 307). Thus Chaucer mentions *agu* 'ague, (malarial) fever' (*NPT* 2960); *apoplexie* 'apoplexy' (*NPT* 2841);[15] *boch* 'tumour, boil, ulcer', also called *postum*, Latin *apostema*, in the same passage

---

15. Chaucer may have intended an apoplectic seizure with the sudden *swap* experienced by the dreamer as the Eagle grabs him in *HF* 541 ff. The ensuing symptoms are similar, as Joseph E. Grennen points out in 'Science and Poetry in Chaucer's *House of Fame*', *Annuale Mediaevale* VIII (1967), 38 ff.

(*Bo* III, pr. 4, 12); *cardynacle* 'palpitations', possibly a cardiac disease (*CT* VI, 313), Harry Bailly's version of *cardiacle*; *fevere terciane* 'intermittent, "tertian" fever' (*NPT* 2959); *frenesye* 'insanity, delirium, frenzy' (*SumT* 2209; *Tr* I, 727); *fumositee* 'an exhalation caused by one of the bodily humours' (*SqT* 358); *goute* 'gout' (*NPT* 2840); *hirnia* 'hernia' (*ParsT* 423); *litargye* 'lethargy, morbid drowsiness', described as 'a comune seknesse to hertes that been desceyved' (*lethargum patitur communem inlusarum mentium morbum*) (*Bo* I, pr. 2, 20); *meselrie* 'leprosy' (*ParsT* 625); *mormal* 'an ulcerous sore' (*Gen Prol* 386); *pose* 'cold in the head, catarrh' (*RvT* 4152; *CT* IX, 62); *qualm* 'plague, pestilence' (*KnT* 2014). In addition, Chaucer ascribes some lesser ailments to his *alter ego* in one or two places, insomnia at the beginning of *The Book of the Duchess*, for example, and headaches due to too much reading and writing at night in *The House of Fame*, 631 ff.

Chaucer's Doctor was world champion ('in al this world ne was ther noon hym lik') at speaking 'of phisik and of surgerye' (*Gen Prol* 412–13), but Chaucer himself has little to say about surgery. He uses an interesting technical term, *sursanure* 'a wound healed only on the surface', in *The Franklin's Tale* with reference to Aurelius's predicament:

> And wel ye knowe that of a sursanure
> In surgerye is perilous the cure.
> (*FranklT* 1113–14)

The word is a straight adoption from Old French *soursanëure*, *sursanure* 'cicatrice' and apart from Lydgate no other English writer, according to the *OED*, has it. Surgeons are prominent among the 'congregacion of folk' assembled in *The Tale of Melibee* (1004 ff.) where they are depicted, as in Renaud's *Livre de Mellibee et Prudence*, as models of professional conduct: 'As to us surgiens aperteneth that we do to every wight the beste that we kan, where as we been withholde, and to oure pacientz that we do no damage; / wherfore it happeth many tyme and ofte that whan twey men han everich wounded oother, oon same surgien heeleth hem bothe' (*Mel* 1012–13). When Prudence later adds that it is the business of surgeons and physicians 'to doon to every wight honour and profit, and no wight for to anoye; / and after hir craft to doon greet diligence unto the cure of hem which that they han in hir governaunce' (1269–70), we realize that Chaucer's Doctor hardly qualifies for membership.

If the so-called 'religion' of courtly love draws some of its terminology from theology, the maladies afflicting the lovers similarly depend for their description on medical jargon. Chaucer's Knight, for all his 'bismotered' exterior no mean classical scholar, has his own phrase for it, 'the loveris maladye / Of Hereos' (*KnT* 1373–4), Eros's disease, defined as

> rather lyk manye,
> Engendered of humour malencolik,
> Biforen, in his celle fantastik,
>
> (*KnT* 1374–6)

in other words rather like a mania, caused by the humour of melancholy, in the front lobe of the lover's brain. Arcite, who is the victim here, displays many of the familiar symptoms of the malady, physical and psychological, and these can be paralleled in other case histories, those of Aurelius, for example, or Troilus. The latter becomes a *pacyent* (*Tr* I, 1090), afflicted with *accesse* 'a feverish illness' (II, 1315, 1543, 1578); he has a 'sikliche manere' (II, 1543), and is liable, at least Pandarus thinks so, of falling into a *frenesie* 'frenzy' (I, 727). Troilus has nightmares which Pandarus ascribes, as Pertelote does in the case of Chauntecleer, to *malencolie* (V, 360; *NPT* 2933) which is at the root of it all. If miraculous cures were unlikely to result from the application of *salves* and *charmes*, however skilfully applied to patients suffering from bodily ailments, lovers were in a different and more fortunate category. Thus the Merchant's Damyan, one moment grievously afflicted with Eros's disease, the next moment:

> Up riseth Damyan the nexte morwe;
> Al passed was his siknesse and his sorwe.
> He kembeth hym, he preyneth hym and pyketh. . . .
>
> (*MerchT* 2009–11)

It is just conceivable that, apart from May's encouragement, Damyan was restored by a healthy swig of Januarie's *ypocras*, not to mention the latter's 'clarree, and vernage / of spices hoote', for however much Chaucer knew about medicine, and he patently knew a good deal, he probably knew *von Haus aus* even more about wine.

He also knew something of the connection between the two, for the Summoner's unfortunate malady was in some way connected with the latter's passion for 'strong wyn, reed as blood', not to mention the 'garleek, oynons, and eek lekes' to which he was also addicted (*Gen Prol* 634–5). What the malady was Chaucer does not say, but the Summoner's portrait and his later angry eruptions against Friar Hubert make up an interesting test-case of Chaucer's competence at describing accurately the symptoms of a particular disease and of the modern reader's competence at diagnosing it. W. C. Curry, from a very thorough study of the Summoner's symptoms, diagnosed alopecia,[16] while Pauline Aiken argues that 'the Summoner's appearance is a remarkably accurate paraphrase of Vincent's [of Beauvais] account of the symptoms of *scabies*'.[17] More recently and most convincingly Thomas J. Garbáty has diagnosed the Summoner's complaint as a form of venereal disease in medical terms which would have delighted Chaucer: 'A rosacea-like secondary syphiloderm with meningeal neurosyphilitic involvement, with chronic alcoholism playing an important part'.[18] The diagnosis appears to fit; it explains Chaucer's choice of words not used anywhere else in his work, *knobbes* 'lumps, nodes', *whelkes* 'pimples', *scalled* 'scabby', *saucefleem* 'having pimples or eruptions', as well as the allusions to the Summoner's lechery, pathological anger ('his herte was so wood / That lyk an aspen leef he quook for ire', *CT* III 1666–7), and his passion for strong drink. Even the passion for strong vegetables fits into the diagnosis, with or without a possible biblical innuendo,[19] and it is only here that Chaucer mentions garlic and onions, while references to leeks are, with the Reeve's one exception (*RvT* 3879), all of the 'not worth a leek' type. It all adds up, therefore, to a careful choice of words in order to build up, in physiological and psychological terms, the image of a depraved rogue afflicted with a type of venereal disease, whose outward appearance is a bitterly ironic comment on his profession as 'watch-dog of morality'.

16. Curry, pp. 37 ff.

17. Pauline Aiken, 'The Summoner's Malady', *Studies in Philology* XXXIII (1936), 44.

18. Thomas J. Garbáty, 'The Summoner's Occupational Disease', *Medical History* VII (1963), 357.

19. See R. E. Kaske, 'The Summoner's Garleek, Oynons, and eek Lekes', *Modern Language Notes* LXXIV (1959), 481–4.

Chaucer' art of portraiture depends a good deal on selecting physical features and appropriate words which are, as in the Summoner's case, indicative of personality traits. His knowledge of medieval physiognomy, a science closely linked with astrology, was no doubt shared by his audience who would respond to allusions like that to Alisoun's eyebrows:

Ful smale ypulled were hire browes two,
And tho were bent and blake as any sloo,
(*MillT* 3245–6)

or to the Wife of Bath's being 'gat-tothed' (*Gen Prol* 468), or to the Pardoner's extraordinary coiffure. Speaking of Criseyde, Chaucer hints how outward appearance, in this case movement, reveals inner characteristics, albeit very different ones from those of Shakespeare's heroine:

And ek the pure wise of hire mevynge
Shewed wel that men myght in hire gesse
Honour, estat, and wommanly noblesse.
(*Tr* I, 285–7)

But as a rule Chaucer does not spell out the psychological traits suggested by prominent physical features, although the total portrait conveys in many cases a pretty clear idea of the personality involved. Here as so often in Chaucer's diction the distribution of significant words is of interest. The only two characters whose hair is *crul* 'curly', suggesting a bit of a dandy, are the Squire and the Miller's Absolon. The only ones to have big, staring eyes are the Pardoner whose eyes were *glarynge*, and the Monk and Host whose eyes were *stepe*: they obviously all three had something in common. The only person whose eyes *twynkled* is the Friar, perhaps a redeeming feature in view of the simile

As doon the sterres in the frosty nyght,
(*Gen Prol* 268)

perhaps a hint of mischief in view of Fortune's 'twinkling' upon Boethius 'with a wikkid eye' (*Bo* II, pr. 3, 70–2). Friar Hubert is also Chaucer's only character to lisp:

Somwhat he lipsed, for his wantownesse,
To make his Englissh sweete upon his tonge.
(*Gen Prol* 264–5)

The Miller's are the only nostrils to receive comment ('blake . . . and wyde'), although noses are in every sense more prominent and physiognomically significant: the miller of Trumpington had a *camus* nose, a turned-up, pug nose, which his daughter inherited; Sir Thopas had a *semely* nose which recalls the Prioress singing divine service

> Entuned in hir nose ful semely,
>
> *(Gen Prol* 123)

while the Knight's great Indian king Emetrius, Arcite's chief ally and the first freckled hero undoubtedly in English literature, has a *heigh* nose. The Miller's nose was adorned with a wart –

> . . . and theron stood a toft of herys,
> Reed as the brustles of a sowes erys –
>
> *(ibid.* 555–6)

the only wart in all Chaucer.

Hair and beard, or their absence, are also significant, and again Chaucer's diction is selective. Several of his men have crew cuts or no hair at all: the Yeoman is given a *not heed* 'a closely cropped head' *(Gen Prol* 109); the Reeve's hair is nicely *yshorn* round the ears, while his *top* is '*dokked* lyk a preest biforn' which goes with his homiletic leanings and the fact that he (like the Summoner's friar) is '*tukked* . . . as is a frere aboute' *(Gen Prol* 589–90, 621); the miller of Trumpington had a bald skull, 'as *piled* as an ape' *(RvT* 3935), while the Summoner's beard, also *piled* 'pilled, bereft of hair', must have been very thin indeed *(Gen Prol* 627). Limbs are also of interest: could it be that the Miller, who was among other things broad and thick, bore some resemblance to square-limbed Diomede? There is certainly some kinship between the Reeve's lean legs and Januarie's lean neck, as there is a no doubt deliberate contrast between the Wife of Bath's large, well-covered hips (in themselves, if one may say so, revealing enough) and her jolly Jankyn's pair

> Of legges and of feet so clene and faire.
>
> *(WBT* 598)

We must not overlook the importance of colour in physiognomical descriptions. That Vulcan should have a 'ful *broun*' face *(HF* 139) is a little odd, because red might have been more appropriate; perhaps the rhyme (with *doun*) explains it. Apart from

him only three of Chaucer's characters are given brown faces: the
Yeoman who was a forester, hence much out of doors; the Shipman tanned by the summer sun; and Perkyn Revelour whose
berry-brown face must have contrasted handsomely with his black
locks 'ykembd ful fetisly' (*CkT* 4369). Red faces suggest many
things, apart from blushing (one recalls Criseyde): rich living,
alcohol, disease, courage, passion – ample scope for some ironic
brush-strokes in Chaucer's portraits. The only two characters to
be *sangwyn*, a proper technical term, are the Franklin and Arcite's
Emetrius, presumably for different reasons, as the one is the
world's best *envyned* man (*Gen Prol* 342), a unique Middle English
word specially adopted from French for the occasion, whereas the
other

> Cam ridynge lyk the god of armes, Mars,
> (KnT 2159)

and Mars' colour is red:

> Thou ferse god of armes, Mars the rede,
> (Anel 1)

and similarly in numerous other places. But red also are the sick
Summoner, *fyr-reed* indeed, and the Wife of Bath, and 'jolif'
Absolon, and the Miller's beard (appropriately, if unflatteringly,
likened to a sow's or fox's skin), and brave Sir Thopas whose
complexion is 'lyk scarlet in grayn', i.e., deeply dyed with co-
chineal (*Thop* 727). Sir Thopas is blessed further with 'lippes rede as
rose' (726), but so is the Prioress, whose mouth was 'ful smal, and
therto softe and reed' (*Gen Prol* 153), a handsome, albeit gently
ironic, compliment to the lady if not to the gentleman. Virginia
has the fairytale colouring appropriate to a beautiful fourteen-year-
old heroine, lily-white and rose-red (*PhysT* 32–4), just as Pertelote
is fittingly and irresistibly *scarlet-reed* about her eyes (*NPT* 3161).
Red is obviously the desirable hue for a medieval complexion, despite the excesses or maladies it might connote, particularly when
associated with whiteness and freshness. Hence one cannot but
grieve as the Canon's Yeoman laments:

> And wher my colour was bothe fressh and reed,
> Now is it wan and of a leden hewe.
> (CYT 727–8)

There is yet another branch of medieval medicine in which Chaucer appears well versed. One needs only to recall his persistent interest in the phenomena of dreams, and the opening lines of *The House of Fame*, for example, to see him manipulating yet another set of technical terms:

> Why that is an *avisioun*
> And this a *revelacioun*,
> Why this a *drem*, why that a *sweven*,
> And noght to every man lyche even;
> Why this a *fantome*, why these *oracles*,
> I not. . . .

(HF 7–12)

Chaucer's curiosity delves into every aspect of dream-lore: their causes, physiological, psychological, astronomical; their meanings: whether *significaciouns* or *vanitee*; their consequences: 'Allas, his wyf ne roghte nat of dremes!' *(NPT 3340)*. He studies his own dreams as he transforms himself into the naive *alter ego* of *The Book of the Duchess* and *The House of Fame*, and ponders on the connection between dream and waking experience:

> The wery huntere, slepynge in his bed,
> To wode ayeyn his mynde goth anon;
> The juge dremeth how his plees been sped;
> The cartere dremeth how his cartes gon;
> The riche, of gold; the knyght fyght with his fon;
> The syke met [dreams] he drynketh of the tonne;
> The lovere met he hath his lady wonne.

(PF 99–105)

Chaucer afflicts Troilus with horrid nightmares *(Tr V, 246 ff.)* which Pandarus tries to dismiss lightly as 'swich fantasie' caused by melancholy, but Chaucer cannot resist the temptation to amplify, so the technical jargon is rehearsed once again: *swevenes, revelaciouns, infernals illusiouns, avysiouns*, and the causes may be *complexiouns*, or *fast*, or *glotonye*, or *impressiouns*,

> 'As if a wight hath faste a thyng in mynde,'
> *(Tr V, 373)*

or 'after tymes of the yer' and 'by the moone'. In a later poem, *The Nun's Priest's Tale*, Chaucer returns to this theme with undiminished gusto and, if anything, with increased technical

expertise. Pertelote the hen explains the close connection between
bodily malfunctioning and such a dream as is frightening her
husband. The passage is rich in jargon:

> '*Swevenes engendren* of *replecciouns*,
> And ofte of *fume* and of *complecciouns*,
> Whan *humours* been to *habundant* in a wight.
> Certes this dreem, which ye han met to-nyght,
> Cometh of the greete *superfluytee*
> Of youre *rede colera*, pardee. . . .'
>
> (*NPT* 2923–8)

Pertelote thus diagnoses Chauntecleer's complaint and prescribes
the appropriate remedies. Chauntecleer remains unconvinced, for
the debate is not solely about dreams, but is part of that larger
debate with which we began this chapter, between experience and
authority, the two approaches to knowledge which characterize
Chaucer's excursions into science. The Doctour of Phisik, whose
portrait, as we have seen, is central to an understanding of
Chaucerian medicine, himself exemplifies the two approaches:
the practical astrological calculating, the 'natural magic', the
prescription of drugs and remedies, on the one hand; and on the
other the impressive catalogue of medical authorities ranging
from ancient Greece to fourteenth-century Oxford. In the texture
of the poetry both elements play a distinctive part by contributing
their share to the learned, often exotic, diction which forms an
important part of Chaucer's total vocabulary.

If medicine is in the Middle Ages first cousin to 'astronomye',
mathematics is even more closely akin. Many mathematical concepts were indispensable to astronomy, as they are to most modern
sciences, and it is often hard to assign particular terms to one or
the other. Chaucer himself distinguishes between *geometrie* and
ars-metrike (both in *KnT* 1898), the former occurring only here, the
latter also as a vulgar pun in *The Summoner's Tale*, 2222. Together
with astronomy and music, these two constituted the quadrivium,
the higher course of medieval academic study. The practitioners
of geometry are the *geometriens* of *Boece*, a word used in a passage
(*Bo* III, pr. 10, 132 ff.) which gave Chaucer also *porismes*, Boethius's
porismata 'deductions', and probably *corolarie*, Boethius's *corollarium* 'corollary', a word also used by Wyclif. The word *proposicions* 'propositions' in the same passage was not a new word in

English, though probably suggested here by Boethius's *demon-stratis propositis*. Chaucer uses it elsewhere in *Boece*, in a gloss in the phrase 'false proposiciouns' (III, m. 11, 15), and to render *colloca-tionem propositionum* as 'the collacioun of proposicions' (IV, pr. 4, 67). It occurs once more, in *Melibee* 1276, rendering the French *proposicion* of Renaud. The word, though uncommon, would not have been wholly unfamiliar in the later fourteenth century. The case is different with *corolarie* and *porisme*, however, and by adding two further equivalents to Boethius's two (*siue porisma siue corollarium*) Chaucer is expressing doubt whether the concept will be understood by his readers. He makes the narrator respond to Philosophy's arguments with '... clepe it as thou wilt, be it corolerie, or porisme, or mede of coroune, or declarynges' (III, pr. 10, 152–3), where *declarynges* takes the place of Philosophy's earlier *declaracions* (135); otherwise the list remains the same. Both *declaracioun* and the verb *declaren* were widely current at this time, but the sense here of a corollary or deduction from a theorem is peculiar to Chaucer, hence perhaps not a very happy attempt at defining a strange term. Whether *mede of coronne* 'reward of crown or garland' was any more enlightening is also doubtful; it too seems to be unique in the sense Chaucer gives it. He derived it no doubt from the *loier de coronne* of the French version of Boethius which he used alongside the Latin. The Latin *corollarium* meant 'a surplus or gratuity' from the custom of presenting distinguished performers with a *corolla*, a little crown, chaplet, or garland, in addition to their usual fee; thus Chaucer's *mede of coroune* literally represents the Latin *corollarium*, though not in the Boethian sense of a deduction or corollary. It is a picturesque figure, but remains decidedly obscure in the context.

Chaucer manages rather better with more straightforward mathematical words, many of which occur in the *Astrolabe*, in *Boece*, and in some passages of technical jargon as in *The House of Fame*, in *The Franklin's Tale*, 1273 ff., or in the description of the lists in *The Knight's Tale*, 1887 ff. But here, too, it is noteworthy that words thoroughly familiar to the modern reader were only just coming into regular written use when Chaucer employed them, such as *adden, dividen, altitude, center, circuit, dymynucioun* 'subtraction, reduction', *divisioun, equacion, multiplicacioun*. Some words may owe their subsequent currency to Chaucer's initiative in first using them in writing, like *circuler*, used once in *Boece*, or

fraccion 'fraction' and *consentrik* 'concentric' used only in the
Astrolabe, or the adjective *proporcionable* and the noun *proporcionel*,
each used once, derived from the noun *proporcioun* then gaining
currency. Such words were not, however, confined to technical
contexts, although in *The Canterbury Tales* they are not usually
ascribed to the less educated pilgrims. In *Troilus and Criseyde*
proporcioun, for example, is used in the hero's portrait:

> And Troilus wel woxen was in highte,
> And complet formed by *proporcioun*.
>> (*Tr* V, 827–8)

Fortune has the lines

> I have thee taught *divisioun* bitwene
> Frend of effect, and frend of countenaunce.
>> (*Fort* 33–4)

Troilus prays that Love may '*cerclen* hertes alle' (*Tr* III, 1767), a
very recent if not newly created verbal derivative from *cercle*,
repeated in the opening lines of *To Rosemounde*:

> Madame, ye ben of al beaute shryne
> As far as cercled is the mapemounde [i.e. map of the world].
>> (*Rosemounde* 1–2)

If we turn from arithmetic and geometry to music, the fourth
discipline in the medieval quadrivium, we find Chaucer using yet
another set of technical terms mainly for descriptive and figurative
purposes. Clair C. Olson has shown that Chaucer displays little
interest in the theoretical aspects of music, but that he has an
educated layman's knowledge of the various types of musical
instruments in use at the time and of the role which music played
in fourteenth-century life.[20] Nearly all the technical terms are of
Romance origin, though there are some exceptions: *baggepipe*,
where the first element probably derives from Old Norse *baggi*
('bag, bundle'), while *pipe* is a common Germanic word; *beme*
'trumpet', O.E. *bīeme*; *fithele* 'fiddle', found in several Germanic
languages, though probably related to, if not actually derived
from, medieval Latin *vitula*, whence *viol*; *glee*, O.E. *glēo*, a general
word meaning 'music, musical entertainment or performance,

20. Clair C. Olson, 'Chaucer and the Music of the Fourteenth Century', *Speculum*
XVI (1941), 64–91.

musical instrument'; *harpe*, O.E. *hearpe*; *horn*, O.E. *horn*; *song*,
O.E. *sang*; *yeddynges* 'songs, ballads', O.E. *gieddung*. Of these words
song is the only really common one, although *harpe* and *horn* occur
about fifteen times each. The Miller's *baggepipe* (*Gen Prol* 565) is
probably the same instrument as the *cornemuse* of *The House of
Fame*, 1218; neither word occurs elsewhere in Chaucer. Similarly,
fithele and *yeddynges* occur only once each, both in *The General
Prologue*, the former in connection with the Clerk (296), who preferred books to, among other things, fiddles, and the latter with
reference to the Friar whose musical accomplishments included
yeddynges, of which 'he baar outrely the pris' (237). These last two
examples illustrate the more casual manner in which Chaucer
generally uses musical terms. There are few sustained passages
about music, the most interesting from the lexical point of view
probably being that describing musicians in the Third Book of
The House of Fame playing a variety of wind instruments: *cornemuse, shalemye, pipe, doucet, rede, flowte, liltyng horn, pipes made of grene
corn, trumpe, beme, claryoun* (*HF* 1214 ff.). An account of musical
entertainment accompanying a wedding feast is given in *The
Merchant's Tale* in the description of Januarie's and May's nuptials,
but it lacks the detailed technical expertise of Chaucer's excursions
into other sciences:

> Thus been they wedded with solempnitee,
> And at the feeste sitteth he and she
> With othere worthy folk upon the deys.
> Al ful of joye and blisse is the paleys,
> And ful of instrumentz and of vitaille,
> The mooste deyntevous of al Ytaille.
> Biforn hem stoode instrumentz of swich soun
> That Orpheus, ne of Thebes Amphioun,
> Ne maden nevere swich a melodye.
> At every cours thanne cam loud mynstralcye. . . .
>   (*MerchT* 1709–18)

As a rule, Chaucer is content to introduce musical allusions and
technical terms casually into narrative and description or to enhance a *descriptio personae* by adding some musical accomplishment.
The Miller, something of a musician himself on the bagpipes,
endows both the heroes of his tale with performing talents.
'Hende' Nicholas, in pointed contrast to the poor scholarly
Oxford Clerk of the pilgrimage, has a *sautrie*, a 'psaltery', plucked

like a harp but somewhat differently constructed, in the place of honour above his bed,

> On which he made a-nyghtes melodie
> So swetely that all the chambre rong;
> And *Angelus ad virginem* he song;
> And after that he song the Kynges Noote.
> Ful often blessed was his myrie throte.
>
> (*MillT* 3214–18)

Not to be outdone, 'jolif' Absolon not only tripped and danced in the best Oxford manner, but knew how to

> pleyen songes on a smal rubible
> Therto he song som tyme a loud quynyble;
> And as wel koude he pleye on a giterne.
>
> (*ibid.* 3331–3)

We have already glanced at some of the uses Chaucer makes of songs in his poetry, hence we need here only note his familiarity with the appropriate instruments used as accompaniment. Nicholas probably accompanied his own singing on his *sautrie* but used it also as a solo instrument:

> He kiste hire sweete and taketh his sawtrie,
> And pleyeth faste, and maketh melodie –
>
> (*ibid.* 3305–6)

one way of giving vent to an overflow of powerful feelings. Absolon sings his serenade to Alisoun to the accompaniment of his *giterne*, an instrument akin to the modern guitar:

> He syngeth in his voys gentil and smal,
> 'Now, deere lady, if thy wille be,
> I praye yow that ye wole rewe on me,'
> Ful wel acordaunt to his gyternynge.
>
> (*ibid.* 3360–3)

Other Chaucerian characters are no less gifted. Phebus, the unfortunate hero, or victim, of *The Manciple's Tale*,

> Pleyen he koude on every mynstralcie,
> And syngen, that it was a melodie
> To heeren of his cleere voys the soun,
>
> (*MancT* 113–15)

where *mynstralcie* means 'musical instrument', later spelt out, when

Phebus 'brak his mynstralcie', as 'bothe harpe, and lute, and gyterne, and sautrie' (*MancT* 268). Chaucer uses the word *myn-stralcie* somewhat idiosyncratically in this sense, much as he and some other fourteenth-century writers used *glee*, for normally it means 'musical entertainment' as in *The Merchant's Tale* above, or simply, 'music', or unflatteringly 'noise' as in *The Knight's Tale*, 2671. It is essentially a poet's usage, for to 'break one's min-strelsy' connotes not only the destruction of the instruments so carefully enumerated, but the ensuing silence and the departure of previous joys. That the playing of musical instruments went to-gether with composing and singing songs and with dancing as necessary equipment for medieval gentlemen, and their ladies too for that matter, is clear from many references in Chaucer, from Blanche and her knight in *The Book of the Duchess* to *Troilus and Criseyde* and *The Canterbury Tales*. But in most cases the references are devoid of the detailed technicalities which distinguish Chau-cer's astronomical passages in particular. The reference to Abso-lon's *quynyble* provides one of the few exceptions, for it shows not only that Chaucer was aware of the singer's melody being sung a fifth above the accompaniment on the *rubible*, but also that this could only be done in a high falsetto ('loud', *MillT* 3332) as a '*smal* rubible' would be high in sound. This accords well with Absolon's voice being described as 'gentil and smal' (3360), and with his dandified appearance and deportment and somewhat *squaymous* disposition.

Where musical references are not used in the ways just described they provide Chaucer with figures of speech, mostly metaphors and similes. Both instruments and song are used here. That memorable freckled hero in *The Knight's Tale*, Emetrius of India, has a voice 'as a trompe thonderynge' (*KnT* 2174); Troilus and Criseyde find delight in each other's words just as birds 'deliten in hire song in leves grene' (*Tr* IV, 1433); a great number of 'love-dayes and acordes', of days of reconciliation and amicable agreements, is represented in *The House of Fame* as larger 'then on instrumentes be cordes' (*HF* 696), an allusion to such a contem-porary instrument presumably as the bass lute which has twenty-four strings, or possibly to a harp of as many as thirty.[21] Bird-

21. See James B. Colvert, 'A Reference to Music in Chaucer's *House of Fame*', *Modern Language Notes* LXIX (1954), 241.

song, martial music, the 'songes, compleintes, roundels, virelayes' of the typical lover, the music of the spheres producing
melody

> That welle is of musik and melodye
> In this world here, and cause of armonye,
>   (*PF* 62-3)

the minstrelsy of marriage feasts, the *floytynge* of lusty bachelors,
and so forth – they all belong to Chaucer's world, shared of course
by his contemporaries, but nonetheless made integral to his
poetry.

Chaucer may not have known much about musical theory; his
humorous reference to *Boece* in *The Nun's Priest's Tale*, 3294,
probably alluding to Boethius's *De Musica*, is the only allusion to a
medieval musical treatise in his work, and a very vague one at
that. Yet there is hardly a character in all his poetry that does not
evince some acquaintance, connection, contact, with music,
whether as a straightforward personal accomplishment or knowing, like Pandarus and the Wife of Bath, 'the olde daunce'. Even
the Parson has to have his say: 'Whoso thanne wolde wel under-
stande thise peynes, and bithynke hym weel that he hath de-
served thilke peynes for his synnes, certes, he sholde have moore
talent to siken and to wepe, than for to syngen and to pleye'
(*ParsT* 228). Chaucer's musical vocabulary is not that of an expert,
but that of an educated fourteenth-century Englishman familiar
with courtly customs, with church music, with a representative
range of instruments, and with other aspects of music encountered
both in his own experience and in his reading. The result is the
almost total absence of jargon and a marked tendency to fit
musical allusions, references, and figures of speech more easily and
colloquially into the verse than is the case with most of his other
technical words. It is significant that Chaucer's musical vocabulary
is singularly free from neologisms; a mere handful of words is
apparently not recorded before he used them, among them such
derivatives from words already current as *clarionynge* (*HF* 1242);
entune (*Tr* IV, 4; *Gen Prol* 123); *floytynge* (*Gen Prol* 91); *melodious*
(*Tr* V, 577); and the compound *carole-wyse* (*LGW* Prol G 201).
The word *musicien*, if Chaucer's coinage, was a happy analogy to
'physician', current since the thirteenth century, when he rendered Boethius's 'Si musica quidem musicos medicina medicos

rhetoricea rhetores facit' as 'also musyke maketh musicyens, and phisyk maketh phisicyeens, and rethoryke, rethoriens' (*Bo* II, pr. 6, 95-7). Chaucer was hardly likely to coin the names of musical instruments or to invent technical terms: if he was the first to use *quynyble* in its musical sense, as the *OED* suggests, the word was probably already in existence in its meaning 'fivefold, quintuple'; and even if words like *balade, cornemuse, floute*, were not in current English use much before the last quarter of the century, they were certainly known to other writers at the time they found their way into Chaucer's verse.

In the Second Book of *The House of Fame* Chaucer uses the sounds produced by a *pipe* and by *harpe-strynges* as illustrations of the Eagle's thesis that 'soun ys noght but eyr ybroken' (*HF* 765) in a lengthy passage devoted to another scientific excursus. Once again technicalities are discussed with the aid of appropriate terminology as Chaucer exploits delightfully the spectacle of a pedantic bird lecturing to a captive auditor on a topic relevant to the house of Fame as well as of intrinsic interest. Once again 'proof by experience' is juxtaposed with suitable authorities,

'As Aristotle and daun Platon,
And other clerkys many oon',
        (*HF* 759-60)

as the Eagle displays his learning, softening its impact by an occasional touch of informality, like addressing his passenger as 'Geffrey' or 'my leve brother' or slipping into a colloquial idiom. The diction, however, is not severely technical and the several familiar illustrations, like the sounds of pipes and harps or throwing a stone into water, are plainly attuned to a pretty 'lewed' understanding. The Eagle is well aware, as Chaucer his maker is not always aware, that

'hard langage and hard matere
Ys encombrous for to here
Attones'.
        (*ibid.* 861-3)

Hence, the passage is not difficult, and one assumes that even the listener's dubious intelligence was able to cope with 'kyndely enclynyng', and 'multiplyinge ever moo', and the peculiar syntax and unfamiliar word in line 847,

'As most conservatyf the soun',

where a preposition seems to have been omitted,[22] and where *conservatyf* may well represent a Chaucerian neologism of some consequence to England's political history, based, as Grennen suggests, on the equivalent Latin word in Walter Burley's commentary on Aristotle's *Physics*. There are a few other passages in Chaucer involving concepts belonging to some branch of physics, but the poet does not make much of them and thus manages with few technical terms. The magic mirror in *The Squire's Tale*, for instance, would lose its peculiar mystery, important to the story, if its secret were unravelled, in the manner of Mrs Radcliffe, according to known natural laws. Admittedly, someone, says the Squire,

> seyde it myghte wel be
> Naturelly, by composiciouns
> Of anglis and of slye reflexiouns,
>
> (*SqT* 228–30)

but Chaucer is hesitant and perhaps insufficiently skilled in optics to do more than refer to a few famous physicists, 'Alocen, and Vitulon, / And Aristotle' and to mention 'queynte mirours' and 'perspectives' (*SqT* 232 ff.), and so he lets the Squire leave it at that.

The very opposite is true of chemistry or its medieval ancestor, alchemy, which affords Chaucer one of the most dazzling displays of scientific jargon found anywhere in his work. John Read, historian of alchemy, once described alchemy as 'a complex and indefinite mixture of chemistry, astrology, philosophy, occultism, magic, and other ingredients',[23] hence at least in part its strong appeal for Chaucer. Much has been written about Chaucer's attitude to alchemy and speculation has been rife whether *The Canon's Yeoman's Tale* is intended as an expression of Chaucer's belief in its mysteries, or a rejection of them, or a religious allegory or a straightforward exposure of a contemporary racket comparable to that of the pardoner. The Canon's Yeoman, himself a victim of his master's, or late master's, activities, refers to alchemy in several interesting, derogatory phrases besides calling it merely 'that art' (*CYT* 716). He calls it 'that slidynge science' (732), an epithet rich in meaning for Chaucer in view of 'slydynge For-

22. See Robinson's note and Joseph E. Grennen's 'Science and Poetry in Chaucer's *House of Fame*', *Annuale Mediaevale* VIII (1967), 43–5.

23. John Read, 'Alchemy and Alchemists', *Folklore* XLIV (1933), 251.

tune' and 'slidynge and desceyvynge hope', both in *Boece* (I, m. 5, 34 and IV, m. 2, 14), and Criseyde being 'aslydynge of corage' (*Tr* V, 825), suggesting a particularly slippery kind of inconstancy. The Yeoman goes on with 'oure elvysshe craft' (*CYT* 751) and 'this elvysshe nyce loore' (842), where *nyce* 'foolish' is moderately critical, but where *elvysshe* probably carried much stronger pejorative connotations than the definitions in the *MED* suggest. Chaucer applies the word elsewhere only to himself *qua* pilgrim, when he makes Harry Bailly say ironically that he 'semeth elvyssh by his contenaunce' (*CT* VII, 703), not a flattering term when we recall the long tradition in England that elves were malignant creatures, a tradition rooted in Anglo-Saxon beliefs as revealed in references to elves, and still alive in several Chaucerian allusions. Maligned by Donegild as the mother of 'so horrible a feendly creature', Constance herself is called 'an elf', hated by everybody (*MLT* 750 ff.), which is clearly a highly opprobrious description; similarly the Wife of Bath equates *elf* with *incubus* (*WBT* 873 ff.), and the Miller's carpenter tries to rouse Nicholas from his trance by exorcizing *elves* and *wightes* with the sign of the cross (*MillT* 3479). The Canon's Yeoman tops his list with 'this cursed craft' (*CYT* 830), and the only person who has anything favourable to say about alchemy is the duped priest of the tale who calls it 'this noble craft and this subtilitee' (1247) where the first half of the phrase is definitely complimentary and the second nicely ambiguous, because *subtilitee* to Chaucer, as to his contemporaries, meant both 'skill, ingenuity, perspicacity' in a favourable sense as well as 'craftiness or nasty cunning'.

The jargon that went with this science had to be as impressive to dupe the 'lewed' as the Pardoner's snatches of Latin, and the Canon's Yeoman had clearly acquired a goodly portion of it. More than that, he is made to be a highly articulate narrator, one of Chaucer's most fluent speakers, whose vocabulary reflects his years of close proximity to a master skilled in persuasive rhetoric, just as his frequent lapses into colloquial turns of phrase indicate the more commonplace linguistic register of his own humble station. He describes the canon of *pars secunda* of his tale, who was obviously modelled on his own ex-master, as gifted with particular linguistic skill:

> In al this world of falshede nis his peer;
> For in his termes he wol hym so wynde,

And speke his wordes in so sly a kynde,
Whanne he commune shal with any wight,
That he wol make hym doten anonright,

(CYT 979–83)

and he refers to the technical jargon of the alchemists as

Oure termes been so clergial and so queynte,

(ibid. 752)

that is, 'scholarly and curious' or 'learned and strange', and that
they certainly are.

Edgar Hill Duncan has classified the technical terms in *The
Canon's Yeoman's Tale* under several heads: materials from which
medicines may be refined, like *arsenyk* or *brymstoon*; middle mi-
nerals, or metallic salts, (a) those suitable for cleansers, like *argoille*
'crude potassium tartrate deposited by wines' or *virtiole* 'crude
salt of sulphuric acid, or the acid itself', and (b) those suitable
for feces in sublimation, like *alkaly* 'impure sodium carbonate' or
chalk; waters and oils, like *watres corosif* or *oille of tartre*; herbs, like
egremoyne 'agrimony' or *lunarie* 'the fern moonwort'; other substances, like *asshes* or *gleyre of an ey* 'white of an egg, albumen';
processes, like *calcinacioun* 'calcination, reducing to powder by
heating' or *induracioun* 'induration, hardening'; and, finally, vessels, like *alambikes* 'upper parts of distilling vessels' or *yngottes*
'moulds for molten metal'.[24] Altogether, there are well over fifty
such terms, mostly concentrated into about a hundred lines close
to the beginning of *prima pars* of the tale. Some of these terms occur
also in Gower's brief description of alchemy in *Confessio Amantis*
IV, 2457 ff., and the names of the various substances referred to are
mostly to be found also in other fourteenth-century writers. Not
so the words describing alchemical processes and the vessels used
in them, however, many of which Chaucer appears to have been
the first to use in literature. As with technical terms in other
sciences, Chaucer probably anglicized alchemical terms straight
from the Latin of whatever source material he had access to,
whether the *Summa Perfectionis Magisterii* and other works of
Geber, or the writings of Arnoldus de Villa Nova who is mentioned in line 1428 of *The Canon's Yeoman's Tale*, or the *Speculum
Naturale* of Vincent of Beauvais, or the 'book Senior' (*CYT*

24. Edgar Hill Duncan, 'The Yeoman's Canon's "Silver Citrinacioun"', *Modern
Philology* XXXVII (1940), 255–7.

1450), now generally identified with the *Tabula chemica* of the tenth-century Arabic philosopher Muhammad ibn Umail.[25] Of the twelve alchemical processes classified by Duncan, at least eight are first described in the given terms by Chaucer, according to the *OED* and *MED*, and similarly seven of the eleven names of vessels. For the words *albificacioun* 'whitening' and *descensories* 'retorts for distillation by condensation (descent)', the *MED* cites no other Middle English occurrences. In some cases Chaucer gave new technical meanings to known words, like *encorporyng* 'the process of forming an amalgam or compound', a verb which Trevisa used in the sense of 'to include or incorporate'; or *cucurbites* 'the lower, gourd-shaped parts of vessels used for distillation' from the sense 'gourd' of the same word. The Canon's Yeoman's lists may be unmethodical, as he disarmingly admits, but they embody, accurately enough, much of the alchemical science known to anyone in the later fourteenth century who took pains to acquaint himself with it, as Chaucer obviously did. To dismiss the Canon's Yeoman, as Spargo did in *Sources and Analogues to Chaucer's Canterbury Tales* as one of 'these servants [who] can repeat like parrots some few of the words which they have heard bandied about, but 'grope' them ever so little and they are lost'[26] is plainly silly. The Yeoman's technical vocabulary is extensive and in describing the two canons of his tale at work he displays full awareness of what goes on during experiments. He also knows something of alchemical theory, of 'the foure spirites and the bodies sevene' (820), he knows the meaning of key terms like *multiplie*, the technical term for transmuting metals into gold, or *sublymyng* 'vaporizing by applying heat', and he can cite authorities and even quote from them. Chaucer's irony in crediting the 'lewed' servant, sceptical yet believing, with greater insight into the whole business of alchemy than the clerks whom he served or helped to deceive is matched by the remarkably controlled diction of the whole tale which marks it as a work of Chaucer's highest maturity. Even the pun on *multiplie* goes deeper in the context of the tale than the rather obvious play on the primary and technical alchemical meanings of the word.[27]

25. See John Webster Spargo in Bryan and Dempster, p. 686.
26. John Webster Spargo, Bryan and Dempster, p. 689.
27. Cp. Joseph E. Grennen, 'The Canon's Yeoman and the Cosmic Furnace: Language and Meaning in the "Canon's Yeoman's Tale"', *Criticism* IV (1962), 226 ff.

In terms of linguistic artistry, *The Canon's Yeoman's Tale* is masterly. What Charles Muscatine has called the narrator's 'chaos of matter, refuse, excrement, [representing] the universe of technology',[28] is at the same time Chaucer's most daring experiment in sustained technical diction without any fear, it seems, that his audience might 'doten anonright'. He achieves this by splitting the Yeoman's catalogues of terms into several sections, by insinuating other technical terms less obtrusively into the narrative, and by allowing the Yeoman's diction to oscillate between quite rare words, some of them possibly neologisms, and thoroughly colloquial language. For example, the first recital of 'termes clergial' (754 ff.) works steadily towards the splendidly anticlimactic

> For lost is al oure labour and travaille;
> And al the cost, a twenty devel waye,
> Is lost also, which we upon it laye.
>
> (*CYT* 781–3)

Similarly, the next instalment (784 ff.) finishes with a beautifully inappropriate 'by my fader kyn!' (829), and there are other oaths, expletives, interjections, including some strong ones like 'by Jhesus!' (967) from the Yeoman himself, or 'in name of Crist' (1122) and 'devel of helle!' (1238) and 'by oure Lady' (1354) from the canon in *pars secunda*. Numerous colloquial turns of speech soften the impact of the technicalities; for example:

> Biforn thise poudres *that I speke of heer*.
> (*ibid.* 763)
> And herbes *koude I telle eek many oon*,
> As egremoyne, valerian, and lunarie,
> And othere swiche, *if that me liste tarie*.
> (*ibid.* 799–801)

And the 'ruggedly dramatic' idiom, in Muscatine's phrase, finds expression in similarly dramatic syntax, sometimes strongly rhetorical and rich in exclamations, rhetorical questions, parentheses and inverted word-order; sometimes colloquially loose and informal:

> Passe over this: I go my tale unto.
> Er that the pot be on the fir ydo,
> Of metals with a certeyn quantitee,

28. Muscatine, p. 220.

My lord hem tempreth, and no man but he –
Now he is goon, I dar seyn boldely –
For, as men seyn, he kan doon craftily.
Algate I woot wel he hath swich a name,
And yet ful ofte he renneth in a blame.
And wite ye how ? ful ofte it happeth so,
The pot tobreketh, and farewel, al is go!

(*ibid*. 898–907)

Many of the words ascribed to the Canon's Yeoman, not only
alchemical terms, do not occur elsewhere in Chaucer. It is as if
Chaucer had saved them up for this rich linguistic feast, or perhaps he had himself only latterly discovered them. Words like
annueleer 'a priest who celebrates anniversary memorial masses for
the dead' (*MED*), *introduccioun, malliable, prolle* 'to prowl', *ram-
myssh* 'ram-like, hence smelling strongly', *residence, verifie*. Others
make so rare an appearance in Chaucer's diction that they impress
one as similarly exotic, words like *crased* 'perforated, cracked', used
also in *The Book of the Duchess* (324); *lucre*, used once in *The Prioress's Tale* (491); *gracelees* 'graceless, improvident, lacking favour',
and *resistence*, each used once in *Troilus and Criseyde* (I, 781, III,
990); and others more.

There is a difference between the two parts of *The Canon's Yeoman's Tale*, or its three parts if we wish to adopt Muscatine's
further division at line 1387, which is in some ways comparable to
the stylistic divisions in the Pardoner's performance. The first
part is more heavily technical: all the lists of alchemical terms occur
here, and there is little dialogue or action except when the pot
explodes and suggestions are offered as to why it happened. It is in
this part that Chaucer taxes his audience most severely:

Yet forgat I go maken rehersaille
Of watres corosif, and of lymaille,
And of bodies mollifacacioun,
And also of hire induracioun;
Oilles, abluciouns, and metal fusible. . . .

(*CYT* 852–6)

The effect on any ordinary listener or reader is comparable to that
of similarly sustained jargon in contemporary English, like this
piece singled out for comment in the London *Times* on 25th
October 1971 (the anniversary, appropriately, of Chaucer's death):

'It comprises a fungistatic high polymer with mycologically active reagents potent against a broad spectrum of bacteria and mould growth combined with negligible toxicity to humans'. One's degree of 'lewedness' clearly determines one's understanding of such jargon as well as the Canon's Yeoman's. On the other hand, the second part of his tale, the 'tale' poper, is less overtly technical. There are still alchemical terms, of course, like *crosselet* 'crucible', not found in Middle English outside this tale; *lemaille* 'metal filings', probably first used by Chaucer and confined to this tale; *mortifye*, apparently also first used by Chaucer in the alchemical sense of 'to change something by chemical action', here specifically quicksilver into silver, a word used elsewhere by the poet only in connection with 'mortifying good works' in *The Parson's Tale*, that is to destroy their effectiveness; *quyksilver*; *teyne* 'a thin metal rod', probably derived from Old Norse *teinn* 'twig, rod', recorded only in *The Canon's Yeoman's Tale*. But in the second part of the tale such terms figure much less obtrusively in the narrative, as do other recondite words which Chaucer succeeds in fusing skilfully with quite familiar diction, sometimes racily colloquial:

God kepe us from his false *dissymulynge*!
(CYT 1073)

    and bad hym hye
The coles for to *couchen* al above
The *crosselet*.
(*ibid.* 1151–3)

    but he is heere and there;
He is so *variaunt*, he abit nowhere.
(*ibid.* 1174–5)

The dialogue moreover adds a dramatic quality to the second part, peppered as it is with a considerable range of oaths and other strong language particularly from the Canon, and thrown into relief by the Yeoman's spirited narrative and his periodic denunciation of the Canon's *falshede* and *doublenesse* acting like a refrain.

In the final hundred lines of the tale, the third part, if we like, a slower pace is re-established, and a more sober, philosophical note is heard as the Yeoman contrasts the 'lusty game' of alchemy as practised by dishonest clerics, 'experimentz of alkenamye, the poeple to deceyue', in Langland's ponderous phrase (*PP* B X, 212), with true scientific inspiration which comes from God. Technical jargon is now at a minimum, but the educated diction and serious moral tone of the 'postscript' finally refute the speaker's earlier claim to be 'a lewed man' (*CYT* 787). Chaucer seems anxious to draw a final and important distinction between true and false *philosophres*, for the word is hammered home insistently, and his usage of it, though nearly always respectful, does permit occasional ambiguity. The word 'scientist' was unknown to the Middle Ages and *philosophre* was the nearest word to it in English, except for those terms describing practitioners of particular sciences, like Chaucer's *astrologer* or *astrologien*, *geometrien*, *musicyen*, *phisicyeen*, *rethorien*, and the nonce *alkamystre* 'alchemist' which he seems to have adapted from the French specially for *The Canon's Yeoman's Tale* (1204). For the most part a *philosophre* was for Chaucer, as for Gower, simply, and etymologically we might say, a lover of wisdom, a wise and learned man, and it is apposite to recall that Langland speaking of philosophers forsaking wealth, 'for they wolde be nedy', changed the 'wyse men' of *Piers Plowman* B XX, 37 into the 'filosofres' of the corresponding line in the C text. Yet for all these poets the word carried the dubious connotations of improper practices, particularly alchemical trickery and unlawful gain. The learned clerk of Orleans whose unholy magic in *The Franklin's Tale* is worth a thousand pounds is called a *philosophre*, and there is irony of the same sort in the punning reference to the pilgrim Clerk of Oxford,

> But al be that he was a philosophre,
> Yet hadde he but litel gold in cofre.
>
> (*Gen Prol* 297–8)

There is irony of a subtler, more poignant, kind in the swindling Canon of *The Canon's Yeoman's Tale* inviting the gullible priest 'in name of Crist, to wexe a philosofre' (1122), for the victim becomes a philosopher in the true sense through bitter experience, wise after the event, through failing to become a *philosophre* in the sense in which the Canon primarily intends the word. One gains the impression that Chaucer, although aware of the ironic potential of the word, was keen to stress its primary, etymological meaning but was somehow hampered by its disparaging connotations as well as by the almost automatic rhyme reflex with *cofre* 'coffer' or, even more suggestively, 'gold in cofre', which occurs several times in his poems. In this connection it is interesting to note that where the F version, probably the earlier, of the Prologue to *The Legend of Good Women* rhymes *philosophre* predictably with 'gold in cofre' (F 380 f.), the G version changes the sense completely and rhymes on *profre* 'proffer'. For Chaucer, science was a serious business which merited for its genuine disciples an appropriately respectful term; and perhaps this was the compelling reason for adopting the word *alkamystre* for the rascally Canon and for trying as a rule to keep the word 'philosopher' for those who had like himself a disinterested concern for 'wysdom and science'.

'This disciplyne and this crafty science' of alchemy may have aroused Chaucer's moral indignation, much as the Pardoner's trade did, but it obviously exerted its fascination too on Chaucer's curious and inquiring mind. Yet he responded to it above all as a poet, in the total shaping of *The Canon's Yeoman's Tale* as much as in the close attention to story, character, and diction, as well as in the manner in which the whole episode of the Canon and his Yeoman is welded into the Canterbury pilgrimage. Before the newcomers are allowed to utter a word Chaucer the narrator is busily rejoicing in the Canon's perspiration with the aid of a simile that acts as a fitting hors d'oeuvre for what is to come, and which illustrates at the same time the rich background of knowledge, observation and inventiveness of Chaucerian imagery;

> But it was joye for to seen hym swete!
> His forheed dropped as a stillatorie,
> Were ful of plantayne and of paritorie.
>
> (*CT* VIII, 579–81)

Stillatorie 'a still, a vessel used in distillation', was a happy invention, or adoption rather, from the medieval Latin, and the two herbs mentioned, plantain and pellitory, were commonly distilled for medicinal purposes. None of these words occurs elsewhere in Chaucer: the precise image of the alchemist distilling sweat from his brow as if it were full of medicinal herbs remains unique and as topically exciting as T. S. Eliot's patient etherized upon a table. Even the omission of the relative pronoun at the beginning of line 581, not uncommon in Chaucer's English, adds to the compactness and memorability of the image. And as with his plant lore, so it is with Chaucer's zoology: both are richly exploited for figurative uses, sometimes commonplace, often strikingly appropriate like the reference to alchemists in vain perfecting their jargon –

> They mowe wel chiteren as doon thise jayes –
> (*CYT* 1397)

where no other bird's chattering could have been quite as apt as that of one known to the expert as *garrulus glandarius*.

Chaucer's botanical and zoological vocabulary is not inconsiderable and as in the case of astronomy or medicine or alchemy he is happy to make use of it incidentally as well as to parade it. But for all his daisy meadows and singing birds Chaucer is not a nature poet. His descriptions of landscapes are stereotyped and the most memorable of his animals are, like Eagle or Chaunticleer, the most recognizably human. The natural world, unlike the sundry folk who peopled it, remained for Chaucer throughout his artistic life very much as he saw it in *The Book of the Duchess*, an ideal landscape,

> Ful thikke of gras, ful softe and swete,
> With floures fele, faire under fete,
> (*BD* 399–400)

where animals frolicked:

> And many an hert and many an hynde
> Was both before me and behynde.
> Of founes, sowres, bukkes, does
> Was ful the woode, and many roes,
> And many sqwirelles, that sete
> Ful high upon the trees and ete. . . .
> (*ibid.* 427–32)

The *Roman de la Rose* provided the pattern of a formal garden,

> by mesuryng,
> Right evene and square in compassing;
> It as long was as it was large,
> (*Rom* 1349–51)

as precisely ordered as the grove in *The Book of the Duchess* where

> every tree stood by hymselve
> Fro other wel ten foot or twelve,
> (*BD* 419–20)

and Chaucer had only to follow the example of the *Roman* and pour into his groves and gardens a plenitude of flowers, herbs, trees, birds, beasts, brooks and fountains to satisfy the most insatiable appetite for rhetorical amplification. Whether or not he rendered the particular version of the *Romaunt of the Rose* included among his works ever since Thynne's edition of 1532 is immaterial; we know that he translated the *Roman*, because he tells us so, and he must have enriched his botanical and zoological vocabulary *inter alia* considerably in doing so. The list of trees in the *Romaunt of the Rose*, 1383 ff., for example, contains nine common European trees, all of which are reproduced together with a further twelve in *The Knight's Tale* in one of those breathless Chaucerian enumerations:

> As ook, firre, birch, aspe, alder, holm ['holly'], popler,
> Wylugh ['willow'], elm, plane, ash, box, chasteyn ['chestnut'],
> lynde ['linden-tree'], laurer,
> Mapul, thorn, bech, hasel, ew, whippeltree ['cornel-tree, dogwood'].
> (*KnT* 2921–3)

These twenty-one trees do not by any means exhaust Chaucer's arboreal vocabulary. There are the more exotic trees and shrubs, like *brasile* 'brazil tree' which produced the red dye referred to in the Host's 'dyen / With brasile' (*CT* VII, 3459); the *cedir grene* of *Troilus and Criseyde* II, 918; the *ciprees* 'cypress' of which Sir Thopas's spear was made (*Thop* 881); the Knight's *mirre* 'myrrh' (*KnT* 2938); the *olyve* 'olive-tree' which with the cypress and palm adds an exotic touch to the more elaborate catalogue in *The Parliament of Fowls* which is made linguistically interesting as well as poetically effective by a variety of epithetical patterns, including single adjectives, phrasal genitives (*of pes*), adjunct nouns (*byldere* 'fit for building', *shetere* 'fit for shooting'), and postmodifying infinitives (*deth to playne*):

> The byldere ok, and ek the hardy asshe;
> The piler elm, the cofre unto carayne;
> The boxtre pipere, holm to whippes lashe;
> The saylynge fyr; the cipresse, deth to playne;
> The shetere ew; the asp for shaftes pleyne;
> The olyve of pes, and eke the dronke vyne;
> The victor palm, the laurer to devyne.
> (*PF* 176–82)

In *The House of Fame* (1278) is 'a table of *sycamour*'; the Miller's Alisoun is more pleasant to behold 'than is the newe *pere-jonette tree*' (*MillT* 3248), a pear tree with fruit that ripens early, a nice comment upon the wench; and *The Merchant's Tale* reaches its climax on and around a *pyrie* 'pear tree'. Although apple trees are not specifically mentioned they are implicit in the beautiful description of autumn coming again 'hevy of apples' in *Boece* IV, m. 6, 32–3. Pandarus is somewhat obsessed with *haselwode*, just as Pertelote is with medicinal herbs and fruit like *gaitrys beryis* (*NPT* 2965), which are the berries of the wild dogwood or 'gaiter tree', recorded in late Old English as *gātetrēow*.

Flowers are as often described in general terms ('and swote smellen floures white and rede', *Tr* I, 158) as named. Roses and lilies occur frequently in figurative use:

And she was fayr as is the rose in May.
(*LGW* 613)

His nayles whitter than the lylye flour.
(*NPT* 2863)

His nekke whit was as the flour-de-lys.
(*Gen Prol* 238)

Other characters also invite botanical comparison: Sir Thopas ironically with the *brembul flour* or 'dog rose' (*Thop* 746), and the Miller's Alisoun once again, this time with the *prymerole* 'primrose, cowslip' (*MillT* 3268). Perhaps the *piggesnye* 'pig's eye' of the same line was also the name of a flower, although the word was used after Chaucer's time invariably as a term of endearment. There is a solitary reference to gathering *vyolettes* 'violets' in *Boece* I, m. 6, 8. But for Chaucer 'the emperice and flour of floures alle' was the *dayesye* which figures so prominently in the Prologue to *The Legend of Good Women* and so unforgettably in the portrait of the Franklin:

Whit was his berd as is the dayesye.
(*Gen Prol* 332)

Except for their figurative and occasional descriptive function in poetry flowers were the business of medieval ladies weaving chaplets, like Emelye gathering

floures, party white and rede,
To make a subtil gerland for hire hede,
(*KnT* 1053–4)

and Chaucer certainly appears more of a herbalist than a horti-
culturist. His knowledge of herbs and spices was probably to
some extent literary; again the *Roman de la Rose* provided appropriate lists. But Chaucer's interest in medicine and alchemy
was the source of further words, and his familiarity with the
pleasures of aristocratic tables and various domestic aromas
brought with it the names of culinary herbs and spices. There
are several herbs in *The Canon's Yeoman's Tale*, some of which we
have already noted: *egremoyne* 'agrimony', *lunarie* 'moonwort',
paritorie 'pellitory', *plantayne* 'plantain', *valerian*; and there is also
papeer 'pepper' (as well as salt). And elsewhere there are herbs, and
aromatic plants, and spices, and laxatives made

> 'Of lawriol, centaure, and fumetere,
> Or elles of ellebor, that groweth there,
> Of katapuce, or of gaitrys beryis,
> Of herbe yve . . .',

> (*NPT* 2963–6)

that is of the foliage of the spurge laurel, of centaury, and fumitory,
of hellebore, of caper spurge, or of the berries of the gaiter tree, of
herb-ive or buck's horn plantain. These are impressive lists, and
there are others in that aromatic poem, *Sir Thopas*, where further
'herbes grete and smale' are mentioned: *lycorys* 'licorice', *cetewale*
'zedoary', *clowe-gylofre* 'clove', *notemuge* 'nutmeg' (760 ff.); and
later, 'roial spicerye of *gyngebreed*', that is, ginger, more *lycorys*,
and *comyn* 'cummin' (853 ff.). Some of these occur also in *The
Miller's Tale*, apropos 'hende' Nicholas whose room is agreeably
perfumed 'with herbes swoote' and whose person is

> as sweete as is the roote
> Of lycorys, or any cetewale.

> (*MillT* 3206–7)

And 'jolif' Absolon, aware of the attraction of sweet body odour,
'cheweth greyn [a spice] and lycorys' (*MillT* 3690) before setting
off in search of amorous adventure, in the course of which he
addresses his beloved among other endearments as 'my sweete
cynamome', that is cinnamon.

Most of these names of herbs and spices occur only once in
Chaucer's work. They were exotic names mostly, fit for appropriate contexts of alchemy or medicine, and for a sparing, hence all
the more effective, irony, as in the case of Absolon's sweetening

his mouth for so disagreeably unaromatic a kiss. Chaucer's zoological vocabulary shows much the same mixture of homely and
exotic names as his botanical vocabulary, probably derived for
the most part from literary sources, and partly from personal
knowledge and observation of the birds and beasts mentioned.
From such sources as the *Roman de la Rose*, the *De Planctu Naturae*
of Alanus de Insulis, or the encyclopedic work of Vincent of
Beauvais, Chaucer could have derived, and probably did, the
suggestion for his lists, the characteristics of some of the birds
enumerated in *The Parliament of Fowls*, and some of the animal
names themselves. Some of the lists are certainly extensive – the
catalogue of birds assembled for the parliament runs to three
dozen – but they do not offer much scope for zoological detail.
J. A. W. Bennett characterizes the descriptions of the qualities
of the birds in the *Parliament* as 'in the language of the Bestiaries',[29]
and there is certainly not much evidence of personal bird-watching
on Chaucer's part. The only glance at a bird's appearance in the
Parliament is at the 'fetheres donne / And grey' of the goshawk
(*PF* 334–5), and there are few instances elsewhere, most of them
conventional, like the 'white swan' (*LGW* 1355), or the 'snow-
whit swan' (*MancT* 133); the 'white doke' swimming 'after hire
drake' (*MillT* 3576); the simile of King Lygurge's hair.

> As any ravenes fethere it shoon for blak;
> (*KnT* 2144)

or the two references to a goose being grey (*MillT* 3317, *WBT*
269). Twice also Chaucer notes the magpie's appearance as being
flekked 'spotted, variegated', a reference presumably to its black
and white plumage (*MerchT* 184–8, *CYT* 565), although Trevisa
applied the same word to a chameleon and Langland to unspeci-
fied multicoloured birds ('With fleckede fetheres and of fele
colours', *PP* C XIV, 138).

Such instances may not reveal much ornithological interest on
Chaucer's part, but occasional references to the movements or the
song of birds suggest that he had at least something of an eye and
rather more of a good ear for them. The Pardoner's likening his
'bisynesse' to the motions of a pigeon's head and neck (*PardT*
395 ff.) is a happy image which smacks of personal observation.
So, as we have noted, is the choice of *chiteren* to describe the noise

29. J. A. W. Bennett, *The Parlement of Foules: An Interpretation* (Oxford, 1957), p. 149.

of the jay (*CYT* 1397), and we might add to this the reference to
the Summoner's friar who '*chirketh* as a sparwe / With his lyppes'
(*SumT* 1804–5), an expressive word with connotations of creaking
doors (*ParsT* 605) and soughing glades (*Bo* I, m. 6, 10) and croak-
ing and grating and gnashing of teeth. That the sparrow is a
lecherous bird (*Gen Prol* 626; in *PF* 351 he is 'Venus sone')
Chaucer could have learnt from Alexander Neckam's *De Naturis
Rerum* or Bartholomew de Glanville's *De Proprietatibus Rerum*, but
that he *chirketh* he must have heard for himself. There is also the
swallow's song, 'loude and yerne' (*MillT* 3257), and the bittern
booming in the bog:

> And as a bitore *bombleth* in the myre.
>
> (*WBT* 972)

Whether Chaucer wrote 'bombleth' or 'bumbith' or 'blumbeth' or
whatever the various manuscripts read does not matter much;
what matters is that he must have had an idea of the bittern's
boom and sought to find the appropriate lechoic word for it.
Presumably Chaucer also listened to nighingales singing, a
pleasure rather more easily gained in fourteenth-century London
and its surrounding country than today, although we cannot be
quite sure just what he meant by the nightingale *brokkynge*
(*MillT* 3377). The *MED* defines the words as 'complaining', the
editors gloss 'trilling' or 'using a quavering or broken voice'. The
clue may be in *Troilus and Criseyde* where the bird is described as
interrupting its song on hearing other sounds:

> And as the newe abaysed nyghtyngale,
> That stynteth first whan she bygynneth to synge,
> Whan that she hereth any herde [shepherd]tale [speak],
> Or in the hegges any wyght stirynge,
> And after siker doth hire vois out rynge,
> Right so Criseyde, whan hire drede stente,
> Opned hire herte, and tolde hym hire entente.
>
> (*Tr* III, 1233–9)

In *The Miller's Tale* it is the serenading Absolon who is *brokkynge*,
presumably interrupted by the carpenter waking up, so that
brokkynge may well be related to O.E. *broc* in the sense of 'fragment', like German *Brocken* 'bit, pieces, snatches of conversation'.
The point is that for all the lore Chaucer may have inherited from

Pliny and the other sources about the nightingale calling forth 'the grene leves newe' (*PF* 352) with its song, he also appears to have observed some of its habits for himself. His ornithology is thus a classic example of the Chaucerian mixture of *auctoritee* and *experience*; even 'roial' Chauntecleer probably owes his splendours as much to the poet's watching a Golden Spangled Hamburg cock pecking and feathering around Aldgate or Eltham as to his knowledge of Bartholomew's treatise and of the *Roman de Renart* or *Reinhart Fuchs*. If the literary influences predominate it is because Chaucer, except where people were concerned, was more a bookworm than an outrider, for all his travels around the English countryside and abroad. He seems capable of odd mistakes, like ascribing a sweet, distinctive fragrance to the common daisy which, *pace* Beryl Rowland,[30] really cannot stand aromatic comparison with 'gomme, or herbe, or tre'; unless, of course, the passage has been persistently misread and the reference is to the whole meadow producing a delicious aroma of grass and various flowers:

Fayr was this medewe, as thoughte me, overal;
With floures sote enbrouded was it al.
As for to speke of gomme, or herbe, or tre,
Comparisoun may non ymaked be;
For it surmountede pleynly alle odoures,
And of ryche beaute alle floures.

(*LGW* Prol G. 107–12)

As Chaucer had just previously referred to the daisy as 'that flour' (106) the syntax is at least ambiguous: 'the collective fragrance and beauty of the whole flowery mead surpassed any individual odours or flowers' is a possible reading, and one that exonerates the poet from a botanical blunder.

The poet's literary indebtedness becomes particularly apparent in the case of exotic or legendary birds and beasts. Among the former are *fenix* 'phoenix' (*BD* 982), *grifphon* 'griffin' (*KnT* 2133), and *popynjay* 'parrot', another bird traditionally reputed lecherous, hence its epithet 'ful of delicasye' (wantonness) in *The Parliament of Fowls*, 359. Among beasts are *basilicok* 'basilisk' (*ParsT* 853), *camaille* 'camel' (*CLT* 1196), probably introduced for the sake of its rhyme into the Clerk's elaborate envoy, *hyene* 'hyena' (*Fort* 35), a

30. Beryl Rowland, 'Chaucer's Daisy', *Notes and Queries* CCVIII (1963), 210.

number of astronomical animals like *Delphyn* (*HF* 1006) or *Dragoun* (*Astr* II, 4, 36), and a few mini-zoos, as in *Boece*: '. . . the serpentz, and the lyoun, and the tigre, and the bere, and the boor' (IV, m. 4, 7–9), or the Monk's 'leouns, leopardes, and beres' (*MkT* 2261), or the Knight's 'wood leon . . . crueel tigre . . . wilde bores' (*KnT* 1656 ff.). There is a number of figures and idioms involving *apes*, but only a solitary mention of *olifauntes* in *Boece* III, pr. 8, 27, except for the giant in *Sir Thopas* whose name is 'sire Olifaunt' (*Thop* 808) in delightful contrast to the wild beasts, 'ye, bothe bukke and hare' (756), of the forest. It is obviously among the latter that both Sir Thopas and Chaucer are more at home. If the comic knight

> koude hunte at wilde deer,
> And ride an haukyng for river
> With grey goshauk on honde,
> (*Thop* 736–8)

the poet knew the difference between 'founes, sowres, bukkes, does . . . and many roes' (*BD* 429–30), that is fawns (young deer), sorrels (three-year-old bucks), bucks (male deer), does (female deer), and roes (a species of deer), as well as 'the hert and hynde' (*PF* 195), male and female of the red deer. There are several occurrences of *hare*, but only one mention of *conyes* 'rabbits' (*PF* 193), and two of *sqwirelles* 'squirrels' (*BD* 431, *PF* 196). There is a solitary *polcat* 'polecat' busily doing away with *capouns* 'capons' in *The Pardoner's Tale* (855–6), and in addition to one Ovidian reference to 'the litel wesele' (weasel, *Mel* 1325) the memorable image of Alisoun's figure

> As any wezele hir body gent and smal.
> (*MillT* 3234)

Pandarus is a sly fox (*Tr* III, 1565), as, of course, is daun Russell in *The Nun's Priest's Tale* or 'the fox Renard' in *The Legend of Good Women*, 2448. There are several mentions of wolves, mostly alluding to their rapacious onslaughts on lambs, whether actual or figurative, as in the Physicians'

> Under a shepherde softe and necligent
> The wolf hath many a sheep and lamb torent,
> (*PhysT* 101–2)

or the Parson's 'Wherfore I seye that thilke lordes that been lyk wolves, that devouren the possessiouns or the catel of povre folk wrongfully, withouten mercy or mesure...' (*ParsT* 775). For the Manciple 'a *she-wolf* hath also a vileyns kynde' (*MancT* 183). In *Troilus and Criseyde* occurs a memorable simile of venerable ancestry, through Boccaccio's *Filostrato* and Dante's *Inferno* back to Virgil's *Aeneid*:

> Right as the wylde *bole* [bull] bygynneth sprynge,
> Now her, now ther, idarted to the herte,
> And of his deth roreth in compleynynge,
> Right so gan he [Troilus] aboute the chaumbre sterte....
> (*Tr* IV, 239–42)

According to Pertelote's medical lore melancholy men cry out in their sleep for fear of black devils and black bears and 'boles blake' (*NPT* 2935).

But on the whole Chaucer is more at home, as it were, among domestic animals than wild ones, even of Sir Thopas's kind. There are many direct and figurative allusions to domestic animals, often reinforcing the colloquial tone of much Chaucerian dialogue and narrative.[31] Of linguistic interest is the unique *vache* 'cow, beast' in *Truth*, 22, probably adopted straight from the French to allow the punning allusion to Sir Philip (de) la Vache first suggested by Edith Rickert in 1913. *Cow* occurs only three times in Chaucer and the plural *keen* 'kine' only once (*NPT* 2831). The sense 'property, chattels' is normal for Chaucer as for his age generally for the Anglo-French word *catel*, although the sense 'livestock, cattle' occurs occasionally in the fourteenth and fifteenth centuries and may be intended by Chaucer in one or two instances, for example in the reference to the poor widow in *The Nun's Priest's Tale* (2827) which is followed in a couple of lines by the inventory of her livestock. Cats, apart from one 'sweynte [slothful] cat' in *The House of Fame* (1783), figure only in the narratives of some of the more lowly pilgrims: Miller, Summoner, Manciple, and the Wife of Bath. The latter indeed has quite a discourse on the imputation that she is herself 'lyk a cat', in the course of which she coins the unique 'goon *a-caterwawed*', go caterwauling (*WBT* 354), a type of adverbial phrase ultimately modelled on the Old English pattern *on huntað* 'a-hunting' found elsewhere in Chaucer: 'goon a-begged', go begging (*FranklT*

31. Cp. above, Chapter 4, pp. 198 ff.

1580), and 'goon a-blakeberyed', go blackberrying (*PardT* 406). It is worth noting that Langland employs the same rare construction in 'gon a-begged' (*PP* C IX, 138) and 'gon abrybeth', go vagabonding (*ibid.* 246).

If cats belong to Chaucer's lower orders, so do dogs as distinct from hounds. The word *dogge*, as the *MED* notes, was usually abusive in early Middle English, and the depreciatory sense persists in Chaucer. Mrs Goodelief Bailly refers to her husband's servants as '*dogges*' (*CT* VII, 1899), and there is little more respect in Pandarus's

> 'Shulle in a strete as dogges liggen dede'.
>
> (*Tr* IV, 626)

The word was also applied to dogs 'trained to track game wounded by the bowmen' (*MED*), hence the phrase 'dogge for the bowe' used in *The Friar's Tale* (1369) and *The Merchant's Tale* (2014). The distinction between Chaucer's *dogge* and *hound*, which appears more carefully observed by him (and by John Trevisa, for that matter) than by some of his contemporaries, is that between the widow's farmyard *dogge*, Colle, in *The Nun's Priest's Tale* (3383), and the Prioress's 'smale houndes' (*Gen Prol* 146). Significantly, there are no dogs in *The Knight's Tale*, only hounds, as when Theseus goes hunting helped along by a tripping alliterating line,

> With hunte and horn and houndes hym bisyde,
>
> (*KnT* 1678)

just as in *Sir Gawain and the Green Knight* there are plenty of hunting *houndez*, but only one pack of (alliterating) *doggez* (1600). At the magnificent reception held in Theseus's palace in honour of the assembled knights, the narrator forbears to describe

> What haukes sitten on the perche above,
> What houndes liggen on the floor adoun,
>
> (*KnT* 2204–5)

a very different picture indeed from Pandarus's *dogges*. In translating Matthew XV:27, Chaucer, like Wyclif, renders Latin *catelli* as *whelpes* (the same word used for the momentary puppy in *The Book of the Duchess*):

Thynk on the womman Cananee, that sayde
That whelpes eten somme of the crommes alle
That from hir lordes table been yfalle.

(SecNT 59–61)

Only the Wife of Bath seems to be out of step when translating the Latin *caneis* of Theophrastus into *houndes* in that catalogue of merchandise 'assayed' before purchase (*WBT* 285). But she is not really out of step, or character, or class; for that penchant for *gentillesse* which distinguishes her would naturally associate 'hors and houndes', as the poet does in *The Book of the Duchess* (349), and one was more likely in any case to buy a hound than a dog – quite apart of course from the rhyme. There is only one occurrence of *curre* 'cur' in Chaucer, a word of rather less pejorative import then than now, though Chaucer's contrast between the noble lion flicking his tail to chase away a fly and the vindictive cur is not flattering to the latter,

for, of his genterye,
Hym deyneth nat to wreke hym on a flye,
As doth a curre, or elles another best.

(LGW Prol G 380–2)

Of canine species, finally, there are some examples in Chaucer: *grehoundes* (*Gen Prol* 190); *spaynel* 'spaniel' (*WBT* 267); *alauntz*, a breed of ferocious dog used in hunting 'at the leoun or the deer' and in bull-baiting (cp. *MED, KnT* 2148); *lymere* in *The Book of the Duchess* (362, 365) is properly a tracking hound, literally a 'leash hound' from Old French *liem* 'leash', but was also specifically applied to the bloodhound.

There are a good many other animals in Chaucer which it would be tedious to enumerate. A few further examples will suffice to complete this sketch of Chaucer's familiarity with terms of natural history. He mentions a number of insects in various contexts, often as symbols of worthlessness; the *gnat*, for instance, which explicitly for the Wife of Bath and the Manciple and implicitly for Pandarus (*Tr* IV, 595), is something of little value. In *The Parliament of Fowls* (353–4) bees (Chaucer has both plurals *bees* and *been* attested in rhyme) are designated as 'foules smale', which Albert S. Cook long since proved to be not a Chaucerian blunder but a classification of venerable patristic and Old English ancestry.[32]

32. See Albert S. Cook's notes in *Modern Language Notes* XXI (1906), 111 f. and XXII (1907), 146.

The Parson refers to 'thise flyes that men clepen bees' (*ParsT* 468) and *Boece* to the 'bytynge of smale flyes' (*Bo* II, pr. 6, 39–40), which illustrate the generic use of *flyes* for any flying insect, while the word also referred specifically to the common housefly. The popular phrase 'nat worth a flye' probably means the latter, as does Harry Bailly's allusion to the Cook's shop:

'For in thy shoppe is many a flye loos'.
(*CT* I, 4352)

Also addressing the Cook, although much later in the poem (*CT* IX, 17), Harry Bailly has Chaucer's only mention of *fleen* 'fleas': 'Hastow had fleen al nyght . . .?' Chauntecleer, who

caste his ye
Among the wortes on a boterflye,
(*NPT* 3273–4)

seems to have had more of an eye for butterflies than his maker, who uses the word only twice elsewhere, again as a measure of worthlessness, in Proserpina's emphatic

'I sette right noght, of al the vileynye
That ye of wommen write, a boterflye!'
(*MerchT* 2303–4)

and the Host's no less forceful

'Swich talkyng is nat worth a boterflye'.
(*CT* VII, 2790)

The biblical moth puts in an appearance in the practical context of the Wife of Bath's household management:

Thise wormes, ne thise *motthes*, ne thise mytes,
Upon my peril, frete hem [i.e. gowns] never a deel,
(*WBT* 560–1)

but the dozen other references to *mytes* in Chaucer are all of the type 'nat worth a myte'. The only ant in Chaucer is the 'angry . . . *pissemyre*, of *The Summoner's Tale* (1825), a word of recent appearance in late fourteenth-century English in contrast to the common word *ampte* and its variants descended from O.E. *ǣmete* 'ant'. *Waspes* 'wasps' occurs once only in the Prioress's somewhat involved figure of the serpent Sathanas having 'in Jues herte his waspes nest' (*PrT* 559), and only in the *Astrolabe* occurs the Old

English word *loppe* 'spider' and the compound *lopwebbe* besides 'webbe of a loppe' (*Astr* I, 3, 5; I, 19, 3; I, 21, 2).

Chaucer's entomological vocabulary shows no particular originality nor does it range widely, and apart perhaps from the 'angry' ant there is little evidence of personally observed facts. Like any of his contemporaries the poet must have been only too familiar with *flyes* of every description; the fact that so many insects were singled out as 'nat worth' anything proves them to have been as plentiful as irritating. On the other hand, as regards the names of fish Chaucer seems to have profited at least from their culinary associations, even if he was not himself a compleat angler, for he anticipated the fifteenth-century cookery books in introducing, as far as we can tell, several such names into literature. Among these is *breem* 'bream' which along with *luce* 'pike' (found also in the third part of the *Romaunt*, 7039) helped to furnish the Franklin's table (*Gen Prol* 350), both words adopted from French like so many other culinary terms, and *pykerel* 'young pike' which figures in the Merchant's splendid gastronomical metaphor of Januarie's marital *desiderata*, though Chaucer's palate here differs from Izaak Walton's:[33]

'Oold fissh and yong flessh wolde I have ful fayn.
Bet is,' quod he, 'a pyk than a pykerel,
And bet than old boef is the tendre veel.'
(*MerchT* 1418–20)

Less of a delicacy, though sometimes used for food, is the *houndfyssh* 'dogfish' whose rough skin furnishes a simile for Januarie's beard (*MerchT* 1825), a word also used for some other species of fish and found recorded before Chaucer. The eighth metrum of Book III of Boethius's *Consolatio* provided Chaucer amid other piscatorial lore with *echynnys*, Latin *echinis*, 'sea urchins', and there is in the gloss in this metrum, as in *Boece* II, m. 5, 14, mention of *schellefyssh*, which figures a third time in 'oistres and muscles and oothir swich schelle-fyssh of the see' in *Boece* V, pr, 5, 29–31. Mussels and oysters were no prized delicacies judging by the friar's comment in *The Summoner's Tale* (2100 ff.) and the poet's own 'nat worth an oystre' in the *General Prologue* (182), perhaps prompted as much by the preceding image of 'a fissh that is waterlees' (*ibid.* 180) and the need for a rhyme with *cloystre* (as in

33. See M. Donovan's note in *Philological Quarterly* XXXI (1952), 441.

The Summoner's Tale) as by the cheapness of oysters in the economy of the thirteen-eighties. Chaucer may not have been much of an angler, but he did know something about catching eels apparently, for in the general mêlée of the concluding lines of *The House of Fame* occurs the simile:

> And troden fast on others heles,
> And stampen, as men doon aftir *eles*.
>
> (*HF* 2153–4)

Stamping or 'stomping' after eels, according to F. P. Magoun's evidence in Robinson's note (p. 788), was a regular mode of catching them and it looks as if Chaucer was using a proper technical term. The only other time he uses *stampe* is in the culinary sense of 'to pound, pulverize' along with 'streyne, and grynde' (*PardT* 538).

At this point it may be as well to leave natural history and to glance briefly, as we have already had occasion to do, at Chaucer's expertise in the terminology of more domestic sciences. In cooking, as we have just seen, verbs once again assume importance, perhaps nowhere more obviously so than in the line

> He koude rooste, and sethe, and broille, and frye,
>
> (*Gen Prol* 383)

from the Cook's portrait, where there is mention also of *boille* and *bake*. As a rule it is with verbs as with other culinary terms, the more elaborate and refined processes like *broille* are described in words of Romance origin, the more commonplace ones like *bake* in words derived from Old English. Among basic English words is *breed* 'bread', now the normal word instead of O.E. *hlāf* 'loaf', of which there were several varieties, the more costly needing French words or epithets to do them justice: the Wife of Bath contrasts 'breed of pured [refined] whete-seed', symbolic of virginity, with common *barly-breed* symbolizing the lesser estate of married women (*WBT* 142 ff.); the fastidious friar in *The Summoner's Tale* asks his hostess for a 'shyvere' of 'youre softe breed' (*SumT* 1840); and the Prioress feeds *wastel-breed* to her dogs (*Gen Prol* 147), that is bread made of the finest flour, 'cake-bread', the form *wastel* being a dialectal equivalent of Old French *gastel* whence derives modern French *gâteau* 'cake'. If Chaucer implies its value ironically in the Prioress's liberality, Langland points it more bluntly:

'For thow hast no good, by good faith! to bygge [buy] the wlth a wastell.'

(*PP* C VII, 341)

Even whiter than white (to borrow a phrase from the language of advertising) was *payndemayn* (*Thop* 725), originally medieval Latin *panis dominicus* 'lord's bread', probably the same as simnel bread which is also made of very fine flour. Gower mentions *paindemeine* as a particular delicacy in *Confessio Amantis* VI, 620, and Langland adds two other words of French derivation, *clerematyn* and *coket* (*PP* C IX, 328), both of which also refer to bread made of fine flour. At the other end of the scale is the plain English 'broun breed' of the poor widow in *The Nun's Priest's Tale* (2844), rather closer to the 'bred ... of benes and of peses' on which the poor reared their children, according to Langland (*PP* C IX, 307), or to the coarse 'houndes bred and horse bred' eaten by beggars (*ibid.* 225). An interesting word is *kechyl*, in the phrase 'a Goddes kechyl' (*SumT* 1747), that is a small cake (O.E. *cēcel*) given in charity. It is a rare word in Middle English literature: the *MED* cites only two occurrences in the *Orrmulum*, and Chaucer does not use the word elsewhere. Chaucer was not yet worried, as Caxton was to be a hundred years later, by having two words for 'egg' to choose from. He uses the word twice, both times in its Old English form *ey* rather than Scandinavian *egg*.

For the modern gastronome a menu sounds more sophisticated in French even if it conceals nothing more exotic than fish and chips, and it would be interesting to know whether French culinary terms produced a similar effect on fourteenth-century English ears. Langland is certainly aware that dishes with French names cost more:

For-thy he eet mete of more cost: *mortrewes* and *potages*,

(*PP* C XVI, 47)

while Chaucer's Cook's repertoire is clearly meant to impress upon the audience the social aspirations of the guildsmen whom he served:

A Cook they hadde with hem for the nones
To boille the chicknes with the marybones,

And poudre-marchant tart and galyngale.
Wel koude he knowe a draughte of Londoun ale.
He koude roosete, and sethe, and broille, and frye,
Maken mortreux, and wel bake a pye.
. . . .
For blankmanger, that made he with the beste.

(Gen Prol 379–87)

Quite apart from the array of verbs testifying to divers culinary
skills, there is clearly something imposing in the exotic flavouring
materials, *poudre-marchant* and *galyngale*, as well as in the dishes
named, particularly *mortreux*, a kind of rich soup, and *blankmanger*,
a dish of fowl or other meat combined with numerous other
ingredients, both of them mentioned together in much the same
way in *Piers Plowman* C XVI, 100 apropos the learned doctor who
knew how to dine well. Other words and phrases create similar
impressions of well-composed menus, though for the modern
reader some words, like Dame Prudence's *hochepot* 'a rich stew'
(*Mel* 1257), modern English 'hotch-potch', originally a legal term,
will have lost some of their fourteenth-century lustre. Twice
Chaucer mentions *galauntine*, a richly concocted sauce, both times
in short poems distinguished by the use of some unusual diction.
In *To Rosemounde* (17) the phrase 'pyk walwed in galauntyne', pike
smothered in galauntine-sauce, conjures up medieval gastronomic exuberance, just as the image it serves, of a lover 'walwed'
in love, strains to excess a familiar trope. In *The Former Age* the
pleasures of the table are as yet unrealized, but it is interesting
that the symbol of cordon bleu excellence for Chaucer appears to
be 'sause of galantyne':

Unkorven and ungrobbed lay the vyne;
No man yit in the morter spyces grond
To clarre [spiced wine], ne to sause of galantyne.

(Form Age 14–16)

Unless a writer goes into details of recipes, however, his culinary
descriptions must needs rely heavily on more general terms, like
brawen 'meat', *fissh*, *potage*, *sauce*, *sewe* 'broth, gravy, stew', *spyce*.
This is how the *Gawain*-poet gives the impression of a sumptuous
meal served to the knight upon his arrival at Hautdesert:

Seggez hym serued semly innoȝe
Wyth sere sewes and sete, sesounde of þe best,

Double-felde, as hit fallez, and fele kyn fischez,
Summe baken in bred, summe brad on þe gledez,
Summe soþen, summe in sewe sauered with spyces,
And ay sawes [sauce] so sleȝe, þat þe segge lyked.
                    (*SGGK* 888–93)

In *The Squire's Tale* (67–8) Chaucer merely hints at exotic dishes by mentioning 'strange sewes', *swannes*, and *heronsewes* 'young herons'. At Sarpedoun's feast all is summed up in the telling line,

That deynte was, al coste it gret richesse,
                    (*Tr* V, 438)

which is elaborated in the Franklin's portrait, although specific culinary terms are still relatively few:

Withoute bake mete was nevere his hous
Of fissh and flessh, and that so plentevous,
It snewed in his hous of mete and drynke,
Of alle deyntees that men koude thynke.
After the sondry sesons of the yeer,
So chaunged he his mete and his soper.
Ful many a fat partrich hadde he in muwe,
And many a breem and many a luce in stuwe.
Wo was his cook but if his sauce were
Poynaunt and sharp, and redy al his geere.
                    (*Gen Prol* 343–52)

One gains the impression from such passages that Chaucer, like his Ricardian colleagues, was familiar with good eating and knew something of the ingredients that went into the dishes he mentions and of the appropriate terms. *The Parson's Tale* with its reference to 'swich manere bake-metes and dissh-metes [food cooked in dishes], brennynge of wilde fir and peynted and castelled with papir' (445) further suggests that like the poet of *Purity* Chaucer was familiar also with some of the more extravagant modes of serving food – '*wast*' the Parson calls them. But the kitchen does not contribute a particularly original element to Chaucer's vocabulary, for all its heavy reliance on words of Romance origin. And much the same is true of the words describing drinks. *Wyn* and *ale* predominate, sometimes qualified by general epithets – 'sweete wyn' (*WBT* 459, *Thop* 851), 'no wyn ne drank she, neither whit ne reed' (*NPT* 2842), 'moyste and

corny [malty] ale' (*CT* VI, 315) – sometimes by more specific
ones, like 'the white wyn of Lepe' (*PardT* 563), a small town in the
Spanish province of Huelva, mentioned in a passage in which
Chaucer displays some familiarity with French and Spanish wines
and with the illegal custom of adulterating French wines of 'the
Rochele' (La Rochelle) and 'Burdeux' (Bordeaux) with Spanish
ones. Most of the drinks mentioned in Chaucer's poetry would
have been familiar to his audience: *clarree* was a sweet spiced drink
made of wine or ale, similar to *pyment*, both words of French
origin and recorded well before Chaucer's time; *mede* or *meeth*
'mead' derives from Old English and its sweetness provides an
apt figure for Alisoun's mouth in *The Miller's Tale* (3261). So does
bragot (*ibid.*), a word of Welsh origin, describing a drink of ale and
honey fermented together, which Chaucer and John Trevisa first
used in English literature at about the same time; Chaucer does
not use the word elsewhere. Another sweet drink is the Italian
wine *vernage* (Italian *vernaccia*) found also in Gower's *Confessio
Amantis* and mentioned by Chaucer in *The Shipman's Tale* (71),
and in *The Merchant's Tale* (1807) as one of the several drinks old
Januarie consumes on his wedding night 't' encreessen his corage'.
The other two are *clarree* and *ypocras*, the latter a word derived
from the proper name of 'Olde Ypocras', Hippocrates, describing a well-strained concoction of red wine, sugar, spices and
other ingredients. The *MED* does not record an earlier use than
Chaucer's. Along with *vernage* in *The Shipman's Tale* Chaucer
mentions 'a jubbe [a large container] of *malvesye*', malmsey, a
word not used by him elsewhere. Perhaps we should not forget
to mention, amid all these sweet and spiced and heady drinks,
Chaucer's simile 'whit as morne *milk*' which occurs in the Franklin's portrait (*Gen Prol* 358) and in that of Alisoun (*MillT* 3236),
or the Parson's 'milk of losengerie [flattery]' (*ParsT* 613), for, as
we have seen, Chaucer's use of such terms is both direct and
figurative and in the context of Chaucer's poetic art the reader's
sensibility is more likely to be 'modified' by these images of
morning milk or Sir Thopas's face white as *payndemayn* or the
Reeve's wine-cask than by glimpses, however enlightening, of
medieval drinking habits.

The class distinction implicit between the poor widow in *The
Nun's Priest's Tale* who had no lack of 'milk and broun breed' and,
say, the Franklin who was well 'envyned' and richly endowed

with 'mete and drynke', is one of the facts of medieval life which Chaucer expresses in numerous ways in his poetry. One that is relevant to our present discussion is the use of technical terms to describe the clothes worn by different characters and the textiles used in their manufacture. Chaucer's command of sartorial vocabulary was considerable and he used it not merely to indicate rank but much as he used his knowledge of astrology and physionomy and medicine to portray character as well. The glimpse of the Monk's sleeves 'purfiled at the hond / With grys, and that the fyneste of a lond' (*Gen Prol* 193–4), that is lined or edged with the finest fur, and of the gold pin he uses to fasten his hood under his chin, sums up the man's character, his attitude to his chosen calling, his self-indulgence, and contrasts sharply with the poverty implicit in the *thredbare* clothing worn by the Clerk. The Knight's *gypon*, a tunic probably worn under the *habergeon* 'hauberk, coat of mail,' made of *fustian*, cloth, frequently coarse, made from cotton, flax or wool, and all *bismotered*, stained or soiled (*Gen Prol* 75–6), contrasts poignantly with Sir Thopas's sumptuous garments, including shirt and pants 'of cloth of lake fyn and cleere' (*Thop* 858), for *lake* was a fine linen, proverbial for its whiteness, the word itself adopted from Dutch. In *The General Prologue* alone a considerable number of technical words is used to describe cloths and clothes, many of them possessing connotations relevant to the person described or to his profession or rank which are often hard for modern readers to recapture. Thus Chaucer distinguishes, for example, in his first few portraits between the garments worn, by varying words appropriately: the Knight's *gypon* of *fustian* we have already noted; the Squire wears a short *gowne*; the Yeoman a green *cote* and *hood*; the Prioress an elegant *cloke*; the Monk's *sleves*, as we saw, were lined with fine fur; the Friar wore a *semycope* 'of double *worstede*'; the Merchant was dressed in *mottelee*; the Clerk wore a threadbare *courtepy*; the Sergeant of the Law was dressed informally 'in a *medlee cote*'; and so on. That most of these and similar words are of Romance origin is no more surprising than in the case of culinary terms, for the French set the tone in both spheres. But Chaucer once again does more than simply use technical expertise for purely descriptive purposes. As in Shakespeare's plays, so in Chaucer's poetry as well as in his prose some striking images are sartorial. Thus Pandarus asks Criseyde to wrap herself in the *mantel* of friendship for Troilus:

'And wry yow in that mantel evere moo',

(Tr II, 380)

and a little later in the poem Criseyde ponders the pros and cons of
her situation as if folding a garment:

And what to doone best were, and what eschue,
That plited [pleated] she ful ofte in many fold.

(ibid. 696–7)

The Wife of Bath's proverbial lore includes the reference to her
fourth husband, the *revelour*, who

sat ful ofte and song,
Whan that his shoo ful bitterly hym wrong,

(WBT 491–2)

and Pandarus, who commands a similarly happy colloquial turn of
phrase, has the words

'Ne knewe hem more than myn olde hat!'

(Tr III, 320)

In *An A B C*, 46, the lover asks his lady to *clothe* him in her grace,
in *Boece* I, pr. 6, 91 ff. misguided minds are said to '*clothen* hem in
false opynyouns', in *Troilus and Criseyde* I, 156 f. the meadow is
'*clothed* ... / With newe grene', in *The Merchant's Tale*

Night with his mantel, that is derk and rude,
Gan oversprede the hemysperie aboute,

(MerchT 1798–9)

and in *The Squire's Tale*, 507, the false tercelet was 'so *wrapped*
under humble cheere', a word that recurs even more picturesquely in the *Astrolabe*: 'For as mochel as a philosofre saith, "he
wrappith him in his frend, that condescendith to the rightfulle
praiers of his frend"' (Intr. 5–8). In *Boece* IV, pr. 6, Philosophy
says that she will '*weve* [weave] to the [thee] resouns *yknyt* by
ordre' (38 f.), and later speaks of 'any thing that *knytteth* and
felawschipeth hymself to thilke myddel poynt' (125 f.).

These and similar figures are perhaps all the more effective for
relying upon the everyday vocabulary of clothing and *clooth-*
makyng, but they give little idea of the range of Chaucer's technical
vocabulary in these fields; hence some further illustrations may
be instructive. Among fabrics Chaucer mentions 'cloth of Reynes'

(*BD* 255), fine linen made at Rennes in France; 'clooth of Tars' (*KnT* 2160), probably silk from Tarsus, St Paul's birthplace, one of the towns of Asia Minor where silk was produced in the Middle Ages; *blanket* (*SumT* 1751), a kind of woollen cloth, generally coarse, one of the two cloths (the other was russet) statutorily prescribed for fourteenth-century ploughmen and others of similar occupation;[34] *cordewane* (*Thop* 732), as in Sir Walter Scott's 'shoes of Spanish cordwain', Cordovan leather, an expensive type of shoe leather named after the Spanish town of Cordoba; *faldyng* (*Gen Prol* 391), coloured woollen cloth, generally assumed to have been coarse as would have befitted the Shipman, although M. Channing Linthicum (in the article cited) argues otherwise. The word occurs elsewhere in Chaucer only in *The Miller's Tale* (3212) where Nicholas's cupboard or storage chest (*presse*) is covered with red *faldyng*. Two other cloths mentioned in *The General Prologue* are the Merchant's *mottelee* (271) and the Man of Law's *medlee* (328), both indicative of colour rather than quality: the former was cloth woven into a particoloured design here indicative of a guild, the latter was cloth of one or several colours made of wool which had been dyed and mingled before being spun into yarn. The colour words *sangwyn* 'red' and *pers* 'blue' are used substantivally to designate cloth of those colours with reference to garments ('In sangwyn and in pers he clad was al', *Gen Prol* 439) and the latter word more specifically to the Reeve's 'long surcote of pers' (617). The Doctor's garments are 'lyned with *taffata* and with *sendal*' (440), both of them silken fabrics. Criseyde wears widow's weeds 'of *samyt* broun' (*Tr* I, 109), also a type of silk. In *The Knight's Tale* 'clooth of gold' (something like Sir Thopas's *syklatoun*, *Thop* 734) is contrasted in the manner of some other romances with *sarge* 'serge' (2568), a woollen fabric here clearly intended to represent something cheap and common, though it was not as coarse or harsh as the *stamyn* which 'this woful lady' Philomela used for her pathetic autobiographical tapestry in *The Legend of Good Women* (2360), and which *inter alia* the Parson considers suitable wear for the penitent: '... in werynge of *heyres* [garments of haircloth], or of *stamyn*, or of *haubergeons* on hire naked flessh, for Cristes sake, and swiche manere penances' (*ParsT* 1052).

34. See M. Channing Linthicum, "Faldyng" and "Medlee"', *Journal of English and Germanic Philology* XXXIV (1935), 39.

Although nearly all these words came into Chaucer's English from Old French, their ultimate origins are varied: *syklatoun* has been traced to Arabic, *taffata* to Persian, *samyt* and *sarge* to classical Latin and Greek. *Worsted*, as already noted, derives from an Old English place-name, the present Worstead in Norfolk; *faldyng*, associated by the *MED* with Old Norse *feldr* 'cloak', could perhaps be connected, as Linthicum has suggested, with Irish *falaing*, the same word as the Welsh *ffaling* 'mantle, cloak'.

How readily even an educated medieval audience would have been able to tell any of these fabrics from the next it is hard to say; many modern readers probably find contemporary textiles and synthetics equally baffling. What Chaucer achieves, however, is in nearly all cases a general understanding provided by contextual clues, whether in the tone of the whole passage, as in the descriptions in *Sir Thopas* with their emphasis on cost (735), mention of foreign places of manufacture (*Brugges*), and use of advertisers' adjectives (*white, fyn, cleere, bright*), or with the help of a single epithet like 'a stamyn *large*' in *The Legend of Good Women* (2360) where size entails cheapness. In the portrait of the Doctor it is the contrasting '*and yet* he was but esy of dispence', moderate in his expenditure (*Gen Prol* 441), which helps to underline the costliness of the exotic *taffata* and *sendal* in the preceding line. It is with the help of such devices, stylistic and syntactical, that Chaucer eases the intelligibility of such technical terms, some of which he was probably once again the first Englishman to use in literature.

Much the same comments apply to items of dress, as distinct from materials. Chaucer handles with astonishing dexterity numerous terms ranging from headgear to footwear, many of which were no doubt familiar to him from his wide reading, some from personal knowledge – *auctoritee* and *experience*. They include items of clothing worn by men and by women, by knights and clerics, by nuns and housewives. They include a number of common garments designated by words of Old English origin, like *barmclooth* 'apron', or *breech* 'underpants', which represents an Old English plural *brēc* – 'Thou woldest make me kisse thyn olde breech' (*PardT* 948) – but developed a new plural, *breches*, in Middle English, as in the Parson's 'they sowed of fige leves a maner of breches to hiden hire membres' (*ParsT* 330); or like *calle* 'caul, hair-net', which the Wife of Bath couples with a *cover-*

chief (*WBT* 1018) and which Chaucer in the *Astrolabe* refers to specifically as 'a wommans calle' (I, 19, 3–4). *Goore*, from O.E. *gāra* 'point of land, promontory', could mean either a triangular piece of cloth forming part of a garment as in the case of Alisoun's *barmclooth* (*MillT* 3237), or a woman's skirt or gown, or a man's coat or robe, as in the common Middle English tag 'under gore', which sometimes has, as in *Sir Thopas* (789), distinctly bawdy connotations. *Hose* derives from O.E. *hosa* and is used either in the singular, as in *The Reeve's Tale* (3933), or in the plural *hosen* (*ibid.* 3955) or *hoses* (*MillT* 3319), though neither of the plural forms is attested in rhyme; the word refers to stockings or leggings as well as tights and is used of both men's and women's garments: no doubt every reader of Chaucer remembers that the Wife of Bath's 'hosen weren of fyn scarlet reed' (*Gen Prol* 456). Another familiar word describing both men's and women's garments was *kirtel*, O.E. *cyrtel* 'man's tunic or woman's gown'; 'jolif' Absolon wears one, of light blue colour, in *The Miller's Tale* (3321). Other common words derived from Old English are *sherte, smok, weede*. An interesting nonce word, derived from a Celtic source and already recorded in the Old English gloss to St Matthew in the Lindisfarne Gospels, is *brat* 'a cloak of coarse cloth', which Chaucer uses in the Canon's Yeoman's poignant description of alchemical addicts reduced to a single *sheete* by night 'and a *brat* to walken inne by daylyght' (*CYT* 881). The *MED* cites no other Middle English occurrence of the word.[35]

On the other hand, Chaucer's vocabulary includes a good many terms of Romance origin pointing to the more fashionable *couture* of the higher orders of medieval society and to specific items of dress worn for social or professional reasons as well as for personal adornment. Criseyde is the only one of Chaucer's women to wear a *barbe*, a word meaning 'beard' in Old French (cp. *barbour* 'barber', *KnT* 2025), which here (*Tr* II, 110) refers to a piece of pleated cloth worn by a widow over or under her chin so as to cover her neck and bosom; it also formed part of a nun's headdress, the wimple, and indeed some of the manuscripts of *Troilus and Criseyde* read *wympel* here, the reading adopted in Root's edition. Both the Man of Law (*Gen Prol* 329) and the Miller's Alisoun

---

35. Henryson (as Dr. I. W. A. Jamieson has reminded me) uses the word in *The Morall Fabillis* (2945): 'now brats laid in pres' or, in the Bannatyne MS, 'now brats to imbrass'.

(*MillT* 3235) – whose husband after all was 'a riche gnof' – wear a
ceynt 'girdle', ornamented in both cases: the Man of Law's was a
silken girdle with small ornamental strips or transverse stripes
(*barres*) probably of gold or silver, as the Parson describes them
(*ParsT* 433); Alisoun's girdle was 'barred al of silk', either, like the
Man of Law's, made of silk and *barred* 'ornamented' with strips
of precious metal, or made of another material and ornamented
with strips of silk. The punctuation generally adopted by the
editors favours the latter, but a slight repunctuating of the line, to
read

> A ceynt she werede, barred, al of silk,
>   (*MillT* 3235)

would yield the former and more likely reading, for silken girdles
are specifically mentioned elsewhere, in Gower's *Confessio
Amantis*, for example: 'Ceinte of Selk' (IV, 857); and in *Sir
Gawain and the Green Knight*, where Gawain himself wears a 'silk
sayn' (589) and later receives the Lady's 'gordel of þe grene silke'
(2035), also called a *saynt* (2431), and ornamented with gold
(1832).

Various other garments could be listed here, from *voluper*, a
kind of headdress, to *galoche*, a kind of footwear, to illustrate
Chaucer's range of more uncommon sartorial terms, but the
point will have been made. Presumably the poet intended his
audience to comprehend these terms, to know what *gypon* was, or
haynselyns, or an *overslope*, or a *dyapred* cloth, or a *purfiled* sleeve; yet,
although he paid them the compliment of hoping that these terms
would be understood, he was also careful to make the task
easier with the aid of such stylistic and syntactical devices as we
have noted earlier. This is more easily achieved in passages of
description in which specific items of appearance contribute to a
total portrait which will emerge with sufficient distinctness even
if not every single detail is clear; but it is much harder to achieve
with isolated terms of a technical nature scattered here and there
through the verse. This is largely the case with such technical
language as that of law or commerce, in both of which Chaucer
was well versed. Admittedly, he uses such technical terms also in
appropriate *descriptiones personarum*, that of the Man of Law, for
example, with its 'patente and . . . pleyn commissioun', its 'fee

symple' an d 'caas and doomes alle' and the rest (*Gen Prol* 309 ff.),
or that of the Merchant

> With his bargaynes and with his chevyssaunce,
>
> (*Gen Prol* 282)

but the intention here may be rather to overwhelm the listener or
reader with the character's professional expertise than to clarify
his understanding of the technicalities involved. That the Man of
Law should use legal terms in the telling of his tale is in keeping
with Chaucer's Platonic contention 'that nedes the wordis moot
be cosynes to the thinges' (*Bo* III, pr. 12, 226–7) or 'to the dede' or
'to the werkyng', as he says elsewhere, a point elaborated in another chapter. Even Harry Bailly is made to spout legal language
as he turns to address the lawyer:

> 'Sire Man of Lawe,' quod he, 'so have ye blis,
> Telle us a tale anon, as *forward* is
> Ye been *submytted*, thurgh youre *free assent*,
> To stonden in this *cas* at my *juggement*.
> *Acquiteth* yow now of youre *biheeste*;
> Thanne have ye do youre *devoir* atte leeste.'
>
> (*CT* II, 33–8)

It is equally appropriate that the tale about the merchant of Seint-
Denys should contain its share of commercial jargon; the subject
invites it, and whatever one might think of the sentiments in
lines 11–19 reflecting a woman's point of view (they might just as
well be taken as referring to the merchant's wife, thinking aloud,
as it were, as to some hypothetical female narrator), the Shipman
who tells the tale knew much about the chapmen whom he so
readily defrauded. Hence the aptness of the jargon in *The Shipman's Tale*: the *countour-hous* and *countyng-bord*, the *acountes* and
rekenynges, the *chevyssaunce* and *reconyssaunce*, the buying and borrow-
ing ('byeth and creaunceth'), the whole merry business of high
finance:

> This marchant, which that was ful war and wys,
> Creanced hath, and payd eek in Parys
> To certeyn Lumbardes, redy in hir hond,
> The somme of gold, and gat of hem his bond;
> And hoom he gooth, murie as a papejay,
> For wel he knew he stood in swich array

That nedes moste he wynne in that viage
A thousand frankes aboven al his costage.
(*ShipT* 365–72)

The Manciple was another character familiar with business matters, being responsible for the provisions of an inn of court. Chaucer refers to him obliquely as an *achatour* 'a buyer' (*Gen Prol* 568), a word previously recorded only as a cognomen, and later uses *achaat* 'buying' (571), a word not previously recorded at all, except in *Boece* where it is explained in a gloss apropos *coempcioun*: 'Coempcioun is to seyn comune achat or beyinge togidre . . .' (*Bo* I, pr. 4, 88–9). The Manciple emerges as an expert whose skill surpasses 'the wisdom of an heep of lerned men' (575). He knew just when to buy and how to pay, whether in cash or on account, 'by taille' (570), a word which provides the wife in *The Shipman's Tale* with a bawdy pun (*ShipT* 416). Money is of course at the heart of all these activities, and Chaucer was no stranger to money even if at the end of his life he had to write those pathetic lines to his *lyght* purse, imploring it with a repeated

Beth hevy ageyn, or elles moot I dye!
(*Purse* 7, 14, 21)

Various currencies figure in the poems: the Venetian *ducat* (*HF* 1348), for example; '*floryns* fyne of gold ycoyned rounde' (*PardT* 770); *frankes* (only in *The Shipman's Tale*); *grotes*, English silver coins worth four pennies each, clearly a princely sum for Pertelote (*NPT* 2958), though negligible for the Pardoner (*PardT* 945), and chickenfeed for Pandarus (*Tr* IV, 586); the solitary Chaucerian *halfpeny* in *The Summoner's Tale* (1749); the small Genoese *jane* or 'Gene' worth about a halfpenny, hence used aptly enough in *The Clerk's Tale* (999), and ironically in *Sir Thopas* (735), for it would indeed take 'many a jane' to pay for Thopas's elegant outfit; the Host's *lussheburghes* (*CT* VII, 1962), so called because they were counterfeit coins introduced into England from Luxembourg. The *mark*, of which the Pardoner made a hundred *per annum* (*PardT* 390), was then worth two-thirds of the *pound*, hence the enormous cost of Aurelius's amorous efforts in *The Franklin's Tale* and the splendid nonchalance of his 'Fy on a thousand pound!' (*FranklT* 1227). Even the alchemist's price of 'fourty pound' for his secret was a considerable sum (*CYT* 1361). The Pardoner asks his village audience to offer 'nobles or sterlynges' (*PardT*

907; cp. also *HF* 1315), *nobles* being worth one third of a pound each and *sterlynges* being the silver pennies, 240 of which made up a pound sterling. A little later the Pardoner, this time addressing not his imaginary villagers but the Canterbury pilgrims asks for 'nobles or pens' (930). There were also French crowns, called in English *sheeldes* after the figure of a shield on one side, each worth one sixth of a pound, mentioned appropriately in *The Shipman's Tale* (331, 352) and in the portrait of the Merchant who made a profit out of foreign exchange transactions:

> Wel koude he in eschaunge sheeldes selle.
> > *(Gen Prol 278)*

Chaucer doing his *rekenynges* (*HF* 653) in the customs house or travelling about on the king's business, his travels abroad, his contact with the law and with affairs of state, all helped no doubt to enrich his knowledge of legal and administrative terms as well as those of trade and commerce. J. A. W. Bennett and D. S. Brewer have pointed to a few well-chosen words with 'a Parliamentary flavour' in *The Parliament of Fowls*: the technical use of *delyvered* (491), for example, in the sense of 'adjourned', of *presente* (531) 'en plein Parlement', of *statut* (387) and 'ryghtful *ordenaunce*' (390), and 'pleyn eleccioun' (528), and others more.[36] And mingled with these are terms of law:

> 'Whan shal youre cursede *pletynge* [pleading] have an ende?
> How sholde a *juge* eyther *parti* leve
> For ye or nay, withouten any *preve*?'
> > *(PF 495-7)*

and of scholastic debate:[37]

> ... the tercelet of the faucoun to *diffyne*
> Al here *sentence*, and as him lest, *termyne*.
> > *(ibid.* 529-30)

Other 'termes queinte of lawe', as the Shipman calls them (*CT* II, 1189), are scattered freely through most of Chaucer's work. Some of them were new to the language, like *arbitracioun* (*Mel* 1753)

36. J. A. W. Bennett, *The Parlement of Foules: An Interpretation* (Oxford, 1957), pp. 140 ff., 165 ff., and D. S. Brewer, ed., *The Parlement of Foulys* (London, 1960), p. 38.
37. See Bernard F. Huppé, 'The Translation of Technical Terms in the Middle English *Romaunt of the Rose*', *Journal of English and Germanic Philology* XLVII (1948), 334-42.

rendering the French *arbitrage*, or *executrice* (*Tr* III, 617) formed from the already current *executen* and *executour*; others have a continuous history of use back to Old English times, like *doom* or *witnesse*. Where the context requires it, the words are used in their strictly technical senses, as when the old woman in *The Friar's Tale* asks the summoner, 'May I nat *axe a libel*, sire somonour?' (*FrT* 1595), that is, see a copy of the indictment, so that she may pass it to her legal agent or *procuratour*; or as when the 'false juge' in *The Physician's Tale* (160 ff.) sat in his *consistorie* 'and yaf his *doomes* upon sondry *cas*', and the 'false cherl' asks for justice 'upon this pitous *bille* [formal plea]' which he has agreed to enter against (*pleyne*) Virginius. At other times Chaucer's meaning is an extension or modification of the legal sense; thus *feffen* 'to enfeoff' is used in its strict technical sense in *The Merchant's Tale*,

> I trowe it were to longe yow to tarie,
> If I yow tolde of every scrit and bond
> By which that she was feffed in his lond,
>
> *(MerchT* 1696–8)

but becomes an effective metaphor in Troilus's wistful

> 'Was ther non other broche [brooch] yow liste lete
> To feffe with youre newe love . . . ?'
>
> *(Tr* V, 1688–9)

The Franklin's Aurelius is capable of some impressive lawyer's English, as when he releases Dorigen from her promise:

> 'I yow relesse, madame, into youre hond
> Quyt every serement [oath] and every bond
> That ye han maad to me as heerbiforn . . .'
>
> *(FranklT* 1533–5)

He also talks about 'this *bargayn* is ful dryve' (*FranklT* 1230) and the learned clerk in the tale talks of having 'holden *covenant*' (1587), a word used in its formal legal sense in the Reeve's portrait in *The General Prologue* (600). Absolon employs *brocage* 'brokerage', hence more generally 'mediation, going-between' (*MillT* 3375) to woo Alisoun; Pandarus talks of 'chartres up to make' (*Tr* III, 340). The Monk speaks of a body of law as Nero's *decree* (*MkT* 2477), much as Arcite does when he talks of 'positif lawe and swich decree' (*KnT* 1167), where 'positif lawe', the Latin *lex positiva*, is man-made law as distinct from what the

Parson calls 'natureel lawe' (*ParsT* 921). A similar collective concept is the Physician's *equitee* (*PhysT* 181) to designate the general principles of justice. The word *verdit* is used by Nature in *The Parliament of Fowls* (525) in its legal sense of a judicial decision, though the proceedings were of course not those of a court of law. Yet it is worth recalling, as J. A. W. Bennett reminds us, 'that parliament was still, in many of its functions, a court of law',[38] hence the peculiar appropriateness of the term to the parliament of the birds. The extended sense of 'opinion' or 'decision' seems to be a Chaucerian innovation; the word is thus used by the narrator as the assembled Canterbury pilgrims ask the Host for his *voirdit* on how to conduct the *disport* of their pilgrimage (*Gen Prol* 787).

That such an extensive technical vocabulary should colour Chaucer's figurative diction is to be expected, for like Job Legh in *Mary Barton* Chaucer clearly 'loved hard words, and lawyer-like forms'. Law, like love, reflects the proper order and ordering of things, so that the poet can say with simple proverbial wisdom,

> That Love is he that alle thing may bynde,
> For may no man fordon the lawe of kynde,
> (*Tr* I, 237–8)

and then proceed to extend the concept of law into various directions, the Franklin's 'lawe of love' (*FranklT* 798), Troilus's 'lawe of compaignie' (*Tr* III, 1748), the Parson's 'lawe of oure membres', 'natureel lawe' and 'lawe of pitee' (*ParsT* 337, 921, 889). Other legal concepts are similarly translated into figurative use: wrath is 'executour of pryde' in *The Summoner's Tale* (2010), much as Fortune was pictured in *Troilus and Criseyde* (III, 617) as 'executrice of wyrdes'. A phrase applied to Fortune in Dante's *Inferno* (VII, 78) – *general ministra* – is by Chaucer transferred to destiny:

> The destinee, ministre general,
> That executeth in the world over al
> The purveiaunce that God hath seyn biforn.
> (*KnT* 1663–5)

Such figurative use of legal language is of course not Chaucer's invention, but his command of the technical vocabulary allowed

38. J. A. W. Bennett, *The Parlement of Foules: An Interpretation* (Oxford, 1957), pp. 168 f.

him to make good use of it. Already in his earliest poem, *An A B C*, Deguilleville's legal metaphors afforded Chaucer the opportunity to seek appropriate English equivalents:

> Beth ye my juge and eek my soules leche.

> Ladi, unto that court thou me ajourne
> That cleped is thi bench.

> > (*ABC* 134, 158–9)

Nor can it be doubted that to the end of his poetic career Chaucer maintained his interest in legal processes and the 'termes queinte' which describe them: in *The Nun's Priest's Tale*, probably one of his latest and most mature poems, Chaucer cannot resist the temptation to relate at some length a *felonye* which demanded 'vengeance and justice' and which led the *ministres* of that town to condemn the culprits to be 'anhanged by the nekke-bon' (*NPT* 2984–3062).

It would be possible to go further yet in our endeavour to demonstrate that Chaucer was 'in science so expert', to discuss his knowledge of the vocabulary of several other 'sciences': architecture, geography, hunting, various trades like 'the barbour, and the bocher [butcher], and the smyth' (*KnT* 2025), and the whole business of medieval knight-errantry with its elaborate armour and *asseges* and *chyvachie* and all the pomp and ritual of *justes* and *tourneiynge*, but in the invariably wise words of Dame Prudence, 'a man sholde nat doon outrage ne excesse'. Hence we shall desist from studying Chaucer any longer at work and instead watch him for a moment at play. Chaucer probably spent much of his own leisure reading 'olde bookes' which he preferred to games (*BD* 50 f.), but he also knew how some other people spent theirs, whether 'huntyng for the hare' or dissolutely haunting *folye,*

> As riot, hasard, stywes [brothels], and tavernes.

> > (*PardT* 465)

He speaks knowingly about dice, 'bicched [cursed] bones' as the Pardoner calls them (*PardT* 656), for allusions to winning and losing throws creep into several verses: 'Sevene is my chaunce, and thyn is cynk [five] and treye [three]!' (*ibid.* 653), or

Youre bagges been nat fild with ambes as,
But with sys cynk, that renneth for youre chaunce.

(MLT 124–5)

Ambes as is two aces, *ambes* ultimately from Latin *ambo* 'both', the lowest possible score, whereas *sys cynk* 'six (and) five' was a winning throw in hazard. The Man of Law's metaphor becomes even more succinct in the Monk's

Thy sys Fortune hath turned into aas.

(MkT 2661)

There are about a dozen mentions of *dys* or *dees* 'dice' in Chaucer's poems, straight references to gambling as in the Cook's enthusiastic tribute to Perkyn Revelour:

For in the toune nas ther no prentys
That fairer koude caste a paire of dys
Than Perkyn koude . . .,

(CkT 4385–7)

or metaphors of changing fortune:

'Wel hath Fortune yturned thee the dys'.

(KnT 1238)

And after that thise dees torned on chaunces,
So was he outher glad or seyde 'allas!'

(Tr II, 1347–8)

When the Parson turns to *hasardrie* he is made to reveal yet more of Chaucer's knowledge of gambling by mentioning *tables*, the usual word for backgammon until the seventeenth century, and *rafles* 'raffles', a game played with three dice (*ParsT* 793). Chaucer himself preferred reading rather 'then play either at ches or tables' (*BD* 51), but both these were obviously quite accepted pastimes, as with the young ladies in *The Franklin's Tale* (900), despite the Parson's gloomy catalogue of disasters consequent upon *hasardrie* and its *apurtenaunces*, to wit 'deceite, false othes, chidynges, and alle ravynes, blasphemynge and reneiynge of God, and hate of his neighebores, wast of goodes, mysspendynge of tyme, and somtyme manslaughtre' (*ParsT* 793) – a veritable epitome of *The Pardoner's Tale*.

The game of chess in *The Book of the Duchess* can stand (modest) comparison with Pope's more justly famous game of ombre in

The Rape of the Lock, even though the odds were plainly on Fortune's side, especially after she had, 'with hir false draughtes [moves]', taken her opponent's *fers* 'queen'. After that

> . . . 'Mat!' in myd poynt of the chekker [board],
> With a poun [pawn] errant, allas!
>
> (*BD* 660–1)

was inevitable. Chaucer may have preferred books, but he knew how to play chess.

One other game deserves mention, if only to record once again as F. P. Magoun did long ago,[39] that Chaucer was the first English man of letters to give it literary respectability: football. That football was well established by Chaucer's time is evident from a reference to it in a proclamation as early as the reign of Edward II which Magoun quotes. Chaucer's allusion is not unambiguous; it occurs in the middle of the great tournament in *The Knight's Tale*:

> Ther stomblen steedes stronge, and doun gooth al;
> He rolleth under foot as dooth a bal,
>
> (*KnT* 2613–4)

but the simile suggests, as does Dryden's rendering ('One rolls along, a football to his foes'), that Chaucer was indeed thinking of football.

Perhaps squash or tennis should be added to football as another sport with which Chaucer was familiar, in view of this passage in *Troilus and Criseyde*:

> 'Thow biddest me I shulde love another
> Al fresshly newe, and lat Criseyde go!
> It lith nat in my power, leeve brother;
> And though I myght, I wolde nat do so.
> But kanstow playen raket, to and fro,
> Nettle in, dok out, now this, now that, Pandare?
> Now foule falle hire for thi wo that care!'
>
> (*Tr* IV, 456–62)

The *OED* is probably wrong in assuming that *raket* is 'some game played with dice', an interpretation apparently based on a misreading of a passage in Lydgate. More probably, to 'playen raket' was a game not unlike squash or tennis, hence its appropriateness

39. F. P. Magoun, Jr., 'Football in Medieval England and in Middle-English Literature', *American Historical Review* XXXV (1929), 33–45.

to a context in which Troilus rebukes Pandarus's advocacy of inconstancy. The idioms 'to and fro', and 'now this, now that' suit both the image of playing *raket* and the theme of inconstancy. So does the reference to the traditional charm recited when rubbing dock leaves over a nettle-sting ('Nettle in, dock out, Dock in, nettle out, Nettle in, dock out, Dock rub nettle out', *OED*), which acquired, in shorter form, proverbial status expressive of inconstancy as well as possessing something of the mesmeric effect of watching a game of squash or tennis.

Few people, even among his most devoted admirers, would wish to claim that Chaucer was, as Goethe was, a considerable man of science in his own time. But Chaucer was possessed, as Shakespeare was, of an insatiable curiosity about people, and this embraced all those diverse activities which have been the subject of our lexical scrutiny in this chapter, 'Al this newe science that men lere' clearly fascinated Chaucer for its own sake, for its human implications, and for its artistic potential. There are some fields, like astronomy or alchemy, in which he acquired considerable expertise; there are others, like music or natural history, in which he displays no more than the familiarity of an educated Englishman of his time. Much of his familiarity, as well as of his expertise, undoubtedly was book-learning: this has been particularly well demonstrated with reference to Chaucer's nautical metaphors, nearly all in *Troilus and Criseyde*, by Paull F. Baum, and on a grander scale in the work of Claes Schaar,[40] but there are, as we have noted, occasional indications of personal *assay*, of Chaucer's keen eye and good ear, and the *Treatise on the Astrolabe* is palpable proof, and possibly the *Equatorie of the Planetis* also, of the poet's personal involvement with at least one important medieval science.

If Chaucer's technical vocabulary – its range, variety, origins – is of linguistic interest for its own sake, it is no less of critical interest for the reader of Chaucer's poetry. Like Donne with his 'new philosophy' or T. S. Eliot drawing the diction of modern technology into the service of poetry, Chaucer innovated with technical terms on a considerable scale. This is perhaps the hardest

40. Paull F. Baum. 'Chaucer's Nautical Metaphors', *The South Atlantic Quarterly* XLIX (1950, 67–73). Claes Schaar, *Some Types of Narrative in Chaucer's Poetry* (Lund, 1954) and *The Golden Mirror: Studies in Chaucer's Descriptive Technique and its Literary Background* (Lund, 1955, repr. 1967).

part of his achievement for the modern reader to gauge adequately, for familiarity with many of Chaucer's rare and novel words, long since grown common in English usage, makes us insensitive to the poignant and memorable novelty many such words clearly possessed for the poet and his audience. This applies not solely to Chaucer's technical vocabulary, but it is particularly true of it; and one can only conclude that many more passages in Chaucer's work must have presented difficulties and obscurities for contemporary readers than we commonly imagine today. In such passages lies a peculiar challenge for us, of course, leading to constant reward in the discovery of new insights, of unsuspected ambiguities and ironies, and of aesthetic satisfaction. For, however much Chaucer delighted in parading his rich technical vocabulary, he was sensitive and sensible enough to employ it with skill and tact. Hence the tempering of alchemical severities with light-hearted colloquialisms, hence the admixture of familiar devotional words into passages of abstruse theology, hence the painstaking explanations, definitions, and glosses of strange words. Moreover, it is the peculiar alchemy of the poet that can transform technical jargon into poetic diction. Chaucer does not always achieve this; there are undoubtedly passages in his poetry where jargon remains jargon, where the accumulated technicalities read like a glossary of 'hard langage', not like poetry. The Franklin's description of the clerk of Orleans at work on his geological miracle is of this kind. It is an exercise in bafflement and as such it succeeds. The poetry comes later, when Dorigen is told of the 'miracle' in a line that stands in sharp contrast to all the astronomical paraphernalia:

'But wel I woot the rokkes been aweye',
(*FranklT* 1338)

and when Chaucer depicts Dorigen's reaction, with a superb economy of language that contrasts even more sharply with all the verbiage that went before:

He taketh his leve, and she astoned stood;
In al hir face nas a drope of blood.
She wende nevere han come in swich a trappe.
(*ibid.* 1339–41)

What redeems the Franklin's passage is, of course, the disarming prefatory avowal 'I ne kan no termes of astrologye', just as the Eagle's or Pertelote's jargon is made sweet through coming from a bird's beak, and the Canon's Yeoman's textbook lore by emanating from a 'lewed' man turned 'philosophre'. For, except in the *Astrolabe*, and even there little Lewis is hovering attentively (one hopes) in the background, Chaucer's science is always closely linked to people (or birds): theology is the Parson 'in his techyng', alchemy is what reduces wealthy and gullible people to a *brat*, medicine is the Doctour of Phisik keeping his patient 'in houres by his magyk natureel', astronomy is the cock knowing 'ech ascencioun', and so on. In such contexts the often new, rare, exotic words of Chaucer's scientific vocabulary may still baffle, but the reader accepts them as part of the total human enigma which Chaucer is exploring and to which they are made to contribute their own share of ambiguity and irony and mystery. It is because Chaucer was 'in science so expert' and because he had mastered and to some extent created the appropriate English vocabulary, that he was able, as a poet, to make such good use of all 'this elvysshe nyce loore'.

CHAPTER 7

The Wordes Moote be Cosyn
to the Dede

🙚🙚🙚🙚🙚

CHAUCER would have approved of Swift's definition of style as 'proper words in proper places'. At least one may think so in view of his adopting as a literary principle the Platonic sentiment which forms the heading of this chapter, 'the wordes moote be cosyn to the dede' (*Gen Prol* 742). The importance of this *sentence* is indicated by its position towards the end of the *Prologue* to *The Canterbury Tales* before the pilgrims are allowed to speak for themselves. It is reiterated later in the poem by the Manciple who refers to himself modestly as 'a man noght textueel' (*Manc T* 235), but who displays at the same time that interesting propensity towards linguistic precision which we have noted in another context.[1] This is the Manciple's wording:

> The wise Plato seith, as ye may rede,
> The word moot nede accorde with the dede.
> If men shal telle proprely a thyng,
> The word moot cosyn be to the werkyng.
>
> (*Manc T* 207–10)

Jean de Meun, from whose portion of the *Roman de la Rose* Chaucer probably derived this idea, mentions Plato and uses the figure of words being *cousines* to deeds, but Chaucer met the Platonic saying also in Boethius's *Consolatio*, so that he rewords it yet again in *Boece*: 'thow hast lernyd by the sentence of Plato that nedes the wordis moot be cosynes to the thinges of whiche thei speken' (*Bo* III, pr. 12, 205–7).

Chaucer had obviously taken this *sentence* to heart and made it something of a touchstone in his 'rehearsing' of other people's words. The passage in *The General Prologue* outlines his reportorial policy for *The Canterbury Tales* in a manner, not without parallel

1. See ch. 4, p. 208.

in medieval literature, obviously designed to absolve him from any imputations of *vileynye* or untruthfulness. The immediate concern is to prepare the way for the 'cherles termes' that are to come, and this is expressed even more overtly in the authorial comments preceding *The Miller's Tale*:

> What sholde I moore seyn, but this Millere
> He nolde his wordes for no man forbere,
> But tolde his cherles tale in his manere.
> M'athynketh that I shal reherce it heere.
> And therfore every gentil wight I preye,
> For Goddes love, demeth nat that I seye
> Of yvel entente, but for I moot reherce
> Hir tales alle, be they bettre or werse,
> Or elles falsen som of my mateere.
>
> *(CT* I, 3167–75)

But we are clearly justified in looking beyond the Miller's and Reeve's *harlotrie* to Chaucer's rehearsal of other pilgrims' tales as well, 'be they bettre or werse'. In the earlier passage no specific speakers are mentioned. Chaucer is enunciating a general principle: his task is 'to telle yow hir wordes and hir cheere' (*Gen Prol* 728), to be accurate, to change or conceal nothing:

> Whoso shal telle a tale after a man,
> He moot reherce as ny as evere he kan
> Everich a word.
>
> *(Gen Prol* 731–3)

And to clinch it all there is not only Plato but Christ:

> Crist spak hymself ful brode [openly] in hooly writ,
> And wel ye woot no vileynye is it.
>
> *(ibid.* 739–40)

Chaucer's primary purpose may well have been to warn his audience that *harlotrie* was in the air, much as Jean de Meun was invoking Plato to sanction the use of coarse language, but his wording is sufficiently general to encourage the belief that he was seeking a kind of verisimilitude not merely in the speech of his vulgar characters. The purpose of the present chapter is to test this belief by examining the language of some of Chaucer's more prominent speakers.

While there is probably general concurrence in Muscatine's

view of the contrasting idioms represented in *Troilus and Criseyde* by Troilus and Pandarus, with Criseyde speaking in both,[2] *The Canterbury Tales*, unfinished and with a much larger number of speakers, presents a different and more complex problem. Some critics consider the ascription of some of the tales to particular tellers fortuitous and find little stylistic and linguistic evidence in favour of more deliberate casting and distinguishing on Chaucer's part. In view of the fragmentary state of the work and of some of the tales, and in the absence of fuller portraits for some of the tellers, it is certainly not possible to be dogmatic. Yet, if Chaucer meant anything at all by 'wordes moote be cosyn to the dede', then it is fair to try to assess how far he may have been attempting to match words and whatever the word *dedes* implies in *The Canterbury Tales*, and how far he was successful. But we must be clear what we are looking for. By 'deeds' Chaucer meant both the 'thinges of whiche thei [his characters] speken' and the manner in which their personalities expressed themselves in speech and action. I find myself on the side of those critics who are suspicious of any 'anxious seeking', as John Lawlor puts it, 'after the certainty of dramatic relevance', or of any 'close congruence of teller and tale'.[3] This certainly exists in some cases, but it is difficult to believe that Chaucer was primarily concerned in *The Canterbury Tales* with the tales as expressions or developments of the characters of the tellers. On the other hand, Chaucer is keenly aware of the way different people speak and there are many indications that he is creating different idioms or, if we so prefer, different registers, for his various characters. This does not mean closely sustained verisimilitude of tone and diction according to any strictly naturalistic canons, but rather a more general labelling of a person's speech which affords the reader occasional moments of pleased recognition. The Man of Law's words, for example, 'weren so wise', we are told in *The General Prologue* (313), which is borne out not by a constant stream of sagacious utterance, but by a happy sprinkling of *wise*, that is, rare, learned, uncommon words, like *argumenten* or *diurnal*, in his tale. The Merchant uttered his opinions 'ful solempnely' (*ibid.* 274), so that we are prepared both for the *solempne* debate on marriage which takes up a third of

2. Muscatine, ch. 5. Cp. also Robert O. Payne, *The Key of Remembrance: A Study of Chaucer's Poetics* (New Haven and London, 1963), pp. 197 ff.
3. John Lawlor, *Chaucer* (London, 1968), pp. 111, 115.

The Merchant's Tale and for the *solempne*, in the sense of 'pompous', manner in which the narrator describes some of the incidents. Even when the 'solemnity' breaks down for the moment, as in 2351-3, the resulting incongruity tends to highlight it even further.

Such 'labelling' of the speech of his characters goes back to Chaucer's earliest poems. The bereaved knight in *The Book of the Duchess* speaks simply and plainly:

> Loo! how goodly spak thys knyght,
> As hit had be another wyght;
> He made hyt nouther towgh ne queynte.

> *(BD* 529-31)

The irony of the situation is that, although the knight did not make his speech hard for his listener, the latter failed to understand what was amiss, or at least pretended to, until the blunt 'She ys ded!' twenty-five lines from the end of the poem. Indeed much of the irony depends upon the knight telling his story in simple terms, 'nouther towgh ne queynte', and of the reader being explicitly reminded of this by the Dreamer's inability to comprehend,

> 'Thou wost ful lytel what thou menest;
> I have lost more than thow wenest',

> *(ibid.* 743-4)

and by the knight's own reiteration,

> 'Allas! myn herte ys wonder woo
> That I ne kan discryven hyt!
> Me lakketh both Englyssh and wit
> For to undo hyt at the fulle;
> And eke my spirites be so dulle
> So gret a thyng for to devyse.
> I have no wit that kan suffise
> To comprehenden hir beaute.

> *(ibid.* 896-903)

There is irony of a different kind in *The House of Fame* where the Eagle prides himself on delivering his scientific discourse in a manner which Bishop Sprat might have approved of –

> 'Withoute any subtilite
> Of speche, or gret prolixite

Of termes of philosophie,
Of figures of poetrie,
Or colours of rethorike' –

(*HF* 855–9)

while at the same time displaying some propensity for precisely
those subtleties and technicalities ('termes of philosophie') which
he is denying. How else should one describe words like *cadence*,
covercle, palpable, renovelaunces, reparacions, sisoures, and others which
no one else uses in Chaucer and some of which the Eagle appears
to have been the first English bird to utter? That the Eagle's
denial of 'colours of rethorike' is to be treated with similar cau-
tion has been well demonstrated.[4] Chaucer here for the first time
couples 'hard langage' with protestations to the contrary: he does
it for the last time, albeit without irony, in the *Astrolabe* where
the assurance of 'naked wordes' and 'light Englissh' is followed,
inevitably, by a good many technicalities couched in appropriate
jargon.

But there is more to the Eagle's personal idiom than this ironic
credibility gap. Clemen has pointed to some of the bird's characteristic turns of speech, his emphatic phrases, his repeated addresses and rejoinders to his listener, and the patronizing tone,[5]
and to these we might add some others. There are the Eagle's
oaths, for example, with their interesting assortment of saints,
'Seynte Marye' (*HF* 573), 'seynt Jame' (885), 'Seynt Julyan' (1022),
'Seynte Clare' (1066), and their highly idiosyncratic, and comi-
cally suggestive, substitution of the usual 'by my trouthe' twice
with 'by *thy* trouthe' (613, 889), and the no less comic juxtaposition
of 'also *God* me blesse' with an immediately following '*Joves* halt
hyt gret humblesse' (629–30). The Eagle is fond of little interjections like 'let see!', 'now wel', 'a ha!', 'ywys', and especially
'lo(o)' which he manages to insert into any suitable opening in
his lines, sometimes in quite rapid succession:

'Til Jupiter, loo, atte laste,
Hym slow, and fro the carte caste.
Loo, ys it not a gret myschaunce . . . ?'

(*HF* 955–7)

4. See Florence E. Teager, 'Chaucer's Eagle and the Rhetorical Colors', *PMLA*
XLVII (1932), 410–18.
5. Clemen, p. 99.

372

or:

'Seynt Julyan, loo, bon hostel!
Se here the Hous of Fame, lo!'

(ibid. 1022–3)

Inevitably, the informal tone to which these interjections contribute their share is sustained in the manner particularly encouraged by the octosyllabic verse, namely by frequent colloquial phrases which may not be unique to the Eagle, as some of his oaths are, but which are an important ingredient of Chaucerian colloquial English, as we have noted elsewhere. They also help to break up the Eagle's sometimes lengthy and syntactically complex sentences, like that prolix *enumeratio* of nearly thirty lines beginning at line 672, in which something of a pause is afforded by a few idioms ('dar I leye', 'no man wot why', 'and over-al wel') and figures ('but as a blynd man stert an hare', 'then greynes be of sondes') of a more conventional kind. In one instance the Eagle permits himself what Robinson calls a 'most peculiar' construction of an adjective taking a direct object:

'As most conservatyf the soun [sound]'.

(ibid. 847)

Chaucer is here treating the adjective *conservatyf* as if it were a participle instead of following it with a preposition as in the case of 'fugityf of Troy contree' in *The House of Fame*, 146. Perhaps he was on somewhat unsure ground, as the word *conservatyf* was not previously recorded in English as far as we know, and other adjectives with the same ending, like *actif* (*Bo* I, pr. 1, 30), *contemplatif* (*ibid.* 32), *fugityf* (*HF* 146), *retentif* (*ParsT* 913), *ymaginatyf* (*FranklT* 1094, *Bo* V, pr. 4, 211), are not common in his work: the occurrences here listed are the only ones. These words function as normal adjectives, usually in postnominal positions. The word *embelif* 'oblique(ly)', which occurs only in the *Astrolabe*, is of different origin, deriving from a phrase, O.Fr. *en be(s)lif*, and is used by Chaucer both as adjective and (like the related *abelef* in *Sir Gawain and the Green Knight*, 2486, 2517) as adverb.

To relish the Eagle's idiom to the full requires that it be heard in its proper setting, the comic dialogue with his captive listener whose generally curt replies stand in sharp contrast to the bird's pedagogic volubility. That Chaucer may have been putting a little of his own expository manner into the Eagle's speech may be gleaned from those magisterial touches which humanize the rather dry technicalities of the *Astrolabe* some years later. But more immediately 'the Eagle is', in Muscatine's words (p. 111), 'a study for Pandarus'. Admittedly, there are some distinctive voices in *The Parliament of Fowls*, but these are momentary utterances, like the *kakelynge* of the goose, and for Chaucer's first major, fully sustained attempt at matching words and deeds we must turn to *Troilus and Criseyde*.

Pandarus's idiom, like Troilus's and Criseyde's, has often been commented upon but usually in very general terms, and while it may be difficult to improve on Muscatine's perceptive remarks in chapter 5 of his *Chaucer and the French Tradition*, it is worth trying to fill in some of the details. No reader of *Troilus and Criseyde* can fail to recognize the bouncing, confident vitality of Pandarus's speech, at least until the final inevitability of the truth renders him speechless – 'I kan namore seye' (*Tr* V, 1743) – but critics have rarely attempted to single out those linguistic features which give it its distinctive tone. Some of the ingredients of Pandarus's speech are the same, as is to be expected, as are found among kindred characters: his sententiousness equals that of the Wife of Bath, his many colloquial idioms recall the Eagle and anticipate several of the Canterbury pilgrims, his vocabulary has affinities with Harry Bailly's. But in creating the common substance of a colloquial level of speech Chaucer was artist enough to vary the accidents: the later characters are no mere repetitions or copies of Pandarus. The latter's idiom emerges and remains in several ways distinctively his own.

Troilus picks on Pandarus's aggressive sententiousness quite early in the poem:

'For thi proverbes may me naught availle',
(*Tr* I, 756)

and for good measure adds a few lines later:

'Lat be thyne olde ensaumples, I the preye'.
(*ibid.* 760)

But some of Pandarus's 'proverbes' and 'olde ensaumples' are much more truly *cosyn* to the man than others. He alone in the poem talks of sweat, hence the aptness of his

'For hym men demen hoot that men seen swete'.

(*Tr* II, 1533)

Having achieved his purpose to bring the lovers togther, Pandarus bows out with an appropriately comic platitude:

'This light, nor I, ne serven here of nought.
Light is nought good for sike folkes yën!'

(*Tr* III, 1136–7)

In the next book, Pandarus gives a nocturnal twist to a common proverbial figure:

'Ek wonder last but nyne *nyght* nevere in towne'.

(*Tr* IV, 588)

And even in the final book of *Troilus and Criseyde*, when the earlier buoyancy has been deflated into a pitiful clinging to whatever 'olde ensaumples' are left to him, Pandarus is still muttering them to himself in his own characteristic voice:

And to hymself ful sobreliche he seyde,
'From haselwode, there joly Robyn pleyde,
Shal come al that that thow abidest heere.
Ye, fare wel al the snow of ferne [previous] yere!'

(*Tr* V, 1173–6)

It is Pandarus who gives but 'a straw for alle swevenes signifiaunce' (*Tr* V, 362), an idiom to be echoed by appropriate voices in *The Canterbury Tales*, who talks of the 'waggyng of a stree [straw]' (II, 1745), and of people disputing 'how this candele in the strawe is falle' (III, 859), rather than getting on with putting the fire out. This mixture of sententious commonplaces and naturalistic imagery is typical of Pandarus's diction. His are the three 'hazelwood' idioms in the poem; he alone refers to a *wheston* 'whetstone', to *slynge-stones* and *milnestones*; he talks of dying 'here as a gnat' (IV, 595) and of laying 'oure jolite on presse' (I, 559) which is a fitting expression to emanate from him, whether *presse* refers to a clothes press, hence meaning putting away, out of sight, or refers to a wine press, with the meaning of squashing, reducing, diminishing – both possible alternatives. Many of Pandarus's colloquial phrases contribute to the distinctive character of his idiom: 'on me is nought along [not my fault] thyn yvel fare' (II, 1001), and 'but it were on hym along' (III, 783), that is his fault;

'to don thyn eris [ears] glowe' (II, 1022); 'by God . . . I hoppe
alwey byhynde' (II, 1107); 'for my bettre arm' (II, 1650), for my
right arm, that is for anything; 'lat se whiche of yow shal bere
the belle' (III, 198), win the prize, take the lead; 'wel worthe of
dremes ay thise olde wives' (V, 379), leave dreams to old women.
Where colloquial turns of phrase occur in clusters, they are often
buttressed by oaths. Pandarus's racy tone is suggested by appropriate
syntactic patterns. These may be a succession of short sentences:

> 'Look up, I seye, and telle me what she is
> Anon, that I may gon about thy nede.
> Knowe ich hire aught? For my love, telle me this.
> Than wolde I hopen rather for to spede',
>
> (Tr I, 862–5)

or an accumulation of clauses:

> 'And nece myn – ne take it naught agrief –
> If that ye suffre hym al nyght in this wo,
> God help me so, ye hadde hym nevere lief, –
> That dar I seyn, now ther is but we two'.
>
> (Tr III, 862–5)

Occasionally, Chaucer puts into Pandarus's speech some grammatical idiosyncrasy sufficiently uncommon to attract notice. He
is the only Chaucerian character to use the rare Middle English
construction 'konne *it counseil kepe*' (I, 992), that is to keep it a
secret, instead of the more usual *kepen counseil* or, in the Wife of
Bath's words, 'a conseil hyde' (*WBT* 966). In II, 379 Pandarus
uses *regneth* 'reigns' transitively, with a direct object 'al this town',
of which there does not appear to be any other Middle English
example. An interesting construction occurs in 'now were it
tyme a lady to gon henne' (III, 630), where modern English
would require a preposition, '*for* a lady'; elsewhere Chaucer
uses this construction twice in prose (*Bo* III, pr. 6, 18–19; *ParsT*
469), and only once in verse (*KnT* 2288). Pandarus has the rare
French plural -*s* ending for the adjective *infernal*, placed before
its noun, ascribed to him by six manuscripts of *Troilus and
Criseyde*, a reading accepted by all recent editors,

> 'That they ben infernals illusiouns',
>
> (Tr V, 368)

but such linguistic subtlety – if that is what is intended – is not typical of Pandarus.

Nor is technical language typical of the man. A rare legalism occurs, like the reference to *chartres* (III, 340), or the use of *feffe* 'to endow, present' (III, 901), here 'with a fewe wordes white' much as Chaucer uses the word in *Boece*: '*tho feffedestow Fortune with glosynge wordes*' (*Bo* II, pr. 3, 64–5). From the liturgical act of contrition, the *Confiteor*, in the sacrament of penance, Pandarus derives, somewhat anachronistically as has been observed, the beating of the breast at the words *mea culpa*:

'Now bet thi brest, and sey to God of Love,
Thy grace, lord, for now I me repente'.
(*Tr* I, 932–3)

He uses the words *mea culpa* in the following book, ascribing them to Troilus talking in his sleep (II, 525). Both passages illustrate strikingly how readily liturgical language could be adapted by a medieval poet to the theme of *fine amour*. Pandarus's knowledge of natural history is largely enshrined in proverbial utterances, as in his comment to Criseyde:

'The harm is don, and fare-wel feldefare!'
(*Tr* III, 861)

This is closely paralleled in 'go, farewel, feldefare' of the *Romaunt of the Rose* (5510), an addition by the translator, but Chaucer's only other certain reference to this bird is as 'the frosty feldefare', concluding the catalogue of birds in *The Parliament of Fowls* (364). The allusion to the fieldfare is usually explained, by the *OED* and elsewhere, as meaning something like 'good riddance', with reference to the bird's departure northwards at the end of winter. But Pandarus's innuendo may be more subtle than that, for the fieldfare, as Gilbert White observed with wonder in *The Natural History of Selborne* (Letter XXVI to Thomas Pennant, December 8, 1769), goes northwards *to breed*. The expression 'nought worth an hawe', that is a haw, the fruit of the hawthorn (III, 854), Pandarus shares with the Wife of Bath; but the expression 'nought worth two fecches' (III, 936), vetches, a variety of bean, he shares with no one else.

It may be a bit foolhardy to claim anything like a 'private' or 'personal' vocabulary for any of Chaucer's characters, and yet the reader of Chaucer cannot help associating at least some words intimately with the speech of some of the characters. The Miller's rich *gnof* springs to mind, the Wife of Bath's *bele chose*, the Pardoner's *a-blakeberyed*, the Friar's *rebekke* and *ribibe*, Harry Bailly's *drasty* and *clobbed* and *coillons* and *fructuous*. Pandarus has quite a number of words which are securely his own within the Chaucer canon and for the most part they are words with an informal, if not always a colloquial, ring about them. He does use some 'learned' words, as most of Chaucer's people do, for Chaucer does not strive for anything resembling total verisimilitude; words are to be 'cousins', nothing closer, hence one feels no shock or surprise to hear Pandarus contributing to Chaucer's vocabulary (if I may put it this way) words like *diffusioun* and *disavaunce* and *hardyment*. But the 'real' voice of Pandarus rings through *Troilus and Criseyde* on a different register with the aid of words more truly cousin to the *werkyng* of such an exceptionally garrulous man. On a par with his strings of sententious offerings and racy colloquialisms, with his 'olde hat' and his 'fy on the devel!' are those of Pandarus's words which, while they may be unique in Chaucer and, so far as we can tell, rare or even unique in written Middle English, yet possess a colloquial flavour and intimacy quite remote from the more studied exoticism of words like *diffusioun*. No one knows quite what a *fare-carte* is, for example, yet it suits Pandarus as he explains away Troilus's fancied vision of the returning Criseyde:

'That I se yond nys but a fare-carte'.

(*Tr* V, 1162)

Not some false creation, apparently just a plain wagon of sorts carrying some load or other 'withoute the yates'. It is indeed just possible that *fare-carte* is a slang term for a common woman: one recalls Conscience referring to Lady Meed 'as comune as a cartwey to eche a knaue that walketh' (*PP* B III, 131), much as Prince Hals calls Doll Tearsheet' 'some road' (*2 Henry IV*, II, ii). But it is mainly verbs which Pandarus makes his own, verbs like *biblotte* 'to cover with stains' (II, 1027), *jompre* 'to jumble' (II, 1037), *jouken* 'to roost, rest, lurk' (V, 409), *motre* 'to mutter' (II, 541), *mucche* 'to munch' (I, 914), *titerying* 'hesitating' (II, 1744); and some memorable adjectives like *scryvenyssh* which loses all its distinctive character when glossed prosaically as 'in the manner of a scrivener, or professional scribe' (II, 1026), or *unapt* (I, 978). The latter belongs to the group of 'un-' words particularly common in *Troilus and Criseyde* and *Boece* to which Pandarus contributed his share, including the line which Spenser's friend E. K. singled out as the opening words of his prefatory epistle to *The Shepheardes Calender*:

'Unknowe, unkist, and lost, that is unsought'.

(*Tr* I, 809)

Pandarus's vocabulary, like the rest of Chaucer's, has many springs, and there is little enlightenment to be derived from tracing his more personal choices to their sources. He was evidently as familiar with words derived from Old French as with Old English ones; of the verbs listed above, several appear to be imitative in origin: *jompre, motre, mucche*. He plays with grammatical categories by turning nouns into verbs:

'And strengest *feythed* ben, I undirstonde'.

(*Tr* I, 1007)

'Han evere thus *proverbed* to us yonge'.

(*Tr* III, 293)

He makes up compounds out of familiar elements as in *wantrust* 'lack of trust' (I, 794), used later once also by the Manciple (*MancT* 281), on the analogy of *wanhope* 'lack of hope'. He helps to keep in circulation less common native words like *hameled* 'maimed, mutilated' (II, 964), from O.E. *hamelian* 'to hamstring', as well as to give impetus to more recent adoptions from Romance sources, like *remors* 'remorse' (I, 554). Pandarus's linguistic 'apparatus' thus reflects the man, his restless activity and energy, his inventiveness and vitality and humour, as well as, in his bourgeois attitudes and folksy wisdom, the limitations of his vision. Both in his own right and as a foil to Troilus, Pandarus demonstrates something of Chaucer's success at making words match 'the werkyng'.

Pandarus is kin to the Wife of Bath and to Harry Bailly, though his English lacks their vulgarity. Of the three, the Host is the crudest, mainly because of the nature and frequency of his swearing, but he knows his station, as a good publican should, and is capable of speaking 'as curteisly as it had been a mayde'

(*CT* VII, 445) when occasion demands it. The contrast between his concluding words to the Shipman and his invitation to the Prioress to tell her tale proves it to a nicety. Chaucer's initial characterization of Harry Bailly's speech is *boold* (*Gen Prol* 755), which the *MED* glosses misguidedly as 'well-spoken' (*s.v. bōld*, adj. 6 (a)). When applied to speech M.E. *bold* connotes several of the qualities appropriate to persons: strength, sturdiness, confidence, even brazenness, but most of the occurrences of the word suggest forthrightness and perhaps crudeness. The owl in *The Owl and the Nightingale* refers to her voice as 'bold and nouht vnorne' (317), forthright and not a whit decrepit, and Robert Mannyng speaks of 'oþys bolde', brazen, shameless oaths, hardly 'well-spoken'. The Manciple's crow tells Phebus 'by wordes bolde', in plain, undisguised language (*MancT* 258), of what took place between Phebus's wife and her *lemman*, and Chaucer himself clinches the point when he refers to Harry Bailly's words in another context thus:

> Thanne spak oure Hoost with rude speche and boold.
> (*CT* VII, 2808)

Everything Harry Bailly says bears out the interpretation of *boold* as forthright to the point of crudeness. That Chaucer, in the same line of *The General Prologue*, paying tribute, tinged with irony, to his practical sagacity, calls him also 'wys, and wel ytaught' does not conflict with this impression of his speech. He was a thoroughly practical man, not without cunning, for 'wily and wys' go well together (cp. *CT* VII, 1940), nor yet without some smattering of higher things than suppers and corny ale. He can bandy about 'pieces and rags' of various learned trades and professions, bits of medical and legal jargon as appropriate, picked up inevitably in his dealings with the sundry folk who passed through his hostelry. But his knowledge was superficial, he was 'nat depe ystert in loore' (*CT* II, 4), he 'kan nat speke in terme' (*CT* VI, 311), he can put up a brave ('boold'!) show of technical expertise, but it does not amount to much. Compared with those of Chaucer's characters who are truly 'in science so expert', Harry Bailly is 'lewed'. His linguistic blunders are further tokens of this, to wit his *cardynacle* for *cardiacle*, his idiosyncratic Latinisms *corpus dominus* and the delightfully enigmatic *corpus Madrian* with its

380

aroma of spicery;[6] so is the instant jargon of 'a large man' (*Gen Prol* 753) blundering amid delicate glassware –

> 'And eek thyne urynals and thy jurdones,
> Thyn ypocras, and eek thy galiones'
> (*CT* VI, 305–6)

– and so also is the uneasy suspicion that 'heigh style' may be beyond him:

> 'Youre termes, youre colours, and youre figures,
> Keepe hem in stoor til so be that ye endite
> Heigh style, as whan that men to kynges write.
> Speketh so pleyn at this tyme, we yow preye,
> That we may understonde what ye seye'.
> (*CT* IV, 16–20)

Courtly diction is not for Harry Bailly, whereas Pandarus can command it and the Wife of Bath's *Tale* is a victory for *gentillesse* in more ways than one. Harry's vocabulary, like Pandarus's, embraces some *termes*, the scraps of jargon, as well as other learned words like *discoloured*, *fructuous*, *jocunde*, *penant* 'penitent', *reclayme*, *sophyme* 'sophism, subtlety', but like Pandarus also his normal register tends the other way, only further still. This is the proper place for the Host's 'personal' vocabulary of 'bold and rude' words: *clobbed*, *coillons*, *dogerel*, *drasty*, *fneseth*, *rampeth*, *sluttish*, *toord*, as well as for other words of the same ilk shared with speakers of the same persuasion: *clappeth*, *labbyng*, and the like. He has his occasional euphemism like Alys of Bath, though for less complex reasons, and can refer to the Monk's supposed or suspected sexual practices in various sly phrases:

> 'Thou woldest han been a tredefowel aright.
> Haddestow as greet a leeve, as thou hast myght,
> To parfourne al thy lust in engendrure,
> Thou haddest bigeten ful many a creature.
>
> . . . .
>
> Religioun hath take up al the corn
> Of tredyng, and we borel men been shrympes.
>
> . . . .
>
> This maketh that oure wyves wole assaye
> Religious folk, for ye mowe bettre paye

6. See above ch. 5, pp. 280–1.

Of Venus paiementz than mowe we;
God woot, no lussheburghes payen ye!'
(*CT* VII, 1945–61)

But he can be as blunt as any churl when addressing his social equal:

'Or hastow with som quene al nyght yswonke,
So that thow mayst nat holden up thyn heed?'
(*CT* IX, 18–19)

Besides such more personal features, the Host's language shares the general characteristics of Chaucer's colloquial English, oaths, tags, clichés, loose syntax, as in the epilogue to *The Merchant's Tale* (*CT* IV, 2419 ff.) or in the prologue to *The Monk's Tale* (*CT* VII, 1913 ff.), and many idiomatic turns of phrase. Harry is fond of 'no fors', no matter, of phrases like 'lat se now' and 'I dar wel sayn'; he does not care a bean, mite, straw, butterfly; he alludes to Lollers (*CT* II, 1173), twice-heated pies ('Jakke of Dovere', *CT* I, 4347), and popular games ('Dun is in the myre', *CT* IX, 5). He has occasion to address all kinds of people and on some he bestows some interesting epithets: 'o Jankin, be ye there?' (*CT* II, 1172); 'thou beel amy' (*CT* VI, 318); 'this were a popet in an arm t'enbrace' (*CT* VII, 701); 'thou woldest han been a tredefowel aright' (*CT* VII, 1945, 3451). He addresses most of his fellow-pilgrims familiarly as *thou*, keeping the polite *ye* for such as the Knight, the Squire, the Prioress, the Clerk of Oxford, and the Friar, rogue though he was. He addresses the Monk politely to start off with, then slips into the familiar *thou* as he expatiates upon the cleric's amorous potential, and then back again into the formal mode as he seconds the Knight's 'styntyng' the Monk of his tale. The Parson, too, Harry addresses as *thou* on several occasions (e.g. *CT* II, 1167; X, 22–9), but then he glides almost imperceptibly into the more formal mode in the final, more solemn words that lead into *The Parson's Tale* (*CT* X, 68–73). The polite form of the pronoun is accompanied by appropriate expressions as the Host addresses his betters:

'Sire Knyght,' quod he, 'my mayster and my lord,
Now draweth cut, for that is myn accord.
Cometh neer,' quod he, 'my lady Prioresse.
And ye, sire Clerk . . .'
(*Gen Prol* 837–40)

the Prioress:

> 'Now wol ye vouche sauf, my lady deere?'
> (*CT* VII, 451)

the Clerk:

> 'Sire Clerk of Oxenford,' oure Hooste sayde,
> 'Ye ryde as coy and stille as dooth a mayde
> Were newe spoused ...'
> (*CT* IV, 1–3)

and the Monk:

> 'But be nat wrooth, my lord, though that I pleye'.
> (*CT* VII, 1963)

When the brawl between the Friar and Summoner first erupts, the Host calms the antagonists, turning his back, as it were, upon the Wife of Bath whose long prologue has just ended:

> Oure Hooste cride 'Pees! and that anon!'
> And seyde, 'Lat the womman telle hire tale.
> Ye fare as folk that dronken ben of ale'.
> (*WBT* 850–2)

And then with a little flourish Harry turns back to 'the womman':

> 'Do, dame, telle forth youre tale, and that is best'.
> (*ibid.* 853)

The Host addresses the assembled pilgrims as *lordynges* or *sires*, as was customary, and they in their turn treat him with considerable respect. The Franklin returns the Host's familiar 'What, Franke-leyn! pardee, sire, wel thou woost' (*CT* V, 696) with a polite 'Gladly, sire Hoost, ... I wole obeye / Unto your wyl' (*ibid.* 703–4), and pilgrim Chaucer responds in much the same way using the plural verb *beth* to the Host in VII, 707, though later slipping into a solitary *wiltow* (*ibid.* 926) before he addresses presumably the whole company and not just the Host with the plural pronoun in the preamble to *The Tale of Melibee*. The Knight distinguishes nicely between Host and Pardoner as he stills their quarrel at the end of *The Pardoner's Tale*:

> 'Sire Pardoner, be glad and myrie of cheere;
> And *ye*, sire Hoost, that been to me so deere,
> I prey *yow* that *ye* kisse the Pardoner.

And Pardoner, I prey *thee*, drawe *thee* neer,
And, as we diden, lat us laughe and pleye'.
                                    (*PardT* 963–7)

As Harry Bailly had no tale to contribute to the pilgrimage,
Chaucer had to rely entirely upon his incidental utterances in
creating a recognizably distinctive voice. Hence the importance
of the few but sharp outlines of the Host's initial portrait: he was a
semely man, big, with glaring eyes, a merry fellow, and 'boold of
his speche'. One can visualize him, and one can certainly distinguish his voice. Again, as in the case of Pandarus and of other
Chaucerian characters yet to be considered, the poet's linguistic
characterization is as selective as is his method of *descriptio personae* in his mature poems: some features are given prominence,
in Harry Bailly's case whatever 'boldness' implied. And what it
implied we have tried to indicate: a generally colloquial level of
English made forceful and forthright by blunt, outspoken language, often crude in its use of low words and particularly of
oaths including some very wicked ones, untroubled by blunders,
free from any social pretensions yet sufficiently attuned to particular speakers to permit some show of politeness and even some
parade of learned jargon wherever Chaucer deemed this socially
or ironically appropriate. Most readers of *The Canterbury Tales*
tend to concentrate on individual tales and thus Harry Bailly is
often overlooked. Charles Muscatine gives him a paragraph of
ten lines, albeit rich in insight; S. S. Hussey in a recent study treats
him rather more generously.[7] And yet Harry Bailly deserves
better. He is Chaucer's only character revealed, as it were, in
instalments. To maintain consistently a distinctively *boold* idiom,
constantly interrupted by long stretches of other people's voices,
was no easy assignment. That Harry emerges on the threshold of
The Parson's Tale as bluff as ever, still swearing lustily by 'cokkes
bones', and echoing his own far distant 'unbokeled is the male'
of I, 3115, at the end of *The Knight's Tale*, with a final invitation to
'sire preest' to

'Unbokele, and shewe us what is in thy male',
                                    (*CT* X, 26)

7. Muscatine, p. 171; S. S. Hussey, *Chaucer: An Introduction* (London, 1971), especially pp. 119–22.

– all this is no mean achievement, even when measured against the total substance of *The Canterbury Tales*.

Harry Bailly expresses a good deal of his character through his oaths, as Pandarus does through his proverbs. There is no great show of learning in the former's utterances, merely the smattering of 'olde clerkes' that goes with his awareness of such words as *sophyme*. He can be as scathing in his dismissal of learning –

> 'What amounteth al this wit?
> What shul we speke alday of hooly writ?'
> *(CT* I, 3901–2)

– as he can be perfunctory in his rare displays of it, as when he couples 'Senec and many a philosophre' with 'Malkynes maydenhede' *(CT* II, 25 ff.) or reduces the wisdom of Solomon to the blunt truism that 'every thyng hath tyme' *(CT* IV, 6). Better use is made of Solomon by the Wife of Bath who cites him *(WBT* 35) as the first authority, next to Christ himself, in support of her claim that the more spouses one has, the better. Alys of Bath combines the sententiousness of Pandarus with Harry Bailly's 'boldness', though Chaucer characterizes her as *boold* of *face* rather than of *speche* *(Gen Prol* 458). We are told little of her speech in the opening portrait except that

> In felaweshipe wel koude she laughe and carpe,
> *(Gen Prol* 474)

a comment worthy of note because Chaucer does not use *carpe* anywhere else. The rhyme with *sharpe* was certainly not an easy one, and elsewhere *harpe* is the normal answer, but one may assume that *carpe* was right for the Wife of Bath, else Chaucer would not have used it. The basic meaning in Middle English is simply 'to speak, talk', and the *MED* points out that the modern Scandinavian meanings evolved from O.N. *karpa* 'to brag, boast, dispute, quarrel', represent a late development. But by the fourteenth century there is enough evidence of M.E. *carpen* being used in the sense of 'to chatter, gossip, argue, carp'. Gower has an expression recalling Pandarus's talkativeness:

> And whom it liketh forto carpe
> Proverbes . . .;
> *(Conf Am* VIII, 1488–9)

and Langland equates *carpen* with empty protestations:

Clerkus and knyghtes carpen of god ofte,
And haueth hym muche in hure mouthe, ac mene men in herte.
(*PP* C XII, 52–3)

The word is common in the alliterative poetry as a useful synonym for 'speak', 'say', and lent itself to alliterative formulas: 'to
carpen other to counsaile', 'carpen of Cryst', 'wyth clene cortays
carp', 'to carp of cumfort'. It is of course possible that Chaucer
meant nothing more specific than 'talk', but it is more probable
that the context of the word as well as some of its contemporary
connotations imply the kind of argumentative garrulousness later
to be displayed by the Wife of Bath. The fifteenth-century
Promptorium Parvulorum glosses *carpen* (*inter alia*) with *garrulo*.[8]

The Wife of Bath's autobiographical *confessio* is certainly 'a long
preamble of a tale', as the Friar points out (*WBT* 831), and even
the word *preamble* appears specially adopted into English literary
usage for the occasion; nor does Chaucer use it elsewhere. There
is a Tennysonian chatter, chatter about Alys's English which adds
to its distinctive flavour. Pandarus also talks a great deal, but his
syntax is never quite as loose as the Wife's; nor does the rhyme
royal stanza favour quite the same breathlessness as the Wife of
Bath displays in the opening lines of her *preamble*:

> 'Experience, though noon auctoritee
> Were in this world, is right ynogh for me
> To speke of wo that is in mariage;
> For, lordynges, sith I twelve yeer was of age,
> Thonked be God that is eterne on lyve,
> Housbondes at chirche dore I have had fyve, –
> If I so ofte myghte have ywedded bee, –
> And alle were worthy men in hir degree.'
> (*WBT* 1–8)

The syntax of the Wife's prologue is often irregular as she shifts
her subject in mid-sentence, mixes her pronouns or omits them
altogether, plays with prepositions, varies normal word-order
to make a point more emphatically – or loses her way altogether
to collapse into a heap of clichés.[9] The whole performance creates
superbly the impression of boundless loquacity. Her vocabulary
adds its share as it ranges from crude words describing sexual

8. *The Promptorium Parvulorum: The First English-Latin Dictionary*, ed. A. L. Mayhew,
E.E.T.S., E. S. 102 (1908), col. 107.
9. For illustrations see ch. 4, pp. 185 ff.

organs to a good many words found mainly in learned clerical discourse. She is much surer of her vocabulary than Harry Bailly, just as she is much better read, and whatever one may think of the logic of her arguments about marriage and virginity, or for that matter of her syntax, she certainly has an interesting and wide-ranging vocabulary.

Once again, Chaucer is restricting certain words to a particular character, in Alys's case a rich variety of words expressive of the two main facets of her personality as she herself describes them: the aggressive, argumentative *Marcien*, and the 'ewig weibliche' *Venerien*. One part of her talks frankly of her *queynte*, the other seeks out genteel euphemisms like 'nether purs' or *quoniam* or *bele chose* or 'do his nycetee'. The slangy side of her inclines towards those vivid terms of endearment which we looked at in another chapter, *lorel* and 'olde dotard shrewe' and 'olde barelful of lyes' and the rest, and calling old men *bacon*, and talking of tickling people's hearts (nobody else tickles in Chaucer). The genteel side of her favours all the little animals, mice and cats and spaniels, which people her discourse, and plumbs her wordhoard for impressive vocables like St Jerome's *octogamye*, or *tormentrie*, or *vacacioun*, or *spectacle*, all of them unique within the Chaucer canon. Such language, however much it may be intended to impress, is at the same time a token of Alys's boundless energy and curiosity; for the linguistic contest within her reflects a complex personality that combines an earthy vitality with a passionate hankering after *gentillesse* which finally blossoms into the miniature sermon on this theme in the tale proper.

Even in the more restricted diction of the *Tale* is heard the other voice of the matriarch of Bath punning, as Chaucer had done once before (in *LGW* 2325–6), on *heed* and *maydenhede*, talking colloquially of a friar saying 'his hooly thynges', scattering oaths, and finishing with a heartfelt prayer for the pestilence to fall upon all 'olde and angry nygardes of dispence' (*WBT* 1263).

In creating for Alys of Bath such a complex personality Chaucer set himself an unusual linguistic task. Criseyde may be thought of as, in this respect, not unlike, for she can hold her own bantering lightly, although not vulgarly, with Pandarus as well as celebrating with Troilus the mysteries of love in appropriately 'heigh style'. But where for Criseyde the appropriate level of discourse was generally provided by the presence of an interlocutor, the Wife of Bath's is a monologue. Hence the inextricable mingling of her two voices, the wistful consciousness of her fading beauty, for example, coupled with a blunt stocktaking of whatever is left of saleable value:

> 'But age, allas! that al wole envenyme,
> Hath me biraft my beautee and my pith.
> Lat go, farewel! the devel go therwith!
> The flour is goon, ther is namoore to telle;
> The bren, as I best kan, now moste I selle'.
>
> (*WBT* 474–8)

Much of the art of the Wife's speech lies in the interweaving of traditional rhetorical colours with strongly colloquial diction carefully observed by Chaucer. Her monologue, for all its seeming lack of sophistication, is carefully structured, and appropriate words and phrases are repeated at intervals to give it cohesion. The words may be structurally important, but are linguistically inconspicuous, like 'I woot wel' (*WBT* 55, 63, 79); 'I sey this' (126) and 'but I seye noght' (135); 'thou seist' and its variant forms (248 ff., some fifteen times); 'now wol I speken' with variants 'now wol I tellen forth' (452, 503, 563, and the rest). Such phrases, whatever their importance in the rhetorical patterning of the Wife's prologue, are of course part of the staple of colloquial Chaucerian English. Like Pandarus and Harry Bailly and the rest, Alys has her indispensable colloquialisms, some common enough, some more distinctively her own, several she shares with only one other of Chaucer's people. Thus she shares with the miller of Trumpington in *The Reeve's Tale* (4096) the expression 'to make someone's beard', that is to trim it, cut down to size, hence outwit him:

> 'Yet koude I make his berd, so moot I thee!'
>
> (*WBT* 361)

She shares with the Merchant the phrase 'ful of ragerye', that is wantonness, and its rhyming association with the magpie:

> 'And I was yong and ful of ragerye,
> Stibourn and strong, and joly as a pye.'
>
> (*WBT* 455–6)

> He was al coltissh, ful of ragerye,
> And ful of jargon as a flekked pye.
>
> (*MerchT* 1847–8)

The word *stibourn* 'stubborn' is used only by the Wife of Bath (456 and 637), and if it is indeed one of her contributions to English literature it is a most appropriate one. Alys shares with Pandarus (*Tr* III, 736) the mention of 'mouses herte' (*WBT* 572), and with the Reeve of 'coltes tooth' in lines identical except for the tense (*WBT* 602, *RvT* 3888). Her 'olde sho' (*WBT* 708) parallels Pandarus's 'olde hat' (*Tr* III, 320); her reference to her fifth husband's knowledge of

> 'mo proverbes
> Than in this world ther growen gras or herbes'
> (*WBT* 773–4)

is echoed by Januarie's derogatory

> 'Straw for thy Senek, and for thy proverbes!
> I counte nat a panyer ful of herbes
> Of scole-termes.'
> (*MerchT* 1567–9)

She herself quotes proverbs readily enough, if necessary taking them straight from some other pilgrim's mouth, as it were. Her

> 'With empty hand men may none haukes lure'
> (*WBT* 415)

is almost identical with clerk John's

> 'With empty hand men may na haukes tulle'
> (*RvT* 4134)

except that the Wife's *lure* is a technical hawking term used also by the Friar and the Host, whereas *tullen* is probably the same as *tollen* 'to attract, entice', a common enough Middle English verb ultimately related to O.E. *fortyllan* 'to seduce'; Chaucer uses it once more as the equivalent of *drawen* in *Boece*: 'but natheles it may nat drawen or tollen swiche hertes' (*Bo* II, pr. 7, 15 f). At one point the Wife produces a memorable proverbial jingle ascribed to her 'joly clerk, Jankyn':

> '"Whoso that buyldeth his hous al of salwes,
> And priketh his blynde hors over the falwes,
> And suffreth his wyf to go seken halwes,
> Is worthy to been hanged on the galwes!"'
> (*WBT* 655–8)

As there is a particular irony in making a loud, crude, hard-swearing publican the master of ceremonies of a pilgrimage to the foremost shrine in England, so there is similar irony in setting up this big, garrulous female, 'the great professional widow of literature', as Chesterton called her, as a kind of marriage guidance counsellor to whom Chaucer could refer not only other characters in his fiction but his real friends, like 'maister Bukton', for all that was needful to know about the married state, from 'hooly writ' and 'proverbes' to what 'experience shal . . . teche' (*Lenvoy de Chaucer a Bukton, passim*). Both these pilgrims speak a natural idiom artfully contrived, both of them illustrate admirably the Chaucerian technique of relating words and deeds.

Something of a natural idiom even more artfully contrived is that of Chaucer's Reeve, who hailed from the vicinity of the village of *Baldeswelle*, Bawdeswell in northern Norfolk (*Gen Prol* 619–20) and was thus particularly well placed to represent the northern idiom of the two students in his tale to the presumably predominantly southern audience of the Canterbury pilgrimage. How well Chaucer's ear was attuned to the northern dialect of his own time has been admirably demonstrated in J. R. R. Tolkien's now classic address to the Philological Society in 1931.[10] The dialect of Aleyn and John is not 'pure' northern speech; as such it would probably have been largely unintelligible to Chaucer's audience, as John Trevisa noted about this time.[11] Instead, Chaucer selected a number of distinctive northern features, phonological, grammatical, and lexical, and inserted these into the speech of the two clerks with sufficient frequency to maintain the impression of their native speech without courting the danger of making it incomprehensible. Those who seek a more naturalistic explanation still may of course regard the northern speech of the two students as being strongly modified by their residence at Cambridge, much as is the native Australian or New Zealand

---

10. J. R. R. Tolkien, 'Chaucer as a Philologist: *The Reeve's Tale*', *Transactions of the Philological Society* (1934), 1–70.

11. In his translation of Higden's Polychronicon, Trevisa writes 'Al þe longage of þe Norþhumbres, and specialych at ȝork, ys so scharp, slytting, and frotyng, and vnschape, þat we Souþeron men may þat longage vnneþe vndurstonde.' Two centuries earlier William of Malmesbury had made a similar observation in the Prologue to Book III of his *De Gestis Pontificum Anglorum*: 'Sane tota lingua Nordanimbrorum, sed maxime in Eboraco, ita inconditum stridet, ut nichil nos australes intelligere possimus' (Rolls Series, 1870, p. 209).

English of several distinguished members of the English faculty
at Oxford at the present time. In a way, therefore, the Reeve's
portrayal of northern English speech is a particularly good illustration of Chaucer's selective method of making words 'cosyn
to the dede', because the features selected are easily isolated.
Even allowing for the vagaries of scribal transmission or even
direct interference there is sufficient manuscript evidence to show
what Chaucer was doing. For his principal phonological criterion
he used the northern [ɑ:], the long *a-* sound retained from Old
English, where southern Middle English has [ɔ:], the long open
o- sound; in the following examples, not intended to be exhaustive,
the southern forms as used by Chaucer elsewhere are given in
parentheses: *alswa (also), atanes (at ones), awen (owene), banes (bones)
bathe (bothe), fra (fro), ga (go), ham (hoom), raa (roo* 'roe'*), swa (so),
waat (woot).* The Old English group *-ang,* corresponding to normal
Chaucerian *-ong,* remains in northern speech: *lange (longe), sang
(song), wrang (wrong).* The northern equivalent of Chaucer's *swich*
'such' is Aleyn's *swilk,* but another northern form, *slyk,* derived
from Scandinavian, is used as well, by John, for example, in a
proverbial utterance with a strong northern colouring:

> '"man sal taa of twa thynges
> Slyk as he fyndes, or taa slyk as he brynges."'
> (R*v*T 4129–30)

Similarly, the southern *which* appears as *whilk.*

The proverb just cited illustrates Chaucer's principal northern
grammatical criterion, the final *-es* or *-s* for the third person singular of the present indicative of verbs, where his normal usage has
-eth or *-th;* for example, *brynges* (the rhyme with the plural noun
thynges establishes the northern verbal form as the one Chaucer
wrote), *falles, fares, fyndes, gas* 'goes', *says, wagges,* and so on. By
contrast, there is only one example of the northern plural ending
in *-s* in 'swa *werkes* ay the wanges' (4030). Other northernisms are,
I is' ('I am'), 'thou is' ('thou art'), 'we / ye are' ('we / ye been'),
gif for *if, heythen* for *hennes* 'hence', *sal* for *shal, thair* for *hir* 'their',
til for *to* (occasionally used by Chaucer elsewhere, especially before a following vowel, as in *Gen Prol* 180), and the contractions
boes for *bihoveth* and *taa* for *take.* The enigmatic forms *geen* 'gone'
(R*v*T 4078) and *neen* 'none' (4185, 4187) which occur in the Ellesmere
manuscript and are accepted by some editors (Robinson, for

example) and rejected by others (such as Manly and Rickert) are unlikely to be true northernisms, particularly in face of the several genuine northern forms *gas* 'goes' (4037), *ga* 'go' (4102, 4254) and *na* (4026 *et al.*), as well as *nafors* 'no matter' (4176).[12]

Several words used by the two students in *The Reeve's Tale* have long been recognized as dialectal. One such word, *capul* 'horse', is used by the Reeve in his own person as narrator (4105) as well as by clerk John. In our discussion of Chaucer's 'cherles termes' we noted that in ascribing the word to Harry Bailly, the Friar, and the Summoner as well as the Reeve, Chaucer clearly branded it as something of a vulgarism. Its occurrence, moreover, mainly in northern and midland speech, made it appropriate both for John and the Reeve himself. Other dialect words are *fonne* 'fool' (4089); *hethyng* 'contempt' (4110); *howgates* 'how, in what way' (4037); *il, ille* (4045, 4174, 4184) and *ilhayl!* (4089), in place of Chaucer's usual word *yvel*; *lathe* 'barn' (4088); *wanges* (4030), generally glossed 'molar teeth', but perhaps, as Tolkien argues, rather the cheeks or the upper sides of the face (as in O.N. *vangi* or German *Wange*) in which case the ailing manciple of the clerks' college would have been suffering from migraine or sinusitis rather than toothache; *wight* 'swift, active' (4086); *ymel* 'among' (4171). Most of these words are unique to *The Reeve's Tale* within the Chaucer canon, but *lathe* occurs also once near the end of *The House of Fame* (2140) as a rhyme for *rathe*, and the Monk once uses the word *wang-tooth* (*MkT* 2044). It is worth noting also that *ille* occurs eight times in rhyming positions in the B section of the English *Romaunt of the Rose*, and the word is common in Middle English mainly in northern and eastern texts. Nor should we forget the aptness of John's swearing at one point by a well-known north-country saint, 'seint Cutberd' (4127), as appropriate as the invocation by the miller's wife of the 'hooly croys of Bromeholm' (4286), a reference to the rood of Bromeholm Priory in Norfolk with which the Reeve must be assumed to have been familiar.

The foregoing comments are not meant to be an exhaustive analysis of the Reeve's dialectal features; this can be found in Tolkien's study. But they will have illustrated what is germane to our present purpose: Chaucer's method of linguistic characterization. It is worthy of note that the Reeve himself betrays few

12. See particularly Tolkien, *op. cit.*, pp. 65-70.

traces of dialect in his own speech as narrator: the word *capul* is not confined to him, nor is the word *greythen* 'to prepare, get ready, dress' (4309), which Chaucer uses once in *Boece* (I, pr. 4, 238) and once ascribes to the Monk (*MkT* 2594), though both words are particularly associated with areas of Scandinavian settlement. But Chaucer astutely opens the Reeve's performance with an unmistakable northernism when he makes the Reeve utter as his first words 'So theek' (3864), that is 'so thee ik', so may I thrive, and then makes him repeat the northern *ik* twice more: 'but ik am oold' (3867) and 'and yet ik have' (3888). Such a signpost was all that was needed at this point to prepare the audience for the linguistic hurdles ahead. When the clerks eventually enter and utter their chosen and choice bits of dialectal English the audience is ready for them: Aleyn's *hayl* 'hail' to start with, which Chaucer uses elsewhere only in *The Miller's Tale* (3579) and *The Friar's Tale* (1384) and which may have possessed dialectal associations, more particularly when used as a noun; his contracted *y-fayth*, used once again a little later and possibly meant to be something of a personal mannerism rather than a dialectal form; and the northern verbal form *fares*; followed in John's first speech by *na* and *boes* and 'swa werkes ay the wanges' and 'is I' and *ham* and *heythen*, all within their first dozen lines.

Such linguistic characterization by dialect was certainly a new thing in English literature and Chaucer's achievement is as original as it is successful. But for good measure Chaucer adds to the Reeve's English some further individual traits, though none as distinctive. The latter has some tendency towards pulpit oratory, what the narrator calls 'this sermonyng' (*CT* I, 3899), which manifests itself in various ways, as in the wistful disquisition on old age, the elaborate simile of the cask, the preacher's characteristic division of matter and enumeration of points –

> 'Foure gleedes [hot coals] han we, which I shal devyse, –
> Avauntyng, liyng, anger, coveitise;
> Thise foure sparkles longen unto eelde'
> (*RvT* 3883–5)

– just like the Parson's 'the causes that oghte moeve a man to Contricioun been sixe' (*ParsT* 133), biblical echoes, the concluding prayer, and so on. Yet at the same time the Reeve is unquestionably a 'churl' and his diction is made to express this in no uncertain terms. This side of him the reader first meets when in the Miller's prologue the theme of *The Miller's Tale* is announced as 'how that a clerk hath set the wrightes cappe' (*CT* I, 3143), that is, how a clerk makes a fool of the carpenter, which is enough to provoke the Reeve's

> 'stynt thy clappe!
> Lat be thy lewed dronken harlotrye.'
>
> (*CT* I, 3144–5)

When the Reeve's turn comes round he echoes the Miller's phrase with his promise to 'somdeel sette his [the Miller's] howve' (*CT* I, 3911), another word for 'cap', and to *quite* him in his own coin:

> 'Right in his cherles termes wol I speke.'
>
> (*CT* I, 3917)

An appropriate malediction is added for good measure and as a token of his expertise in 'cherles termes':

> 'I pray to God his nekke mote to-breke'.
>
> (*ibid.* 3918)

The Reeve's announcement of the manner in which he proposes to tell his tale is interesting as a restatement from the pilgrim himself of what the narrator of *The Canterbury Tales* had said at some length before embarking on *The Miller's Tale*, but there is no reason whatever to believe that the Miller's 'cherles termes' are not his, the Reeve's, also. He has a proper command of rustic diction as befits one whose house stood 'ful faire upon an heeth' (*Gen Prol* 606) and whose business was with grain and harvesting and livestock as well as with carpentry. He talks of a *mullok* 'heap of refuse' (*CT* I, 3873), a word used elsewhere only by the Canon's Yeoman, and of a *market-betere* 'a person given to loafing around markets' (*RvT* 3936), not used elsewhere by Chaucer; his similes include 'as water in a dich' (3964), and 'as a draf-sak', sack of husks, and as two pigs wallowing in a poke (4278). He has a fair command also of slang and coarse language, talks of old men having 'a grene tayl' (*CT* I, 3878), 'so myrie a fit' (*RvT* 4230) and 'he priketh harde and depe as he were mad' (4231), and makes Aleyn pun on *esement* (4179 ff.) and talk of 'swyving' the miller's daughter (4178) and of his 'swynk to-nyght' (4253) and address his mate affectionately as 'thou swynes-heed' (4262). The Reeve has several memorable words unique to himself in Chaucer's work, quite apart from the northernisms already mentioned, words that reflect fittingly his professional interests, his homiletic bent, and his command of 'cherles termes'. His is the first reference to Sheffield cutlery in English literature in the description of the heavily armed miller: 'a Sheffeld thwitel' (3933), *thwitel* being a large knife, while *poppere* (3931) is a kind of short dagger and *panade* (3929) a cutlass; his also is the only reference in Chaucer to *chalons* (4140), woollen bedspreads so named because the material was of a type manufactured at Châlons-sur-Marne in France, and to *sokene* (3987), the right of a particular mill to grind the corn of tenants in a given district. He alone in Chaucer uses *bisemare* and *hoker*, both words popular in homiletic writings, both in line 3965, meaning respectively 'mockery, derision' and 'scorn, contempt', and *unhardy* (4210) 'cowardly, timorous', and he shares with the Parson the censorious use of the rare word *unsaunt* (3940) 'accustomed, addicted'. He enriches the Chaucerian vocabulary with several words we have noted in another context: *camus* 'pug-nosed', *cokenay* 'sissy, milksop', *daf* 'fool', possibly a dialectal word, of which Langland is fond, *quakke* 'hoarseness', *toty* 'unsteady, dizzy', *yexeth* 'hiccoughs'.

The Reeve's English, moreover, has its proper share of colloquial idioms: 'and straunge he made it of hir mariage' (3980), he made an issue of it, made difficulties about it, an idiom Chaucer uses in somewhat different form as the narrator in *The General Prologue*, 785 'noght worth to make it wys', although the sense is much the same; 'he craketh boost' (4001), brags, threatens vociferously; 'made fare' (3999), made a fuss, as in *Boece*: 'with so greet a noyse and with so greet a fare' (*Bo* II, pr. 5, 113–14): 'so was hir joly whistle wel ywet' (4155); 'yet kan a millere make a clerkes berd' (4096), an idiom shared, as we have seen, with the Wife of Bath. Here, too, could be listed once again the several rich oaths which grace the speech particularly of the Reeve's two students, but perhaps the evidence is sufficient to demonstrate the distinctiveness of the Reeve's idiom. Yet once again Chaucer clearly visualized a unique human being, long and lean, irascible (*colerik*), competent at his job, 'dokked lyk a preest biforn' and 'tukked . . . as is a frere aboute' with a sermonizing tendency to match, yet as coarse and slangy as the Miller whom he sets out to requite, and withal familiar with dialectal forms of fourteenth-century English which impart to his tale a flavour all its own. Whatever Chaucer's own views may have been on the universities of Oxford and Cambridge, in the tales of the Miller and the Reeve and in the persons of Nicholas and Aleyn and John he certainly provided modern undergraduates at these institutions with lusty ancestors well equipped with appropriate gifts of the gab.

The colloquial element which forms such an important part of the English of the characters thus far considered belongs also to others, like the Miller who was 'a janglere and a goliardeys', a fluent purveyor of 'synne and harlotries' as well as a buffoon (*Gen Prol* 560–1), or the Shipman if he is the person intended as the one who scorns to talk philosophy or legal jargon, and supports his disclaimer that

'Ther is but litel Latyn in my mawe'

(*CT* II, 1190)

by an appropriately obscure, because probably ignorant, mention of something he calls *phislyas* (*ibid.* 1189), whatever that may be. At least there is no question that the tale finally assigned to the Shipman, despite the feminine tone of lines 10–19, is rich in colloquialisms (one recalls such gems as 'What! yvel thedam on his monkes snowte!', *ShipT* 405, or 'the devel have part on alle swiche rekenynges!', *ibid.* 218), obscene puns, mouth-filling oaths, and the like. By contrast, the colloquial element is reduced to insignificance wherever Chaucer was aiming to reflect a more learned and serious register of English as in the two edifying tales of long-suffering women told respectively by the Sergeant of the Law and the Clerk of Oxford. The Man of Law is described as 'war and wys' (*Gen Prol* 309), epithets implying prudence and sound judgment. He appears to be *discreet* 'prudent, circumspect', at least 'his wordes weren so wise' (*Gen Prol* 313), which means that they were full of sense and sagacity, carefully chosen, 'proper words in proper places', with a suggestion of adequate erudition to make intelligent selection possible. It is generally believed that the tale of Constance was not originally intended for the Man of Law because the latter concludes his discussion of the work of the poet Chaucer with a shrugging admission that to follow Chaucer as a story-teller can only mean very plain fare, 'though I come after hym with hawebake' (*CT* II, 95), baked haws being a pretty meagre dish. He then adds the comment

> 'I speke in prose, and lat hym rymes make',
> (*CT* II, 96)

which may have been intended to refer to a following tale in prose, possibly *The Tale of Melibee* originally, as some critics have surmised, but it obviously need not mean this. Skeat thought quite sensibly (notwithstanding Robinson's comment 'wholly unlikely') that the Man of Law is saying something like 'I generally have to speak in prose in the law courts; so that if my tale is prosy as compared with Chaucer's, it is only what you would expect'. I would reduce this simply to 'I (normally) speak in prose; poetry is Chaucer's business'. 'I speke in prose' is a very different utterance from those that introduce the two prose tales in *The Canterbury Tales*, as Robinson ought to have noted, both using the auxiliary *wol* with future intention as Chaucer frequently does; this is how *Melibee* is announced:

> 'I wol yow telle a litel thyng in prose',
> (*CT* VII, 937)

and these are the Parson's words:

> 'I wol yow telle a myrie tale in prose'.
> (*CT* X, 46)

The same construction is used by other speakers referring to their tales, viz. the Miller's 'for I wol speke' (*CT* I, 3133), the Reeve's 'right in his cherles termes wol I speke' (*CT* I, 3917), the Clerk's 'I wol yow telle a tale' (*CT* IV, 26), the Squire's 'a tale wol I telle' (*CT* V, 6), the Monk's 'first, tragedies wol I telle' (*CT* VII, 1971), and the Canon's Yeoman's

> 'But nathelees yow wol I tellen part.
> Syn that my lord is goon, I wol nat spare;
> Swich thyng as that I knowe, I wol declare.'
> (*CYT* 717–19)

The last line quoted illustrates plainly the semantic difference between the two constructions.

The point is not of tremendous importance; there are several instances of changes of intention and lack of revision in *The Canterbury Tales*, but the evidence of 'I speke in prose' is patently insufficient to cast doubt upon the ascription of the tale of Constance to the Man of Law. On the other hand, there is adequate ground for accepting the tale as emanating from one whose 'wordes weren so wise', in the sense suggested earlier. That the Man of Law uses a fair number of legal words has been noted before, including one or two not used elsewhere in Chaucer, like *ligeance* 'the duty of fidelity of a subject to his sovereign' (*MLT* 895), but equally interesting is the considerable number of other words, perhaps three dozen or more, ascribed by Chaucer to the teller of this tale which are not used by anyone else in his work, and which may confidently be described as *wise*, well chosen to make their point. Such words include *ceriously* 'minutely, in detail', *cristyanytee*, *dilatacioun*, *diurnal*, *eggement*, *extenden*, *femynynytee*, *indigence*, *mysdeparteth*, and the reading *inprudent* (or *im*) in line 309, adopted by Manly and Rickert and preferable to Robinson's earlier *impudent*. Half of these words at least are not recorded before Chaucer, others are only lately found in writing. That the Man of Law should talk of a *constable* is not surprising, although he means not a policeman but the governor of a castle, but that he should be the first character in medieval English fiction to talk of a *constablesse* is wholly appropriate, or for that matter of an *embassadrie*. Numerous other words which occur in *The Man of Law's Tale* are used very sparingly by Chaucer, and it is not difficult to detect patterns of distribution of many rare words among appropriate pilgrims in *The Canterbury Tales* or in suitable contexts in other poems and in the prose. The point is that such words are 'proper' in *The Man of Law's Tale*; they belong to the idiom of a serious, learned, prudent man with a subtle enough intellect to seek for linguistic precision of the kind favoured by lawyers. That is presumably what Chaucer meant by saying that no one could find fault with his writing,

Ther koude no wight pynche at his writyng.
(*Gen Prol* 326)

Among such words we might note *abasshed*, *abusioun*, the verb *argumenten*, *ignorance*, *iniquitee*, *motyf*, *plages* 'regions', *renegat* 'renegade', *reneyed* 'renounced', *resigne*, *subjeccioun*, *successour*.

Perhaps even more in character still is the sobriety of tone which controls the diction of *The Man of Law's Tale*, not least the almost total absence of those lively colloquial tags and clichés, inter-

jections and oaths, which are found in such abundance elsewhere in Chaucer's poetry. Apart from his opening *depardieux*
the Man of Law hardly swears at all, nor do the characters of his
tale, although some of them might well have been constitution-
ally prone to swearing, or at least provoked into it by their share
of the disasters enumerated. Nor can such expressions as 'if I shal
nat lye', 'withouten doute', 'be as be may', 'it is no drede', be
considered as anything but the most colourless of clichés. There
are few exceptions to the formality of the diction. One such is the
unique use of *grenehede* 'greenness' to denote the inexperience or
foolishness of youth (*MLT* 163); another is the equally unique,
strongly abusive 'cursed krone' (432), applied to the old sultaness,
krone or *crone* 'old hag', apparently derived from Anglo-French
carogne 'carrion', being the closest the Man of Law ever gets to
slang; yet another is the description of the drunken messenger
sleeping 'as a swyn' (745) and on his return once again drinking
more than is good for him and snoring in his stupor:

> He drank, and wel his girdel underpighte;
> He slepeth, and he fnorteth in his gyse
> Al nyght.

> (*MLT* 789–91)

Of course it might be argued that the pitiful tale of Constance is
not the place for levity of language, nor for humour or occasional
lewdness or relaxed informality, yet these are precisely the ingredients Pandarus contributes to the tale of 'the double sorwe
of Troilus', also in rhyme royal, so that the verse form at least can
hardly be regarded as inhibiting. What little humour is permitted
to creep into *The Man of Law's Tale* appears almost adventitious,
like the sultaness's attitude to baptism:

> 'Coold water shal nat greve us but a lite!'
> (*ibid.* 352)

or the narrator's reluctant admission that even the most virtuous
of wives

> moste take in pacience at nyght
> Swiche manere necessaries as been plesynges
> To folk that han ywedded hem with rynges,
> And leye a lite hir hoolynesse aside,
> As for the tyme, – it may no bet bitide,
> (*ibid.* 710–14)

or the narrator's final confession

> I am so wery for to speke of sorwe.
>
> (*ibid.* 1071)

Clearly, at such moments Chaucer 'wol out' despite his creature. But the total impression of the tale remains one of *discreet* language, sober, formal, rich in *wise* words, precise even in such details as the language a Roman princess might speak to the natives when shipwrecked on the coast of far *Northhumberlond*.[13] Even the frequent use of *occupatio*, the somewhat restless cutting short and passing from one topic to the next, in *The Man of Law's Tale* is in character with one who 'semed bisier than he was' (*Gen Prol* 322). Admittedly, the tale is a very long one, and Chaucer often makes use of expressions recalling the *occupatio* and *praecisio* of the rhetoricians, but the fact that they occur elsewhere, in *The Knight's Tale* for instance, does not invalidate their aptness here in reinforcing the impression that the Man of Law really has to get on with his tale because there was so much else for him to attend to. Sometimes these expressions take on something of a legal air, as in the last part of the tale where they are particularly frequent:

> I wol no lenger tarien in this cas.
>
> (*MLT* 983)

> I may nat tellen every circumstance.
>
> (*ibid.* 1011)

Perhaps it is just as well that the Man of Law forbore to 'tellen every circumstance', for his tale is long enough for modern taste; moreover, it lacks what E. T. Donaldson calls the 'human profundity'[14] of the Clerk's tale of that other long-suffering heroine, patient Griselda. Chaucer is a good deal more explicit about the Clerk's habits of speech than he is about the Man of Law's, or most other pilgrims' for that matter:

> Noght o word spak he moore than was neede,
> And that was seyd in forme and reverence,
> And short and quyk and ful of hy sentence;
> Sownynge in moral vertu was his speche.
>
> (*Gen Prol* 304–7)

---

13. Chaucer calls it 'a maner Latyn corrupt', a kind of pidgin Latin, on which see J. Burrow's informative note in *Medium Aevum* XXX (1961), 33–7.

14. Donaldson, p. 912.

The comment that he never said 'moore than was neede' may strike the modern reader as somewhat incongruous when confronted with the almost 1,200 lines of *The Clerk's Tale*; yet the tale has a steady momentum which never flags, the narrative proceeding with a controlled rhythm brought about largely by making the majority of the rhyme royal stanzas complete sentence units, and by rarely allowing more than two sentences in any one stanza. Despite this element of regularity there is enough rhythmic and syntactic variety to prevent monotony or boredom. Where the narrative is interrupted it is to make room for 'moral vertu', for comments by the narrator on the monstrousness of Walter's obsession or on Griselda's constancy to her vow. There is little amplification of any kind. When Griselda is stripped of 'hir olde geere', which the five ladies-in-waiting were reluctant to touch (*CLT* 372 ff.), the narrator refuses to elaborate: 'of hire array what sholde I make a tale?' (383), a common enough figure, of course, but again thoroughly true to one whose speech was 'short and quyk' and eschewed superfluities. There is a sense of decorum about *The Clerk's Tale* which is one of the connotations of the Clerk's speech being 'in forme', the decorum being linguistic as well as social and moral. There is no offence against good taste, no crudeness or vulgarity, no lewd swearing, no banter.

The Clerk's Tale thus accords with the brief but informative sketch given to us by Chaucer of the narrator's English; and it also fulfils to a large extent Harry Bailly's request for *pleyn* speech (*CT* IV, 19), free from rhetorical adumbration and all that appertains to 'heigh style'. There is much art in the telling, of course, the sudden change in the rhythm of a stanza, for instance, as when Janicula, Griselda's father, hears of Walter's proposal (*CLT* 316–22), or the occasional phrase or figure that impresses itself on the memory: 'this flour of wyfly pacience' (919), 'and she ay sad and constant as a wal' (1047), or

> Wel ofter of the welle than of the tonne [wine-cask]
> She drank.
>
> (*CLT* 215–16)

Particularly effective is Chaucer's accumulation of negatives whenever Griselda re-affirms her vow of constancy, or when (as in 920 ff.) her constancy is described by the narrator. Doubling or multiplying of negatives is a common feature of Chaucer's

English, nor does an even number make the statement affirmative, and there can be considerable gain in emphasis:

'How that bitwixen youre magnificence
And my poverte *no* wight kan *ne* may
Maken comparison; it is *no nay.*
I *ne* heeld ne *nevere* digne in *no* manere
To be youre wyf, *no, ne* youre chamberere.'

(*CLT* 815–19)

The Clerk's diction, for all his *studie*, is less learned than the Man of Law's. In this respect, too, the Host's request 'that we may understonde what ye seye' (*CT* IV, 20) has been taken to heart. Words which are unique to the Clerk in the Chaucer canon are for the most part 'short and quyk' words, rather than long and Latinate, like *flokmeele* 'in groups' (*CLT* 86), the O.E. *floccmǣlum*, also used in the Wyclifite Bible to render Latin *gregatim*, or *crabbed* 'angry, spiteful' (1203), or *smoklees* 'without smock or shift' (875), or 'houses of office *stuffed* with plentee' (264), or *torace* 'tear to pieces' and *ugly* (572, 673), both of them words also used in *Sir Gawain and the Green Knight*. Among other words unique to *The Clerk's Tale* or of very rare occurrence in Chaucer are several further derivatives like *smoklees*, formed from words which were familiar enough to a late fourteenth-century audience. In the Envoy to the tale occurs, for example, *archewyves* (1195), found elsewhere only in Lydgate, though its components are of course familiar, and *bidaffed* 'outwitted' (1191), unique in Middle English apparently, although *daf* 'fool' occurs several times in *Piers Plowman* and once in *The Reeve's Tale*. There are also nouns formed from familiar adjectives, like *hoomlinesse* (429), known also to Wyclif and Trevisa among Chaucer's contemporaries, and *sturdinesse* (700), which makes its appearance in written English at about the same time, and *mazednesse* (1061), which seems to have been first used by Chaucer. There are rare adjectives or participles with the prefix *un-*, like *undiscreet* (996), also used once by the Nun's Priest's fox; *unsad* 'inconstant' (995), another word common to Chaucer, Wyclif and Trevisa; *untressed* 'unbraided' (379), also in *The Knight's Tale* and *The Parliament of Fowls*; and *undigne* 'unworthy' (359), a word current in the fourteenth and fifteenth centuries and probably here suggested to Chaucer by Petrarch's *indignam*.

Chaucer's use as the basis for *The Clerk's Tale* of Petrarch's Latin prose version of the story of Griselda, itself based on the last tale of Boccaccio's *Decameron*, and of an anonymous French prose version of Petrarch, has long been accepted. Chaucer makes his Clerk acknowledge for himself his debt to 'Fraunceys Petrak, the lauriat poete' (*CT* IV, 31). A comparison of the versions printed by J. Burke Severs in *Sources and Analogues of Chaucer's 'Canterbury Tales'* with *The Clerk's Tale* reveals how much Chaucer managed to alter the whole tone of the story without in any way changing the sequence of events; for our purpose it is instructive to note how small, relatively speaking, is the number of nonce or rare words in the tale derived from these sources, and what kind of words they are. Here are some examples from Petrarch's Latin: *equitee*, suggested by *equitate*, used also in other poems and in *Boece*; *successour*, Petrarch's *successore*, used once in *The Man of Law's Tale*; *suspect*, Petrarch's *suspecta*, used in *The Physician's Tale* and *Melibee*; *undigne*, Petrarch's *indignam*, used once in *Boece* and once in *The Parson's Tale*. The French *Livre Griseldis* probably suggested *dispensacion* (identical in the French), used once in *Boece*; *dowere*, *dowaire* 'dower' (Fr. *douaire*), not used elsewhere; *humanitee* (Fr. *humanité*), not used elsewhere; *publiced* 'published, made known' (Fr. *publioit*), used twice in the tale as well as in *Boece* and *Troilus and Criseyde*; *servitute* (identical in the French), used once in *The Parson's Tale*. For Chaucer these are all uncommon words; what is surprising is not their adoption from the texts he was working with, for he did this in other cases as well (one recalls *Melibee*, for example), but the fact that he did not adopt many more. The reason may well be that in trying to make *The Clerk's Tale* conform to the Clerk's declared mode of speaking as well as to Harry Bailly's request for plain English, the poet deliberately tailored his diction accordingly. Even the Envoy to the tale with its severe restriction of rhyme manages to avoid a heavy preponderance of unusual words. Of the eighteen words rhyming in *-aille*, for example, only seven are uncommon in Chaucer's diction: *camaille* 'camel' and *countretaille* 'retort, reply' occur only here, *aventaille* 'piece of armour protecting the neck and upper chest' and *maille* 'mail armour' occur also in *Troilus and Criseyde*, *quaille* 'quail' (bird) in *The Parliament of Fowls*, *governaille* 'mastery, control' in *Boece*, and *entraille* in *The Prioress's Tale* and *Boece*.

In its sober tone *The Clerk's Tale* is like the Man of Law's except
that its author allows more of his own 'hy sentence' to come to the
surface. Generally his comments are phrased in harmony with the
rest of the narrative –

> But hye God somtyme senden kan
> His grace into a litel oxes stalle.
> (*CLT* 206–7)

> And for he saugh that under low degree
> Was ofte vertu hid, the peple hym heelde
> A prudent man, and that is seyn ful seelde.
> (*ibid.* 425–7)

> This storie is seyd, nat for that wyves sholde
> Folwen Grisilde as in humylitee,
> For it were inportable, though they wolde.
> (*ibid.* 1142–4)

Occasionally a slightly more colloquial note enters, faintly reflecting a different register, as in the apostrophe to the fickle mob:

> 'Delitynge evere in rumbul that is newe,
> For lyk the moone ay wexe ye and wane!
> Ay ful of clappyng, deere ynogh a jane [small coin]!
> Youre doom is fals, youre constance yvele preeveth;
> A ful greet fool is he that on yow leeveth.'
> (*ibid.* 997–1001)

Such a touch now and again as 'ay ful of clappyng' well accords
with the character of one who could finish the story of Griselda
with the wry comment that

> It were ful hard to fynde now-a-dayes
> In al a toun Griseldis thre or two,
> (*ibid.* 1164–5)

but too much colloquial informality would have offended against
proper 'forme and reverence'.

A more evenly balanced mingling of formal and informal
English than Chaucer thought appropriate for the Clerk, he
created in *The Merchant's Tale*. If *The Clerk's Tale* reads somewhat
like *Troilus and Criseyde* with Pandarus left out, *The Merchant's Tale*
reads a little like a *conversazione* between the Sergeant of the Law
and the Wife of Bath. For the Merchant, pompous in the manage-

ment of his affairs and 'solempne' in voicing his opinions '(his resons he spak ful solempnely', *Gen Prol* 274), was also a man who had his wits about him ('this worthy man ful wel his wit bisette', *ibid.* 279), although this did not apparently prevent his contracting a disastrous marriage. The phrase 'his resons he spak ful solempnely' is all we are told of the Merchant's manner of speech, but *solempne* in its various senses of 'ceremonial, formal, dignified, pompous' matches that other telling epithet in the Merchant's portrait, *estatly* (*ibid.* 281), which connotes much the same qualities. The word does not seem to have been recorded before Chaucer, but it clearly appealed to him: Criseyde is described as 'charitable, estatlich, lusty, and fre' (*Tr* V, 823), while the Prioress tries to be 'estatlich of manere' (*Gen Prol* 140); Julius Caesar, according to the Monk, loved 'estaatly honestee', that is an honourable character befitting his rank (*MkT* 2712), and 'Duc Jasoun' in the Legend of Hypsipyle and Medea possessed a 'statly aparaunce' (*LGW* 1372), a shortened form of the same word. In this respect at least Chaucer's Merchant is in select company, and apart from the twice repeated 'worthy man', with its ironic undertone, these are the only epithets applied to him in *The General Prologue*.

When it comes to the telling of the Merchant's tale the 'solempne' tone of voice is not forgotten, whether in the pompous utterances of Placebo, or the learned passages of astronomical lore, or the dignified reference to May's going to the lavatory. It is there also in a good many rare *wise* words of the type the Man of Law favours: *diurnal* says the latter, *diurne* says the Merchant, neither found elsewhere in Chaucer, neither recorded earlier. And other words not used elsewhere in Chaucer once again add their distinctive note, as in the case of similar characters: *emplastre*, for example, which means literally to treat something with a medicinal plaster, is used figuratively in *The Merchant's Tale* with the sense of 'to whitewash, gloss over'; or *encombraunce*, *mysconceyveth*, *superlatyf*, *terrestre*. But diction of this 'solempne' kind is only half of the Merchant's rich word-hoard; it is the Man of Law's contribution to the *conversazione*. From Alys of Bath we expect more racy language, oaths, interjections, loose sentence structure and loose language generally, and her idiom provides the other half of the piece. Of course it is not that the Merchant is deliberately made to echo any of the earlier pilgrims; it comes

naturally to him, for beneath his dignified exterior with his
'Flaundryssh bever hat' and 'his bootes clasped faire and fetisly
[elegantly]' (*Gen Prol* 272–3), there lurks a vulgar, disillusioned
man, as opinionated and disagreeable as the Januarie of his tale,
and just as blind to the truth of things and to the ironies which
link his situation with that of his tale. And Chaucer once again
succeeds in making words 'cosyn to the dede'. Januarie's pompous diction cannot conceal for long the sensuality revealed by
his daydreams or by the figurative language he employs when
contemplating a young wife:

> 'She shal nat passe twenty yeer, certayn;
> Oold fissh and yong flessh wolde I have ful fayn.
> Bet is,' quod he, 'a pyk than a pykerel,
> And bet than old boef is the tendre veel.'
> (*MerchT* 1417–20)

Nor can the Merchant as narrator conceal for long the tension
between his own (and Januarie's) romantic vision of love and the
sordid realities of sexual union as he knows it, whether in the
grotesque intimacy of Januarie's and May's bridal chamber, or in
the adulterous encounter between May and Damyan on the pear
tree. In linguistic terms this side of the Merchant expresses itself
in many of those characteristics of colloquial Chaucerian English
which we have noted before. He utters an oath, 'by Seint Thomas
of Ynde', before he even begins his tale (*CT* IV, 1230), and takes
God's name in vain more than thirty times before he finishes it,
not to mention Christ or Saint Mary or other oaths uttered by
himself or his characters. He has his share of colloquial expressions like 'but I woot best where wryngeth me my sho' (*MerchT*
1553), or 'straw for thy Senek, and for thy proverbes!' (1567), or
'she preyseth nat his pleyying worth a bene' (1854). He may well
be intending an obscene pun, echoing words used by the Reeve
(*CT* I, 3878–9), when he says

> That every man that halt hym worth a leek,
> Upon his bare knees oughte al his lyf
> Thanken his God that hym hath sent a wyf.
> (*MerchT* 1350–2)

And for all his protestations of modesty (1962 ff., 2362 ff.), and
his echoes of the Song of Songs (2138 ff.), and his cursing of the

author of the treatise *De Coitu* (1810–11), the Merchant can be just
as blunt as any of Chaucer's *cherles* and is even able to glean a truth
about himself in the process:

> I kan nat glose, I am a rude man.
>
> (*ibid.* 2351)

For so indeed he is.

What the language of *The Merchant's Tale* does is to complement
the other facets of Chaucer's art, particularly the story itself and
its pattern of ironies, to reveal the truth about the teller, to show
up the 'estatly' demeanour as a mere pose and the 'solempne'
words as but a veneer. The greatest irony is of course that the
Merchant, despite his momentary awareness of himself as 'a rude
man', remains blind to the end.

Other Chaucerian characters say similar things about themselves, but, when Chaucer's ironic spirit is at work, one cannot
always simply take such sayings at their face value. The Franklin's
self-effacement as he introduces his tale, for example, 'I am a burel
man' (*FranklT* 716), sounds much like the Merchant's 'I kan nat
glose, I am a rude man', but 'a burel man' is different from a *rude*
one, *burel* implying lack of learning and education rather than
coarseness, despite its derivation from the noun *burel, borel* (as in
WBT 356) which designates a kind of coarse woollen cloth. 'Burell
folk', as the friar in *The Summoner's Tale* makes clear, may be
living 'in richesse and despence / Of mete and drynke' (*SumT*
1874–5), precisely as the Franklin does, and yet lack essential
spiritual and moral qualities. The Franklin's situation is not that
he is 'burel' in the sense in which he elaborates the word – that is,
uneducated –

> 'Have me excused of my rude speche.
> I lerned nevere rethorik, certeyn;
> Thyng that I speke, it moot be bare and pleyn',
>
> (*FranklT* 718–20)

but rather in the Summoner's friar's sense. The Franklin is clearly
not uneducated, his tale is a model of narrative art, rich in all
those ingredients that delighted a medieval audience and still
delight a modern one, at the same time controlled in structure
and movement and diction, but he clearly has some hankering for
vertu, avowedly for his son, who contrasts so unfavourably with

the Squire of the Canterbury pilgrimage, but presumably no less for himself. Like the Wife of Bath he makes true *gentillesse* the *leitmotif* of his tale, hence the emphasis on those qualities which spring from it, as *franchise* and *fredom* and

> Trouthe is the hyeste thyng that man may kepe',
> (*ibid.* 1479)

a sentiment to be echoed ironically long after in *The Canon's Yeoman's Tale* (1044).

We must thus interpret the Franklin's self-portrait with some care, all the more so since Chaucer says nothing about his manner of speech in *The General Prologue*. The modesty trope employed by the Franklin is of course familiar enough to any reader of Chaucer's verse but, as we have seen, the irony here is precisely that while *The Franklin's Tale* shows its narrator to be a thoroughly well-educated and well-spoken man, perfectly familiar with the 'colours of rethoryk' which he disclaims, he yet remains 'a burel man' – in a different sense. And much as the Franklin denies any knowledge of rhetoric or 'termes of astrologye', so the Squire, employing the same trope, calls himself 'a dul man' (*SqT* 279), but proves himself no less competent a story teller, in what we have of *The Squire's Tale*, than most of his fellow pilgrims.

Yet another pilgrim to adopt the pose of self-abasement is the Prioress who not only speaks of her weak *konnyng* (*PrT* 481), but compares her linguistic competence to that of a little child:

> 'But as a child of twelf month oold, or lesse,
> That kan unnethes any word expresse,
> Right so fare I'.
>
> (*PrT* 484–6)

However absurd if taken literally, the sentiment is at least in harmony with the emphasis on the 'mouth of innocentz' (*PrT* 608) rendering praise to God and to the Virgin throughout the tale as well as in the opening words of the Prioress's prologue which paraphrase the first verses of the eighth Psalm. *The Prioress's Tale* is no nursery performance, of course, but its choice of words no less than its subject matter helps to keep the image of childhood before the listener's or reader's eyes, words, some of them constantly reiterated, like *boy, child, innocent, litel, smal, tendre, yong.*

Theme and diction are thereby closely integrated, words are made cousin 'to the werkyng' with particular aptness but – be it noted – without any attempt to adapt the telling to the Prioress's one linguistic accomplishment singled out for comment in *The General Prologue*, her French. Whether or not Chaucer meant to disparage the Prioress's Anglo-French 'after the scole of Stratford atte Bowe' (*Gen Prol* 125) is for the moment irrelevant (and critical opinion continues to be divided); what matters is her command of it, the fact that she spoke it 'ful faire and fetisly' (124), competently and elegantly, and of this there is no indication in her tale. The case is markedly different from the judicious use of dialect in *The Reeve's Tale* to which the Prioress's might have been analogous if Chaucer had seen fit to give it something of a French, particularly a Stratford French, flavour. The reason for his refraining from doing so is perhaps not difficult to surmise: it is essentially a question of good taste. To diversify a miracle of the Virgin, a pathetic tale of young martyrdom, with linguistic appurtenances inappropriate to it, however characteristic of the teller, might have detracted seriously from its powerfully sobering impact, and would undoubtedly have weakened the strong emotive force of the tale's liturgical echoes. Instead of reminding the audience of the Prioress's linguistic talents and her courtly aspirations, Chaucer chose to recall her 'tendre herte' and her religious background. The language of the liturgy, of the little office of the Blessed Virgin Mary and the Mass of Innocents' Day, is wholly fitting to one who sang 'ful weel'

> the service dyvyne,
> Entuned in hir nose ful semely.
> (*Gen Prol* 122–3)

Just how rich and effective these liturgical echoes are has been shown by Beverly Boyd and G. H. Russell;[15] what is of further interest here is Chaucer's use of some distinctively 'clerical' words to enhance further the strong religious impression of *The Prioress's Tale*. One such word is *expounden* which Chaucer uses three times with reference to Troilus's dream in Book V of *Troilus and*

15. Beverly Boyd, *Chaucer and the Liturgy* (Philadelphia, 1967), especially ch. 5, and G. H. Russell, 'Chaucer: The Prioress's Tale', in *Medieval Literature and Civilization: Studies in Memory of G. N. Garmonsway*, ed. D. A. Pearsall and R. A. Waldron (London, 1969), pp. 214 ff.

Criseyde, but for the rest confines to several of his clerical pilgrims, the Monk, the Nun's Priest, the Second Nun, and the Prioress. Most recorded Middle English occurrences of the word are to be found in biblical or theological contexts. The word *laude* 'praise' occurs three times in *The Prioress's Tale* and may have been suggested by the Latin of the Vulgate, *ex ore infantium et lactentium perfecisti laudem*, which is part of the psalm paraphrased by Chaucer in the opening stanza of the Prioress's prologue. The word is not common in Chaucer: it occurs three times in *The House of Fame*, where Aeolus's trumpet is called 'Clere Laude' (*HF* 1575), and Troilus once uses it in his paean to Love (*Tr* III, 1273). It occurs once in *Boece* in the phrase 'so large preysynge and laude' (*Bo* II, pr. 3, 61–2), but in *The Canterbury Tales* is again restricted to clerical pilgrims, the Prioress, the Friar, and the Monk. In the plural the usual sense is the canonical hour of lauds as in *The Miller's Tale*, 3655: 'the belle of laudes gan to rynge'. The rare word *lucre* the Prioress shares only with the Canon's Yeoman, whose seven years of clerical service equipped him well with appropriate terms; Wyclif uses it, so does Gower several times, once, like Chaucer, in connection with the 'lusty game' of the alchemists (*Conf Am* IV, 2590). With *lucre* the Prioress links *usure*, a word used elsewhere only by Friar and Parson, and possessing for Chaucer and his contemporaries obvious theological overtones. Another word with similar overtones is *doctrine*, which could be applied to secular concepts, Cicero's, for example (*Mel* 1201), or Plato's (*Bo* III, m. 11, 44), but apart from *Melibee* figures in *The Canterbury Tales* only in the vocabulary of Prioress, Nun's Priest, and Parson. That words like *antiphoner*, *clergeon* 'chorister', *grammeere* 'grammar', *prymer* 'primer', should be unique to *The Prioress's Tale* within the Chaucer canon is not surprising in view of the theme of the story; their contribution to the religious diction and powerful emotiveness of the tale was perhaps all the stronger.

The Prioress's English is carefully sustained at the same level throughout her tale: she does not eschew 'clerical' words, as we have seen, but for the most part her diction would have done credit to Wordsworth's contribution to *Lyrical Ballads*. She avoids colloquialisms and she does not swear, not even by 'Seinte Loy'. Her desire 'to been estatlich of manere' (*Gen Prol* 140) is certainly accomplished in the dignity of her speech.

The same is only partly true of Criseyde whom Chaucer calls *estatlich* (*Tr* V, 823) among other attributes. Criseyde has two voices, the colloquial, bantering tone of much of her discourse with Pandarus, and the courtly, dignified tone which she adopts towards Troilus and which she affects *strangely*, oddly, that is, as well as distantly, towards Diomede (*Tr* V, 955).[16] Perhaps it is the latter rather than the former mode which Chaucer implies with his comment that Criseyde was 'goodly of hire speche in general' (*Tr* V, 822), pleasing, delightful, that is, much as Blanche's speech was 'goodly, softe' (*BD* 919). Criseyde's colloquial English has all the familiar Chaucerian ingredients: oaths and exclamations like

'Nay, therof spak I nought, ha, ha!' quod she;
'As helpe me God, ye shenden every deel!'
(*Tr* II, 589–90)

or

'Ye, holy God,' quod she, 'what thyng is that?
What! bet than swyche fyve? I! nay, ywys';
(*ibid.* 127–8)

colloquial modes of address, as in 'ey, uncle myn' (II, 87); loose syntax, as in the phrase 'in a wordes fewe' (IV, 1280), which Criseyde shares with one of the Pardoner's revellers (*PardT* 820), whereas the more usual construction is 'in fewe wordes', as in *The Franklin's Tale*, 1525; idiomatic turns of speech, like

'Now, my good em [uncle], for Goddes love, I preye,'
Quod she, 'come of, and telle me what it is!'
(*Tr* II, 309–10)

or 'unhappes fallen thikke / Alday for love' (II, 456–7); and occasional proverbs, as her soliloquizing

'But al to late comth the letuarie [remedy],
Whan men the cors unto the grave carie.'
(*Tr* V, 741–2)

Criseyde's formal tone is marked by a more distinctive vocabulary, although she uses some rare words also in her more colloquial dialogue with Pandarus, for example:

16. Cp. Donaldson, *Speaking*, p. 78. It is worth noting, incidentally, that *goodly* occurs much more frequently in *Troilus and Criseyde* than in all the rest of Chaucer's work taken together; surely this is no accident.

'I am, til God me bettre mynde sende,
At *dulcarnoun*, right at my wittes ende',
(*Tr* III, 930–1)

a word, meaning 'puzzle, dilemma', ultimately derived from the
Arabic name for a difficult proposition in Euclid (*MED*), which
Pandarus echoes forthwith, but which does not appear to have
been recorded elsewhere in Middle English. In much of her discourse with Troilus, Criseyde's diction takes on a noticeably
more elevated tone as a more formal vocabulary is employed:

'And som so ful of furie is and despit
That it surmounteth his repressioun.
But, herte myn, ye be nat in that plit,
That thonke I God; for whiche youre passioun
I wol nought calle it but illusioun,
Of habundaunce of love and besy cure,
That doth youre herte this disese endure.'
(*Tr* III, 1037–43)

Rare words like *devoir*, the noun *disjoynte* 'plight', *disseveraunce*,
hemysperie, *voluptuous*, and words unique to Criseyde in Chaucer's
writings, like *amphibologies* 'ambiguities' (not recorded elsewhere
in Middle English), *marcial* 'martial', *ordal* 'ordeal', *satiry and
fawny* 'satyrs and fawns', all help to elevate the diction to a more
stately formality, a more *estatlich*, level. So do some of Criseyde's
unique Chaucerian *un-* words: *undeserved*, *ungiltif*, *unshethe*, *untriste*.
She is as formal and elegantly affectionate in her terms of address
to Troilus as she can be casual towards her uncle: 'deere herte
and al my knyght' (III, 176);

'myn owen hertes list,
My ground of ese, and al myn herte deere'.
(*Tr* III, 1303–4)

'Welcome, my knyght, my pees, my suffisaunce!'
(*ibid.* 1309)

A rare glimpse of the passion underlying this veil of courtliness is
afforded by the deceptively simple device of letting Criseyde use
the second person singular in declaring her love, all the more
effective for being set off by the more formal plural pronouns
surrounding it:

'And that ye me wolde han as faste in mynde
As I have yow, that wolde I yow biseche.

. . . .

But herte myn, withouten more speche,
Beth to me trewe, or elles were it routhe;
For I am *thyn*, by God and by my trouthe!'
                                   (*Tr* III, 1506 ff.)

Criseyde's idiom varies according to situation, interlocutor, or mood, expressing that element of instability in her character which Chaucer calls *slydynge* (*Tr* V, 825). Troilus's idiom is sustained at a more formal, rhetorically structured, level throughout the poem. His is the 'heigh style' which Harry Bailly prefers to do without, not so much because of its *termes*, although Troilus has his share of distinctive words, but more because of its 'colours, and ... figures'.[17] Even Troilus's more casual utterances have an air of formal eloquence about them:

'What! holde youre bed ther, thow, and ek thi Morwe!
I bidde God, so yeve yow bothe sorwe!'
                                   (*Tr* III, 1469–70)

'Whi nyl I make atones riche and pore
To have inough to doone, er that she go?
Why nyl I brynge al Troie upon a roore?
Whi nyl I slen this Diomede also?
Why nyl I rather with a man or two
Stele hire away? Whi wol I this endure?
Whi nyl I helpen to myn owen cure?'
                                   (*Tr* V, 43–9)

Troilus's share of distinctive words includes further *un-* words not found elsewhere in Chaucer: *unespied, unholsom, unpreyed, unresty, unneste* –

'O soule, lurkynge in this wo, unneste,
Fle forth out of myn herte, and lat it breste',
                                   (*Tr* IV, 305–6)

and that very poignant word 'to *unloven* yow' (V, 1698). Troilus is given the Italian word *palestral* in 'pleyes palestral', games of wrestling (*Tr* V, 304), from Boccaccio's 'mio palestral giuoco' (*Teseida* VII, 27), just as Criseyde's *poeplissh* 'popular, vulgar' ('as

17. Cp. Robert O. Payne, *The Key of Remembrance: A Study of Chaucer's Poetics* (New Haven and London, 1963), especially pp. 197 ff.

rudenesse and poeplissh appetit', *Tr* IV, 1677) probably derives straight from the *popolesco* of *Filostrato* IV, 165, where it is used by Troilo. Neither word occurs elsewhere in Chaucer. Criseyde has another unique word in *-ish*, although not in direct speech: *goosish* (III, 584), not recorded elsewhere in Middle English, and the narrator of *Troilus and Criseyde* adds others: *snowisshe* (III, 1250) and *wommanysshe* (IV, 694), the latter not to be confused with the more common *wommanliche*.

Something of the often elaborate rhetorical structure of Troilus's English can be gleaned from such utterances as the passage in III, 127–47, all one long sentence neatly encased between the opening 'What that I mene, O swete herte deere?' and the closing 'lo, this mene I, myn owen swete herte'. But the rhetoric does not always come off, and some of Chaucer's syntactical weaknesses occasionally spoil the effect, like the accumulation of *that*'s in Troilus's letter to Criseyde:

'And *that* defaced is, *that* may ye wite
The teris which *that* fro myn eyen reyne,
That wolden speke, if *that* they koude, and pleyne',
(*Tr* V, 1335–7)

or that astonishingly prosaic moment, vaguely reminiscent of a classic Churchillian utterance, in Troilus's Boethian excursus on predestination and free will which Root (p. 519) described as 'probably the least poetical line that Chaucer ever wrote':

'And further over now ayeynward yit'.
(*Tr* IV, 1027)

Pandarus's heartfelt reaction was clearly not without good cause:

'O myghty God,' quod Pandarus, 'in trone,
I! who say evere a wis man faren so?'
(*ibid.* 1086–7)

The combination in one poem of a more naturalistic idiom as represented by Pandarus's English and to some extent by Criseyde's with the formal, courtly rhetoric of Troilus is most closely paralleled in Chaucer's poetry by *The Knight's Tale*. The composition of the latter cannot have been far removed in time from that of *Troilus and Criseyde*. Both poems are based on poems by Boccaccio, both show markedly the influence of Boethius, probably recently translated by Chaucer, both deal against a classical background with 'the loveris maladye / Of Hereos', each in its own distinctive way. Not the least part of the distinctiveness of *The Knight's Tale* is its sustained emphasis upon knightly virtues and appurtenances couched in the appropriate terms. This is wholly in keeping with the one, negative comment made by Chaucer on the Knight's manner of speaking, a comment that is as much a linguistic as a moral one, if we recall that one of the senses of *vileynye* is, according to the *OED*, 'wicked, low, obscene, or opprobrious language':

> He nevere yet no vileynye ne sayde
> In al his lyf unto no maner wight.
>
> *(Gen Prol* 70–1)

What this comment does not prepare us for, however, any more than the Knight's own modest avowal

> I have, God woot, a large feeld to ere,
> And wayke been the oxen in my plough,
>
> *(KnT* 886–7)

are the touches of colloquial English scattered through the tale. Arcite, rather more the soldier and man of action than Palamon, has some unmistakably colloquial turns of phrase: 'this is the short and playn' (1091); 'ech man for hymself' (1182); 'he that dronke is as a mous' (1261). Moreover, he swears rather more readily than anyone else in the poem, not only by God and Jupiter, be it remembered, but by his *pan*. More surprisingly still, perhaps, are the colloquial touches that brighten the wisdom and 'greet solempnytee' of Theseus who shares with the narrator of *Troilus and Criseyde* the saying about 'pipen in an yvy leef' (1838), and who reacts to the spectacle of Palamon and Arcite fighting up to their ankles in blood for the blissfully unaware Emelye with a mouthful of popular idioms:

> 'But this is yet the beste game of alle,
> That she for whom they han this jolitee
> Kan hem therfore as muche thank as me.
> She woot namoore of al this hoote fare,
> By God, than woot a cokkow or an hare!'
>
> *(KnT* 1806–10)

Humorous, colloquial, idiomatic elements thus exist in *The*

Knight's Tale alongside the more formal, courtly language used by the narrator and his characters, whether in dialogue or description or narrative, but *vileynye* there is none.

One inescapable ingredient in the tale is the sense of urgency which characterizes the narration and finds expression in numerous phrases of the type 'but shortly for to speken of this thyng' (985), or 'what nedeth wordes mo?' (1029), or 'shortly for to seyn' (1341), or 'as shortly as I kan, I wol me haste' (2052), a theme on which Chaucer was able to play an astonishingly large number of variations. The reason here was primarily the constant sense of compression as Chaucer worked hard to reduce his tale into little more than a quarter of the length of Boccaccio's poem, but it suits the Knight's own restlessness to narrate like this. One who had travelled so widely, 'no man ferre [further]', ever since he first began 'to riden out', might well find long-winded storytelling irksome: *occupatio* is properly his favourite rhetorical device. *The Knight's Tale* thus expresses in more ways than one the Knight's personality, character, and appropriate linguistic register.

There are other Canterbury pilgrims about whose speech Chaucer makes comments, without committing himself very far towards matching words and deeds. The Friar's lisp, for example, was a 'foppish affectation', as the *OED* glosses *wantownesse* here, whether it was a soft, amorous mode of speaking, as in Elizabethan usage, or a proper lisp. If the latter, it might have been reproduced by Chaucer in spelling had he been writing at the time of Dickens or P. G. Wodehouse, but we can only guess how far the poet may have imitated a lisp when reading *The Friar's Tale* aloud. A few of the Summoner's inebriated scraps of Latin ('a fewe termes hadde he, two or thre', *Gen Prol* 639) find their way into his tale in addition to the *Questio quid iuris* and *Significavit* mentioned in *The General Prologue*.

The Pardoner's *smal*, goat-like voice must be left to the reader's imagination like Friar Hubert's lisp, but the announcement of his accomplished eloquence and polished rhetoric is fully borne out by the subsequent performance:

Wel koude he rede a lessoun or a storie,
But alderbest he song an offertorie;
For wel he wiste, whan that song was songe,

He moste preche and wel affile his tonge
To wynne silver, as he ful wel koude;
Therefore he song the murierly and loude.

(Gen Prol 709–14)

The Pardoner's prologue and tale are indeed a remarkable linguistic and stylistic achievement. I have discussed elsewhere[18] the possibility that what might appropriately be called the Pardoner's 'spiel' is directed specifically against the Host. What is of more immediate interest here is Chaucer's creation of an exceptional command of appropriate registers of language as the Pardoner loosens his tongue at the same time as he unbuckles his *male*, his *walet*, his bag of tricks. There are several distinct, but closely interwoven, 'scenes' in the Pardoner's performance, each one of which has a distinctive linguistic colouring of its own. The prologue (*PardT* 329–462) reveals to the Canterbury pilgrims the Pardoner's shameless frauds and offers a sample of his technique of addressing a 'lewed' village congregation. The two audiences, the pilgrims and the villagers, are kept apart by appropriate terms of address: *lordynges* and *sires* are used by the Pardoner, as elsewhere in *The Canterbury Tales*, to the pilgrims; whereas the medieval preacher's 'goode men' (352, 904), 'ye wyves' (910), 'goode men and wommen' (377) neatly conveys the Pardoner's patronizing tone towards the credulous yokels whose gullibility furnishes him with his considerable annual income. The diction of both the mock sermon to the villagers and the running commentary addressed to the pilgrims is thoroughly colloquial throughout. No attempt is made to dress the stark realities of the Pardoner's practices in rhetorical garb; statements are made in plain English:

'I wol have moneie, wolle, chese, and whete';

(PardT 448)

even slangy English:

'I rekke nevere, whan that they been beryed,
Though that hir soules goon a-blakeberyed!'

(ibid. 405–6)

The domestic imagery ('as dooth a dowve sittynge on a berne',

---

18. Ralph W. V. Elliott, 'Our Host's "Triacle": Some Observations on Chaucer's "Pardoner's Tale"', *Review of English Literature* VII, 4 (1966), 61–73. Cp. above, ch. 5, pp. 258 f.

397) and rustic allusions ('be it whete or otes', 375, and the like)
keep the imagined village setting constantly in mind. At the same
time Chaucer manages to convey not only the patronizing tone to
the villagers but also the confidential air assumed in the Pardoner's
revelations to the pilgrims: the word *hauteyn*, in the Pardoner's
lines

> 'in chirches whan I preche,
> I peyne me to han an hauteyn speche,
> And rynge it out as round as gooth a belle',

> *(ibid.* 329–31)

means 'loud and clear', as the simile indicates, but it also carries
the sense of 'arrogant, proud, haughty', as in the Parson's 'for
somtyme detraccion maketh an hauteyn man be the moore humble'
(*ParsT* 614). The references to the villagers as the 'lewed peple'
(392, 437) are certainly in keeping with the *hauteyn* modes of
address to them mentioned earlier. In contrast are the revelations to the pilgrims with their intimate, confidential air, whether
in the casual 'what, trowe ye, . . .?' (439) or the more direct
comments 'thanne telle I forth' (341), 'thanne shewe I forth' (347),
'thus spitte I out my venym' (421), or the emphatic denials, 'nay,
nay, I thoghte it nevere, trewely!' (442), 'nay, I wol drynke licour
of the vyne' (452).

At line 463 it looks as if the tale proper is about to begin; but
not yet, for the second scene is composed of two parts, a *predicacioun* on gluttony, gambling, swearing, and the tale or *exemplum*
of the three revellers seeking Death. The disquisition on the vices
of the tavern is not 'saffroned' with bits of Latin, as hinted earlier
(344–5), but it is full of Latinate diction. The style is now highly
rhetorical, the diction *repleet* with erudite words, many of them
uncommon in Chaucer, others confined almost wholly to clerical
characters or learned contexts, some of them apparently not
recorded in English before Chaucer; words like *disfigured, fumositee,
mesurable, original, repleet* in the first group; *homycide, superfluitee,
talent* in the second; *dominacioun, embassadour, policye* in the third. In
place of the sheep and *potage* and blackberries of the prologue, the
Pardoner now turns to scholastic philosophy and talks of 'turnen
substaunce into accident' (539), or preaches, as the Parson was to
do later, that drunkenness is

'verray sepulture
Of mannes wit and his discrecioun',[19]

(*PardT* 558–9)

or that

'Hasard is verray mooder of lesynges,
And of deceite, and cursed forswerynges,
Blaspheme of Crist, manslaughtre, and wast also
Of catel and of tyme'.[20]

(*ibid.* 591–4)

The tone and diction are those of the preacher; so is the rhetoric: the repeated apostrophes, the biblical allusions, the hammer blows of repeated words. In the thirty-five lines between lines 590 and 624 the words *hasard, hasardour, hasardrye* occur altogether nine times, and more tightly packed still are the occurrences of *sweryng* and *swere* eight times in thirteen lines (631–43). Compared with the slow, measured prose of the Parson's sermon, the Pardoner's *predicacioun* is a virtuoso performance.

And so too, but in a different mode again, is his tale of the three revelling young men in their search for Death. The tale is one of the *'ensamples . . . | Of olde stories longe tyme agoon'* (435–6) which the Pardoner is wont to recite to his village audiences; hence the resumption of a plainer style, of simpler diction, than in the rhetorical outburst against the sins of revelry just concluded. In the tale proper the storyteller's unadorned narrative style is punctuated by the colloquial oaths and outbursts of the young men, expressed in short, pithy, syntactically simple sentences, in their turn contrasted with the old man's courteous speech with its longer, syntactically more complex sentences. He uses the polite form of address; they the familiar, patronizing 'thou'. He addresses them as 'lordes' and as 'sires'; they call him 'carl' and 'olde cherl'. He prays that 'God save yow, that boghte agayn mankynde' (766); they swear vulgarly 'by God, and by the hooly sacrement' (757), and worse still,

19. Cp. the Parson's 'dronkenesse, that is the horrible sepulture of mannes resoun' (*ParsT* 822).

20. Cp. the Parson's 'Now comth hasardrie with his apurtenaunces, as tables and rafles, of which comth deceite, false othes, chidynges, and alle ravynes, blasphemynge and reneiynge of God, and hate of his neighebores, wast of goodes, mysspendynge of tyme, and somtyme manslaughtre' (*ParsT* 793).

And many a grisly ooth thanne han they sworn,
And Cristes blessed body al torente.
(*PardT* 708–9)

The words are no longer learned and clerical, but plain, familiar, evocative, often monosyllabic:

'Ne dooth unto an oold man noon harm now'.
(*ibid.* 745)

That oon of hem the cut broghte in his fest.
(*ibid.* 802)

For al the nyght he shoop hym for to swynke.
(*ibid.* 874)

All the more electrifying is the sudden reversion to the 'heigh style' of the preceding oration at the conclusion of the tale:

O cursed synne of alle cursednesse!
O traytours homycide, O wikkednesse!
O glotonye, luxurie, and hasardrye!
Thou blasphemour of Crist with vileynye
And othes grete, of usage, and of pride!
(*ibid.* 895–9)

All the threads are now being gathered. Another brief reminder of the village sermon to the 'goode men' and 'ye wyves', a final comment aside to the pilgrims ('And lo, sires, thus I preche', 915), a concluding formula in the proper medieval sermon manner, and the scene is set for the Pardoner's jocular assault upon Harry Bailly:

'For he is moost envoluped in synne',
(*ibid.* 942)

a splendid dart of irony to come from Chaucer's most depraved creature. The Host's retort descends into slangy vulgarity as he talks of the Pardoner's 'olde breech', his *fundement*, his *coillons*, and of 'an hogges toord'. And Chaucer's final touch of genius is to leave the Pardoner, that eloquent master of rhetoric, that accomplished manipulator of language, that 'saffroned' preacher and lively narrator, speechless:

This Pardoner answerde nat a word;
So wrooth he was, no word ne wolde he seye.
(*ibid.* 956–7)

What Chaucer had promised us in the Pardoner's portrait and in the latter's own remarks, he fulfilled to good measure. It is all there: the 'feyned flaterye and japes', the 'hauteyn speche', the fact that 'wel koude he rede a lessoun or a storie', the ability to 'wel affile his tonge' and to *saffron* his *predicacioun* with Latin and Latinate *wordes*, and the tongue that goes

'so yerne
That it is joye to se my bisynesse.'
(ibid. 398–9)

We have looked in the preceding pages at fifteen of Chaucer's creatures in order to ascertain how far the poet succeeded in applying his maxim that

If men shal telle proprely a thyng,
The word moot cosyn be to the werkyng,
(MancT 209–10)

not merely to the attainment of harmony between the theme of a story and its telling, but of congruence between the telling and what we know of the speech or speech habits of the teller. At least one may put it this way regarding the story-telling pilgrims in *The Canterbury Tales*; in the case of characters in the other poems or of Harry Bailly it is in dialogue or occasional soliloquy that any matching of *wordes* and *dede* must be sought. At the simplest level of establishing some individuality of speech are occasional mannerisms, like the Canon's Yeoman's idiosyncratic 'er this' *(CYT* 985, 1106, 1180, 1256, 1362), but generally Chaucer was clearly aiming to be more ambitious in drawing attention in his narrative comments to some speech characteristic which then had to be made part of dialogue or story-telling to fulfil the reader's or listener's expectations. Sometimes the hint is oblique, as in the Reeve's Norfolk origin, more often it is direct, as in the 'wisdom' of the Man of Law's words, the 'solemnity' of the Merchant's, or the elaborate comments on the Clerk's *speche*. Sometimes the hint is not followed up, as is the case with the Prioress's French, .or modified as in the Pardoner's Latin words which, apart from his *oon* text, turn out to be Latinate rather than Latin.

And yet in all these cases. and in others, as we have seen, considerable success is achieved in translating some given observation about speech or character or both into recognizably individual utterance. Chaucer's aim, we may assume, was to *suggest* such individuality rather than attempt anything 'as round as gooth a belle', hence he had to start from the commonly shared basis in any given register of English, whether vulgar or polite, colloquial or courtly, from which more individualized speech habits, patterns of diction, choice and range of vocabulary, syntactical preferences, linguistic idiosyncrasies, and the like, could be developed. The result is the first appearance in English literature of a number of individual voices: they not only attempt to make their words 'cosynes to the thinges of whiche thei speken', but their English confirms to varying degree the personalities and linguistic propensities which their maker has bestowed upon them: 'By the fruyt of hem shul ye knowen hem.'

Select Bibliography

🔳🔳🔳🔳🔳🔳

I EDITIONS OF CHAUCER'S WORKS

Donaldson, E. T., ed. *Chaucer's Poetry: An Anthology for the Modern Reader*. New York, 1958.

Manly, John M., and Rickert, Edith, eds. *The Text of the Canterbury Tales*. 8 vols, Chicago and London, 1940.

Pollard, Alfred W., Heath, Frank H., Liddell, Mark H., and McCormick, W. S., eds. *The Works of Geoffrey Chaucer*. London, 1898, repr. 1960.

Price, Derek J., ed. *The Equatorie of the Planetis*. Cambridge, 1955.

Robinson, F. N., ed. *The Works of Geoffrey Chaucer*. Boston, 1933, 2nd edn, Boston and London, 1957.

Root, Robert Kilburn, ed. *The Book of Troilus and Criseyde*. Princeton, 1926.

Skeat, Walter, W., ed. *The Complete Works of Geoffrey Chaucer*. 7 vols, Oxford, 1894–7, 2nd edn, 1899.
A Treatise on the Astrolabe by Geoffrey Chaucer. E.E.T.S., E.S. 16, 1872, repro. 1968.

Sutherland, Robert, ed. *The Romaunt of the Rose and Le Roman de la Rose: A Parallel-Text Edition*. Oxford, 1967.

II OTHER TEXTS

'Boethius' *De Consolatione* by Jean de Meun'. Edited by V. L. Dedeck-Héry. *Medieval Studies* XIV, (1952), 165–275.

Boethius. *The Theological Treatises and The Consolation of Philosophy*. Translated by H. F. Stewart and E. K. Rand. Loeb Classical Library, London, 1918, repr. 1968.

Bryan, W. F., and Dempster, Germaine, eds. *Sources and Analogues of Chaucer's Canterbury Tales*. Chicago, 1941, repr. New York, 1958.

Chambers, R. W., and Daunt, Marjorie. *A Book of London English 1384–1425*. Oxford, 1931, repr. 1967.

Gower, John. *The English Works of John Gower*. Edited by G. C. Macaulay. 2 vols. E.E.T.S., E.S. 81, 82, 1900–1.

Langland, William. *Piers the Plowman and Richard the Redeless*. Edited by Walter W. Skeat, 2 vols, Oxford, 1886, repro. 1954.
Piers Plowman: The A Version. Edited by George Kane. London, 1960.

Bibliography

Sir Gawain and the Green Knight. Edited by J. R. R. Tolkien and E. V. Gordon, revised by Norman Davis. Oxford, 1967.

Patience. Edited by J. J. Anderson. Manchester and New York, 1969.

Pearl. Edited by E. V. Gordon. Oxford, 1953.

Purity. Edited by Robert J. Menner. Yale Studies in English LXI, 1920, repro. 1970.

III DICTIONARIES

Anglo-Saxon Dictionary. Edited by Joseph Bosworth, T. Northcote Toller and Alistair Campbell. Oxford, 1972.

A Concise Anglo-Saxon Dictionary. Edited by John R. Clark Hall. 4th edn. with Supplement by Herbert D. Meritt. Cambridge, 1960.

A Concordance to Five Middle English Poems. Edited by Barnet Kottler and Alan M. Markham. Pittsburgh, 1966.

A Concordance to the Complete Works of Geoffrey Chaucer. Edited by John S. P. Tatlock and Arthur G. Kennedy. Washington, 1927, repro. 1963.

The Middle English Dictionary. Edited by Hans Kurath, Sherman M. Kuhn, and John Reidy. Ann Arbor, 1954 *et seq.*

Origins: A Short Etymological Dictionary of Modern English. Edited by Eric Partridge. London, 1958, 4th edn., 1966.

The Oxford Dictionary of English Etymology. Edited by C. T. Onions. Oxford, 1966.

The Oxford Dictionary on Historical Principles. Edited by J. A. H. Murray, Henry Bradley, W. A. Craigie, and C. T. Onions. Oxford, 1884–1928. Corrected reissue with Supplement, 13 vols, 1933.

Promptorium Parvulorum: The First English-Latin Dictionary. Edited by A. L. Mayhew, E.E.T.S., E.S. 102, 1908.

IV GENERAL WORKS

Baum, Paull F. *Chaucer: A Critical Appreciation.* Durham, N. C., 1958. 'Chaucer's Puns'. *PMLA* LXXI (1956), 225–46, and LXXIII (1958), 167–70.

Baxter, Edna L. 'Chaucer's Use of Literary Terms'. Microfilmed M.A. thesis, University of Washington, 1946.

Bennett, J. A. W. *The Parlement of Foules: An Interpretation.* Oxford, 1957.

Berndt, Rolf. *Einführung in das Studium des Mittelenglischen unter Zugrundelegung des Prologs der Canterbury Tales.* Halle, 1960.

Boyd, Beverly. *Chaucer and the Liturgy.* Philadelphia, 1967.

Braddy, Haldeen. 'Chaucer's Bawdy Tongue'. *Southern Folklore Quarterly* XXX (1966), 214–22, repro. in H. Braddy, *Geoffrey Chaucer: Literary and Historical Studies,* Port Washington, 1971.

Brewer, D. S. *Chaucer*. London, 1953.
⸻ ed. *Chaucer and Chaucerians: Critical Studies in Middle English Literature*. London, 1966.

Brunner, Karl. *An Outline of Middle English Grammar*. Translated by Grahame Johnston. Oxford, 1963.

Burrow, J. A. *Ricardian Poetry*. London, 1971.

Cawley, A. C., ed. *Chaucer's Mind and Art*. Edinburgh, 1969.

Chesterton, G. K. *Chaucer*. London, 1932, repr. 1962.

Clemen, Wolfgang. *Chaucer's Early Poetry*. Translated by C. A. M. Sym. London, 1963.

Coghill, Nevill. *The Poet Chaucer*. Oxford, 1949, 2nd edn., London, 1960.

Cottle, Basil. *The Triumph of English 1350–1400*. London, 1969.

Craik, T. W. *The Comic Tales of Chaucer*. London, 1964.

Curry, E. C. *Chaucer and the Mediaeval Sciences*. Oxford, 1926, rev. edn., London, 1960.

Curtius, Ernst Robert. *European Literature and the Latin Middle Ages*. Translated by Willard R. Trask. New York, 1953.

Dedeck-Héry, V. L. 'Jean de Meun et Chaucer, Traducteurs de la Consolation de Boèce'. *PMLA* LII (1937), 967–91.

Dobson, E. J. *English Pronunciation 1500–1700*. Vol. I: *Survey of the Sources*, Vol. II: *Phonology*. Oxford, 1957.

Donaldson, E. Talbot. *Speaking of Chaucer*. London, 1970.

Eliason, Norman E. *The Language of Chaucer's Poetry: An Appraisal of the Verse, Style, and Structure*. Anglistica, Vol XVII, Copenhagen, 1972.

Everett, Dorothy. 'Chaucer's "Good Ear"'. *Essays on Middle English Literature*. Oxford, 1955.

Fansler, Dean S. *Chaucer and the Roman de la Rose*. New York, 1914, repr. Gloucester, Mass., 1965.

Fisiak, Jacek. *Morphemic Structure of Chaucer's English*. Alabama, 1965.
⸻ *A Short Grammar of Middle English*. Warsaw and London, 1968.

Gordon, Ida L. *The Double Sorrow of Troilus: A Study of Ambiguities in Troilus and Criseyde*. Oxford, 1970.

Hall, V. T. 'Oaths and Swearing in Chaucer's Writing'. Microfilmed M.A. thesis, University of Washington, 1934.

Huppé, Bernard F. *A Reading of the Canterbury Tales*. Albany, N.Y., 1964, rev. edn, 1967.

Hussey, Maurice. *Chaucer's World: A Pictorial Companion*. Cambridge, 1967.
⸻ Spearing, A. C., and Winny, James. *An Introduction to Chaucer*. Cambridge, 1965.

Hussey, S. S. *Chaucer: An Introduction.* London, 1971.
　　　　'The Minor Poems and the Prose'. Vol. I of the Sphere
　　　　Library *History of Literature in the English Language.*
　　　　Edited by W. F. Bolton. London, 1970.

Jefferson, Bernard L. *Chaucer and the Consolation of Philosophy of Boethius.*
　　　　Princeton, 1917, repr. New York, 1968.

Jordan, Richard. *Handbuch der mittelenglischen Grammatik (Lautlehre).*
　　　　Heidelberg, 1925.

Kean, P. M. *Chaucer and the Making of English Poetry.* Vol. I: *Love Vision
　　　　and Debate,* Vol II: *The Art of Narrative.* London and Boston,
　　　　1972.

Kerkhof, J. *Studies in the Language of Geoffrey Chaucer.* Leiden, 1966.

Kittredge, George Lyman. *Chaucer and His Poetry.* Cambridge, Mass.,
　　　　　　　　1915, repr. 1967.
　　　　　　　　*Observations on the Language of Chaucer's
　　　　　　　　Troilus.* London, 1891, repr. New York,
　　　　　　　　1969.

Klaeber, Friedrich. *Das Bild bei Chaucer.* Berlin, 1893.

Kökeritz, Helge. *A Guide to Chaucer's Pronunciation.* Stockholm and
　　　　　　New Haven, 1954, 1961, New York, 1962.
　　　　　　'Rhetorical Word-Play in Chaucer'. *PMLA* LXIX
　　　　　　(1954), 937–52.

Lawlor, John. *Chaucer.* London, 1968.

Magoun, Francis P., Jr. *A Chaucer Gazeteer.* Chicago and Uppsala, 1961.

Manly, John M. 'Observations on the Language of Chaucer's Legend
　　　　of Good Women'. *Harvard Studies and Notes in Philology and Literature*
　　　　II (1893), 1–120.

Masui, Michio. *The Structure of Chaucer's Rime Words: An Exploration
　　　　into the Poetic Language of Chaucer.* Tokyo, 1964.

Mersand, Joseph. *Chaucer's Romance Vocabulary.* New York, 1937,
　　　　2nd edn., 1939, repro. 1968.

Mossé, Fernand. *A Handbook of Middle English.* Translated by James A.
　　　　Walker. Baltimore, 1952.

Muscatine, Charles. *Chaucer and the French Tradition: A Study in Style and
　　　　Meaning.* Berkeley and Los Angeles. 1957, repr. 1966.

Mustanoja, Tauno F. *A Middle English Syntax.* Part I: *Parts of Speech.*
　　　　Helsinki, 1960.

Payne, Robert O. *The Key of Remembrance: A Study of Chaucer's Poetics.*
　　　　New Haven and London, 1963.

Remus, Hans. *Die kirchlichen und speziell-wissenschaftlichen Romanischen
　　　　Lehnworte Chaucers.* Halle, 1906.

Richardson, Janette. *Blameth Nat Me: A Study of Imagery in Chaucer's
　　　　Fabliaux.* The Hague, 1970.

Robertson, D. W., Jr. *A Preface to Chaucer: Studies in Medieval Perspective*. Princeton, 1963.

Robinson, Ian. *Chaucer's Prosody: A Study of the Middle English Verse Tradition*. Cambridge, 1971.

Rowland, Beryl, ed. *Companion to Chaucer Studies*. Toronto, 1968.

Ruggiers, Paul G. *The Art of the Canterbury Tales*. Madison, 1965.

Russell, G. H. 'Chaucer: The Prioress's Tale'. *Medieval Literature and Civilization: Studies in Memory of G. N. Garmonsway*. Edited by D. A. Pearsall and R. A. Waldron. London, 1969.

Schaar, Claes. *The Golden Mirror: Studies in Chaucer's Descriptive Technique and its Literary Background*. Lund, 1955, repr. 1967.
    Some Types of Narrative in Chaucer's Poetry. Lund, 1954.

Schlauch, Margaret. 'Chaucer's Colloquial English: Its Structural Traits'. *PMLA* LXXVII (1952), 1103–16.

Schoeck, Richard J., and Taylor, Jerome, eds. *Chaucer Criticism: An Anthology*, Vol I: *The Canterbury Tales*, Vol II: *Troilus and Criseyde and the Minor Poems*. Notre Dame, Indiana, 1960–1.

Skeat, Walter W. *The Chaucer Canon*. Oxford, 1900.

Smyser H. M. 'Chaucer's Use of *Gin* and *Do*'. *Speculum* XLII (1967), 68–83.

Southworth, James G. *Verses of Cadence: An Introduction to the Prosody of Chaucer and his Followers*. Oxford, 1954.

Starr, Herbert W. 'Oaths in Chaucer's Poems'. *West Virginia University Bulletin: Philological Studies* IV (1943), 44–63.

ten Brink, Bernhard. *The Language and Metre of Chaucer*. Translated by M. Bentinck Smith. London, 1901.

Thompson, W. M. 'Chaucer's Translation of the Bible'. *English and Medieval Studies Presented to J. R. R. Tolkien*. Edited by Norman Davis and C. L. Wrenn. London, 1962.

Tolkien, J. R. R. 'Chaucer as a Philologist: *The Reeve's Tale*'. Transactions of the Philological Society (1934), 1–70.

Wagenknecht, Edward, ed. *Chaucer: Modern Essays in Criticism*. New York, 1959.

Whiting, Bartlett Jere. *Chaucer's Use of Proverbs*. Cambridge, Mass., 1934.

Wild, Friedrich. *Die Sprachlichen Eigentümlichkeiten der wichtigeren Chaucer-Handschriften und die Sprache Chaucers*. Wien and Leipzig, 1915.

Wilson, R. M. 'Linguistic Analysis'. *The Equatorie of the Planetis*. Edited by Derek J. Price. Cambridge, 1955.

Index of Words

꧁꧂꧁꧂꧁꧂

We have singled out for inclusion in the Index of Words those of Chaucer's words and phrases which seemed of particular interest or importance in the discussion. The Index is meant to be used in conjunction with the General Index where a good many additional references will be found under appropriate headings.

been along on, 95f.
beere, 87
bele chose, 217, 223, 387
beme, 318
benedicitee, 257, 263
berd, make his, a clerkes, 388, 395
bibbed, 206
biblotte, 378
bidaffed, 402
bifel, (it.), 73ff.
bisemare, 395
bishrewen, 260
blabbe, 201
blanket, 253
blankmanger, 348
boch, 308f.
boes, 393
boille, 346
bombleth, 338
bones, by Goddes, Cokkes, corpus, 271f.
boold, 380
boole armonyak, 307
boterflye, 344
boy, 38
bragot, 350
brasile, 334
brat, 355
breech, breches, 354
breed, 346f.
breem, 345
brocage, 360
broille, 346
brokkynge, 338
brother, 43
broun, 313f.
brybe, 215
bryd, 231f.
bryngere out of bisynesse, 162
burdoun, 206, 221, 280
burthe, 304
burel, 407f.
bytynge bysynesse, 166f.

cadence, 120f.
calculed, 137
Calkas, 81
calkulynge, 81, 285
calle, 354f.
camaille, 339, 403
camus, 207, 313, 395
can, 62, 94
capel, 199f., 392, 393

capouns, 340
cardynacle, 309, 380
carole-wyse, 322
carpe, 385f.
catel, 341
cause, 305
celebrable, 159
celebrete, 159
celerer, 294
center, 317
cerclen, 318
ceriously, 398
certes, 144
certeyn, a, 91
ceynt, 356
chaast, chaced, 221
chalons, 79, 395
chargeaunt, 144
charite, 289f.; for seinte—, 283, 291; par—, 284
cherl, carl, 226f.
chirketh, 338
chiteren, 333, 337
chyncherie, 177
circuit, 317
circuler, 317
clappe, 202
clappen, 202f.
clarionynge, 322
clarree, 350
clergeon, 295, 410
clobbed, 204
clom, 214
cloth of Reynes, 352f.;—of Tars, 353;—of gold, 353
cloysterer, 294
clymat, 136
coeterne, 161
coillons, 216f.
cokenay, 215, 395
colera, rede, 316
colt, 199
combust, 138
come to hous upon, 96
comedye, 119
compaignye, 28: par—, 206
compassioun, 112ff.
compeer, 214
compilator, 119, 137
compilen, 119
compleynt, 98, 129, 237
concupiscence, 150
confiture, 308

General Index

ᩒᩒᩒᩒᩒᩒ

This index is selective. Chaucer's works and characters are referred to only where the passage quoted directly illuminates those works and characters.